Copyright © 2021 by Cynthia Bricker -All rights r_____ ___.

No part of this book may be reproduced or transmitted in any form or by any means, electronic or mechanical, including photocopying and recording, or by any information storage and retrieval system, without permission in writing from the publisher. This is a work of fiction. Names, places, characters and incidents are either the product of the author's imagination or are used fictitiously, and any resemblance to any actual persons, living or dead, organizations, events or locales is entirely coincidental. The unauthorized reproduction or distribution of this copyrighted work is ilegal.

Please note the information contained within this document is for educational and entertainment purposes only. All effort has been executed to present accurate, up to date, reliable, complete information. No warranties of any kind are declared or implied. Readers acknowledge that the author is not engaged in the rendering of legal, financial, medical, or professional advice. The content within this book has been derived from various sources. Please consult a licensed professional before attempting any techniques outlined in this book. By reading this document, the reader agrees that under no circumstances is the author responsible for any losses, direct or indirect, that are incurred as a result of the use of the information contained within this document, including, but not limited to, errors, omissions, or inaccuracies.

CONTENTS

INTRODUCTION

What is a gas griddle?

Natural Gas, Propane, Electric. A griddle is a cooking device consisting of a broad flat surface heated by gas, electricity, wood, or coal, with both residential and commercial applications. In industrialized countries, a griddle is most commonly a flat metal plate, elsewhere typically a brick slab or tablet.

Different Types of Gas Griddle

Let's go over the major types of gas griddles on the market.

• **Dedicated**: These are the largest type of gas griddle and can even be placed next to your regular outdoor grill. These often have wheels for easy transportation and storage. They can cook more food at the same time than smaller griddles due to their increased surface area. These griddles also tend to be the most expensive, but they can provide good value for money if you run a small restaurant or do frequent cookouts for many people at once.

• **Tabletop/Portable**: These have less cooking surface area and are more affordable in general due to their smaller size. These griddles are designed to be small enough to be placed on a tabletop or counter, although there are smaller standing varieties around as well. These standing griddles can be easily moved throughout a kitchen or backyard. Portable griddles typically use 1-pound disposable propane tanks or canisters. Due to their small size, they are excellent choices for cooking while camping.

• **Placed on Existing Grill**: These are innovative plates that you place over the top of your existing grill. These griddle covers then warm from the heat of the grill. These retain the same versatile benefits of a griddle but heat up quickly thanks to the grill being its source of heat. Because they're so small and compact, they're often extremely lightweight and affordable and are great attachments if you enjoy grilling frequently but would like to add eggs or a similar food to your backyard cookouts, for instance.

Buying Factors to Consider

Before you make a final decision concerning an outdoor gas griddle, keep these key aspects in mind so you can choose the best one for your needs.

Griddle Size

Obviously, the size of the griddle impacts how many folks you can cook for, and where. Smaller griddles can be used both indoors and outdoors and can be implemented relatively easily with an existing cookout layout. For instance, you can combine them with existing grills with no trouble at all. Smaller griddles usually have surface areas of around 300 in.^{2} or less and are perfect for cooking for a small family. Larger griddles will require dedicated space but can cook more food. They usually have cooking surface areas of 500 in.^{2} or more and can cook for a large family.

Number of Burners

Griddles have hot and cold zones due to their burners. Essentially, the space directly above the burner will be hotter while spaces near the edges will be cooler. Having more burners beneath your griddle surface will let you heat the entire surface area more quickly and thoroughly. This can be important if you plan to cook a lot of food at the same time. More burners is always a good thing since you can always turn burners off to keep a "cooler" or warming area. You get more temperature control over the griddle with more burners.

Material

Gas griddle surface areas can be made from a variety of materials. Stainless steel or chrome griddles are excellent picks, as these are very resistant to rust damage. However, these often tend to be more expensive. Cheaper options can be made from regular steel or aluminum, but you should check to see if there's any additional coating of heat-resistant material to ensure that the surface will function effectively for a decent period of time. Also, check out what else the griddle has to offer in terms of storage space or shelves; these add value for money to any individual griddle and can make your cooking tasks a lot easier.

Price

Finally, keep an ideal budget in mind when searching for your perfect gas griddle. Smaller griddles will be around the $100 to $200 mark, while larger griddles can easily go upwards of $300 or $400. The best way to determine your ideal budget is to predict how much you'll be using the griddle in the weeks and months to come. If you plan on cooking for a lot of people frequently, a more expensive griddle will be well worth the cost. On the other hand, if you only use the griddle sparingly, perhaps a cheaper option is in order.

After cooking, it's imperative that you clean your griddle to preserve its surface and avoid rust formation, even if you have a rust-resistant surface like stainless steel.

- After the grill has cooled down, scrape away any hard debris or larger chunks of grease with your grill spatula.

- Then use a paper towel with a little water to get rid of the rest of the residue.

- A nylon scouring pad is a great idea after using a paper towel, as this will get even more of the grease and debris off the cooking surface.

- Rinse the cooking area thoroughly once this is all done and dry the griddle with a soft cloth. Finally, add a little oil over the surface and spread it with another paper towel to stop rust from forming.

When it comes to storing your gas griddle, try to find a place that is dry and cool so that your propane tanks will not be in danger blowing their tops off and leaking propane. You can use a propane tank gauge to check if you have enough fuel in the tank before each cooking session. A garage or storage shed is a great idea, provided that you have a cover for the griddle so that dust and other debris doesn't fall onto the cooking surface and scratch or damage it. Don't stack anything on top of your griddle, as this can damage the cooking surface and the griddle as a whole and will lower the tool's overall lifespan.

BREAKFAST RECIPES

1.   Pigs In A Blanket

Servings: 4
Cooking Time: 10 Minutes
Ingredients:
- Buttermilk Pancake batter
- 8 breakfast sausage links

Directions:
1.   Preparing the Ingredients.
2.   Make the buttermilk pancake batter.
3.   Bring the griddle grill to medium-high heat.
4.   Grilling
5.   Cook the breakfast sausage links until they are completely cooked through, with the juices running clear, or when they reach an internal temperature of 165°F, then set aside and keep warm.
6.   Follow the directions for making buttermilk pancakes. Using your spatula, coax the pancake to roll around the sausage link like a blanket. Allow to continue Grilling with the sausage in the middle until the pancake is fully cooked.

2.   Chocolate Lava Cake

Servings: 8
Cooking Time: 30 Minutes
Ingredients:
- ½ pound (2 sticks) butter, plus softened butter for the pan
- 8 ounces dark chocolate, chopped
- 4 eggs
- 4 egg yolks
- ½ cup sugar
- 4 teaspoons all-purpose flour
- ½ teaspoon salt

Directions:
1.   Preparing the Ingredients.
2.   Generously coat the inside of a 9- or 10-inch cast-iron skillet with softened butter; make sure not to miss any spots, or the cake will stick.
3.   Place the ½ pound butter in a heatproof bowl and melt it in the microwave or over hot water in a double boiler. Add the chocolate to the hot butter and mix until it's melted.
4.   Place the whole eggs and egg yolks in another bowl. Add the sugar and Whisk with an electric mixer on high speed (or enthusiastically with a whisk) until light and thick, about 1 minute. On low speed (or whisking) Whisk the egg mixture, flour, and salt into the melted chocolate and butter until combined. Pour the batter into the prepared pan. (At this point you can refrigerate the batter for up to 3 hours; take the pan out of the refrigerator 30 Minutes before you intend to bake it.)

5.   If using a Griddle, heat for medium direct
6.   Grilling
7.   The grill temperature should be 500° to 600°F; it could mean all the burners are on medium or medium-low, depending on your particular grill.
8.   Place the pan on the grill directly. Grill-bake until the cake puffs up around the edge but the center still jiggles slightly when shaken, 5 to 15 Minutes. (It's better to underbake than to overbake the cake; start checking it after 3 Minutes.) Let sit for at least 10 Minutes before slicing, or the insides will ooze all over the pan.

3.   Mexican Scramble

Servings: 4
Cooking Time: 10 Minutes
Ingredients:
- 8 eggs, beaten
- 1 lb Chorizo
- 1/2 yellow onion
- 1 cup cooked black beans
- 1/2 cup green chilies
- 1/2 cup jack cheese
- 1/4 cup green onion, chopped
- 1/2 teaspoon black pepper
- vegetable oil

Directions:
1.   Preheat a griddle to medium heat. Brush the griddle with vegetable oil and add the chorizo to one side and the onions to the other side.
2.   When the onion has softened, combine it with the chorizo and add the beans and chilies.
3.   Add the eggs, cheese, and green onion and cook until eggs have reached desired firmness.
4.   Remove the scramble from the griddle and season with black pepper before serving.
Nutrition Info: Calories: 843, Sodium: 1554 mg, Dietary Fiber: 9.2g, Fat: 54.1.g, Carbs: 38.2g Protein: 50.7g

4.   Lemon-garlic Artichokes

Servings: 4 Slices
Cooking Time: 15 Minutes
Ingredients:
- Juice of 1/2 lemon
- 1/2 cup canola oil
- 3 garlic cloves, chopped
- Sea salt
- Freshly ground black pepper
- 2 large artichokes, trimmed and halved

Directions:

1. Preheat the griddle to medium high.
2. While the unit is preheating, in a medium bowl, combine the lemon juice, oil, and garlic. Season with salt and pepper, then brush the artichoke halves with the lemon-garlic mixture.
3. Place the artichokes on the Grill, cut side down. Gently press them down to maximize grill marks. Grill for 8 to 10 minutes, occasionally basting generously with the lemon-garlic mixture throughout cooking, until blistered on all sides.
Nutrition Info: (Per serving): Calories: 285kcal; Fat: 28g; Carbs: 10g; Protein: 3g

5.   Cauliflower Hash Browns

Servings: 6
Cooking Time: 10 Minutes
Ingredients:
- 1 egg
- 3 cups cauliflower, grated
- 3/4 cup cheddar cheese, shredded
- 1/8 tsp pepper
- 1/4 tsp garlic powder
- 1/4 tsp cayenne pepper
- 1/2 tsp salt

Directions:
1. Preheat the griddle to medium-low heat.
2. Add all ingredients into the bowl and mix well.
3. Spray griddle top with cooking spray.
4. Make 6 hash browns from mixture and place on hot griddle top and cook until golden brown from both sides.
5. Serve and enjoy.
Nutrition Info: (Per Serving): Calories 80 ;Fat 5 g ;Carbohydrates 3 g ;Sugar 1 g ;Protein 5 g ;Cholesterol 46 mg

6.   Blistered Green Beans

Servings: 4 Slices
Cooking Time: 10 Minutes
Ingredients:
- 1 pound haricots verts or green beans, trimmed
- 2 tablespoons vegetable oil
- Juice of 1 lemon
- Pinch red pepper flakes
- Flaky sea salt
- Freshly ground black pepper

Directions:
1. Preheat the griddle to medium high.
2. While the unit is preheating, in a medium bowl, toss the green beans in oil until evenly coated.
3. Place the green beans on the Grill and grill for 8 to 10 minutes, tossing frequently until blistered on all sides.

4. When cooking is complete, place the green beans on a large serving platter. Squeeze lemon juice over the green beans, top with red pepper flakes, and season with sea salt and black pepper.
Nutrition Info: (Per serving): Calories: 100kcal; Fat: 7g; Carbs: 10g; Protein: 2g

7.   Steak With Balsamic Sauce

Servings: 2
Cooking Time: 10 Minutes
Ingredients:
- 2 tablespoons butter
- 8 cremini mushrooms, sliced
- 1 tablespoon minced garlic
- 1 teaspoon salt, plus more to taste
- 1 teaspoon pepper, plus more to taste
- Balsamic Griddle Sauce, as needed
- 6-ounce beef tenderloin fillet, cut in half lengthwise
- 2 prepared crepes
- Grilling oil, as needed

Directions:
1. Preparing the Ingredients.
2. Over medium heat, melt the butter and sauté the mushrooms with the garlic and 1 teaspoon each of salt and pepper.
3. The salt will help release the moisture from the mushrooms. When this begins, add ¾ cup of the Balsamic Griddle Sauce to the mushrooms and cover. Mix occasionally for 6 to 8 Minutes, and set aside to keep warm.
4. Increase the heat on the griddle grill to medium high and while it is heating, scrape and clean any residual balsamic sauce from the Grilling surface so it does not burn.
5. Pat the beef dry with paper towels, and season liberally with salt and pepper.
6. Grilling
7. Add Grilling oil to the griddle, and when it begins to shimmer, add the steak and sear for 3 Minutes. Flip and sear for an additional 1 to 3 Minutes, based on your desired doneness.
8. Allow the steak to rest for 10 Minutes, then cut across the grain into thin slices. Arrange the steak on a crepe and top with mushrooms.

8.   Classic Eggs Benedict

Servings: 2
Cooking Time: 10 Minutes
Ingredients:
- 1 medium red or green bell pepper
- 2 English muffins
- 2 eggs

- 4 slices Canadian bacon
- ½ cup very finely shredded Jarlsberg cheese
- butter, as needed

Directions:
1. Preparing the Ingredients.
2. Bring the griddle grill to medium heat. Cut the uneven bottom off the bell pepper, then cut two rings of pepper about ½ inch thick.
3. Grilling
4. Coat the griddle with a good amount of butter. Separate the English muffins and place the uncut-sides on the griddle to begin warming. Place the bell pepper rings on the griddle and cook for 2 Minutes. Flip the peppers, then flip the English muffins to heat the other sides.
5. Crack an egg and carefully drop it into one of the bell pepper rings. Scoot the other pepper ring close by and repeat with the second egg. Using a cover that's just bigger than the peppers, cover the eggs and allow them to cook for 1 minute.
6. While the eggs are Grilling, warm the Canadian bacon on the grilling surface.
7. Remove the cover from the eggs and squirt water around the grilling surface very close to the eggs, and immediately cover the eggs again to capture the steam and assist with Grilling the whites and yolks. Cook for another minute, then cover each of the eggs with half of the cheese. The finer the cheese is grated, the more quickly it will melt, so I use a very fine grater or even a Microplane. Squirt the perimeter of the eggs again and cover to catch the steam, allowing the cheese to melt.
8. Remove the English muffins from the griddle and Place 2 slices of Canadian bacon on top of each. Uncover the eggs, and using a spatula, remove the pepper ring containing the egg and slide it onto the Canadian bacon.

9. Bacon Egg And Cheese Sandwich

Servings: 4
Cooking Time: 10 Minutes
Ingredients:
- 4 large eggs
- 8 strips of bacon
- 4 slices cheddar or American cheese
- 8 slices sourdough bread
- 2 tablespoons butter
- 2 tablespoons vegetable oil

Directions:
1. Heat your griddle to medium heat and place the strips of bacon on one side. Cook until just slightly crispy.
2. When the bacon is nearly finished, place the oil on the other side of the griddle and crack with eggs onto the griddle. Cook them either sunny side up or over medium.
3. Butter one side of each slice of bread and place them butter side down on the griddle. Place a slice of cheese on 4 of the slices of bread and when the cheese has just started to melt and the eggs are finished, stack the eggs on the bread.
4. Add the bacon to the sandwiches and place the other slice of bread on top. Serve immediately.

Nutrition Info: Calories: 699, Sodium: 1148 mg, Dietary Fiber: 1.5g, Fat: 47.7g, Carbs: 37.8g Protein: 29.3g

10. Old Fashioned Easy Apple Crisp

Servings: 6
Cooking Time: 30 Minutes
Ingredients:
- 5 tablespoons cold butter, cut into bits, plus softened butter for the pan
- ⅔ cup brown sugar
- ½ cup rolled oats (not instant)
- ½ cup all-purpose flour
- Pinch salt
- 6 cups sliced cored apples (2 to 2¼ pounds; peeling is optional)
- Juice of ½ lemon

Directions:
1. Preparing the Ingredients.
2. Place the cold butter, all but 1 tablespoon of the brown sugar, the oats, flour, and salt in a food processor and pulse a few times, until everything is combined but not too finely ground. (To mix by hand, mash it together between your fingers.) Transfer the topping to a bowl and refrigerate until you're ready to use it.
3. Generously coat the inside of a 10-inch cast-iron skillet with softened butter. Toss the apples with the lemon juice and remaining tablespoon brown sugar in a large bowl. When you're ready to grill, spread them out in the prepared pan in an even layer. (You can leave them in the bowl, cover, and refrigerate until you're ready to bake.)
4. Grilling
5. When you're ready for dessert, crumble the topping evenly over the apples. Place the skillet on the grill directly. Bake for 5 Minutes, then check. If the topping seems to be browning too fast, turn the heat off under the pan and turn it up on the other burners for a Griddle. Bake, checking every few Minutes, until the topping is browned and the apples are tender, 5 to 20 Minutes more. Carefully transfer to a rack and let cool until you are ready to serve.

11. Hash Brown Scramble

Servings: 4
Cooking Time: 10 Minutes
Ingredients:
- 2 russet potatoes, shredded, rinsed, and drained
- 8 eggs, beaten
- 1 cup cheddar cheese
- 6 slices bacon, cut into small pieces
- 1/3 cup green onion, chopped
- vegetable oil

Directions:
1.   Preheat griddle to medium heat and brush with vegetable oil.
2.   On one side, place the potatoes on the griddle and spread in a 1/2 inch thick layer. Cook the potatoes until golden brown and then flip. Add the bacon to the other side of the griddle and cook until the fat has rendered.
3.   Add the eggs and cheese to the top of the hash browns and stir in the bacon and green onion. Cook until the cheese has melted and divide equally among 4 plates.

Nutrition Info: Calories: 470, Sodium: 965 mg, Dietary Fiber: 2.8g, Fat:30.2g,Carbs: 18.8g Protein: 30.6g

12. Grilled Peaches With Ginger Ice Cream

Servings: 4
Cooking Time: 40 Minutes
Ingredients:
- 1 pint vanilla ice cream, softened just a bit
- ¼ cup chopped candied ginger
- 2 or 4 ripe peaches, depending on their size
- 4 tablespoons (½ stick) butter, melted
- ¼ cup Demerara sugar, or more as needed
- Fresh mint sprigs for garnish

Directions:
1.   Preparing the Ingredients.
2.   Place the ice cream and ginger in a bowl and mash together with a wooden spoon until the ginger is mixed throughout the ice cream. This can be done several days ahead; Place it back in the ice cream container and freeze at least a couple hours.
3.   Grilling
4.   Heat your Griddle to medium heat. When you're ready for dessert, cut the peaches in half through the stem end and remove the pits. Brush with the melted butter. Place the sugar on a plate and dredge the cut side of each peach in it.
5.   Place the peaches on the grill directly, cut side up. Cook until they soften, 10 to 15 Minutes depending on their size and ripeness. Turn them cut side down and cook until the sugar caramelizes to a golden brown, 2 to 5 Minutes. Transfer to a platter. To serve, Place the warm peaches on plates or in dessert bowls, cut side up. Divide the ice cream between them, or pass the ice cream at the table. Garnish with the mint.

13. Strawberry, Banana, Crepes

Servings: 2
Cooking Time: 10 Minutes
Ingredients:
- 6 tablespoons hazelnut-chocolate spread
- 2 prepared crepes
- 8 large strawberries, sliced
- 1 banana, sliced
- powdered sugar

Directions:
1.   Preparing the Ingredients.
2.   Spread half the hazelnut-chocolate spread on each of the crepes and divide the fruit evenly as a topping.
3.   Fold the crepes over the filling and garnish with powdered sugar.

14. Cauliflower Fritters

Servings: 6
Cooking Time: 15 Minutes
Ingredients:
- 2 eggs
- 1 large head cauliflower, cut into florets
- 1 tbsp butter
- 1/2 tsp turmeric
- 1 tbsp nutritional yeast
- 2/3 cup almond flour
- 1/4 tsp black pepper
- 1/2 tsp salt

Directions:
1.   Add cauliflower florets to a large pot.
2.   Pour enough water to cover the cauliflower florets. Bring to boil for 8-10 minutes.
3.   Drain cauliflower well and transfer in food processor and process until it looks like rice.
4.   Transfer cauliflower rice into the large bowl.
5.   Add remaining ingredients except for butter to the bowl and stir to combine.
6.   Preheat the griddle to medium heat.
7.   Melt butter onto the hot griddle top.
8.   Make small patties from cauliflower mixture and place on hot griddle top and cook for 3-4 minutes on each side or until lightly golden brown.
9.   Serve and enjoy.

Nutrition Info: (Per Serving): Calories 155 ;Fat 10 g ;Carbohydrates 11.1 g ;Sugar 3.9 g ;Protein 8.1 g ;Cholesterol 60 mg

15. Flaky South Asian Flatbread

Servings: 4
Cooking Time: At Least 1 Hour
Ingredients:
- 1½ cups whole wheat flour, plus more as needed
- 1½ cups all-purpose flour, plus more for kneading and dusting
- 1 teaspoon salt
- ¾ cup warm water, plus more as needed
- About 4 tablespoons (½ stick) butter, melted, or good-quality vegetable oil

Directions:
1. Preparing the Ingredients.
2. Beat the flours and salt together in a large bowl. Add the water and mix with a heavy spoon until the mixture can be formed into a ball and is slightly sticky. If it's dry, add more water, 1 tablespoon at a time, until you get the right consistency; in the unlikely event that the mixture is too sticky, add flour 1 tablespoon at a time. (You can also make this in a food processor. First pulse the dry ingredients together, then add the water through the feed tube.) Turn the dough out onto a lightly floured work surface; knead a few times until it becomes smooth. Cover with plastic wrap or a clean, damp dish towel and let rest at room temperature for at least 30 Minutes or up to 2 hours. (At this point, the dough can be wrapped tightly in plastic and refrigerated for up to a day or frozen for up to a week; bring to room temperature before proceeding.)
3. Divide the dough into 8 to 12 even-sized pieces. Flouring the work surface and dough as necessary, roll each piece out to a 4-inch disk. Brush on one side with some of the melted butter. Roll up like a cigar, then into a coil (kind of like a cinnamon bun); set aside until you finish all the pieces. Don't let them touch or they will stick to one another. Press each coil flat, then roll out into a thin disk, about the size of a tortilla.
4. Grilling
5. Working in batches, Place the paratha on the grill directly.
6. Cook until lightly browned on the bottom, 3 to 5 Minutes. Brush the tops with butter, turn with tongs, and brown the second side, another few Minutes. Brush the tops with butter, turn, cook for another minute, until lightly browned and cooked through. Transfer to the prepared plate. Repeat with the remaining paratha and butter and serve as soon as possible.

16. Spicy Egg Scrambled

Servings: 2
Cooking Time: 10 Minutes
Ingredients:
- 4 eggs
- 2 tbsp cilantro, chopped
- 1/3 cup heavy cream
- 1 tomato, diced
- 3 tbsp butter
- 1 Serrano chili pepper, chopped
- 2 tbsp scallions, sliced
- 1/4 tsp pepper
- 1/2 tsp salt

Directions:
1. Preheat the griddle to medium heat.
2. Melt butter on top of the hot griddle.
3. Add tomato and chili pepper and sauté for 2 minutes.
4. In a bowl, whisk eggs with cilantro, cream, pepper, and salt.
5. Pour egg mixture over tomato and chili pepper and stir until egg is set.
6. Garnish with scallions and serve.

Nutrition Info: (Per Serving): Calories 355 ;Fat 33 g ;Carbohydrates 3 g ;Sugar 1.7 g ;Protein 12 g ;Cholesterol 401 mg

17. Naan Bread

Servings: 4
Cooking Time: 2½ Hours
Ingredients:
- ¼ cup yogurt
- 2 tablespoons good-quality vegetable oil, plus more for the bowl
- 1 tablespoon sugar
- 2¼ teaspoons (1 package) instant yeast
- 3½ cups all-purpose flour, plus more as needed
- ½ cup whole wheat flour
- 2 teaspoons salt
- 1½ cups warm water, plus more as needed
- 6 tablespoons (¾ stick) butter, melted and still warm

Directions:
1. Preparing the Ingredients.
2. Beat the yogurt, oil, sugar, and yeast together. Mix the flours and salt together in a large bowl. Add the yogurt mixture and combine. Add the water ½ cup at a time, stirring until the mixture comes together in a cohesive but sticky dough; you may need to add another tablespoon or 2 water.
3. Turn the dough out onto a floured work surface and knead by hand for a minute or so to form a smooth dough. Shape into a round ball, Place in a lightly oiled bowl, and cover with plastic wrap. Let

rise until doubled in size, 1 to 2 hours. Or you can let the dough rise in the refrigerator for up to 8 hours.

4. Punch the dough down. Using as much flour as necessary to keep the dough from sticking to the work surface or your hands, roll it into a snake about 2 inches in diameter, then tear into 12 equal-sized balls. Space the balls out on the work surface. Cover with plastic wrap or a clean, damp dish towel and let rest for 10 Minutes. Roll each dough ball into an oval roughly 6 to 8 inches long and 3 to 4 inches wide.

5. Heat a Griddle for hot direct

6. Grilling

7. Make sure the grates are clean. Have the melted butter handy.

8. Working in batches, Place the naan on the grill directly. If the grill temperature is 600°F or above, it will only take 20 to 30 seconds for the first side to brown. It should smell toasty, not burning. the visible side should be bubbled. Quickly turn with tongs. The other side will take about the same time or a little less to cook. When you grab it with tongs, the bread should feel firm and springy, and both sides should be browned in spots, with a little charring. Transfer to a platter and immediately brush with the butter. Repeat with the remaining naan and butter and serve as soon as possible.

18. Easy Cheese Omelet

Servings: 2
Cooking Time: 10 Minutes
Ingredients:
- 6 eggs
- 7 oz cheddar cheese, shredded
- 3 oz butter
- Pepper
- Salt

Directions:
1. In a bowl, whisk together eggs, half cheese, pepper, and salt.
2. Preheat the griddle to medium heat.
3. Melt butter on the hot griddle top.
4. Once butter is melted then pour egg mixture onto the griddle top and cook until set.
5. Add remaining cheese fold and serve.

Nutrition Info: (Per Serving): Calories 892 ;Fat 80 g ;Carbohydrates 2.4 g ;Sugar 1.6 g ;Protein 41.7 g ;Cholesterol 687 mg

19. Broccoli Omelet

Servings: 2
Cooking Time: 10 Minutes
Ingredients:
- 4 eggs

- 1 cup broccoli, chopped and cooked
- 1 tbsp olive oil
- 1/4 tsp pepper
- 1/2 tsp salt

Directions:
1. In a bowl, beat eggs with pepper, and salt.
2. Preheat the griddle to medium heat. Add oil to the griddle top.
3. Pour broccoli and egg mixture onto the hot griddle top and cook until set. Flip omelet and cook until lightly golden brown.
4. Serve and enjoy.

Nutrition Info: (Per Serving): Calories 203 ;Fat 16 g ;Carbohydrates 4 g ;Sugar 1.5 g ;Protein 12 g ;Cholesterol 327 mg

20. Mini Corn Muffins

Servings: 8
Cooking Time: 25minutes
Ingredients:
- 2 tablespoons butter, melted, or good-quality olive oil, plus softened butter for the pan
- 1½ cups cornmeal
- ½ cup all-purpose flour
- 1 teaspoon baking soda
- 1 teaspoon salt
- 1 egg
- 1½ cups buttermilk or yogurt, plus more as needed

Directions:
1. Preparing the Ingredients.
2. Heat a Griddle for medium-high heat.
3. Grilling
4. The grill temperature should be between 500° and 600°F; if using gas, all your burners might be on medium or medium-low. Coat the insides of a 24-cup heavy-duty mini muffin pan with softened butter.
5. Combine the cornmeal, flour, baking soda, and salt in a large bowl. Beat the egg into the buttermilk. Mix the buttermilk mixture into the dry ingredients just enough to eliminate streaks; lumps are okay. Add the melted butter and mix until just incorporated; avoid overmixing. Spoon or pour the batter into the muffin cups, almost to the top.
6. Place the pan on the grill directly. Grill-bake until the muffins have domed and a skewer inserted in the center comes out clean, 5 to 10 Minutes; don't walk away from the grill. Transfer the pan to a rack to cool for a few Minutes, then transfer the muffins to a clean dish towel or napkin, wrap loosely, and serve warm.

21. Grilled Pizza With Eggs And Greens

Servings: 2 Slices
Cooking Time: 8 Minutes
Ingredients:
- 2 tbsps. all-purpose flour, plus more as needed
- 1/2 store-bought pizza dough (about 8 ounces)
- 1 tbsp. canola oil, divided
- 1 cup fresh ricotta cheese
- 4 large eggs
- Sea salt
- Freshly ground black pepper
- 4 cups arugula, torn
- 1 tbsp. extra-virgin olive oil
- 1 tsp. freshly squeezed lemon juice
- 2 tbsps. grated Parmesan cheese

Directions:
1. Preheat the griddle to medium high.
2. Dust a clean work surface with flour. Place the dough on the floured surface, and roll it into a 9-inch round of even thickness. Dust your rolling pin and work surface with additional flour, as needed, to ensure the dough does not stick.
3. Brush the surface of the rolled-out dough evenly with 1/2 tablespoon of canola oil. Flip the dough over and brush with the remaining 1/2 tablespoon oil. Poke the dough with a fork 5 or 6 times across its surface to prevent air pockets from forming during cooking.
4. Place the dough to the grill and cook for 4 minutes.
5. After 4 minutes, flip the dough, then spoon teaspoons of ricotta cheese across the surface of the dough, leaving a 1-inch border around the edges.
6. Crack one egg into a ramekin or small bowl. This way you can easily remove any shell that may break into the egg and keep the yolk intact. Imagine the dough is split into four quadrants. Pour one egg into each. Repeat with the remaining 3 eggs. Season the pizza with salt and pepper.
7. Continue cooking for the remaining 3 to 4 minutes, until the egg whites are firm.
8. Meanwhile, in a medium bowl, toss together the arugula, oil, and lemon juice, and season with salt and pepper.
9. Transfer the pizza to a cutting board and let it cool. Top it with the arugula mixture, drizzle with olive oil, if desired, and sprinkle with Parmesan cheese. Cut into pieces and serve.
Nutrition Info: (Per serving): Calories: 788kcal; Fat: 46g; Carbs: 58g; Protein: 34g

22. Bacon And Gruyere Omelet

Servings: 2
Cooking Time: 15 Minutes

Ingredients:
- 6 eggs, beaten
- 6 strips bacon
- 1/4 lb gruyere, shredded
- 1 teaspoon black pepper
- 1 teaspoon salt
- 1 tablespoon chives, finely chopped
- vegetable oil

Directions:
1. Add salt to the beaten eggs and set aside for 10 minutes.
2. Heat your griddle to medium heat and add the bacon strips. Cook until most of the fat has rendered, but bacon is still flexible. Remove the bacon from the griddle and place on paper towels.
3. Once the bacon has drained, chop into small pieces.
4. Add the eggs to the griddle in two even pools. Cook until the bottom of the eggs starts to firm up. Add the gruyere to the eggs and cook until the cheese has started to melt and the eggs are just starting to brown.
5. Add the bacon pieces and use a spatula to turn one half of the omelet onto the other half. Remove from the griddle, season with pepper and chives and serve.
Nutrition Info: Calories: 734, Sodium: 855 mg, Dietary Fiber: 0.3g, Fat: 55.3.g, Carbs: 2.8g Protein: 54.8g

23. Potato Pancakes

Servings: 2
Cooking Time: 10 Minutes
Ingredients:
- 2 eggs
- ¼ cup milk
- 1½ cups russet potato, peeled and shredded
- ¼ cup all-purpose flour
- ¼ cup finely diced onion
- ¼ cup finely chopped green onion
- 1 teaspoon baking powder
- 1 teaspoon salt
- 1 teaspoon pepper
- Grilling oil, as needed

Directions:
1. Preparing the Ingredients.
2. In a large bowl, Whisk the eggs and milk until frothy. Add the remaining ingredients and mix to combine. The batter should be moist throughout but not pooling with liquid. Allow to rest for 20 Minutes while the grill heats up.
3. Bring the griddle grill to medium-high heat.

4. Add a thin coat of oil to the Grilling surface, and when it begins to shimmer, add about ¼ cup of potato pancake batter to the griddle for each pancake.
5. Grilling
6. Press the batter to flatten and cook each side for 3 to 4 Minutes until golden brown.

24. Diner Cilantro-style Omelet

Servings: 1
Cooking Time: 10 Minutes
Ingredients:
- ½ cup diced red bell pepper
- ½ cup sliced mushrooms
- ½ teaspoon garlic salt
- 2 eggs plus 2 egg yolks
- ½ cup shredded cheddar-Jack cheese blend, or 2 slices cheese
- butter, as needed
- salt and pepper, to taste
- cilantro, to serve (optional)

Directions:
1. Preparing the Ingredients.
2. Bring the griddle grill to medium-low heat.
3. Butter a portion of your griddle grill and begin to slowly sauté the peppers and mushrooms. After about 3 Minutes, give the veggies a mix and sprinkle on the garlic salt, then cover.
4. Whisk the eggs in a medium bowl until quite frothy. With a large spatula, move the pepper and mushroom mixture to the side of the griddle. Melt plenty of butter over a large area on the griddle and very slowly pour the eggs onto the Grilling surface. The eggs will run a bit, and if you are able to use the side of the spatula to shape them into a circle or square, they will be easier to flip later on.
5. Grilling
6. Allow the eggs to cook slowly without much poking or prodding. After about 3 Minutes, you will see the eggs start to bubble as they cook. Some portions of the omelet will be firm, and some portions will be runny and raw. Distribute the peppers and mushrooms evenly across the omelet the same way you would top a pizza, in a thin layer. When about 80 percent of the egg has solidified, add the cheese in an even layer.
7. At this point, your omelet should have very little runny or visibly raw egg remaining. With a long spatula, scrape under the omelet with a quick wrist motion to make sure the egg is released from the griddle before you attempt to finish. To fold the omelet in half, slide the spatula under the omelet until the entire width of the spatula is covered, and with a lift and twist, lift the spatula and twist your wrist so the omelet folds over and flops onto itself.

8. Cook for about another minute and serve with salt and pepper to taste. Garnish with cilantro, if desired

25. Tomato Scrambled Egg

Servings: 2
Cooking Time: 5 Minutes
Ingredients:
- 2 eggs, lightly beaten
- 2 tbsp fresh basil, chopped
- 1 tbsp olive oil
- 1/2 tomato, chopped
- Pepper
- Salt

Directions:
1. Preheat the griddle to medium heat.
2. Add oil on top of the griddle.
3. Add tomatoes and cook until softened.
4. Whisk eggs with basil, pepper, and salt.
5. Pour egg mixture on top of tomatoes and cook until eggs are set.
6. Serve and enjoy.
Nutrition Info: (Per Serving): Calories 125 ;Fat 12 g ;Carbohydrates 1 g ;Sugar 0.8 g ;Protein 5.8 g ;Cholesterol 164 mg

26. Healthy Oatmeal Pancake

Servings: 2
Cooking Time: 10 Minutes
Ingredients:
- 6 egg whites
- 1 cup steel-cut oats
- 1/4 tsp vanilla
- 1 cup Greek yogurt
- 1/2 tsp baking powder
- 1 tsp liquid stevia
- 1/4 tsp cinnamon

Directions:
1. Preheat the griddle to medium-low heat.
2. Add oats to a blender and blend until a fine powder is a form.
3. Add remaining ingredients into the blender and blend until well combined.
4. Spray griddle top with cooking spray.
5. Pour 1/4 cup batter onto the hot griddle top.
6. Cook pancake until golden brown from both sides.
7. Serve and enjoy.
Nutrition Info: (Per Serving): Calories 295 ;Fat 4 g ;Carbohydrates 37 g ;Sugar 9 g ;Protein 23 g ;Cholesterol 7 mg

27. French Toast Sticks

Servings: 2
Cooking Time: 10 Minutes
Ingredients:
- 2 eggs
- 4 bread slices, cut each bread slice into 3 pieces vertically
- 2/3 cup milk
- 1/4 tsp ground cinnamon
- 1 tsp vanilla

Directions:
1. Preheat the griddle to medium-low heat.
2. In a bowl, whisk eggs with cinnamon, vanilla, and milk.
3. Spray griddle top with cooking spray.
4. Dip each bread piece into the egg mixture and coat well.
5. Place coated bread pieces onto the hot griddle top and cook until golden brown from both sides.
6. Serve and enjoy.

Nutrition Info: (Per Serving): Calories 166 ;Fat 7 g ;Carbohydrates 14 g ;Sugar 5 g ;Protein 10.4 g ;Cholesterol 193 mg

28. Orange Quick Bread

Servings: 8
Cooking Time: 40 Minutes
Ingredients:
- ½ cup good-quality olive oil, plus more for the pan
- 2 cups all-purpose flour
- 1 cup sugar
- 1½ teaspoons baking powder
- ½ teaspoon baking soda
- 1 teaspoon salt
- 1 tablespoon grated orange zest
- ¾ cup fresh orange juice
- 2 eggs
- 1 cup grated zucchini
- ½ cup chopped pecans or walnuts

Directions:
1. Preparing the Ingredients.
2. If using a Griddle, heat it for medium-high direct
3. Grilling
4. The grill temperature should be 500° to 600°F; it could mean all the burners are on medium or medium-low, depending on your particular grill. Rub the inside of a 9- or 10-inch cast-iron skillet with oil.
5. Beat the flour, sugar, baking powder and soda, and salt together in a large bowl. Place the ½ cup oil, orange zest and juice, and eggs in a separate bowl; Beat to combine. (You can prepare the recipe to this point up to several hours ahead; refrigerate the egg mixture.)

6. Pour the wet mixture into the dry ingredients; mix just enough to combine. Don't overmix; it's okay if the batter has lumps. Fold in the zucchini and nuts. Pour the batter into the prepared pan.
7. Place the pan on the grill directly. Grill-bake for 7 Minutes. If the top is brown and the sides have pulled away but the bread still isn't cooked through in the center, turn the heat off under the pan and turn it up on the other burners for a gas gril. Bake, checking frequently, until the top is golden brown, the bread has pulled away from the pan, and a toothpick inserted into a couple of different places comes out almost entirely clean, 3 to 10 Minutes more, depending on how hot it is. Carefully transfer to a rack to cool for at least 15 Minutes. You can cut and serve this right out of the pan. Wrapped, it will keep at room temperature for a couple days.

29. Grilling Repes

Servings: 8
Cooking Time: 15 Minutes
Ingredients:
- 1 cup all-purpose flour
- 1½ cups milk
- ½ cup water
- 2 eggs
- 1 teaspoon grated lemon zest
- 2 pinches salt
- 2 tablespoons melted butter, plus more as needed for the griddle

Directions:
1. Preparing the Ingredients.
2. Place all the ingredients except the butter in a blender and Mixfor 30 to 45 seconds until a smooth batter forms. If necessary, scrape down the sides of the blender so all the ingredients are incorporated, and Mixagain. Allow the batter to rest for 30 Minutes.
3. Bring the griddle grill to medium heat. Butter about a 10-inch square on the griddle grill, then pour ¼ cup of the batter in the center.
4. Grilling
5. Spread the crepe batter into a circle with the measuring cup or use a crepe spreader to create a thin, round layer on the griddle. Cook for about 90 seconds or until most of the batter has set. Flip and cook for another 60 to 90 seconds until it is between yellow and golden brown in color. (You can cook the crepes to your desired doneness, but I find Grilling them to a yellowish color leaning toward golden brown is best for rolling and stuffing.)

30. Upside-down Plum Cake

Servings: 8

Cooking Time: 30 Minutes

Ingredients:
- 8 tablespoons (1 stick) butter
- ½ cup brown sugar
- 1½ pounds small ripe red plums, halved and pitted (if the plums are large and/or hard, slice them to make sure they cook through)
- 1 cup buttermilk
- 2 eggs
- ½ cup granulated sugar
- 2 cups all-purpose flour
- 1 teaspoon baking soda
- ¼ teaspoon salt

Directions:
1. Preparing the Ingredients.
2. Melt 4 tablespoons (½ stick) of the butter in a 9- or 10-inch cast-iron skillet over low heat; remove from the heat. Sprinkle the brown sugar evenly over the bottom of the pan and arrange the plums in a single layer over the brown sugar, cut side down.
3. Melt the remaining 4 tablespoons (½ stick) butter. Add it to the buttermilk, eggs, and granulated sugar in a medium-sized bowl and Beat until foamy. In a large bowl, Beat the flour, baking soda, and salt. (You can make the cake ahead to this point. If not grilling within 30 Minutes, refrigerate the buttermilk mixture.)
4. If using a Griddle, heat it for medium-high direct
5. Grilling
6. The grill temperature should be 500° to 600°F; it could mean all the burners are on medium or medium-low, depending on your particular grill.
7. When you're ready to bake, gradually add the egg mixture to the dry ingredients and mix until well incorporated. Spoon the batter over the plums and spread gently with a spatula until it's evenly thick.
8. Place the skillet on the grill directly. Bake for 10 Minutes, then check. If the cake seems to be browning too fast, turn the heat off under the pan and turn it up on the other burners on a Griddle. Keep checking every few Minutes until the top of the cake is golden brown and a toothpick inserted into the center comes out clean, 5 to 15 Minutes more, depending on how hot it is. Carefully transfer the skillet to a rack and let the cake cool for no more than 5 Minutes. Run a knife around the edge to loosen the cake. Place a serving plate on top of the skillet and carefully invert the hot pan over the plate. The cake should fall out. If it sticks, turn it right side up again, run the knife along the edge again, and use a spatula to gently lift around the edge. Invert again and tap. Remove any stuck fruit from the bottom of the pan with a knife and fit it back into any gaps on the top of the cake.

31. Easy Banana Pancakes

Servings: 6
Cooking Time: 10 Minutes

Ingredients:
- 2 eggs
- 2 tbsp vanilla protein powder
- 1 large banana, mashed
- 1/8 tsp baking powder

Directions:
1. Preheat the griddle to medium-low heat.
2. Meanwhile, add all ingredients into the bowl and mix well until combined.
3. Spray griddle top with cooking spray.
4. Pour 3 tablespoons of batter onto hot griddle top to make a pancake.
5. Cook pancake until lightly browned from both sides.
6. Serve and enjoy.

Nutrition Info: (Per Serving): Calories 79 ;Fat 1.6 g ;Carbohydrates 5.5 g ;Sugar 3 g ;Protein 11 g ;Cholesterol 55 mg

32. Pumpkin Pancake

Servings: 4
Cooking Time: 10 Minutes

Ingredients:
- 4 eggs
- 1/2 tsp cinnamon
- 1/2 cup pumpkin puree
- 1 cup almond flour
- 2 tsp liquid stevia
- 1 tsp baking powder

Directions:
1. Preheat the griddle to medium-low heat.
2. In a bowl, mix almond flour, stevia, baking powder, cinnamon, pumpkin puree, and eggs until well combined.
3. Spray griddle top with cooking spray.
4. Drop batter onto the hot griddle top.
5. Cook pancakes until lightly golden brown from both sides.
6. Serve and enjoy.

Nutrition Info: (Per Serving): Calories 235 ;Fat 18.5 g ;Carbohydrates 9.6 g ;Sugar 2.4 g ;Protein 11.9 g ;Cholesterol 164 mg

33. Baked Egg And Bacon-stuffed Peppers

Servings: 4
Cooking Time: 15 Minutes

Ingredients:
- 1 cup shredded Cheddar cheese

- 4 slices bacon, cooked and chopped
- 4 bell peppers, seeded and tops removed
- 4 large eggs
- Sea salt
- Freshly ground black pepper
- Chopped fresh parsley, for garnish

Directions:
1. Preheat the griddle to medium high.
2. Divide the cheese and bacon between the bell peppers. Crack one of the eggs into each bell pepper, and season with salt and pepper.
3. Place each bell pepper to the grill and cook for 10 to 15 minutes, until the egg whites are cooked and the yolks are slightly runny.
4. Remove the peppers, garnish with parsley, and serve.

Nutrition Info: (Per serving): Calories: 326kcal; Fat: 23g; Carbs: 10g; Protein: 22g

34. Grilled Apple With Rum

Servings: 1
Cooking Time: 30 Minutes
Ingredients:
- 1 pineapple
- 8 tablespoons (1 stick) butter
- 2 tablespoons spiced or dark rum
- 2 tablespoons coconut milk

Directions:
1. Preparing the Ingredients.
2. Remove the core of the apple carefully, without puncturing the bottom or side. (A swivel vegetable peeler does an excellent job, or use a paring knife.) Mash the butter, brown sugar, and cinnamon with the back of a fork until thoroughly mixed. Stuff the mixture into the cavity of the apple.
3. Grilling
4. In either case, clean the grates.
5. Place the apple on the grill directly. Cook until it feels soft when gently squeezed and the filling is melted, 8 to 10 Minutes, depending on its size. Transfer to plate and let cool a few Minutes before serving.

35. Potato Bacon Hash

Servings: 6 – 8
Cooking Time: 3 Hours
Ingredients:
- 6 slices thick cut bacon
- 2 russet potatoes, cut into 1/2 inch chunks
- 1 yellow onion, chopped
- 1 red bell pepper, chopped
- 1 clove garlic, finely chopped

- 1 teaspoon salt
- 1/2 teaspoon black pepper
- 1 tablespoon Tabasco sauce

Directions:
1. Set your griddle to medium heat and cook the bacon until just crispy.
2. Add the potato, onion, and bell pepper to the griddle and cook until the potato has softened. Use the large surface of the griddle to spread out the ingredients.
3. When the potato has softened, add the garlic, salt, and pepper.
4. Chop the bacon into small pieces and add it to the griddle. Stir the mixture well and add the hot sauce right before removing the hash from the griddle. Serve immediately.

Nutrition Info: Calories: 154, Sodium: 475 mg, Dietary Fiber: 1.8g, Fat: 10.2g, Carbs:11.3g Protein: 4.5g

36. Classic Steak And Eggs

Servings: 4
Cooking Time: 10 Minutes
Ingredients:
- 1 pound Sirloin, cut into 4 1/2-inch thick pieces
- 8 large eggs
- 3 tablespoons vegetable oil
- salt and black pepper

Directions:
1. Preheat griddle to medium-high heat on one side and medium heat on the other.
2. Season the steaks with a generous amount of salt and pepper.
3. Place steaks on the medium high side and cook for 3 minutes and add the oil to the medium heat side.
4. Flip the steaks and crack the eggs onto the medium heat side of the griddle.
5. After 3 minutes remove the steaks from the griddle and allow to rest 5 minutes. Finish cooking the eggs and place two eggs and one piece of steak on each plate to serve. Season the eggs with a pinch of salt and pepper.

Nutrition Info: Calories: 444, Sodium: 215 mg, Dietary Fiber: 0g, Fat: 27.2g, Carbs: 0.8g Protein: 47g

37. Grape Focaccia

Servings: 4
Cooking Time: 20 Hours
Ingredients:
- 2 cups all-purpose flour, plus more for dusting
- 1 cup whole wheat flour
- 1¼ teaspoons salt, plus more for the topping
- ¼ teaspoon instant yeast

- 1½ cups plus 2 tablespoons warm water
- Up to ½ cup cornmeal for dusting
- 4 tablespoons good-quality olive oil
- Leaves from 1 large sprig fresh rosemary
- Black pepper
- 1 cup red or green seedless grapes

Directions:
1. Preparing the Ingredients.
2. Beat the flours, salt, and yeast together in a large bowl to combine. Add the water and mix with a heavy spoon until a sticky, shaggy dough forms; it doesn't have to be completely smooth. Cover the bowl with plastic wrap and let it sit in a warm spot for anywhere between 12 and 20 hours.
3. The dough will be wet and bubbly. Transfer it to a lightly floured work surface; sprinkle the top with a little more flour and fold the dough over on itself once or twice. Use a metal bench scraper, plastic pastry scraper, or spatula to keep it from sticking to the surface as you fold. Cover it loosely with plastic and let rest about 15 Minutes.
4. Generously coat a cotton dish towel (not terry cloth) with a layer of cornmeal. Using just enough flour to keep the dough from sticking to the work surface and your fingers, gently and quickly gather the dough into a loose ball and transfer it to the prepared towel; dust the top with more cornmeal. Cover with another clean towel and let the dough rise until it more than doubles in size and will hold the indentation for a moment when you poke it with your finger, 1½ to 2 hours.
5. Place 2 tablespoons of the oil in a small bowl with the rosemary leaves and a sprinkle of salt and pepper. Mix with a small spoon, using the back to muddle the leaves.
6. Heat a Griddle for medium-high indirect
7. Grilling
8. 450°F with the grill closed is ideal. Place a 10-inch ovenproof skillet in the grill over the indirect side of the grill; Bring the dough, still in the towels, out to the grill, along with the grapes and oil mixture.
9. When the grill is ready and the skillet is scorching hot, after 10 to 15 Minutes, carefully remove the skillet. Pour in the remaining 2 tablespoons oil and swirl it to coat. Use the towel to transfer the dough to the skillet. Scatter the grapes on top and spry with the rosemary–olive oil mixture. Shake the pan a few times to distribute the dough if necessary, return it to the indirect side of the grill. Bake, undisturbed, until the focaccia almost fills and separates from the pan and is golden on the top and edges, 30 to 40 Minutes. (The temperature should register between 205° and 210°F on an instant-read thermometer.) Transfer the pan to a wire rack and let the focaccia cool in the pan until you can touch the bottom. Cut into slices and serve.

38. Sausage And Vegetable Scramble

Servings: 4
Cooking Time: 20 Minutes
Ingredients:
- 8 eggs, beaten
- 1/2 lb sausage, sliced into thin rounds or chopped
- 1 green bell pepper, sliced
- 1 yellow onion, sliced
- 1 cup white mushrooms, sliced
- 1 teaspoon salt
- 1/2 teaspoon black pepper
- vegetable oil

Directions:
1. Preheat the griddle to medium-high heat.
2. Brush the griddle with vegetable oil and add the peppers and mushrooms. Cook until lightly browned and then add the onions. Season with salt and pepper and cook until the onions are soft.
3. Add the sausage to the griddle and mix with the vegetables. Cook until lightly browned.
4. Add the eggs and mix with the vegetables and cook until eggs reach desired doneness. Use a large spatula to remove the scramble from the griddle and serve immediately.

Nutrition Info: Calories: 342, Sodium: 1131 mg, Dietary Fiber: 1.2g, Fat: 24.9.g, Carbs: 6.3g, Protein: 23.2g

39. Classic French Toast

Servings: 4
Cooking Time: 10 Minutes
Ingredients:
- 6 eggs, beaten
- 1/4 cup "half and half" or heavy cream
- 8 slices thick cut white or sourdough bread
- 2 tablespoons sugar
- 1 tablespoon cinnamon
- 1 teaspoon salt
- butter
- powdered sugar
- maple syrup

Directions:
1. Heat your griddle to medium heat.
2. In a large bowl, combine the eggs, cream, sugar, cinnamon, and salt. Mix well until smooth.
3. Lightly grease the griddle with butter or vegetable oil.
4. Dip each slice of bread in the mixture until well saturated with egg then place onto the griddle.

5. When the French toast has begun to brown, flip and cook until the other side has browned as well. About four minutes.
6. Remove the French toast from the griddle, dust with powdered sugar, and serve with warm maple syrup.
Nutrition Info: Calories: 332, Sodium: 593 mg, Dietary Fiber: 2.4g, Fat: 10.5.g, Carbs: 44.2g Protein: 16g

40. Chocolate Pancake

Servings: 4
Cooking Time: 10 Minutes
Ingredients:
- 2 eggs
- 1/2 tsp baking powder
- 2 tbsp erythritol
- 1 1/2 tbsp cocoa powder
- 1/4 cup ground flaxseed
- 2 tbsp water
- 1 tsp nutmeg
- 1 tsp cinnamon
- 1/4 tsp salt

Directions:
1. In a bowl, mix ground flaxseed, baking powder, erythritol, cocoa powder, spices, and salt.
2. Add eggs and stir well.
3. Add water and stir until batter is well combined.
4. Preheat the griddle to medium-low heat.
5. Spray griddle top with cooking spray.
6. Pour a large spoonful of batter on a hot griddle top and make a pancake.
7. Cook pancake for 3-4 minutes on each side.
8. Serve and enjoy.
Nutrition Info: (Per Serving): Calories 138 ;Fat 12 g ;Carbohydrates 11 g ;Sugar 8 g ;Protein 4.5 g ;Cholesterol 82 mg

41. Light And Fluffy Buttermilk Pancakes

Servings: 2
Cooking Time: 10 Minutes
Ingredients:
- 2 cups all-purpose flour
- 3 tablespoons sugar
- 2 teaspoons baking powder
- 2 teaspoons baking soda
- pinch kosher salt
- 2 eggs
- 2½ cups buttermilk

Directions:
1. Preparing the Ingredients.

2. Sift the flour, sugar, baking powder, baking soda, and salt together in a large bowl.
3. In a medium bowl, Beat the eggs, buttermilk, and melted butter together until frothy, then pour into the dry ingredients. Mix until well combined but do not overmix. Small lumps will be fine. Let sit at room temperature for 20 to 30 Minutes while your grill heats up.
4. Bring the griddle grill to medium-high heat. Oil the griddle and allow it to heat until the oil is shimmering but not smoking.
5. Grilling
6. Pour about ¼ cup batter onto the griddle grill for each pancake. The pancakes should slowly begin to form bubbles. After 2 to 4 Minutes, when the bubbles pop and leave small holes, flip the pancake. Cook for an additional 2 Minutes.

42. Simple French Crepes

Servings: 4
Cooking Time: 15 Minutes
Ingredients:
- 1 1/4 cups flour
- 3/4 cup whole milk
- 1/2 cup water
- 2 eggs
- 3 tablespoons unsalted butter, melted
- 1 teaspoon vanilla
- 2 tablespoon sugar

Directions:
1. In a large bowl, add all the ingredients and mix with a whisk. Make sure the batter is smooth. Rest for 1 hour.
2. Heat your Blackstone Griddle to medium heat and add a thin layer of butter. Add about ¼ cup of the batter. Using a crepe spreading tool, form your crepe and cook for 1-2 minutes. Use your Crepe Spatula and flip. Cook for another minute.
3. Top with Nutella and strawberries for a sweet crepe, or top with scrambled eggs and black forest ham for a savory crepe
Nutrition Info: Calories: 303, Sodium: 112mg, Dietary Fiber: 1.1g, Fat: 12.7g, Carbs: 38.2g Protein: 8.4g

43. Grilled Ham And Swiss Crepes

Servings: 2
Cooking Time: 10 Minutes
Ingredients:
- 2 tablespoons oil
- ½ red bell pepper, thinly sliced
- 6 thin slices Black Forest ham
- 4 thin slices Swiss cheese

- 2 prepared crepes
- 2 teaspoons Dijon mustard

Directions:
1. Preparing the Ingredients.
2. Bring the griddle grill to medium and heat the oil. Sauté the bell pepper strips for 5 to 7 Minutes, until wilted. Set aside and keep warm.
3. Spread ham slices out on the griddle grill and warm them for about 5 Minutes on one side. Flip the ham and arrange into two piles of three slices, letting the slices overlap.
4. Place two slices of cheese on each of the piles of ham, add a few tablespoons of water to the griddle, and cover to help the cheese melt.
5. Grilling
6. While the cheese is melting, warm the crepes on the griddle and spread half the mustard on each. Top with the ham and melted cheese and sauteed bell peppers. Fold and serve.

44. Grilled Cinnamon Toast With Berries And Whipped Cream

Servings: 4 Slices
Cooking Time: 10 Minutes
Ingredients:
- 1 (15-ounce) can full-fat coconut milk, refrigerated overnight
- 1/2 tablespoon powdered sugar
- 1-1/2 teaspoons vanilla extract, divided
- 1 cup halved strawberries
- 1 tablespoon maple syrup, plus more for garnish
- 1 tablespoon brown sugar, divided
- 3/4 cup lite coconut milk
- 2 large eggs
- 1/2 teaspoon ground cinnamon
- 2 tablespoons unsalted butter, at room temperature
- 4 slices challah bread

Directions:
1. Turn the chilled can of full-fat coconut milk upside down (do not shake the can), open the bottom, and pour out the liquid coconut water. Scoop the remaining solid coconut cream into a medium bowl. Using an electric hand mixer, whip the cream for 3 to 5 minutes, until soft peaks form.
2. Add the powdered sugar and 1/2 teaspoon of the vanilla to the coconut cream, and whip it again until creamy. Place the bowl in the refrigerator.
3. Preheat the griddle to medium high.
4. While the unit is preheating, combine the strawberries with the maple syrup and toss to coat evenly. Sprinkle evenly with ½ tablespoon of the brown sugar.

5. In a large shallow bowl, whisk together the lite coconut milk, eggs, the remaining 1 teaspoon of vanilla, and cinnamon.
6. Place the strawberries on the grill top. Gently press the fruit down to maximize grill marks. Grill for 4 minutes without flipping.
7. Meanwhile, butter each slice of bread on both sides. Place one slice in the egg mixture and let it soak for 1 minute. Flip the slice over and soak it for another minute. Repeat with the remaining bread slices. Sprinkle each side of the toast with the remaining 1/2 tablespoon of brown sugar.
8. After 4 minutes, remove the strawberries from the grill and set aside. Decrease the temperature to medium low. Place the bread on the Grill and cook for 4 to 6 minutes, until golden and caramelized. Check often to ensure desired doneness.
9. Place the toast on a plate and top with the strawberries and whipped coconut cream. Drizzle with maple syrup, if desired.

Nutrition Info: (Per serving): Calories: 386kcal; Fat: 19g; Carbs: 49g; Protein: 7g

45. Fried Pickles

Servings: 4
Cooking Time: 10 Minutes
Ingredients:
- 20 dill pickle slices
- 1/4 cup all-purpose flour
- 1/8 tsp. baking powder
- 3 tbsps. beer or seltzer water
- 1/8 tsp. sea salt
- 2 tbsps. water, plus more if needed
- 2 tbsps. cornstarch
- 1-1/2 cups panko bread crumbs
- 1 tsp. paprika
- 1 tsp. garlic powder
- 1/4 tsp. cayenne pepper
- 2 tbsps. canola oil, divided

Directions:
1. Preheat the griddle to medium-high.
2. Pat the pickle slices dry, and place them on a dry plate in the freezer.
3. In a medium bowl, stir together the flour, baking powder, beer, salt, and water. The batter should be the consistency of cake batter. If it is too thick, add more water, 1 teaspoon at a time.
4. Place the cornstarch in a small shallow bowl.
5. In a separate large shallow bowl, combine the bread crumbs, paprika, garlic powder, and cayenne pepper.
6. Remove the pickles from the freezer. Dredge each one in cornstarch. Tap off any excess, then coat

in the batter. Lastly, coat evenly with the bread crumb mixture.

7.   Set on the griddle top and gently brush the breaded pickles with 1 tablespoon of oil. Cook for 5 minutes.

8.   After 5 minutes, turn and gently brush the pickles with the remaining 1 tablespoon of oil and resume cooking.

9.   When cooking is complete, serve immediately.

Nutrition Info: (Per serving): Calories: 296kcal; Fat: 10g; Carbs: 44g; Protein: 7g

46. Easy Pita Bread

Servings: 6
Cooking Time: 2 Hours
Ingredients:
- 3 cups all-purpose or bread flour, plus more as needed
- 2 teaspoons instant yeast
- 2 teaspoons salt
- ½ teaspoon sugar
- 3 tablespoons good-quality olive oil
- 1 cup warm water, plus more as needed
- Melted butter for brushing (optional)

Directions:
1.   Preparing the Ingredients.
2.   Beat the flour, yeast, salt, and sugar together in a large bowl. Add the oil and water and mix with a heavy spoon. Continue to add water 1 tablespoon at a time, until the dough forms a ball and is slightly sticky; in the unlikely event that the mixture gets too sticky, add flour 1 tablespoon at a time.
3.   Turn the dough onto a lightly floured work surface and knead for a minute to form a smooth, round ball. Place the dough in a bowl and cover with plastic wrap; let rise in a warm spot until it doubles in size, 1 to 2 hours. Or you can let the dough rise more slowly, in the refrigerator, for up to 8 hours.
4.   Divide the dough into 6 to 12 even-sized pieces; roll each into a ball. Place each ball on a lightly floured surface and cover with plastic wrap or a clean dish towel. Let rest until they puff slightly, about 20 Minutes.
5.   On a lightly floured surface, roll each ball out to about ⅛ inch thick. Cover and let rest while you prepare the grill.
6.   Heat a Griddle for medium-high heat.
7.   Grilling
8.   Make sure the grates are clean.
9.   Working in batches, Place the breads on the grill directly. Cook turning once, until they're slightly colored and puffed, 4 to 8 Minutes per side. Don't walk away from the grill. To use the pitas folded over fillings, cook them only until soft and pliable. If you're going to cut the pita in wedges for a dip or spread,

you can grill them longer; move and rotate them for even Grilling. Transfer to a platter, brush with melted butter if you like, and serve.

47. Figs With Honey

Servings: 4
Cooking Time: 25 Minutes
Ingredients:
- 8 ripe figs, stemmed
- 2 tablespoons walnut oil or good-quality olive oil
- 8 walnut halves, toasted
- ¼ cup honey

Directions:
1.   Preparing the Ingredients.
2.   Brush the figs with the walnut oil, then cut an X in the stem ends. Push 1 walnut half into each fig.
3.   Grilling
4.   Heat your Griddle to medium heat.
5.   Place the figs on the grill, stem side up. Cook until the fruit softens, 5 to 10 Minutes. Transfer to a platter, spry with the honey, and serve.

48. Smoky Paprika Shrimp Skewers

Servings: 6
Cooking Time: 20 Minutes
Ingredients:
- 2 pounds 16-20 count shrimp, shelled and deveined
- Marinade:
- 2 tablespoons finely chopped fresh ginger root
- 2 cloves garlic, finely chopped
- 4 tablespoons sesame oil
- ½ cup Japanese rice wine
- 1 tablespoon clover or orange honey
- 2 tablespoons molasses
- 4 green onions, chopped
- 1 teaspoon blackened seasoning (see below)
- ¼ teaspoon dry mustard
- 1 tablespoon butter
- BLACKENING SPICES:
- 4 teaspoons paprika
- 1 teaspoon ground oregano
- 1 teaspoon ground thyme
- 1 teaspoon cayenne powder (or more to taste)
- ½ teaspoon black pepper
- ½ teaspoon finely ground white pepper
- ½ teaspoon garlic powder
- Soak 4-6 bamboo skewers in hot water for 20 Minutes.

Directions:
1.   Preparing the Ingredients.

2. Mix marinade ingredients in small bowl, then pour into Ziploc bag and add shrimp. Drain and bring shrimp to room temperature. Boil remaining marinade for 10 Minutes, adding 1 tablespoon butter, then cool and set aside.
3. Mix blackening spices in small bowl. Preheat grill to medium hot (450° to 500°).
4. Grilling
5. Place 4-5 shrimp on each skewer. Sprinkle both sides with blackening spices. Grill shrimp for 1-2 Minutes on each side, turning once.
6. Serve with cooled marinade as a dip or pouring sauce.

49. Grilled Asian-style Broccoli

Servings: 4 Slices
Cooking Time: 10 Minutes
Ingredients:
- 4 tablespoons soy sauce
- 4 tablespoons balsamic vinegar
- 2 tablespoons canola oil
- 2 teaspoons maple syrup
- 2 heads broccoli, trimmed into florets
- Red pepper flakes, for garnish
- Sesame seeds, for garnish

Directions:
1. Preheat the griddle to medium high.
2. While the unit is preheating, in a large bowl, whisk together the soy sauce, balsamic vinegar, oil, and maple syrup. Add the broccoli and toss to coat evenly.
3. Place the broccoli on the Grill and grill for 8 to 10 minutes, until charred on all sides.
4. When cooking is complete, place the broccoli on a large serving platter. Garnish with red pepper flakes and sesame seeds. Serve immediately.
Nutrition Info: (Per serving): Calories: 133kcal; Fat: 8g; Carbs: 13g; Protein: 5g

50. Special Homemade Marshmallows

Servings: 48
Cooking Time: 1 Hour
Ingredients:
- Good-quality vegetable oil for the pan
- 3 1-ounce packages unflavored gelatin
- 2 cups granulated sugar
- 1 cup light corn syrup
- ¼ teaspoon salt
- 2 teaspoons vanilla extract
- ½ cup confectioners' sugar
- ½ cup cornstarch

- Graham crackers and bar chocolate as needed for the s'mores
Directions:
1. Preparing the Ingredients.
2. Lightly oil a 9- × 13-inch baking pan. Line the bottom and sides with parchment paper, then lightly oil the paper.
3. Place the gelatin in a large heatproof bowl and add ½ cup cold water. Mix to combine.
4. Place the granulated sugar, corn syrup, salt, and ½ cup water in a heavy medium-sized saucepan over high heat and clip a candy thermometer to the side of the pot. Bring the mixture to a boil, stirring just until the sugar dissolves. Once the syrup is boiling, do not stir; that can cause the sugar to crystallize. Let the syrup continue to boil until the temperature reaches 240°F. Immediately remove the pan from the heat. Slowly pour the hot syrup into the bowl with the softened gelatin, mixing continuously with an electric mixer, initially on low speed and then on high speed once all the syrup has been added. Be careful not to pour the syrup directly on the Whiskers and splatter scalding hot syrup everywhere. Whisk until the mixture expands greatly in volume, becomes stiff, and cools, 10 to 12 Minutes. Whisk in the vanilla. Transfer the mixture to the prepared pan and spread it evenly with a rubber spatula. Let set, uncovered, at room temperature, until firm, at least 4 hours or overnight.
5. Mix the confectioners' sugar and cornstarch together and sift a third of it over a large cutting board. Turn the baking pan over onto the board, unmold the marshmallow onto the sugar mixture, and remove the parchment. Sift more of the cornstarch-sugar mixture over the marshmallow to coat. Cut across into 1½-inch-wide strips, and the strips into 1½-inch squares. Sift the remainder of the cornstarch-sugar mixture over the marshmallows and toss to coat them completely. Working in small batches, Place them in a fine-mesh strainer and shake off the excess sugar coating. Store the marshmallows in an airtight container. (They'll keep for up to a couple of weeks.)
6. Grilling
7. Heat for hot direct Grilling.
8. Skewer the marshmallows and toast them, turning until they're as brown as you like. Sandwich the hot marshmallow with a piece of chocolate between 2 graham crackers. Eat and repeat.
9. S'Mores with Homemade Orange Marshmallows
10. Orange and chocolate are made for one another: Substitute 1 teaspoon orange extract for the vanilla and add 2 tablespoons grated orange zest with it.
11. S'Mores with Homemade Brown Sugar–Bourbon Marshmallows
12. These are for the grown-ups: Decrease the granulated sugar to 1 cup and the corn syrup to ½

cup. Add 1 cup dark brown sugar and ½ cup bourbon along with them.

13. S'Mores with Homemade Espresso Marshmallows

14. For a little pick-me-up: Add 2 tablespoons instant espresso in step 3 along with the sugar, corn syrup, salt, and water. Omit the vanilla.

51. Crispy Chicken, Bacon, & Artichoke

Servings: 2
Cooking Time: 10 Minutes
Ingredients:
- 4 slices bacon
- 8 ounces chicken breast, cut into small cubes
- White Wine Griddle Sauce
- 3 marinated artichoke hearts, quartered
- 2 prepared crepes
- ⅓ cup ranch dressing
- salt and pepper, to taste

Directions:
1. Preparing the Ingredients.
2. Bring the griddle grill to medium-high heat and cook the bacon. Remove and keep warm.
3. In the bacon fat, sauté the cubed chicken with salt and pepper for 4 Minutes, with very little movement, allowing the chicken to brown. Add the White Wine Griddle Sauce as needed and cover to finish Grilling an additional 4 to 6 Minutes, or until the chicken is done. Remove and keep warm.
4. Grilling
5. Sauté the marinated artichokes in the residual bits of cooked chicken on the griddle grill for 3 to 5 Minutes until warm and slightly brown.
6. Spread about half of the ranch dressing on each crepe. Fill the crepes with chicken, bacon, and artichoke pieces.

52. Toad In A Hole

Servings: 4
Cooking Time: 5 Minutes
Ingredients:
- 4 slices white, wheat, or sourdough bread
- 4 eggs
- 2 tablespoons butter
- salt and black pepper

Directions:
1. Preheat griddle to medium heat add the butter, spreading it around.
2. Cut a hole in the center of each slice of bread.
3. Place the slices of bread on the griddle and crack an egg into the holes in each slice of bread.
4. Cook until the bread begins to brown, then flip and cook until the egg whites are firm.

5. Remove from the griddle and season with salt and black pepper before serving.
Nutrition Info: Calories: 206, Sodium: 311 mg, Dietary Fiber: 0.8g, Fat: 10.7g, Carbs: 18.4g Protein: 9.4g

53. Sausage Mixed Grill

Servings: 4 Slices
Cooking Time: 22 Minutes
Ingredients:
- 8 mini bell peppers
- 2 heads radicchio, each cut into 6 wedges
- Canola oil, for brushing
- Sea salt
- Freshly ground black pepper
- 6 breakfast sausage links
- 6 hot or sweet Italian sausage links

Directions:
1. Preheat the griddle to medium high.
2. Brush the bell peppers and radicchio with the oil. Season with salt and black pepper.
3. Place the bell peppers and radicchio on the Grill and cook for 10 minutes, without flipping.
4. Meanwhile, poke the sausages with a fork or knife and brush them with some of the oil.
5. After 10 minutes, remove the vegetables and set aside. Decrease the heat to medium. Place the sausages on the Grill and cook for 6 minutes.
6. Flip the sausages and cook for 6 minutes more. Remove the sausages from the Grill.
7. Serve the sausages and vegetables on a large cutting board or serving tray.
Nutrition Info: (Per serving): Calories: 473kcal; Fat: 34g; Carbs: 14g; Protein: 28g

54. Jalapeño Stuffed Burger

Servings: 4
Cooking Time: 50 Minutes
Ingredients:
- Burger Mixture
- 2 lb. ground beef
- 1 tsp. sea salt
- 1 tsp. ground black pepper
- 3 tbsp. cilantro, chopped ½ small onion, peeled & minced
- 1 jalapeño, seeded & chopped

Directions:
1. Preparing the Ingredients.
2. Combine ground beef, sea salt, pepper, cilantro, onion, and jalapeño. Divide ground beef mixture into 4 balls. Stuff each ball with a chunk of cheddar. Rub burgers with olive oil. Grill
3. Grilling

4.   About 5 Minutes per side or to desired doneness. Top burgers with sliced cheddar.
5.   Spread each roll with margarine. Grill to desired doneness. Serve burgers topped with pickled jalapeños. 4 ½ oz. cheddar cheese, cut into chunks 2 tbsp. olive oil,4 slices cheddar cheese,4 brioche rolls ¼ cup margarine,16 pickled jalapeño rings. If you have fresh sliced jalapeños, heat 1 cup vinegar and ¼ cup sugar, then pour over the peppers and let sit for 30 Minutes for a quick pickle.

55.   Fruit Skewers With Syrup

Servings: 4
Cooking Time: 35 Minutes
Ingredients:
- ½ cup sugar
- Zest of 1 large orange, taken off in strips
- 1 tablespoon whole cloves
- 1 small pineapple
- 2 star fruit

Directions:
1.   Preparing the Ingredients.
2.   Place the sugar, orange zest, cloves, and ½ cup water in a small saucepan over medium heat; mix until the sugar dissolves. Bring to a boil, reduce the heat, and gently bubble for 5 to 10 Minutes. Remove from the heat and let sit for at least 30 Minutes and up to several hours to let the flavor develop. When you are happy with the flavor of the syrup, strain it and use or refrigerate in an airtight container; it will keep for at least a week.
3.   Grilling
4.   Heat your Griddle to medium heat.
5.   If you're using bamboo or wooden skewers, soak them in water for 30 Minutes.
6.   Trim, peel, and core the pineapple, then cut it into 2-inch chunks. Cut the star fruit into ½-inch-thick slices. Skewer the fruit; using 2 skewers makes them easier to turn. Skewer the star fruit through the points of the star on two sides. Brush lightly with the orange-clove syrup.
7.   Place the skewers on the grill. Cook turning once, until the pineapple chunks brown in spots, 4 to 8 Minutes per side, depending on how the grill is; brush the fruit several times with the syrup while it grills. When the fruit is done, brush it once more with syrup. Transfer to a platter and serve hot or warm.

56.   Pineapple Rings

Servings: 6
Cooking Time: 30 Minutes
Ingredients:
- 1 pineapple

- 8 tablespoons (1 stick) butter
- 2 tablespoons spiced or dark rum
- 2 tablespoons coconut milk

Directions:
1.   Preparing the Ingredients.
2.   Cut the top and bottom off the pineapple, then remove the peel by standing the pineapple upright and running the knife down from top to bottom, working all around, without taking much of the flesh. Lay the pineapple on its side and cut it across into 1- to 1½-inch rings. Cut the core out of each ring. (An easy way to do this is to use a small cookie cutter or swivel peeler, or with a paring knife.) If not using immediately, Place the rings in an airtight container; they will keep in the refrigerator for up to 2 days.
3.   Melt the butter in a small saucepan over medium heat. When it foams, add the rum and coconut milk and bring to a gentle bubble. Without boiling, stirring occasionally, until the mixture reduces a bit and gets syrupy, 4 to 5 Minutes. Remove from the heat. Brush the pineapple rings on both sides with the glaze; reserve the remaining glaze.
4.   Grilling
5.   Heat your Griddle to medium heat. Place the pineapple rings on the grill. Cook turning once, until they develop grill marks and are heated all the way through, 4 to 8 Minutes per side, depending on how hot it is. Transfer to a plate and serve spryd with the remaining glaze (reheat it if necessary).

57.   Caramelized Oranges

Servings: 4
Cooking Time: 25 Minutes
Ingredients:
- ¼ cup sugar
- ½ teaspoon five-spice powder (to make your own
- 2 large oranges
- ¼ cup chopped fresh mint

Directions:
1.   Preparing the Ingredients.
2.   Mix the sugar and five-spice powder together on a small plate. Cut a sliver off the top and bottom of each orange so that it will sit flat on the grates without rolling, then turn them on their sides and cut in half through the equator. Remove any seeds. Press the cut side of each half into the sugar. Let sit until the sugar is absorbed and/or you are ready to grill.
3.   Grilling
4.   Heat your Griddle to medium heat. Place the orange halves on the grill directly, sugared side up.
5.   Until they are warm all the way through, 5 to 10 Minutes. (Be careful not to let them stay on too long, or their juice will evaporate.) Turn them over and

cook just until the cut sides brown, 2 to 3 Minutes. Transfer to individual serving plates, sprinkle with the mint, and serve with a knife and fork or with grapefruit spoons, if you have them.

58. Piña Colada Tacos With Coconout

Servings: 4
Cooking Time: 40 Minutes
Ingredients:
- ½ ripe pineapple, peeled, cored, and cut into 1-inch cubes
- ¼ cup dark rum
- ¼ cup coconut milk
- 4 tablespoons (½ stick) butter, softened
- 4 7-inch flour tortillas
- 1 tablespoon sugar, or as needed
- Lime wedges for serving (optional)
- ½ cup shredded coconut, toasted (see below)

Directions:
1. Preparing the Ingredients.
2. Place the pineapple, rum, and coconut milk in a bowl and toss to combine. Let the fruit macerate for at least 20 Minutes, or up to several hours in the refrigerator.
3. Grilling
4. Heat your Griddle to medium heat. If you're using bamboo or wooden skewers, soak them in water for 30 Minutes.
5. Spread the butter on both sides of the tortillas, then sprinkle with the sugar. Thread the pineapple cubes onto 4 skewers, letting excess marinade drip back in the bowl.
6. Place the skewers on the grill directly. Cook until the pineapple is caramelized, 5 to 10 Minutes per side, depending on how hot it is. Transfer the skewers to a platter. Place the tortillas on the grill directly, Cook turning once, until they lightly brown, 1 to 2 Minutes per side.
7. To serve, Place a skewer on top of each tortilla, squeeze with some lime if you like, and sprinkle with toasted coconut. To eat, pull out the skewer.

59. Almond Pancakes

Servings: 2
Cooking Time: 10 Minutes
Ingredients:
- 1 egg
- 1/2 cup almond flour
- 1/2 tsp baking powder
- 1/2 tbsp heavy whipping cream
- 1 1/2 tbsp Swerve

Directions:
1. Preheat the griddle to medium-low heat.

2. In a bowl, mix almond flour, Baking powder, sweetener, and salt.
3. In another bowl, whisk egg and heavy whipping cream.
4. Add dry ingredients into the wet and mix well.
5. Spray griddle top with cooking spray.
6. Drop batter onto the hot griddle top.
7. Cook pancakes until lightly golden brown from both sides.
8. Serve and enjoy.
Nutrition Info: (Per Serving): Calories 90 ;Fat 7 g ;Carbohydrates 13 g ;Sugar 11 g ;Protein 4 g ;Cholesterol 87 mg

60. Best Johnny Cakes

Servings: 2
Cooking Time: 10 Minutes
Ingredients:
- 2 eggs
- 1⅓ cups milk
- 1 tablespoon honey
- ¼ cup Grilling oil
- 1½ cups all-purpose flour
- ½ cup fine cornmeal
- 4 teaspoons baking powder
- 1 tablespoon sugar
- 1 teaspoon salt

Directions:
1. Preparing the Ingredients.
2. Beat the eggs, milk, honey, and oil in a medium bowl until frothy. Combine the flour, cornmeal, baking powder, sugar, and salt in a large bowl and mix to combine.
3. Add the wet ingredients to the dry ingredients and mix until well-incorporated and free of clumps. Let sit for 20 Minutes while your grill heats up.
4. Bring the griddle grill to medium-high heat. Oil the griddle and allow it to heat until the oil is shimmering but not smoking.
5. Grilling
6. Pour about ¼ cup of batter onto the griddle grill for each pancake. The pancakes should slowly begin to form bubbles. After 2 to 4 Minutes, when the bubbles pop and leave small holes, flip the pancakes. Cook for an additional 2 Minutes.

61. French Toast With Ice Cream

Servings: 4
Cooking Time: 10 Minutes
Ingredients:
- 1 cup melted vanilla ice cream
- 3 eggs
- 1 teaspoon vanilla extract

- pinch of ground cinnamon
- 8 slices Texas toast or other thick-cut bread
- Grilling oil, as needed

Directions:
1. Preparing the Ingredients.
2. Combine the melted ice cream, eggs, vanilla extract, and cinnamon in a bowl wide enough for the bread to be easily dipped into. Mix very well or until frothy.
3. Bring the griddle grill to medium-high heat and coat the surface with oil. When the oil begins to shimmer, dip each side of the bread into the egg batter so it lightly coats each side. Allow any additional batter to drain back into the bowl.
4. Grilling
5. Place the bread on the griddle. Cook for 3 to 4 Minutes per side, or until the French toast is golden brown. Repeat with the remaining ingredients.

62. Grilled Fruit Salad With Honey-lime Glaze

Servings: 4
Cooking Time: 4 Minutes

Ingredients:
- 1/2 pound strawberries, washed, hulled and halved
- 1 (9 oz.) can pineapple chunks, drained, juice reserved
- 2 peaches, pitted and sliced
- 6 tbsps. honey, divided
- 1 tbsp. freshly squeezed lime juice

Directions:
1. Preheat your griddle to medium high.
2. While the unit is preheating, combine the strawberries, pineapple, and peaches in a large bowl with 3 tablespoons of honey. Toss to coat evenly.
3. Place the fruit on the grill top. Gently press the fruit down to maximize grill marks. Grill for 4 minutes without flipping.
4. Meanwhile, in a small bowl, combine the remaining 3 tablespoons of honey, lime juice, and 1 tablespoon of reserved pineapple juice.
5. When cooking is complete, place the fruit in a large bowl and toss with the honey mixture. Serve immediately.

Nutrition Info: (Per serving): Calories: 178kcal; fat: 1g; Carbs: 47g; Protein: 2g

63. Coconut Orange Pound Cake

Servings: 6
Cooking Time: 1½ Hours
Ingredients:

- ½ pound (2 sticks) butter, softened, plus more for the pan
- 2 cups cake or all-purpose flour
- 1½ teaspoons baking powder
- ¼ teaspoon freshly grated nutmeg (optional)
- ½ teaspoon salt
- 1 cup sugar, plus 1 tablespoon to sprinkle over the oranges
- 5 eggs
- 2 teaspoons vanilla extract
- 6 medium oranges, peeled, sectioned, and seeded if necessary
- Grated zest and juice of 1 lime
- ½–¾ cup shredded coconut, toasted
- 2 tablespoons chopped fresh mint for garnish

Directions:
1. Preparing the Ingredients.
2. Heat the oven to 325°F. Coat the inside of a 9- × 5-inch loaf pan with butter.
3. Beat the flour, baking powder, nutmeg if you're using it, and salt together in a bowl.
4. Place the ½ pound butter in a large bowl; use an electric mixer to Whisk it until smooth. Add ¾ cup of the sugar and Whisk until it's well blended, then add another ¼ cup. Whisk until the mixture is light in color and fluffy, scraping down the side of the bowl if necessary. Whisk in the eggs one at a time. Add the vanilla and Whisk until blended. Add the dry ingredients and mix by hand just until smooth; do not overmix and do not Whisk.
5. Pour and scrape the batter into the prepared pan. Bake until a toothpick inserted into the center comes out clean, 1 to 1¼ hours.
6. Let the cake rest in the pan for 5 Minutes, then invert it onto a wire rack. Remove the pan, then turn the cake right side up. Let cool completely. Store at room temperature, covered with wax paper, for up to 2 days.
7. Place the orange sections in a bowl and sprinkle with the remaining 1 tablespoon sugar and the lime zest and juice. Toss lightly to mix. Let macerate at room temperature for 30 Minutes or up to several hours.
8. Grilling
9. Cut the pound cake into 1-to 1½-inch slices. Place them on the grill directly. Cook turning once, until the slices develop grill marks, 2 to 3 Minutes per side. To serve, spoon the oranges over the cake with some of their liquid, sprinkle with the coconut, and garnish with the mint.

64. Simple Cheese Sandwich

Servings: 1
Cooking Time: 10 Minutes

Ingredients:
- 2 bread slices
- 2 tsp butter
- 2 cheese slices

Directions:
1. Preheat the griddle to medium-low heat.
2. Place cheese slices on top of one bread slice and cover cheese with another bread slice.
3. Spread butter on top of both the bread slices.
4. Place sandwich on hot griddle top and cook until golden brown or until cheese is melted.
5. Serve and enjoy.

Nutrition Info: (Per Serving): Calories 340 ;Fat 26 g ;Carbohydrates 9.8 g ;Sugar 1 g ;Protein 15.4 g ;Cholesterol 79 mg

65. Onion, Pepper, And Mushroom Frittata

Servings: 4 Slices
Cooking Time: 10 Minutes
Ingredients:
- 4 large eggs
- 1/4 cup whole milk
- Sea salt
- Freshly ground black pepper
- 1/2 bell pepper, seeded and diced
- 1/2 onion, chopped
- 4 cremini mushrooms, sliced
- 1/2 cup shredded Cheddar cheese

Directions:
1. Preheat the griddle to medium high.
2. In a medium bowl, whisk together the eggs and milk. Season with the salt and pepper. Add the bell pepper, onion, mushrooms, and cheese. Mix until well combined.
3. Pour the egg mixture into the Ninja Multi-Purpose Pan or baking pan, spreading evenly.
4. Place the pan directly to the grill and cook for 10 minutes, or until lightly golden.

Nutrition Info: (Per serving): Calories: 153kcal; Fat: 10g; Carbs: 5g; Protein: 11g

66. Pain Perdu With Roasted Strawberries

Servings: 4
Cooking Time: 20 Minutes
Ingredients:
- 3 cups sliced hulled strawberries (about 1½ pounds)
- 2–3 tablespoons sugar
- 1 tablespoon balsamic vinegar
- 2 eggs

- ½ cup milk
- 1 teaspoon vanilla extract
- Pinch salt
- 4 slices bread
- Black pepper (optional)

Directions:
1. Preparing the Ingredients.
2. Place the strawberries in a bowl, sprinkle with 1 to 2 tablespoons of the sugar (depending on their sweetness), and toss gently to coat. Add the vinegar and toss again. Let macerate at room temperature until you're ready for dessert, up to several hours.
3. Whisk the eggs lightly in a large shallow bowl, then Whisk in the milk, the remaining 1 tablespoon sugar, vanilla, and salt. Refrigerate until you're ready to use it (or up to several hours).
4. Grilling
5. Heat your Griddle to medium heat.
6. Give each slice of bread a quick dip in the egg wash on both sides, Place on a large plate, and immediately take out them to the grill. Place the bread on the grill directly. Cook until the bread develops grill marks, 2 to 3 Minutes per side. Transfer to a clean platter. To serve, top each grilled toast with a spoonful of the balsamic strawberries. Let diners add freshly ground black pepper to their strawberries, if they like.

67. Classic Buttermilk Pancakes

Servings: 4
Cooking Time: 10 Minutes
Ingredients:
- 2 cups all purpose flour
- 3 tablespoons sugar
- 1 1/2 teaspoons baking powder
- 1 1/2 teaspoons baking soda
- 1 1/4 teaspoons salt
- 2 1/2 cups buttermilk
- 2 eggs
- 3 tablespoons unsalted butter, melted
- vegetable oil

Directions:
1. In a large bowl, combine the flour, sugar, baking soda, baking powder, and salt.
2. Stir in the buttermilk, eggs, and butter, and mix until combined but not totally smooth.
3. Heat your griddle to medium heat and add a small amount of oil. Using a paper towel, spread the oil over the griddle in a very thin layer.
4. Use a ladle to pour the batter onto the griddle allowing a few inches between pancakes.
5. When the surface of the pancakes is bubbly, flip and cook a few additional minutes. Remove the

pancakes from the griddle and serve immediately with butter and maple syrup.

Nutrition Info: Calories: 432, Sodium: 458 mg, Dietary Fiber: 1.7g, Fat: 12.8.g, Carbs: 65.1g Protein: 14.4g

68. Lebanese Bread

Servings: 8
Cooking Time: 1½ Hours
Ingredients:
- 1 tablespoon instant yeast
- 2 teaspoons salt
- 1 teaspoon sugar
- 1 cup warm water, plus more as needed
- 3 cups all-purpose flour, plus more as needed
- 3 tablespoons za'atar (to make your own
- 3 tablespoons good-quality olive oil

Directions:
1. Preparing the Ingredients.
2. Beat the yeast, salt, sugar, and 1 cup water together in a large bowl. Add the flour and mix with a heavy spoon until the mixture can be formed into a ball; it should be slightly sticky. If it's dry, add more water 1 tablespoon at a time until you get the right consistency; in the unlikely event that the mixture is too sticky, add flour 1 tablespoon at a time. Turn the dough out onto a lightly floured work surface; knead a few times until smooth. Place the dough in a bowl and cover with plastic wrap; let rise until it doubles in size, about 1 hour.
3. Heat a Griddle for medium-high heat.
4. Grilling
5. Make sure the grates are clean.
6. Beat the za'atar into the oil in a small bowl.
7. When the dough is ready, transfer it to a well-floured work surface and knead for a few Minutes, until smooth and pliable. Cut into 8 equal-sized pieces. Roll each piece into an oval roughly 6 to 8 inches long and 3 to 4 inches wide. Stack them between wax paper or parchment and bring the breads to the grill along with the za'atar oil, a brush, and a baking sheet. Working in batches, just before Grilling, brush the za'atar oil over the breads to within ½ inch of the edge; make sure to get plenty of the sesame seeds and thyme that are suspended in the oil.
8. One at a time, use your hands to pick up an oval by the long ends and drop it onto the grate directly, with the long side perpendicular to the grates. Cook until the dough bubbles up on top, the outer edges start to brown, and the bottom develops grill marks; depending on how hot it is, this will take 1½ to 3 Minutes. Start checking at 1½ Minutes, then every 30 seconds after that. Use a spatula to transfer the breads to the baking sheet and repeat with the remaining dough and za'atar oil. Serve warm or within several hours.

69. Hearts Of Romaine With Marinade Sauce

Servings: 4
Cooking Time: 20 Minutes
Ingredients:
- 3 tablespoons red wine vinegar
- 1 tablespoon Dijon mustard
- Salt and pepper
- ½ cup good-quality olive oil
- 4 hearts of romaine lettuce

Directions:
1. Preparing the Ingredients.
2. Heat a Griddle for medium heat.
3. Grilling
4. Make sure the grates are clean.
5. Place the vinegar and mustard in a large bowl with some salt and pepper and Beat to combine. While still whisking, add the oil in a steady stream; keep whisking until thick.
6. Trim the bottoms of the romaine just enough to remove the tough ends but keep the leaves attached. Remove any damaged outer leaves. Transfer the lettuce to the bowl and coat with the vinaigrette, using your hands to work it into the heads as much as you can without bruising the leaves.
7. Place the romaine on the grill directly. Cook turning once, until softened and darkly colored in places, 2 to 5 Minutes per side, depending on how hot it is. Transfer to a platter and serve warm or at room temperature with more pepper sprinkled on top.

70. Easy Roasted Okra With Sea Salt

Servings: 4
Cooking Time: 30 Minutes
Ingredients:
- 1½ pounds okra pods, stem ends trimmed
- 2 tablespoons good-quality olive oil
- 2 teaspoons coarse sea salt

Directions:
1. Preparing the Ingredients.
2. Heat a Griddle for medium heat.
3. Grilling.
4. Make sure the grates are clean.
5. Place the okra in a bowl. Spry with the oil and toss to coat completely. Sprinkle with the salt and toss again.
6. Place the okra on the grill directly. Cook turning them once or twice, until the pods turn bright green and a knife inserted in the thickest part goes through without resistance, 5 to 10 Minutes total. Transfer to a platter and serve hot or at room temperature.

71. Savory Cabbage Pancakes (okonomiyaki)

Servings: 4
Cooking Time: 15 Minutes
Ingredients:
- 2 cups shredded cabbage
- ¼ cup plus 1 tablespoon minced green onion, divided
- 2 cups Buttermilk Pancake batter
- 4 strips thinly sliced bacon or pork belly
- ½ cup barbecue sauce
- ¼ cup hoisin sauce
- ½ cup mayonnaise
- 1 teaspoon mirin
- black sesame seeds, for garnish

Directions:
1. Preparing the Ingredients.
2. In a large bowl, add the shredded cabbage and green onions to the pancake batter and mix to combine.
3. Bring the griddle grill to medium heat. Cut the bacon or pork belly in half slices so you have 8 shorter pieces. Slowly cook the bacon in 2 batches of 4 strips each, in separate areas of the griddle. Adjust the heat if necessary to make sure it is Grilling, but not browning and getting crispy just yet, 3 to 5 Minutes. A nice pool of rendered bacon fat should be visible.
4. Flip each pile of bacon into the rendered fat and arrange the strips very close together, touching but not overlapping. Using a 1 cup measure, pour the pancake and cabbage mixture onto one of the groups of bacon. The remaining batter goes on the other.
5. Slowly cook the pancake undisturbed for about 5 Minutes or until bubbles form and burst, leaving small craters where the bubbles were.
6. Grilling
7. Run a long, sturdy spatula under the pancake, taking care to release the bacon from the griddle. When the pancake feels released and slides easily, give it a flip and do the same with the other one. Cook for 3 Minutes more.
8. In a small bowl, mix the barbecue sauce with the hoisin. In a separate bowl, mix the mayonnaise with the mirin.
9. Remove the pancakes from the griddle and while they are hot, brush on a thin layer of the hoisin barbecue sauce.
10. Place the mayonnaise mixture in a squeeze bottle and adorn the top of the cabbage cakes with thin ropes of mayonnaise. Garnish with the

remaining green onion and sprinkle with black sesame seeds.

72. Crisp Broccoli

Servings: 4
Cooking Time: 30 Minutes
Ingredients:
- 1½ pounds broccoli
- 2 tablespoons good-quality olive oil
- Salt and pepper

Directions:
1. Preparing the Ingredients
2. Heat a Griddle for medium-high heat. Grilling. Make sure the grates are clean.
3. Cut the broccoli into florets or spears, as you like. Place on a baking sheet, pour over the oil, sprinkle with salt and pepper, and toss until the broccoli is evenly coated. If grilling florets, transfer to a perforated grill pan right before you take them out to the grill.
4. Place the broccoli on the grill directly.
5. Grilling
6. Turning often, until crisp tender, 5 to 15 Minutes total, depending on how crunchy or charred you want it. Transfer to a platter, taste and adjust the seasoning, and serve.

73. Grill-baked Potatoes

Servings: 4
Cooking Time: 90 Minutes
Ingredients:
- 4 baking potatoes or sweet potatoes
- Good-quality olive oil for brushing
- Salt and pepper

Directions:
1. Preparing the Ingredients.
2. Heat a Griddle for medium indirect
3. Grilling
4. Prick the potatoes in several spots with a knife or fork. Brush them all over with oil and sprinkle with salt and pepper.
5. Place the potatoes on the indirect side of the grill. Cook until you can insert a skewer through the thickest part with no resistance, 60 to 90 Minutes, depending on their size. Turn, move, and rotate the potatoes every 30 Minutes for even Grilling.
6. To crisp the skins, move them directly until they brown, turning a few times, 2 to 3 Minutes per side. Transfer to a plate and serve.

74. Rosemary Mushrooms

Servings: 4
Cooking Time: 35 Minutes
Ingredients:
- 4 large portobello mushrooms, or 1½ pounds shiitake, button, or cremini mushrooms
- ⅓ cup good-quality olive oil
- 1 tablespoon minced shallot, scallion, onion, or garlic
- 1 tablespoon chopped fresh rosemary
- Salt and pepper

Directions:
1. Preparing the Ingredients.
2. Heat a Griddle for medium heat.
3. Grilling.
4. Make sure the grates are clean.
5. Rinse and trim the mushrooms to remove any tough stems. Combine the oil, shallot, rosemary, and some salt and pepper in a small bowl. Brush the mushrooms all over with about half of the mixture; reserve the rest. Skewer the mushrooms if they're small or Place them in a perforated grill pan.
6. Place the mushrooms on the grill directly. Cook turning or shaking the pan to cook evenly, until they soften and a knife pierces the center with no resistance, 5 to 20 Minutes total depending on the size of the mushrooms. Brush with the remaining oil as they cook. Transfer to a platter. Portobellos can be served whole or cut into wedges or slices. All are good hot, warm, or at room temperature.

75. Thai-style Coleslaw

Servings: 8
Cooking Time: 20 Minutes
Ingredients:
- 1 small head cabbage (1 pound)
- ¼ cup fresh lime juice
- ¼ cup fish sauce
- 1 tablespoon minced garlic
- 1 tablespoon sugar
- 1 small red chile (like Thai), chopped, or ½ teaspoon red chile flakes or more to taste
- ¼ cup chopped fresh mint

Directions:
1. Preparing the Ingredients.
2. Discard any discolored outer leaves from the cabbage, cut it into quarters, and remove the core. Cut across into thin ribbons or shred on the largest holes of a box grater or in a food processor with the shredding disk.
3. Beat the lime juice, fish sauce, garlic, sugar, and chile together in a large bowl. Add the shredded cabbage and mint and toss with the dressing until

completely coated. Serve immediately, or cover and refrigerate until you're ready to serve.

76. Scallions With Cilantro And Lime

Servings: 4
Cooking Time: 30 Minutes
Ingredients:
- 2 bunches scallions
- Good-quality olive oil for brushing
- Salt and pepper
- 2 limes, 1 halved, 1 cut into wedges
- Tender fresh cilantro sprigs for garnish

Directions:
1. Preparing the Ingredients.
2. Heat a Griddle for medium-high heat.
3. Grilling
4. Make sure the grates are clean.
5. Trim the root ends of the scallions and the ragged ends of the greens; leave as much of the greens on as possible. Brush or rub the scallions with the oil until well coated; sprinkle with salt.
6. Place the scallions on the grill directly, perpendicular to the grates so they don't fall through. Cook turning once or twice, until deeply colored and tender, 5 to 10 Minutes total, depending on their thickness. Transfer to a platter, sprinkle with pepper, and squeeze the juice of the lime halves over all. Serve hot, warm, or at room temperature, garnished with the cilantro and lime wedges.

77. Fennel-orange Slaw

Servings: 4
Cooking Time: 55 Minutes
Ingredients:
- ½ cup rice vinegar
- ¼ cup sugar
- 1 small red onion, halved, thinly sliced, and pulled apart
- 2 pounds fennel
- 2 tablespoons good-quality olive oil, plus more for brushing
- 3 navel oranges
- 1 teaspoon minced fresh rosemary
- Salt and pepper

Directions:
1. Preparing the Ingredients.
2. Place the vinegar and sugar in a small nonreactive saucepan and bring to a boil. Remove from the heat, add the onion, and mix to combine. Or you can do this earlier in the day, cover, and let sit at room temperature.
3. Heat a Griddle for medium heat. Grilling. Make sure the grates are clean.

4. Trim the fennel bulbs, reserving the feathery fronds. Cut the fennel in half from stalk end to base; brush with some oil. Cut the peel from the oranges with a small knife, deep enough to remove the white pith. Slice the oranges across into ¼-inch rounds, then cut the rounds into wedges. Place in a large bowl.
5. Place the fennel on the grill directly.
6. Grilling.
7. Turning once, until the fennel is crisp-tender and browned or charred in spots, 3 to 5 Minutes per side. Transfer to a cutting board and thinly slice across into crescents. Add to the oranges. Use a slotted spoon to transfer the onion to the bowl; reserve the brine. Mince enough fennel fronds to make 2 tablespoons.
8. Add the oil, 1 tablespoon of the brine, the rosemary, the minced fronds, and some salt and pepper. Toss to coat, taste and adjust the seasoning, and serve. Or prepare the slaw up to a day ahead, cover, and refrigerate.

78. Southern Fried Turkey Strips With Stuffed Mushrooms

Servings: 4 Slices
Cooking Time: 15 Minutes
Ingredients:
- 4 * 4 oz. turkey steaks
- 4 large portabella mushrooms
- 1/3 cup extra virgin olive oil
- 2 tbsps. tomato paste
- 1/2 c. almonds
- 1 tsp. black pepper
- 1 tsp. cayenne pepper
- 1 tsp. paprika powder
- 1 tsp. salt
- 1/2 cup shredded cheddar cheese

Directions:
1. Place the almonds, black pepper, cayenne pepper, paprika powder and salt into the food processor and blend until the almonds become fully powdered.
2. Once the almonds and other ingredients have become fully powdered, add them to the mixing bowl along with the extra virgin olive oil, then mix them together with the wooden spoon to form a marinade.
3. Once the marinade ingredients are fully mixed, add the turkey steaks to the mixing bowl and coat them fully in the marinade.
4. Once the turkey steaks are fully coated in marinade, pour them into the sealable container and put the container into the refrigerator for a minimum of 4 hours to allow the marinade to fully soak into the turkey steaks. If you have time, turn the turkey

steaks halfway through to ensure that the marinade soaks into them evenly.

5.   Prepare griddle for medium heat. Lightly oil. Place on chicken on griddle. Cover with basting cover. Add a little water to the surface before you cover. Until cooked through.

6.   Spread an equal amount of tomato paste on the base of each portabella mushroom and then top with an equal amount of shredded cheddar cheese. Place on griddle, cover until cheese is melted.

7.   Place one southern fried turkey steak and one stuffed portabella mushroom onto each of the four plates, serve and enjoy.

Nutrition Info: (Per serving):calories 175.9kcal; fat 3g; protein 5.3 g; carbohydrates 2.9 g

79. Beets And Greens With Vinaigrette

Servings: 4
Cooking Time: 60 Minutes
Ingredients:
•   1½ pounds small beets, with fresh-looking greens still attached if possible
•   ½ cup plus 2 tablespoons good-quality olive oil
•   Salt and pepper
•   3 tablespoons fresh lemon juice
•   2 tablespoons minced fresh dill
Directions:
1.   Preparing the Ingredients.
2.   Heat a Griddle for medium to medium-low direct
3.   Grilling
4.   Make sure the grates are clean.
5.   Cut the greens off the beets. Throw away any wilted or discolored leaves; rinse the remainder well to remove any grit and drain. Trim the root ends of the beets and scrub well under running water. Pat the leaves and beets dry. Toss the beets with 2 tablespoons of the oil and a sprinkle of salt until evenly coated.
6.   Place the beets on the grill directly. (No need to wash the bowl.) Cook turning them every 5 to 10 Minutes, until a knife inserted in the center goes through with no resistance, 30 to 40 Minutes total. Transfer to a plate and let sit until cool enough to handle.
7.   Toss the beet greens in the reserved bowl to coat in oil. Place the greens on the grill directly. Cook tossing once or twice, until they're bright green and browned in spots, 2 to 5 Minutes total. Keep a close eye on them; if they're on too long, they'll crisp up to the point where they'll shatter. Transfer to a plate.
8.   Place the remaining ½ cup oil and the lemon juice in a serving bowl and Beat until thickened. Mix in the dill and some salt and pepper. Peel the skin from the beets and cut into halves or quarters. Cut the stems from the leaves in 1-inch lengths; cut the

leaves across into ribbons. Place the beets, leaves, and stems in the bowl and toss with the vinaigrette until coated. Serve warm or at room temperature. Or make up to several hours ahead, cover, and refrigerate to serve chilled.

80. Steak

Servings: 4-5 Slices
Cooking Time: 10 Minutes
Ingredients:
•   1 steak
•   1 salt
•   1 pepper
Directions:
1.   This recipe is for any number of steaks including sirloin, T-bone, ribeye, etc.
2.   Season your steak with salt and pepper, or any other seasoning of your choice.
3.   Prepare griddle for medium-high heat. Lightly oil. Place steak on griddle.
4.   When one side develops a crust, flip once. Until the steak is done to your desired doneness.
5.   The most important point to remember when griddling a steak is to leave it alone. Let the juices, the seasoning and the heat make an excellent steak.
Nutrition Info: (Per serving): Calories: 919kcal, Carbs: 4g, Protein: 61g, Fat: 73g

81. Grilled Kale With Lemon

Servings: 4
Cooking Time: 25 Minutes
Ingredients:
•   1½ pounds lacinato kale
•   ¼ cup good-quality olive oil
•   Salt and pepper
•   ½ lemon, cut into wedges
Directions:
1.   Preparing the Ingredients.
2.   Heat a Griddle for medium heat.
3.   Grilling.
4.   Make sure the grates are clean.
5.   Cut the stems from the leaves; save them for another use if you like. Rip the leaves into pieces if you like (but not too small). Place the oil in a large bowl. Add the leaves and massage them around until they are completely coated. Sprinkle with salt and pepper, and toss. (You can prepare the kale to this point up to several hours ahead and refrigerate in a plastic zipper bag until you're ready to grill.)
6.   Place the leaves on the grill directly; it's okay if they overlap. Cook until the leaves develop some char, 2 to 4 Minutes. Turn and cook, spreading them into a single layer as they shrink, until charred on the

other side, another 1 to 3 Minutes. As they finish, immediately transfer to a platter. Serve with the lemon wedges.

82. Grilled Onions

Servings: 4
Cooking Time: 50 Minutes
Ingredients:
- 1½ pounds onions, peeled
- About 2 tablespoons good-quality olive oil
- Salt and pepper

Directions:
1. Preparing the Ingredients.
2. Heat a Griddle for medium to medium-low heat.
3. Grilling
4. Make sure the grates are clean.
5. Cut the onions through the equator (not root end to stem end) into slices at least 1 inch thick. (If the onions are flat-shaped, simply halve them.) Brush the slices with oil and carefully sprinkle with salt and pepper on both sides.
6. Place the onion slices on the grill directly. Cook turning once, until they brown and are soft all the way through, 10 to 15 Minutes per side. Check them a few Minutes after you Place them on; if they're coloring too quickly. Transfer to a platter and serve hot, warm, or at room temperature.

83. Sizzling Chicken Mushroom Recipe

Servings: 4 Slices
Cooking Time: 15 Minutes
Ingredients:
- 1/2 lb. chicken breast, cut into strips
- 1/2 cup button mushrooms, sliced
- 1/2 cup frozen green peas, thawed
- 1/2 cup water
- 1 tbsp. soy sauce
- A pinch ground black pepper
- 1 tsp. cornstarch
- 1 tsp. onion powder

Directions:
1. Make sure you got all of your ingredients ready to go.
2. Prepare your griddle to medium-high and place the chicken on it until cooked.
3. Add the mushrooms and the peas and cook for 3 minutes.
4. To make the sauce or the gravy, mix together the water, soy sauce, ground pepper, onion powder and cornstarch.
5. Place aluminum roasting pan on your flat top. Combine the chicken, mushrooms and peas mixture

in roasting pan. It will thicken immediately. Stir for another 3 to 5 minutes. Take off the heat and serve.
6. The dish easily serves two persons and the recipe can be easily doubled to feed more. Enjoy!
Nutrition Info: (Per serving): Calories: 206kcal | Carbs: 2g | Protein: 23g | Fat: 11g

84. Maple-balsamic Boneless Pork Chops

Servings: 4 Slices
Cooking Time: 10 Minutes
Ingredients:
- 1 tbsp. extra virgin olive oil
- 4 (4-oz.) boneless pork chops
- Salt and black pepper, to taste
- 1/2 cup balsamic vinegar
- 2-1/2 tbsps. real maple syrup

Directions:
1. Prepare griddle for medium heat. Lightly oil.
2. Season pork chops on each side with salt and pepper, to taste, and add to the pre-heated griddle. Brown pork chops on each side, approximately 3 minutes per side. Remove pork chops from pan and set aside on a rimmed dish.
3. Place small aluminum roasting pan to your flat top. Heat this heat zone to high. Add balsamic vinegar and maple syrup and bring to a boil, stirring constantly.
4. Reduce heat to medium and cook mixture until it is reduced to about 1/3 of its original volume. When ready, the glaze will become thick and syrupy. (Do not overcook or the mixture will become hard and sticky).
5. Transfer chops to a serving platter or individual serving plate and drizzle with pan sauce. Serve immediately with griddled Brussels sprouts or your choice of sides.
Nutrition Info: (Per serving):Calories 351.2kcal; protein 25.7 g; carbs 33.2 g; fat 20g

85. Asian Style Beef Broccoli Recipe

Servings: 2-4 Slices
Cooking Time: 10 Minutes
Ingredients:
- 1/2 lb. sukiyaki cut beef (very thin across the grain slices)
- 3 cups Chinese broccoli
- 1/3 cup brown sugar
- 1/3 cup water
- 1/3 cup soy sauce
- 3 tbsps. cooking oil
- 2 tbsps. browned chopped garlic (you may use garlic flakes)
- 2 tbsps. sesame oil

- 1/2 tsp. red chili flakes
- 1/2 tsp. freshly grounded black pepper

Directions:

1. Get all of your ingredients together.
2. Prepare griddle for medium heat. Lightly oil. Place on broccoli on flat top. Cover with basting cover. Add a little water to the surface before you cover to steam Chinese broccoli until it is done but not soggy. It is important to retain the bright green color for the visual appeal of the meal; plus the crunchy texture of the cooked vegetable add a certain freshness to the dish.
3. Cook the beef in the cooking oil until browned. It would only take 3 minutes in medium to high heat because the beef is very thinly cut.
4. Once the beef has been cooked and browned, add in the water, soy sauce, brown sugar, half of the garlic, the red chili flakes and black pepper. Simmer for 3 minutes.
5. On a serving dish, arrange the Chinese broccoli and spoon the cooked beef and the sauce over it. Top with the rest of the garlic flakes and drizzle in the sesame oil.
6. Serve and enjoy! This recipe serves 2-4 individuals depending if the dish is to be served as a side dish or a main dish. It's a visual treat for sure!

Nutrition Info: (Per serving):calories 331.4kcal; protein 21.7 g; carbs 13.3 g; fat 15g.

86. Lemon Pepper Marinated Pork

Servings: 4 Slices
Cooking Time: 10 Minutes
Ingredients:

- Red onion sliced into rings
- Juice of 1 lemon
- 1 tsp. ground black pepper
- 1/2 tsp. chili powder
- 1/4 cup soy sauce
- 2 cloves garlic chopped
- 1 tbsp. coconut sugar (or use 1 tsp. honey)
- 1 lb. sukiyaki cut lean pork (any tender part)
- 1 tbsp. oil for frying
- Green onion for garnish

Directions:

1. In a bowl, combine the pork, soy sauce, lemon juice, chili powder, black pepper, coconut sugar, and garlic.
2. Mix everything together and let stand for 30 minutes in room temperature or up to overnight in the fridge.
3. Preheat griddle to medium heat and prepare with oil

4. Add the pork to your flat top. Cook both sides for about 2 minutes each, spoon the marinade or pork and cook until marinade dries up.
5. Add the red onion rings and sauté for about 2 more minutes.
6. Transfer to a serving dish.
7. Top with chopped green onions and serve with rice or just lettuce. Serves 2-4

Nutrition Info: (Per serving): Calories: 379kcal; fat: 12g; Carbs: 2.1g; Protein: 40.7 g

87. Smoked Pork Sausage Hakka Noodles Recipe

Servings: 4 Slices
Cooking Time: 15 Minutes
Ingredients:

- 1 packet Hakka Noodles
- 5 Smoked Pork Sausages
- 50g Coriander Leaves
- 1 tbsp. Soya Sauce
- 50g Mint Leaves
- 1 Onion
- 3 Green Chilies
- 1 Capsicum
- Salt to Taste

Directions:

1. Cut and slice all the pork vegetables and keep it aside.
2. Then cook the packet of Hakka noodle in a container. Make sure to add a little bit of oil so that they don't stick together. Boil the noodles for 5-6 minutes.
3. Take the noodles and transfer them to a strainer and wash them under the tap so that they stop cooking.
4. Then add a little bit of oil and soya sauce to the noodles. Once this is ready, we are ready to cook the rest of the meal.
5. Prepare griddle for medium heat. Lightly oil. Add the onions and chilies till they turn light brown.
6. Then add the smoked pork sausages and cook it for 5 – 7 minutes.
7. Add the coriander and mint leaves and cook for another 5 minutes. The major aroma will be from the coriander and mint leaves.
8. Then add the cauliflower, capsicum and salt to taste.
9. Then add the noodles and then cook it for another 5 minutes.
10. Take it off the griddle and then serve it with mint leaves.

Nutrition Info: (Per serving):Calories 220.2kcal; protein 25.7 g; carbs 33.2 g; fat 23g

88. Dry-brined Steak

Servings: 1
Cooking Time: 10 Minutes
Ingredients:
- 1 (8-ounce) New York strip steak, 1-inch thick
- 1 teaspoon kosher salt
- 2 tablespoons clarified butter
- pepper, to taste

Directions:
1. Preparing the Ingredients.
2. Two to four hours before Grilling, evenly season both sides of the steak with kosher salt. Ideally, Place the steak on a small cooling rack over a plate and let it rest in the refrigerator until ready to cook, but simply resting on a plate will do fine as well. Through osmosis, the salt will penetrate the meat, initially pulling out some juices and then sucking them back in.
3. When it is time to cook, remove the steak from the refrigerator and transfer it to a room temperature plate. Allow the steak to sit at room temperature for 30 to 45 Minutes as you preheat your grill.
4. The hotter you preheat your griddle grill, the quicker the steak will cook, so I prefer bringing my grill to medium-high heat. Place half the clarified butter on the griddle surface and spread it with a spatula to a pool not much larger than the size of your steak. Blot the steak dry with a paper towel or clean kitchen towel and place it in the pool of clarified butter.
5. Use a bacon press to weigh down the steak for about 1 minute and then remove it and cover the meat.
6. Grilling
7. Add the remaining clarified butter to the griddle in a pool, and once it begins to shimmer, flip the steak into the pool of butter. Cover the meat and continue to cook for about 4 Minutes more. The only real way to accurately cook the steak to your desired doneness is with a probe thermometer. Shoot for a finished temperature of 135°F for medium rare. I will often pull a steak at 131°F and allow it to rest for a few Minutes, covered and undisturbed, which allows the temperature to rise a few more degrees to the 135°F I am searching for.

89. Watermelon Steaks

Servings: 4
Cooking Time: 80 Minutes
Ingredients:
- 1 small watermelon
- ¼ cup good-quality olive oil
- 1 tablespoon minced fresh rosemary
- Salt and pepper
- Lemon wedges for serving

Directions:
1. Preparing the Ingredients.
2. Heat a Griddle for medium heat.
3. Grilling
4. Make sure the grates are clean.
5. Cut the watermelon into 2-inch-thick slices, with the rind intact, and then into halves or quarters, if you like. If there are seeds, use a fork to remove as many as you can without tearing up the flesh too much.
6. Place the oil and rosemary in a small bowl, sprinkle with salt and pepper, and stir. Brush or rub the mixture all over the watermelon slices. (You can prepare the watermelon for the grill up to 2 hours ahead; wrap tightly in plastic wrap to keep it from drying out and refrigerate.)
7. Place the watermelon on the grill directly. Cook turning once, until the flesh develops grill marks and has dried out a bit, 4 to 5 Minutes per side. Transfer to a platter and serve with lemon wedges.

90. Herb-rubbed, Bone-in Pork Chops

Servings: 4 Slices
Cooking Time: 5 Minutes
Ingredients:
- 2 tbsps. Kosher salt
- 8 large fresh basil leaves, torn into pieces
- 2 stems fresh rosemary, leaves stripped from stems and crushed
- 2 tbsps. fresh thyme leaves, crushed with fingers
- 3 cloves garlic, smashed, peeled and roughly chopped
- 1 tbsps. salt
- 4 thick-cut bone-in pork chops, approximately 1" thick

Directions:
1. Combine salt, basil, rosemary, thyme, garlic and pepper thoroughly in a small bowl. Rub mixture over all sides of pork chops until thoroughly covered.
2. Prepare griddle for medium heat. Lightly oil. Place on griddle. Cook for 7-8 minutes, turn once. Cover with basting cover. Add a little water to the surface before you cover. If your chops are thinner or thicker than 1", adjust cook time accordingly.
3. Remove chops from heat, cover and let rest for 3 - 5 minutes before serving. Serve with a summer vegetable medley and top with a pat of compound butter seasoned with the same herbs used in the rub.
Nutrition Info: (Per serving):calories 221kcal, fat 11g, carbs 1g, protein 26g

91. Green Beans

Servings: 4
Cooking Time: 40 Minutes
Ingredients:
- 3 tablespoons good-quality olive oil
- 4 cloves garlic, or more to taste, thinly sliced
- Salt and pepper
- 1½ pounds green beans, trimmed

Directions:
1. Preparing the Ingredients.
2. Place the oil and garlic in a large skillet over the lowest heat possible.
3. Grilling.
4. Shaking the pan occasionally and adjusting the heat if necessary, until the garlic is sizzling steadily. Keep a close eye on the garlic; it shouldn't color at all, but will puff and become quite fragrant. Remove from the heat, sprinkle with salt and pepper, and let sit at room temperature.
5. Heat a Griddle for hot direct Grilling. Make sure the grates are clean.
6. Place the green beans on the grill directly, perpendicular to the grates if you're not using a grill pan. Cook until charred in places and a knife inserted into the center of a bean goes in without any resistance, 3 to 5 Minutes depending on their thickness.
7. If the oil is no longer warm, while the beans are on the grill, Place the skillet back over low to medium heat. Warm the oil just until the garlic starts to sizzle again, then remove from the heat. Transfer the beans directly to the skillet, toss to coat well, taste and adjust the seasoning, and serve.

92. Corn On The Cob

Servings: 4
Cooking Time: 30 Minutes
Ingredients:
- 4 ears fresh corn
- Salt and pepper
- Butter (optional)

Directions:
1. Preparing the Ingredients.
2. Heat a Griddle for medium heat.
3. Grilling.
4. Make sure the grates are clean.
5. Shuck the corn, removing the husks and silks.
6. Place the corn on the grill directly. Cook turning the ears every few Minutes, until some of the kernels char a bit, 8 to 12 Minutes total. Serve with salt, pepper, and butter if you like.

93. Mediterranean Pork Chops

Servings: 6
Ingredients:
- 6 pork chops, thick cut ¼ cup olive oil
- 1 tbsp. sea salt
- 1 tsp. ground black pepper

Directions:
1. Preparing the Ingredients.
2. Rub pork chops with olive oil, sea salt, and pepper.
3. Grilling
4. Grill about 5-7 Minutes per side or until internal temperature reaches 165° F. In a bowl, combine all salad ingredients. Toss. Serve pork chops with salad and your favorite side dishes. Salad ½ cup kalamata olives 1 clove garlic, peeled & minced 1 pint cherry tomatoes, quartered 4 cups feta cheese 3 tbsp. red wine vinegar 1 sprig oregano, fresh ¼ cup extra virgin olive oil 1 cup cannellini beans

94. Avocado With Lemon

Servings: 4
Cooking Time: 25 Minutes
Ingredients:
- 2 ripe avocados
- Good-quality olive oil for brushing
- 1 lemon, halved
- Salt and pepper

Directions:
1. Preparing the Ingredients.
2. Heat a Griddle for medium heat.
3. Grilling
4. Make sure the grates are clean.
5. Cut the avocados in half lengthwise. Carefully strike a chef's knife into the pit, then wiggle it a bit to lift and remove it. Insert a spoon underneath the flesh against the skin and run it all the way around to separate the entire half of the avocado. Repeat with the other avocado. Brush with oil, then squeeze one of the lemon halves over them thoroughly on both sides so they don't discolor. Cut the other lemon half into 4 wedges.
6. Place the avocados on the grill directly, cut side down. Cook turning once, until browned in places, 5 to 10 Minutes total. Serve the halved avocados as is, or slice and fan them for a prettier presentation. Sprinkle with salt and pepper and garnish with the lemon wedges.

95. Easy Grilled Asparagus

Servings: 4
Cooking Time: 20 Minutes

Ingredients:
- 1½–2 pounds asparagus
- 1–2 tablespoons good-quality olive oil or melted butter
- Salt

Directions:
1. Preparing the Ingredients.
2. Heat a Griddle for hot direct
3. Grilling.
4. Make sure the grates are clean. Cut the tough bottoms from the asparagus. If they're thick, trim the ends with a vegetable peeler. Toss with the oil and sprinkle with salt.
5. Place the asparagus on the grill directly, perpendicular to the grates so they don't fall through. Cook turning once, until the thick part of the stalks can barely be pierced with a skewer or thin knife, 5 to 10 Minutes total. Transfer to a platter and serve.

96. Buttery Butternut Squash

Servings: 4
Cooking Time: 1½ Hours
Ingredients:
- 2 pounds butternut squash, cut into large pieces and seeded
- 4 tablespoons (½ stick) butter, melted
- Salt and pepper

Directions:
1. Preparing the Ingredients.
2. Heat a Griddle for medium-high heat.
3. Grilling
4. Make sure the grates are clean.
5. Brush the cut sides of the squash with about half of the melted butter, then sprinkle with salt and pepper.
6. Place the squash on the grill directly, skin side down. Cook until a skewer can be inserted through the center of each chunk without resistance, about 1 hour depending on their thickness. Transfer to a cutting board.
7. When cool enough to handle, slice away the blackened skin, then cut the squash into bite-sized cubes. Place in a serving bowl and spry with the remaining melted butter. Taste and adjust the seasoning, toss to combine, and serve.

97. Classic Crab Sliders With Tartar Sauce

Servings: 8
Cooking Time: 50 Minutes
Ingredients:
- 4 tablespoons (½ stick) butter, melted and cooled slightly
- 1 egg

- 2 tablespoons fresh lemon juice
- 1 teaspoon Worcestershire sauce
- ¼ cup saltine cracker crumbs
- 1 pound crabmeat, picked over for shells and cartilage
- ½ cup mayonnaise
- 1 tablespoon chopped bread-and-butter pickles or cornichons
- ½ teaspoon pickle juice, or more to taste
- ½ teaspoon spicy brown mustard
- Salt and pepper
- 8 slider buns (like potato or dinner rolls)
- Lemon wedges

Directions:
1. Preparing the Ingredients.
2. Place the butter, egg, 1 tablespoon of the lemon juice, and the Worcestershire in a medium bowl; Beat until smooth. Fold in the cracker crumbs with a rubber spatula until fully incorporated. Add the crabmeat and gently fold until fully incorporated.
3. With your hands, form the mixture into 8 equal-sized sliders. Without handling them too much, press each just enough so it stays together without gaps and cracks. Place the patties on a plate, cover, and refrigerate for at least 3 hours for the butter in the mixture to completely harden.
4. To make the tartar sauce, Place the mayonnaise, pickles and pickle juice, mustard, and the remaining 1 tablespoon lemon juice in a small bowl; Beat to combine. Sprinkle with salt and pepper; taste and adjust the seasoning. Refrigerate until you're ready to serve.
5. Heat a Griddle for hot direct
6. Grilling
7. Make sure the grates are clean.
8. Place the crab patties on the grill directly. Cook turning once, until they brown and heat through, 4 to 5 Minutes per side. While the second side is browning, toast the buns on the grill if you like. Squeeze some lemon juice over the sliders and serve on the buns, topped with a dollop of tartar sauce.

98. Orange-glazed Carrots Or Parsnips

Servings: 4
Cooking Time: 50 Minutes
Ingredients:
- 8 tablespoons (1 stick) butter or good-quality olive oil
- 1½ pounds carrots or parsnips, trimmed and peeled
- Salt and pepper
- Grated zest of 1 large orange
- 2 tablespoons fresh orange juice

- Chopped fresh parsley, dill, mint, basil, or chervil leaves for garnish (optional)

Directions:
1. Preparing the Ingredients.
2. Heat a Griddle for medium indirect
3. Grilling.
4. Make sure the grates are clean.
5. Melt the butter in a small saucepan over medium heat. Remove from the heat. Sprinkle with salt and pepper and mix in the orange zest and juice. Brush the carrots with the butter; keep the remaining butter mixture warm.
6. Place the carrots on the grill directly, with the thick ends just over indirect heat. Cook turning them every 5 Minutes or so, until a knife inserted at the thickest part goes in without resistance, 20 to 40 Minutes total. (Cook less if you prefer them more crisp-tender.)
7. Transfer to a cutting board, cut into pieces, and Place in a serving dish. Spry over the remaining flavored butter and toss to coat. Sprinkle with fresh herbs if you're using them and serve.

99. Shrimp With Yogurt Sauce

Servings: 4
Cooking Time: 30 Minutes
Ingredients:
- 4 scallions, trimmed and cut into pieces
- 2 cloves garlic, peeled
- 1 small bunch fresh parsley, thick stems removed (thin stems are fine)
- 1 cup yogurt
- Salt and pepper
- 2 pounds large or jumbo shrimp, peeled (and deveined if you like)
- Lemon wedges for serving

Directions:
1. Preparing the Ingredients.
2. Place the scallions, garlic, parsley, and yogurt in a blender or food processor, sprinkle with salt and pepper, and purée until smooth. Transfer to a large bowl, add the shrimp, and toss to coat fully with the marinade. Marinate at room temperature while the grill heats up, or cover and refrigerate for up to several hours.
3. 2 Heat a Griddle for hot direct
4. Grilling
5. Make sure the grates are clean.
6. Place the shrimp on the grill directly. Cook turning once, until the shrimp are opaque all the way through, 3 to 5 Minutes per side, depending on their size and how hot the it is. Discard any remaining marinade. Transfer to a platter and serve with lemon wedges.

100. Crab Sliders With Classic Tartar Sauce

Servings: 8
Cooking Time: 50 Minutes
Ingredients:
- 4 tablespoons (½ stick) butter, melted and cooled slightly
- 1 egg
- 2 tablespoons fresh lemon juice
- 1 teaspoon Worcestershire sauce
- ¼ cup saltine cracker crumbs
- 1 pound crabmeat, picked over for shells and cartilage
- ½ cup mayonnaise
- 1 tablespoon chopped bread-and-butter pickles or cornichons
- ½ teaspoon pickle juice, or more to taste
- ½ teaspoon spicy brown mustard
- Salt and pepper
- 8 slider buns (like potato or dinner rolls)
- Lemon wedges

Directions:
1. Preparing the Ingredients.
2. Place the butter, egg, 1 tablespoon of the lemon juice, and the Worcestershire in a medium bowl; Beat until smooth. Fold in the cracker crumbs with a rubber spatula until fully incorporated. Add the crabmeat and gently fold until fully incorporated.
3. With your hands, form the mixture into 8 equal-sized sliders. Without handling them too much, press each just enough so it stays together without gaps and cracks. Place the patties on a plate, cover, and refrigerate for at least 3 hours for the butter in the mixture to completely harden.
4. To make the tartar sauce, Place the mayonnaise, pickles and pickle juice, mustard, and the remaining 1 tablespoon lemon juice in a small bowl; Beat to combine. Sprinkle with salt and pepper; taste and adjust the seasoning. Refrigerate until you're ready to serve.
5. Heat a Griddle for hot direct
6. Grilling
7. Make sure the grates are clean.
8. Place the crab patties on the grill directly. Cook turning once, until they brown and heat through, 4 to 5 Minutes per side. While the second side is browning, toast the buns on the grill if you like. Squeeze some lemon juice over the sliders and serve on the buns, topped with a dollop of tartar sauce.

101. Roast Prime Rib

Servings: 8
Ingredients:

- 12-15 pound prime rib with bone-in, cap off
- 1 cup kosher salt
- 1 cup coarse cracked black pepper
- ½ cup Tang (orange breakfast drink)
- ¼ cup granulated garlic
- 5 whole garlic cloves sliced thinly

Directions:
1. Preparing the Ingredients
2. Rub the prime rib all over with salt, pepper, Tang and granulated garlic.
3. With a sharp knife cut slits in meat and insert slices of garlic in each slit.
4. Place an aluminum 9x12 pan on the Griddle filled with 1-2 inches of water. When the grill heat , at approximately 350° to 400°, place the prime rib on the grill,
5. Grilling
6. Turn gas jets on medium high on side away from meat.
7. At the 2-hour point, check the rib with a meat thermometer to determine doneness; remove at 130° F for rare, 140° F for medium rare, 160° for medium, and so on, adding 4° F for each degree of doneness.
8. Remove from heat, seal in foil, and allow to rest for 30 Minutes before slicing.

102.Baby Potatoes With Sea Salt

Servings: 4
Cooking Time: 30 Minutes
Ingredients:
- 1½ pounds fingerling or baby potatoes
- 3 tablespoons good-quality olive oil
- 1 tablespoon coarse sea salt

Directions:
1. Preparing the Ingredients.
2. Heat a Griddle for medium heat.
3. Grilling
4. Make sure the grates are clean.
5. Place the potatoes in a large bowl. Spry them with the oil and toss to coat completely. Sprinkle with the salt and toss again.
6. Place the potatoes on the grill directly. Cook turning them once or twice, until a knife inserted in the center of a potato goes through without any resistance, 10 to 20 Minutes total. Transfer to a platter and serve.
7. Fingerling or Baby Potatoes with Rosemary and Lemon Zest
8. I love lemon with potatoes: When you season the potatoes, add pepper. Toss the grilled potatoes with 1 tablespoon chopped fresh rosemary and the grated zest of 1 lemon before serving.
9. Fingerling or Baby Potatoes with Oregano and Garlic

10. The perfect side for grilled steak or chicken: When you season the potatoes, add pepper. Toss the grilled potatoes with 1 tablespoon chopped fresh oregano and 2 teaspoons minced garlic before serving.
11. Fingerling or Baby Potatoes with Grill-Roasted Garlic
12. For a mellow garlic flavor: When you season the potatoes, add pepper. Toss the grilled potatoes with 2 tablespoons mashed Grill-Roasted Garlic, or more to taste, before serving.

103.Eggplant With Garlic

Servings: 4
Cooking Time: 30 Minutes
Ingredients:
- 2 medium or 1 large eggplant (1½–2 pounds)
- 1 tablespoon minced garlic, or more to taste
- 6 tablespoons good-quality olive oil
- Salt and pepper
- Chopped fresh parsley for garnish

Directions:
1. Preparing the Ingredients.
2. Heat a Griddle for medium-high heat.
3. Grilling.
4. Make sure the grates are clean.
5. Peel the eggplant if you like and cut it across into ½-inch slices. Mix the garlic into the oil along with salt and pepper; brush on the slices on both sides.
6. Place the eggplant slices on the grill directly. Cook turning and basting with the garlic oil, until the slices are browned and fork-tender, 10 to 15 Minutes total. Transfer to a platter, spry with any remaining oil, sprinkle with parsley, and serve hot, warm, or at room temperature. Or transfer to an airtight container and refrigerate for up to a few days.

104.Bbq Lamb Leg

Servings: 4
Ingredients:
- 2-3 pound leg of lamb—
- 3-4 garlic cloves, sliced thinly
- 3 lemons, seeded
- 3 small oranges
- 1 cup olive oil
- 1 cup white or red wine
- 1 large sweet onion
- 1 lime, seeded
- black pepper to taste
- Sea salt to taste
- 5-6 fresh rosemary sprigs

Directions:

1. Preparing the Ingredients.
2. Bone out and butterfly the leg of lamb (lie flat and insert 2-3 skewers all the way through horizontally to keep flat). Take small sharp knife and cut slits into lamb, on both sides. Insert thin slices of garlic. Break up 1-2 large sprigs of rosemary into 2-3 smaller lengths and insert in meat as well. Salt and pepper the meat.
3. Squeeze juice out of 3 lemons and 2 oranges. Remove peel of third orange and reserve, discarding the rest of the orange. Add ½ cup olive oil and ½ cup white or red wine. Cut up onion into thin slices, and chop one seeded lemon, one seeded lime and one orange peel into small pieces and add to liquid.
4. Place lamb in flat Pyrex glass dish and pour marinade over. Cover it with plastic wrap and marinate 6-8 hours or overnight. Take out of refrigerator in the morning, remove plastic wrap, and let meat come to room temperature.
5. Grilling
6. Place lamb on very hot griddle grill (500° to 600°), then just as you place meat on grill, adjust heat (turning down gas) to lower it to medium(400° to 500°). Cook for ½ to ¾ hour, turning only once. Keep an eye on the lamb to make sure it does not burn. If you like tender lamb cook for a little under 35 Minutes for a slightly pink center, or 45 Minutes if you like it cooked a little more. Lamb can become dry and tasteless if overdone so watch your times carefully. Take off Griddle and let the meat rest, covered, for 10 Minutes. Slice and arrange on platter with fresh rosemary sprigs for garnish.

105.Grill-braised Potatoes

Servings: 4
Cooking Time: 45 Minutes
Ingredients:
- 1½ pounds potatoes, cut into ¼-inch-thick slices
- 3 cloves garlic, sliced
- 2 tablespoons good-quality olive oil
- 1 tablespoon chopped fresh marjoram
- Salt and pepper
- 1 tablespoon vegetable broth or water

Directions:
1. Preparing the Ingredients.
2. Heat a Griddle for medium heat.
3. Grilling
4. Place the potatoes, garlic, oil, marjoram, and salt and pepper to taste in a large bowl and toss to combine. Transfer to the center of a 12-inch piece of heavy-duty foil and pour over the broth. Fold over the foil to cover, and crimp the sides shut; you don't want any steam escaping from the packet.
5. Place the packet on the grill directly. Cook until the potatoes are fork tender, 20 to 30 Minutes.

6. Transfer the packet to a platter; the potatoes will keep hot in it for at least 15 Minutes. Be careful of the steam when you undo the foil; transfer to a dish and serve.

106.Grilled Pork Shoulder

Servings: 4
Ingredients:
- Two 12 oz. cans of SPAM
- ½ cup prepared yellow mustard
- 3 tablespoon brown sugar
- ¼ teaspoon ground cloves
- ¼ teaspoon ground ginger
- ¼ teaspoon black pepper
- 1 tablespoon chopped green onion

Directions:
1. Preparing the Ingredients.
2. Serve with baked beans, corn on the cob, potato salad and lots of cold adult beverage. After several adult beverages it'll taste like crown roast of pork.
3. Open both cans of SPAM and cut into ½-inch slices, you should get 12 slices from two cans, or 6 slices from one can, or 198 slices from 33 cans. (Multiply other ingredients if you do 33 cans however!).
4. In separate bowl mix remaining ingredients until a thick paste is formed. Reserve at room temperature.
5. Place slices on very hot grill (500° to 600°).
6. Grilling
7. until bottom is charred with grill marks and browned, approximately 3 Minutes. Turn meat slices over and carefully spoon one tablespoon of mustard-sugar paste onto the cooked side of each slice, taking care not to spill gas flame.
8. After 2-3 Minutes meat is ready to remove to a heated platter for serving.

107.Summer Squash With Sea Salt

Servings: 4
Cooking Time: 30 Minutes
Ingredients:
- 1½ pounds summer squash or zucchini
- Good-quality olive oil for brushing
- Salt

Directions:
1. Preparing the Ingredients.
2. Heat a Griddle for medium heat.
3. Grilling.
4. Make sure the grates are clean.
5. Trim the ends from the squash and cut in half lengthwise, or through the equator if using pattypan.

Brush with oil on all sides, and sprinkle the cut sides with salt.

6. Place the squash on the grill directly. Cook turning once, until fork-tender, 3 to 5 Minutes per side. Transfer to a platter and serve.

108.Morel Mushroom Gravy

Cooking Time: 40 Minutes
Ingredients:
- ¼ cup water
- ⅛ cup brown sugar
- ¼ cup rice wine vinegar
- 1 tablespoon balsamic vinegar
- 3 tablespoons butter
- 1 ¼ pounds fresh morels, washed and trimmed
- ¼ cup minced shallots
- ½ teaspoon chopped parsley
- 2 cups chicken stock
- 2 cups white wine, fruity

Directions:
1. Preparing the Ingredients.
2. In a large saucepan over high heat, boil the water with the sugar, without stirring, until golden caramel color, about 15-20 Minutes. Remove the pan from the heat and slowly spry the rice wine and balsamic vinegar into the sugar water. Return pan to the stove, over medium heat for 2-3 Minutes, mix the mixture until caramel is absorbed.
3. Heat the butter in a cast iron pan over high heat on grill (500° to 600°)
4. Cookig
5. Until the butter bubbles. Move pan to a cooler part of the grill (medium heat), or turn down the gas, then add the washed and trimmed morels and shallots, stirring over until the liquid from the mushrooms evaporates, and the shallots are golden brown, about 5 Minutes. Remove mixture to a bowl..
6. Add the wine and stock to the cast iron pan and stir, Grilling until the liquid reduces to approximately 1 cup. Remove from the heat and mix in the caramel mixture, then add the morel-shallot mixture. Mix once or twice and let the gravy sit for 3-4 Minutes. Taste it and add salt & pepper as desired.

109.Beef With Buttered Noodles

Servings: 4
Cooking Time: 18 Minutes
Ingredients:
- 6 strips bacon
- 1 cup diced onion
- 1 pound thin cut sirloin tip or eye of round beef (about 8 slices)
- ½ cup yellow mustard
- 8 long thin dill pickle slices, cut into ribbons
- 16 ounces American-style lager
- 16 ounces beef stock
- 4 cups noodles, cooked and cooled
- ½ cup finely chopped fresh parsley, for garnish
- Grilling oil, as needed
- salt and pepper, to taste

Directions:
1. Preparing the Ingredients.
2. Bring the griddle to medium-high heat. Cook the bacon for about 10 Minutes until crisp. Cool, crumble into small bits, and set aside.
3. Sauté the diced onion in the bacon grease for about 5 Minutes, until the onions are translucent. Any browned bits of bacon that you can get to release from the griddle and onto the onions will reward you with additional flavor. Allow the onions to cool.
4. To assemble the roulade, sprinkle both sides of a slice of beef with salt and pepper and lay it on a cutting board. If necessary, square off the sides and ends to make a rectangle. Slather a thin coat of mustard on the beef. Place about 2 tablespoons each of the crumbled bacon and onion along one long edge of the beef slice, taking care to leave a perimeter of ¾ inch free of toppings. Add ribbons of pickles to the top of the onion and bacon mixture.
5. Starting at the covered edge of the beef slice, tightly roll the beef, bacon, onions, and pickles toward the opposite side, into a cigar shape. Take care to keep the roulade tight to keep the ingredients inside. Repeat with remaining beef slices and ingredients.
6. Grilling
7. To cook, bring the griddle grill to about medium-high heat. Add Grilling oil to the grill and when it shimmers, place the roulades directly on the griddle with the seam sides down. You want the seam of the roulade to seal as it sears to keep the ingredients from falling out. Allow the seam side to cook for 3 Minutes, then roll the roulades to brown the rest of the meat for another 2 to 3 Minutes per side or until you get a consistently browned exterior.
8. To braise the roulades, place a skillet directly on the griddle surface. Place all of the roulades inside of the skillet in a single layer. In a large bowl, mix the lager and broth and use 1 to 2 cups as braising liquid, or enough so the meat is about 80 percent covered in liquid. (If you prefer to omit the beer, you can simply double the amount of beef broth.)
9. Cover the skillet and leave a small gap so the steam can escape. Allow the liquid to reduce by about half, 15 to 20 Minutes, then carefully rotate the roulades so the portion that was not in the braising liquid is now covered. Add an additional 1 to 2 cups of liquid and allow it to reduce over medium heat for 15 to 20 Minutes. The meat should be fork tender

with just the right amount of give from your initial searing efforts.

10. While the liquid is reducing, coat a clean part of your griddle with butter and cook the noodles in the butter. Flip with a large spatula to get some brownness and texture on them.

11. To **serve**, place a bed of noodles on each plate with two roulades on top. Any reduced braising liquid can be whimsically spryd on top of the noodles and beef for an additional boost of flavor. Garnish with chopped parsley.

110.Tomatoes With Basil

Servings: 4
Cooking Time: 80 Minutes
Ingredients:
- 3 or 4 fresh tomatoes (1½ pounds)
- Good-quality olive oil for brushing
- Salt and pepper
- ⅓ cup or more torn or chopped fresh basil leaves
- Freshly grated Parmesan cheese (optional)

Directions:
1. Preparing the Ingredients.
2. Heat a Griddle for medium heat.
3. Grilling
4. Make sure the grates are clean.
5. Core the tomatoes and cut each across into 3 or 4 thick slices. Brush them with oil and sprinkle with salt and pepper on both sides.
6. Place the tomato slices on the grill directly. Cook turning once, until they are soft but not mushy, 3 to 5 Minutes per side. (They should be just on the verge of falling apart; you should be able to barely lift them from the grill with a spatula.) Transfer the slices to a platter, sprinkle with basil and some cheese if you like, and serve hot, warm, or at room temperature.

111.Honey Paprika Chicken Tenders Recipe

Servings: 4 Slices
Cooking Time: 10 Minutes
Ingredients:
- 1 lb. chicken tenders, sliced into finger-thick slices
- 1/2 cup honey
- 1/3 cup dark soy sauce
- 3 tbsps. olive oil
- 1 tbsp. paprika
- 2 tbsps. curry powder
- Salt and pepper to taste

Directions:

1. Preheat your griddle to medium-high.
2. Slice the chicken into half an inch-thick strips so they will cook faster and absorb more flavor.
3. In a bowl, combine the soy sauce, paprika, curry powder, honey, and olive oil.
4. Dump in the chicken and mix. Season with salt and pepper to taste.
5. Let the mixture stand for 10-15 minutes.
6. Place on griddle to cook half-way through.
7. Remove from flat top and transfer to a roasting pan and spread evenly so that the chicken pieces are just 1 layer.
8. Cover with aluminum foil and place roasting pan back on flat top until fully cooked through. Approximately 10 – 12 minutes.
9. Garnish with spring onion and enjoy!

Nutrition Info: (Per serving): Calories: 619kcal, fat: 13g; Carbs: 39g; Protein: 4g

112.Scallops And Asparagus Tips

Servings: 2
Cooking Time: 15 Minutes
Ingredients:
- 2 cups asparagus tips
- 8 large dry scallops
- White Wine Griddle Sauce, as needed
- butter, as needed
- Grilling oil, as needed
- salt and pepper, to taste

Directions:
1. Preparing the Ingredients.
2. Bring the griddle grill to medium-high heat.
3. Grilling
4. Coat the griddle with Grilling oil, and when it begins to shimmer, place the asparagus on the grill. Allow to cook for 2 Minutes, stirring frequently.
5. Cover the asparagus and place the scallops on the griddle with plenty of room between them. Scallops will only cook for 2 Minutes per side, so set a timer.
6. Just before you flip the scallops, give the asparagus a squirt of the White Wine Griddle Sauce and add a pat of butter. Flip the scallops and allow them to cook for another 2 Minutes until done. Season with salt and pepper to taste.
7. Serve the asparagus alongside the scallops.

113.Easy Pork Ramen

Servings: 2
Cooking Time: 15 Minutes
Ingredients:
- ¼ pound ground pork
- ¼ cup soy sauce

- 2 tablespoons minced ginger
- 2 tablespoons minced garlic
- 2 tablespoons sesame oil
- 2 (6-ounce) packages cooked ramen noodles
- 2 cups chopped cabbage
- ¾ cup chopped kale
- ⅓ cup shredded carrot
- Asian Griddle Sauce, as needed
- Grilling oil, as needed

Directions:
1. Preparing the Ingredients.
2. Bring the griddle grill to medium-high heat. Place the ground pork on the griddle and using a spatula, or spatula and scraper, cook the pork, chopping it into fine pieces to promote even Grilling and texture.
3. After about 4 Minutes, add the soy sauce, ginger, garlic, and sesame oil to the pork. Continue to cook for another 1 to 2 Minutes until the liquids have reduced, and slide to a cooler area on the griddle.
4. Grilling
5. Add oil to your Grilling surface and allow it to heat until shimmering. Spread the cooked ramen noodles in a thin layer across the griddle, taking advantage of the surface area it provides. The noodles are hydrated with water, and we want the water to evaporate some, eventually making the noodles crispy. In the process, the noodles will go from wet to gooey and gummy, and then begin turning brown and crispy. It is important to allow the noodles to cook, but not burn on the griddle. When you first flip the noodles, after about 5 Minutes, work in batches and make sure to scrape as many of the noodle bits from the grilling surface as you can. Add more oil as needed to prevent sticking and promote browning, but use it sparingly.
6. Add the cabbage, kale, carrot, and pork onto half of the noodles. Layer the other noodles on top of the mixture and allow the noodles to help wilt the veggies. Spread all the ingredients out across the griddle and flip the noodles and veggies from the outside inward to help the veggies make more contact with the griddle, and add some Asian Griddle Sauce for additional flavor.
7. As the griddle sauce reduces, and eventually evaporates, you will notice the noodles and veggies start to brown and get quite crispy. This is what you are after. The outer layer of the noodle cake should be crispy and crunchy, and the inner noodles should still be a bit supple, balancing the textures.

114.Brussels Sprouts With Thyme

Servings: 4
Cooking Time: 50 Minutes
Ingredients:

- 1½ pounds Brussels sprouts, trimmed and any discolored leaves removed
- 2 tablespoons good-quality olive oil
- Salt and pepper
- 1 tablespoon fresh thyme leaves

Directions:
1. Preparing the Ingredients.
2. Heat a Griddle for medium to medium-high indirect
3. Grilling
4. Make sure the grates are clean.
5. If the Brussels sprouts are large, cut them in half through the stem. Place the sprouts and oil in a bowl; toss to coat the sprouts evenly with the oil. Sprinkle with salt and pepper to taste and toss again.
6. Place the sprouts on the indirect side of the grill. Cook turning them once, or shaking the grill pan, until they're tender enough for a fork or skewer to pierce the stem, 15 to 35 Minutes, depending on how hot it is. If you want deeper color and a little char, move them directly, turning them frequently, for 2 to 3 Minutes. Transfer to a serving dish, add the thyme, toss to coat evenly, and serve.

115.Beef Honey Curry Stir Fry Recipe

Servings: 3-4 Slices
Cooking Time: 10 Minutes
Ingredients:

- 1/2 lb. sukiyaki cut beef
- 1/2 cup honey
- 1/2 cup soy sauce
- 4 tbsps. curry powder
- 4 tbsps. oil
- 1 tsp. ground black pepper
- 1 medium sized red onion, sliced
- 1 medium sized red bell pepper, sliced into strips
- 1 medium sized green bell pepper, sliced into strips
- 1 medium sized yellow bell pepper, sliced into strips
- Roasting pan

Directions:
1. Prepare all the ingredients that you'll need.
2. Marinate the beef with marinade made of soy sauce, curry powder, honey and ground black pepper and let it stand for 15 minutes.
3. Prepare your flat top to medium high heat. Oil and sauté the red bell pepper, green bell pepper, red onion and yellow bell pepper for a few minutes (usually just a little over a minute), taking care that the vegetables are cooked but not wilted. They should remain crunchy for great texture. Take the cooked vegetables off the pan and set aside.

4. Remove beef from marinate mixed and place on griddle until halfway cooked. Remove and place in roasting pan.
5. Place roasting pan on griddle and add in the remaining half of the oil and marinade and cook the beef together with the marinade over medium heat until the sauce thickens, and the beef is cooked through. This only takes 5-7 minutes. Turn off the heat.
6. Toss the cooked vegetables with the beef in the pain to coat it with some of the sauce and bring all flavors together. Serve over steaming hot rice, mashed potato, or even pasta! This recipe makes for about 3-4 servings.
Nutrition Info: (Per serving): Calories: 473.68kcal Carbs: 16.02g Protein: 24.21g Fat: 34.34g

116.Grill-roasted Plum Tomatoes

Servings: 4
Cooking Time: 3½ Hours
Ingredients:
• 4 plum tomatoes (or as many as you have room for)
• Good-quality olive oil for brushing
• Salt and pepper
Directions:
1. Preparing the Ingredients.
2. Heat a Griddle for medium to low indirect
3. Grilling
4. Make sure the grates are clean.
5. Cut the tomatoes in half lengthwise. Brush them with oil and sprinkle the cut sides with salt and pepper.
6. Place the tomatoes on the indirect side of the grill, cut side up. If the temperture is closer to medium, keep the tomatoes some distance from the heat to avoid charring. Close the grill and cook until shriveled but you can still see signs of moisture, at least 1 hour and up to 3 hours. About halfway through, move and rotate the tomatoes so they cook evenly.
7. Transfer to a platter and serve hot, warm, or at room temperature. These will keep in an airtight container in the refrigerator for up to a week and in the freezer for several months.

117.Chicken Ranch Pizza

Servings: 6
Ingredients:
• 1 pizza dough
• 2 cups cheddar, shredded
• 2 cups cooked rotisserie chicken, shredded
• 4 strips bacon, cooked crispy & crumbled

• ¼ cup scallions ½ cup ranch dressing
Directions:
1. Preparing the Ingredients.
2. Arrange pizza dough to fit onto the Grill Pan
3. Grilling
4. Preheat the oven to 400° F. On medium heat, grill pizza on both sides until golden.
5. Sprinkle shredded cheddar onto the dough. Top with chicken, bacon, and scallions.
6. Place the Grill Pan into the oven. Bake until the cheese is melted and the dough is cooked through. Spry ranch dressing over the pizza immediately before serving.Make it a club by topping with chopped lettuce, tomato and avocado!

118.Radicchio With Balsamic Glaze

Servings: 4
Cooking Time: 25 Minutes
Ingredients:
• 4 small or 2 large heads radicchio (about 1 pound total)
• 2 tablespoons good-quality olive oil
• ¼ cup balsamic vinegar
• 1 tablespoon brown sugar or honey
• Salt and pepper
Directions:
1. Preparing the Ingredients.
2. Heat a Griddle for medium-high heat. Grilling. Make sure the grates are clean.
3. Leaving just enough at the bottom to keep the wedges intact, core the radicchio and cut the heads into halves or quarters, depending on their size. Rub or brush them with the oil. Beat the vinegar and sugar together in a small bowl until the sugar dissolves.
4. Place the radicchio wedges on the grill directly, cut side down.
5. Grilling
6. For a minute or 2, then carefully turn them. Brush or spry with the balsamic mixture. Cook until just starting to crisp and char around the edges, another couple of Minutes. Transfer to a platter and sprinkle with salt and lots of black pepper. Serve hot, warm, or at room temperature.

119.Crispy Asian-seared Salmon

Servings: 2
Cooking Time: 15 Minutes
Ingredients:
• 2 (4-ounce) salmon fillets
• ¾ cup Asian Griddle Sauce, plus more as needed
• Grilling oil, as needed
• salt and pepper, to taste

Directions:
1. Preparing the Ingredients.
2. Wash the salmon fillets and pat dry. Check for pin bones by placing salmon skin-side down on a cutting board and gently running your fingers across the thicker parts of the fillet. If you feel any bones, use a pair of tweezers to remove them before Grilling.
3. Flip the salmon over, skin-side up. Typically, the salmon will resemble the shape of an airplane wing: thick, oval-round on one end, and tapering off to a very thin side on the other end. Make three or four ¼-inch cuts across the skin on the thickest part of the filet. This will allow the filet to cook a bit more evenly and with less curling when it is on the griddle. Season both sides of the filet with salt and pepper and make sure to get some seasoning into the areas where you scored the skin.
4. Grilling
5. Bring the griddle grill to medium-high heat and add Grilling oil to the surface. When the oil is shimmering, place the salmon skin-side down and cook for 3 or 4 Minutes without disturbing. This develops a crispy crust on the salmon skin that many people find quite delicious.
6. When you are ready to flip, place the spatula on the griddle grill at an aggressive 15-degree angle and scrape under the skin to release and flip the salmon.
7. Shake the Asian Griddle Sauce well and add about ¾ cup to the griddle near the salmon. Slide the salmon into the sauce, cover it, and allow it to steam cook for another 5 Minutes. If desired, flip the salmon an additional time and allow it to bathe in the Asian Griddle Sauce before plating.

120.Easy Chickpea Falafel

Servings: 4
Cooking Time: 15 Minutes
Ingredients:
- 1 (16-ounce) can chickpeas, drained
- ¾ cup diced sweet onion
- ¼ cup diced shallot
- 2 tablespoons freshly chopped parsley
- 4 cloves garlic, minced
- 1 teaspoon ground cumin
- 1 teaspoon paprika
- 1 teaspoon olive oil
- 1 teaspoon salt
- 1 teaspoon pepper
- ¼ cup all-purpose flour
- 1 teaspoon baking powder
- Grilling oil, as needed

Directions:
1. Preparing the Ingredients.

2. Combine all the ingredients except the flour and baking powder in a food processor or blender. Mixuntil smooth with some small chunks remaining, scraping the sides of the bowl 2 to 3 times to make sure all of the ingredients are incorporated.
3. Transfer the falafel mix to a medium bowl. Sift and then mix in the flour and baking powder. Mix by hand until the mixture absorbs the flour and becomes firmer. Cover tightly and allow to rest in the refrigerator for at least an hour.
4. Bring the griddle grill to medium heat and form the falafel into 4 patties just under 1 inch thick.
5. Grilling
6. Add a generous amount of oil to your Grilling surface and allow it to heat until shimmering. Place the patties in the hot oil and allow to cook 3 to 4 Minutes, covered. Flip and cook, covered, for an additional 3 to 4 Minutes, until heated through and a golden crust has formed.

121.Grill-steamed Leeks

Servings: 4
Cooking Time: 30 Minutes
Ingredients:
- 4 leeks (1–1½ pounds)
- Salt and pepper
- Good-quality olive oil

Directions:
1. Preparing the Ingredients.
2. Heat a Griddle for medium to medium-low heat.
3. Grilling.
4. Make sure the grates are clean.
5. Trim the root ends of the leeks and cut away the tough green tops. Make a long vertical slit through the center of the leek from the root end through the remaining green part, but not cutting all the way through to the other side. Rinse well to get the sand out from between the layers. Sprinkle both sides with salt.
6. Open up the leeks and Place them on the grill directly, cut side down, pressing down gently with a spatula to make sure the layers fan out over the heat. Cook until they have fully softened, 6 to 8 Minutes, depending on their thickness. Brush with some oil, turn, and cook until the bottom browns, 1 to 3 Minutes. Brush the top with oil, turn, and cook another 1 to 3 Minutes. Transfer the leeks to a plate, sprinkle with pepper, and serve hot, warm, or at room temperature.

122.Skirt Steak Sandwich

Servings: 4
Ingredients:

- 1 lb. skirt steak
- 1 shallot, peeled & minced
- 3 tbsp. balsamic vinegar ¼ cup olive oil ½ tsp. sea salt

Directions:
1. Preparing the Ingredients.
2. In a shallow pan, marinate steak with shallots, balsamic vinegar, olive oil, sea salt, and pepper for 1 hour. Combine tapenade ingredients in a bowl. Set aside.
3. Grilling
4. Grill the steak to desired temperature. Let rest 10 Minutes before slicing. Assemble sliced steak andtapenade open-face on focaccia. Serve with your favorite side dish. ½ tsp. course ground black pepper 3 slices focaccia, grilled. Tomato Red Onion Tapenade ¼ cup olive oil 2 tbsp. red wine vinegar 1 clove garlic, peeled & minced ½ tsp. sea salt ¼ tsp. ground black pepper 3 roma tomatoes, chopped ¼ red onion, diced 6 basil leaves, chopped. Don't forget to let your steak rest for 5-10 Minutes so it stays juicy. It's also important to slice the meat against the grain. For an extra special treat, add a little crumbled Gorgonzola cheese, I promise you won't be disappointed!

123.Savory Applesauce On The Grill

Servings: 2
Cooking Time: 45 Minutes
Ingredients:
- 1½ pounds whole apples
- Salt

Directions:
1. Preparing the Ingredients.
2. Heat a Griddle for medium heat.
3. Grilling
4. Make sure the grates are clean.
5. Place the apples on the grill directly. Cook until the fruit feels soft when gently squeezed with tongs, 10 to 20 Minutes total, depending on their size. Transfer to a cutting board and let sit until cool enough to touch.
6. Cut the flesh from around the core of each apple; discard the cores. Place the chunks in a blender or food processor and process until smooth, or Place them in a bowl and purée with an immersion blender until as chunky or smooth as you like. Add a generous pinch of salt, then taste and adjust the seasoning. Serve or refrigerate in an airtight container for up to 3 days.

POULTRY RECIPES

124. Hawaiian Chicken Skewers

Servings: 4 - 5
Cooking Time: 15 Minutes

Ingredients:
- 1 lb. boneless, skinless chicken breast, cut into 1 ½ inch cubes
- 3 cups pineapple, cut into 1 ½ inch cubes
- 2 large green peppers, cut into 1 ½ inch pieces
- 1 large red onion, cut into 1 ½ inch pieces
- 2 tablespoons olive oil, to coat veggies
- For the marinade:
- 1/3 cup tomato paste
- 1/3 cup brown sugar, packed
- 1/3 cup soy sauce
- 1/4 cup pineapple juice
- 2 tablespoons olive oil
- 1 1/2 tablespoon mirin or rice wine vinegar
- 4 teaspoons garlic cloves, minced
- 1 tablespoon ginger, minced
- 1/2 teaspoon sesame oil
- Pinch of sea salt
- Pinch of ground black pepper
- 10 wooden skewers, for assembly

Directions:
1. Combine marinade ingredients in a mixing bowl until smooth. Reserve a 1/2 cup of the marinade in the refrigerator.
2. Add chicken and remaining marinade to a sealable plastic bag and refrigerate for 1 hour.
3. Soak 10 wooden skewer sticks in water for 1 hour.
4. Preheat the griddle to medium heat.
5. Add red onion, bell pepper and pineapple to a mixing bowl with 2 tablespoons olive oil and toss to coat.
6. Thread red onion, bell pepper, pineapple and chicken onto the skewers until all of the chicken has been used.
7. Place skewers on griddle and grab your reserved marinade from the refrigerator; cook for 5 minutes then brush with remaining marinade and rotate.
8. Brush again with marinade and sear about 5 additional minutes or until chicken reads 165°F on a meat thermometer.
9. Serve warm.

Nutrition Info: Calories: 311, Sodium: 1116 mg, Dietary Fiber: 4.2 g, Fat: 8.8 g, Carbs: 38.1 g, Protein: 22.8g.

125. Hawaiian Chicken

Servings: 5
Cooking Time: 10 Minutes

Ingredients:
- 8 slices Italian bread
- 8 fresh basil leaves
- 8 thinly sliced tomatoes
- 16 slices of Black Pepper Turkey Breast
- 4 pieces of mozzarella cheese
- 4 tbsps. mayonnaise
- Olive oil

Directions:
1. Add chicken into the large zip-lock bag. Mix together ginger, garlic, brown sugar, pineapple juice, and soy sauce and pour over chicken.
2. Seal zip-lock bag shake well and place in the refrigerator overnight.
3. Heat griddle grill to a medium heat.
4. Remove chicken from the zip-lock bag and set aside. Pour marinade in a medium saucepan and simmer for 5-10 minutes.
5. Place chicken on the hot grill and brush with the hot marinade and grill until chicken is cooked or until the internal temperature of the chicken reaches 165 F. Serve.

Nutrition Info: (Per serving):Calories 523, Carbs 53g, Fat 23g, Protein 27g

126. Sizzling Southwestern Cheddar Chicken

Servings: 4
Cooking Time: 20 Minutes

Ingredients:
- 1 lb. Boneless skinless chicken breasts
- 4oz taco seasoning
- 1 tsp. Cayenne pepper
- Kosher salt
- 2 cloves minced garlic
- 1 chopped small red onion
- 2 chopped red bell peppers
- 15-oz. Can black beans (drained)
- 2 cups shredded cheddar
- 1/2 cup chopped fresh cilantro

Directions:
1. Preheat Griddle Grill to High.
2. Sprinkle the chicken with the taco seasoning, cayenne pepper and salt.
3. Add it to the griddle and cook for 6 minutes on each side. Take chicken out when done.
4. Next, add the rest of the ingredients and cook for 7 minutes.
5. Re-add chicken to the griddle and cook for 2 minutes with cheese mixture.
6. Garnish and serve.

Nutrition Info: (Per serving):Calories 530 kcal, Fat 15 g, Carbs 9g, protein 4.5 g

127.Southwestern Turkey Panini

Servings: 4
Cooking Time: 5 Minutes
Ingredients:
- 1 medium Avocado peeled and seeded
- 1/2 tbsp. Cilantro leaves finely chopped
- 1/2 tsp. Lime juice
- Salt to taste
- Chipotle mayonnaise (store bought or homemade)
- 4 slices large Sourdough bread
- 8 slices Colby Jack Cheese
- 8 slices Blackened Oven Roasted Turkey Breast
- 4 slices Tomato

Directions:
1. Preheat the Griddle Grill to Medium-High.
2. Mash and mix the avocado, lime and cilantro, and then salt and pepper to taste.
3. Spread the chipotle mayonnaise on one side of every piece of bread. On 2 pieces of bread with the mayonnaise side facing up place a layer of cheese, then turkey, then tomato, then avocado mixture, then turkey, and finally cheese again. Top with another piece of bread with the mayonnaise side touching the cheese.
4. Cook the sandwiches for 5 minutes, and make sure to check halfway through. The bread should be toasted, and the cheese should be melted.
Nutrition Info: (Per serving):Calories 280, Fat 10.5g, Carbs 43g, Protein 13g

128.Honey Balsamic Marinated Chicken

Servings: 4
Cooking Time: 20 Minutes
Ingredients:
- 2 lbs. boneless, skinless chicken thighs
- 1 teaspoon olive oil
- 1/2 teaspoon sea salt
- 1/4 teaspoon black pepper
- 1/2 teaspoon paprika
- 3/4 teaspoon onion powder
- For the Marinade:
- 2 tablespoons honey
- 2 tablespoons balsamic vinegar
- 2 tablespoons tomato paste
- 1 teaspoon garlic, minced

Directions:
1. Add chicken, olive oil, salt, black pepper, paprika, and onion powder to a sealable plastic bag. Seal and toss to coat, covering chicken with spices and oil; set aside.
2. Whisk together balsamic vinegar, tomato paste, garlic, and honey.
3. Divide the marinade in half. Add one half to the bag of chicken and store the other half in a sealed container in the refrigerator.
4. Seal the bag and toss chicken to coat. Refrigerate for 30 minutes to 4 hours.
5. Preheat a griddle to medium-high.
6. Discard bag and marinade. Add chicken to the griddle and cook 7 minutes per side or until juices run clear and a meat thermometer reads 165°F.
7. During last minute of cooking, brush remaining marinade on top of the chicken thighs.
8. Serve immediately.
Nutrition Info: Calories: 485, Sodium: 438 mg, Dietary Fiber: 0.5 g, Fat: 18.1 g, Carbs: 11 g, Protein: 66.1 g.

129.Chicken Fajitas

Servings: 4
Cooking Time: 15 Minutes
Ingredients:
- 4 boneless, skinless chicken breasts, sliced
- 1 small red onion, sliced
- 2 red bell peppers, sliced
- ½ cup spicy ranch salad dressing, divided
- ½ teaspoon dried oregano
- 8 corn tortillas
- 2 cups torn butter lettuce
- 4 avocados, peeled and chopped

Directions:
1. 1 Preparing the Ingredients. Place the chicken, onion, and pepper in a bowl. Drizzle with 1 tablespoon of the salad dressing and add the oregano. Toss to combine.
2. 2 Bring the griddle grill to high heat. When the griddle is hot, put the chicken and cook for 10 to 14 Minutes or until the chicken is 165°F on a food thermometer. Transfer the chicken and vegetables to a bowl and toss with the remaining salad dressing. Serve the chicken mixture with the tortillas, lettuce, and avocados and let everyone make their own creations.
Nutrition Info: (Per Serving): CALORIES: 783; FAT: 38G; PROTEIN:72; FIBER:12G

130.Tarragon Chicken Tenders

Servings: 4
Cooking Time: 5 Minutes
Ingredients:
- FOR THE CHICKEN:
- 1½ pounds chicken tenders (12 to 16
- tenders)

- Coarse salt (kosher or sea) and freshly
- ground black pepper
- 3 tablespoons chopped fresh tarragon
- leaves, plus 4 whole sprigs for garnish
- 1 teaspoon finely grated lemon zest
- 2 tablespoons fresh lemon juice
- 2 tablespoons extra-virgin olive oil
- FOR THE SAUCE (OPTIONAL):
- 2 tablespoons fresh lemon juice
- 2 tablespoons salted butter
- ½ cup heavy (whipping) cream

Directions:
1. Preparing the Ingredients
2. Make the chicken: Place the chicken tenders in a nonreactive baking dish just large enough to hold them in a single layer. Season the tenders generously on both sides with salt and pepper. Sprinkle the chopped tarragon and lemon zest all over the tenders, patting them onto the chicken with your fingertips. Drizzle the lemon juice and the olive oil over the tenders and pat them onto the chicken. Let the tenders marinate in the refrigerator, covered, for 10 Minutes.
3. Drain the chicken tenders well by lifting one end with tongs and letting the marinade drip off. Discard the marinade.
4. Bring the griddle grill to high heat. When the griddle is hot, place the chicken tenders on the griddle. The chicken tenders will be done after cooking 3 to 5 Minutes. Use the poke test to check for doneness; the chicken should feel firm when pressed.
5. Transfer the chicken tenders to a platter or plates. If making the sauce, place the lemon juice and the butter in a small saucepan or in the grill pan over medium heat. Add the cream and bring to a boil (use a wooden spoon to scrape up the brown bits from between the ridges of the grill pan). Let the sauce boil until thickened, 3 to 5 Minutes. Pour the lemon cream sauce over the chicken tenders and serve at once.

131.Greek Chicken

Servings: 2
Cooking Time: 15 Minutes
Ingredients:
- 2 chicken breasts, skinless and boneless
- 2 tbsp olive oil
- 1 tsp Italian seasoning
- 1 1/2 cup grape tomatoes, cut in half
- 1/2 cup olives
- 1/4 tsp pepper
- 1/4 tsp salt

Directions:

1. Season chicken with Italian seasoning, pepper, and salt.
2. Preheat the griddle to medium-low heat. Add oil to the griddle top.
3. Add season chicken onto the hot griddle top and cook for 4-6 minutes on each side. Transfer chicken on a plate.
4. Add tomatoes and olives onto the griddle top cook for 2-4 minutes.
5. Pour olive and tomato mixture on top of the chicken and serve.

Nutrition Info: (Per Serving): Calories 468 ;Fat 29.4 g ;Carbohydrates 7.8 g ;Sugar 3.8 g ;Protein 43.8 g ;Cholesterol 132 mg

132.Flavorful Chicken Kababs

Servings: 3
Cooking Time: 15 Minutes
Ingredients:
- 2 chicken breasts, cut into cubes
- 1 onion, cut into quarters
- 1 bell pepper, cut into squares
- For marinade:
- 1 tsp nutmeg
- 1 tsp Italian seasoning
- 2 tsp sweet paprika
- 1/2 cup olive oil
- 1 lemon juice
- 2 garlic cloves, chopped
- 1/4 tsp cardamom
- 1/4 tsp paprika
- 1 tsp salt

Directions:
1. In a small bowl, mix together all marinade ingredients.
2. Add chicken, onions, and peppers in a large bowl.
3. Pour marinade over chicken and vegetables and coat well, cover, and place in the refrigerator for 1 hour.
4. Thread marinated chicken and vegetables onto the skewers.
5. Preheat the griddle to medium-low heat.
6. Spray griddle top with cooking spray.
7. Place skewers onto the hot griddle top and cook for 15 minutes or until chicken is cooked through. Turn skewers often.
8. Serve and enjoy.

Nutrition Info: (Per Serving): Calories 515 ;Fat 42 g ;Carbohydrates 8.2 g ;Sugar 4 g ;Protein 29 g ;Cholesterol 88 mg

133.Sizzling Chicken Fajitas

Servings: 4

Cooking Time: 25 Minutes
Ingredients:
- 4 boneless chicken breast halves, thinly sliced
- 1 yellow onion, sliced
- 1 large green bell pepper, sliced
- 1 large red bell pepper, sliced
- 1 teaspoon ground cumin
- 1 teaspoon garlic powder
- 1 teaspoon onion powder
- 2 tablespoons lime juice
- 1 tablespoon olive oil
- 1/2 teaspoon black pepper
- 1 teaspoon salt
- 3 tablespoons vegetable oil
- 10 flour tortillas

Directions:
1. In a zipperlock bag, combine the chicken, cumin, garlic, onion, lime juice, salt, pepper, and olive oil. Allow to marinate for 30 minutes.
2. Preheat griddle to medium heat.
3. On one side of the griddle add the olive oil and heat until shimmering. Add the onion and pepper and cook until slightly softened.
4. On the other side of the griddle add the marinated chicken and cook until lightly browned.
5. Once chicken is lightly browned, toss together with the onion and pepper and cook until chicken registers 165°F.
6. Remove chicken and vegetables from the griddle and serve with warm tortillas.

Nutrition Info: Calories: 408, Sodium:664 mg, Dietary Fiber: 5.5 g, Fat: 18.3g, Carbs:37.1g, Protein: 25.9g.

134.Grilled Chicken Drumsticks

Servings: 6
Cooking Time: 10 Minutes
Ingredients:
- Chicken drumsticks – 12.
- Mustard – 1 tsp.
- White vinegar – 2 tbsps.
- Soy sauce – 1 cup, low-sodium.
- Brown sugar –1/2 cup.
- Granulated sugar – 1/2 cup.
- Tomato sauce – 15 oz.

Directions:
1. Add all ingredients except chicken to a large pot and heat over a medium-high heat.
2. Stir well and bring mixture to boil. Add chicken drumsticks and turn heat to medium-low.
3. Cover and simmer for about 20-30 minutes or until chicken is cooked. Remove chicken drumsticks to a plate.

4. Heat the griddle grill to a high heat and oil grates. Place chicken drumsticks on the hot grill and cook for 3-5 minutes.
5. Turn chicken drumsticks and cook for 3-5 minutes more. Serve.

Nutrition Info: (Per serving):Calories 208, Carbs 21g, Fat 7g, Protein 15g

135.Honey Sriracha Grilled Chicken Thighs

Servings: 6
Cooking Time: 35 Minutes
Ingredients:
- 2.5 lbs. boneless chicken thighs
- 3 tablespoons butter, unsalted
- 1 tablespoon fresh ginger, minced
- 2 garlic cloves, minced
- 1/4 teaspoon smoked paprika
- 1/4 teaspoon chili powder
- 4 tablespoons honey
- 3 tablespoons Sriracha
- 1 tablespoon lime juice

Directions:
1. Preheat griddle to medium high.
2. Melt butter in a small saucepan on medium low heat; when melted add ginger and garlic. Stir until fragrant, about 2 minutes.
3. Fold in smoked paprika, ground cloves, honey, Sriracha and lime juice. Stir to combine, turn heat to medium and simmer for 5 minutes.
4. Rinse and pat chicken thighs dry.
5. Season with salt and pepper on both sides.
6. Spray griddle with non-stick cooking spray.
7. Place chicken thighs on grill, skin side down first. Grill for 5 minutes. Flip the chicken over and grill on the other side for 5 minutes.
8. Continue to cook chicken, flipping every 3 minutes, so it doesn't burn, until the internal temperature reads 165ºF on a meat thermometer.
9. During the last 5 minutes of grilling brush the glaze on both sides of the chicken.
10. Remove from grill and serve warm.

Nutrition Info: Calories: 375, Sodium: 221 mg, Dietary Fiber: 0.3g, Fat: 22.5g, Carbs: 14.7g Protein: 32g

136.Creole Chicken Stuffed With Cheese & Peppers

Servings: 4
Cooking Time: 20 Minutes
Ingredients:
- 4 boneless, skinless chicken breasts

- 8 mini sweet peppers, sliced thin and seeded
- 2 slices pepper jack cheese, cut in half
- 2 slices colby jack cheese, cut in half
- 1 tablespoon creole seasoning, like Emeril's
- 1 teaspoon black pepper
- 1 teaspoon garlic powder
- 1 teaspoon onion powder
- 4 teaspoons olive oil, separated
- Toothpicks

Directions:
1. Rinse chicken and pat dry.
2. Mix creole seasoning, pepper, garlic powder, and onion powder together in a small mixing bowl and set aside.
3. Cut a slit on the side of each chicken breast; be careful not to cut all the way through the chicken.
4. Rub each breast with 1 teaspoon each of olive oil.
5. Rub each chicken breast with seasoning mix and coat evenly.
6. Stuff each breast of chicken with 1 half pepper jack cheese slice, 1 half colby cheese slice, and a handful of pepper slices.
7. Secure chicken shut with 4 or 5 toothpicks.
8. Preheat the griddle to medium-high and cook chicken for 8 minutes per side; or until chicken reaches an internal temperature of 165°F.
9. Allow chicken to rest for 5 minutes, remove toothpicks, and serve.

Nutrition Info: Calories: 509, Sodium:1117 mg, Dietary Fiber: 3.4 g, Fat: 25.1g, Carbs: 19.8g, Protein: 51.4g.

137.Salt-and-pepper Boneless Chicken

Servings: 4
Cooking Time: 15 Minutes
Ingredients:
- 1½ pounds boneless, skinless, chicken breasts
- 2 tablespoons good-quality olive oil
- Salt and pepper

Directions:
1. Preparing the Ingredients.
2. Pat the chicken dry with paper towels, then pound to an even thickness if necessary. Brush with the oil and sprinkle with salt and pepper on both sides.
3. Turn control knob to the high position, when the griddle is hot, place the chicken breasts and cook for 10 to 14 Minutes.
4. Transfer the chicken to a platter, let rest for 5 Minutes, slice across the grain if you like, and serve.

138.Chicken Tacos With Avocado Crema

Servings: 4-5

Cooking Time: 10 Minutes
Ingredients:
- 1 1/2 lbs. Boneless, skinless chicken breasts, sliced thin
- For the chicken marinade:
- 1 serrano pepper, minced
- 2 teaspoons garlic, minced
- 1 lime, juiced
- 1 teaspoon ground cumin
- 1/3 cup olive oil
- Sea salt, to taste
- Black pepper, to taste
- For the avocado crema:
- 1 cup sour cream
- 2 teaspoons lime juice
- 1 teaspoon lime zest
- 1 serrano pepper, diced and seeded
- 1 clove garlic, minced
- 1 large hass avocado
- For the garnish:
- 1/2 cup queso fresco, crumbled
- 2 teaspoons cilantro, chopped
- 1 lime sliced into wedges
- 10 corn tortillas

Directions:
1. Mix chicken marinade together in a sealable plastic bag. Add chicken and toss to coat well.
2. Marinate for 1 hour in the refrigerator.
3. Combine avocado crema ingredients in a food processor or blender and pulse until smooth.
4. Cover and refrigerate until you are ready to assemble tacos.
5. Preheat griddle to medium heat and grill chicken for 5 minutes per side; rotating and turning as needed.
6. Remove from griddle and tent loosely with aluminum foil. Allow chicken to rest 5 minutes.
7. Serve with warm tortillas, a dollop of avocado crema, queso fresco, cilantro and lime wedges.
8. To meal prep: simply divide chicken into individual portion containers with a serving of the garnish, and take with tortillas wrapped in parchment paper to warm in a microwave to serve.

Nutrition Info: Calories: 703, Sodium: 357 mg, Dietary Fiber: 6.3 g, Fat: 44.5 g, Carbs:30.5g, Protein: 47.9g.

139.Tasty Chicken Patties

Servings: 4
Cooking Time: 10 Minutes
Ingredients:
- 1 lb ground chicken
- 1/4 tsp red pepper flakes
- 1/2 tsp chili seasoning

- 1/2 tsp ground cumin
- 1 tsp paprika

Directions:
1. Add all ingredients into the large bowl and mix well to combine.
2. Make four small round patties from the mixture.
3. Preheat the griddle to high heat.
4. Spray griddle top with cooking spray.
5. Place patties on hot griddle top and cook for 5 minutes on each side.
6. Serve and enjoy.

Nutrition Info: (Per Serving): Calories 219 ;Fat 8 g ;Carbohydrates 0.8 g ;Sugar 0.1 g ;Protein 33 g ;Cholesterol 101 mg

140.Chicken Breasts Grilled With Feta And Fresh Mint

Servings: 4
Cooking Time: 14 Minutes
Ingredients:
- 2 whole skinless, boneless chicken breasts
- 1piece (1½ ounces) feta cheese, thinly
- sliced
- 8 fresh mint leaves, rinsed, blotted dry,
- and cut into thin slivers
- Coarse salt (kosher or sea)
- Freshly ground black pepper
- 1 tablespoon fresh lemon juice
- 1 tablespoon extra-virgin olive oil
- Lemon wedges, for serving
- YOU'LL ALSO NEED:
- Wooden toothpicks

Directions:
1. Preparing the Ingredients.
2. If using whole chicken breasts, cut each in half. Trim any sinews or excess fat off the chicken breasts and discard. Remove the tenders from the chicken breasts and set them aside. Place a half breast at the edge of a cutting board. Cut a deep horizontal pocket in the breast, taking care not to pierce the edges. Repeat with the remaining breast halves. Place 2 or 3 slices of feta and a few slivers of mint in the pocket of each chicken breast. Pin the pockets shut with lightly oiled toothpicks. Place the breasts in a baking dish just large enough to hold them. Season the breasts on both sides with salt and pepper and sprinkle any remaining mint over them. Drizzle the lemon juice and olive oil over both sides of the chicken breasts, patting them onto the meat with your fingers. Let the chicken breasts marinate in the refrigerator, covered, for 20 Minutes, turning once or twice.
3. Turn control knob to the high position, when the griddle is hot, place the chicken breasts on the griddle and cook for 10 to 14 Minutes. Insert an instant-read meat thermometer into the thick part of a breast through one end: The internal temperature should be about 160°F.
4. Transfer the chicken breasts to a platter or plates and remove and discard the toothpicks. Serve the chicken at once with lemon wedges.

141.Chicken Roast With Pineapple Salsa

Servings: 2
Cooking Time: 45 Minutes
Ingredients:
- ¼ cup extra virgin olive oil
- ¼ cup freshly chopped cilantro
- 1 avocado, diced
- 1-pound boneless chicken breasts
- 2 cups canned pineapples
- 2 teaspoons honey
- Juice from 1 lime
- Salt and pepper to taste

Directions:
1. Preparing the Ingredients.
2. 1 Season the chicken breasts with lime juice, olive oil, honey, salt, and pepper.
3. 2 Bring the griddle grill to high heat. When the griddle is hot, place on the griddle and cook for 45 Minutes.
4. Flip the chicken every 10 Minutes to grill all sides evenly.
5. Once the chicken is cooked, serve with pineapples, cilantro, and avocado.

Nutrition Info: (Per Serving): CALORIES: 744; FAT: 32.8G; PROTEIN:4.7G; SUGAR:5G

142.Chicken Satay With Thai Peanut Sauce

Servings: 4
Cooking Time: 8 Minutes
Ingredients:
- 3 large boneless skinless chicken breasts or 6 boneless skinless thighs
- satay sticks
- THAI PEANUT SAUCE
- 1 cup creamy peanut butter
- ¾ cup coconut milk
- 3 Tbsp. soy sauce
- 3 Tbsp. fresh lime juice
- 3 Tbsp. brown sugar
- 2 Tbsp. sesame oil
- 2 tsp. crushed red pepper flakes
- 1 Tbsp. fish sauce
- 1 Tbsp. sriracha sauce
- 1 (3-in.) piece of ginger, peeled and diced
- 2 cloves garlic, minced

- ¼ cup chopped cilantro

Directions:
1.   Preparing the Ingredients
2.   Cut chicken into 1.5-inch squares and place onto satay sticks. Lightly season with salt. Combine all ingredients for sauce except the cilantro into a saucepan. Place saucepan over medium heat, mix ingredients together using a whisk, and let simmer for 5 Minutes. Once ingredients have melded together, use either a blender or an immersion blender to blend until smooth. Pour into bowl and top with cilantro.
3.   Turn control knob to the high position, when the griddle is hot, place the chicken breasts and cook for 8 Minutes. Because the chicken is cut into small pieces, it will cook rather quick. But don't risk undercooked chicken. Ensure internal temperature meets minimum requirements of 165° Fahrenheit. Remove from grill.
4.   Serve with sauce and cilantro.

143.Healthy Chicken Fajitas

Servings: 4
Cooking Time: 15 Minutes
Ingredients:
- 2 chicken breasts, cut into chunks
- 2 carrots, sliced
- 2 zucchini, sliced
- 2 bell peppers, sliced
- 1 sweet potato, clean and cut into fries shape
- 1 tbsp olive oil
- 1/2 tsp dried oregano
- 1 tsp ground cumin
- 1 tbsp dried chives
- 2 tbsp paprika
- 1/4 tsp pepper
- 1 1/2 tsp salt

Directions:
1.   Add all ingredients into the large mixing bowl and toss well.
2.   Preheat the griddle to medium-low heat.
3.   Spray griddle top with cooking spray.
4.   Transfer chicken mixture onto the hot griddle top and cook until vegetables are tender and chicken is cooked.
5.   Serve and enjoy.
Nutrition Info: (Per Serving): Calories 255 ;Fat 9.9 g ;Carbohydrates 19.1 g ;Sugar 8.4 g ;Protein 24.4 g ;Cholesterol 65 mg

144.Root Beer Can Chicken

Servings: 2 -4
Cooking Time: 20 Minutes

Ingredients:
- 1 lb. boneless chicken thighs
- 3 (12 ounce) cans root beer, like A&W
- Olive oil
- For the rub:
- 1 tablespoon garlic powder
- 3/4 tablespoon sea salt
- 1/2 tablespoon white pepper
- 2 teaspoons smoked paprika
- 2 teaspoons garlic powder
- 1 teaspoon dried thyme
- 1/8 teaspoon cayenne pepper

Directions:
1.   Combine rub ingredients in a bowl; reserve half in a separate air tight container until ready to cook.
2.   Rub chicken thighs evenly with olive oil and coat each with some rub.
3.   Lay chicken in a 13 by 9 inch baking dish. Cover with 2 cans of root beer.
4.   Preheat grill to medium-high heat.
5.   Discard marinade and brush grill with olive oil.
6.   Gently fold remaining rub and a half of the third can of root beer in a small bowl.
7.   Sear chicken for 7 minutes on each side, basting often with root beer rub mix.
8.   Serve when cooked through or chicken reaches 165°F and juices run clear.
Nutrition Info: Calories: 363, Sodium: 1185 mg, Dietary Fiber: 0.9g, Fat: 12.1g, Carbs: 29.9g, Protein: 33.4g.

145.Flavorful Grilled Chicken Wings

Servings: 6
Cooking Time: 20 Minutes
Ingredients:
- Chicken wings – 3 lbs.
- Garlic – 1-1/2 tsps., minced.
- Fresh thyme leaves – 1 tbsp., chopped.
- Fresh parsley – 1 tbsp., chopped.
- Lemon zest – 2 tsps., grated.
- Soy sauce – 3 tbsps.
- Dijon mustard – 1 tbsp.
- Brown sugar – 3 tbsps.
- Olive oil –1/2 cup.
- Pepper – 3/4 tsp.
- Salt – 1 tsp.

Directions:
1.   Add chicken wings into the zip-lock bag.
2.   In a medium bowl, whisk together the remaining ingredients and pour over the chicken wings. Seal zip-lock bag and place in the refrigerator for 8 hours.
3.   Heat the griddle grill to a medium-high heat.

4. Remove chicken wings from the marinade and place on a hot grill and cook for 10 minutes per side. Serve.
Nutrition Info: (Per serving):Calories 313, Carbs 5g, Fat 14g, Protein 30g

146.Five-spice Squab

Servings: 4
Cooking Time: 20 Minutes
Ingredients:
- 3 tablespoons hoisin sauce
- 2 tablespoons rice wine or dry sherry
- 1 tablespoon soy sauce
- 1 tablespoon rice vinegar
- 2 teaspoons sugar
- 1 teaspoon five-spice powder
- squabs (10–18 ounces each, semiboneless or spatchcocked)

Directions:
1. Preparing the Ingredients
2. 1 Whisk the hoisin sauce, rice wine, soy sauce, vinegar, sugar, and five-spice powder together in a small bowl. Brush the mixture evenly over both sides of the squabs. (You can marinate the squabs for several hours in the refrigerator before grilling.)
3. 2 Bring the griddle grill to high heat. When the griddle is hot, let excess marinade drip off the squabs and put them on the griddle, skin side up and cook, turning once, until they are crisp on the outside and rosy pink inside, 5 to 10 Minutes per side depending on their size. Carve into pieces if you like, transfer to a platter, and serve.

147.Sweet Chili Lime Chicken

Servings: 4
Cooking Time: 15 Minutes
Ingredients:
- ½ cup sweet chili sauce
- ¼ cup soy sauce
- 1 teaspoon mirin
- 1 teaspoon orange juice, fresh squeezed
- 1 teaspoon orange marmalade
- 2 tablespoons lime juice
- 1 tablespoon brown sugar
- 1 clove garlic, minced
- 4 boneless, skinless chicken breasts
- Sesame seeds, for garnish

Directions:
1. Whisk sweet chili sauce, soy sauce, mirin, orange marmalade, lime and orange juice, brown sugar, and minced garlic together in a small mixing bowl.
2. Set aside ¼ cup of the sauce.

3. Toss chicken in sauce to coat and marinate 30 minutes.
4. Preheat your griddle to medium heat.
5. Put the chicken on the griddle and cook each side for 7 minutes.
6. Baste the cooked chicken with remaining marinade and garnish with sesame seeds to serve with your favorite sides.
Nutrition Info: Calories: 380, Sodium: 1274 mg, Dietary Fiber: 0.5 g, Fat: 12 g, Carbs:19.7g, Protein: 43.8 g.

148.Buffalo Chicken Wings

Servings: 6 - 8
Cooking Time: 20 Minutes
Ingredients:
- 1 tablespoon sea salt
- 1 teaspoon ground black pepper
- 1 teaspoon garlic powder
- 3 lbs. chicken wings
- 6 tablespoons unsalted butter
- 1/3 cup buffalo sauce, like Moore's
- 1 tablespoon apple cider vinegar
- 1 tablespoon honey

Directions:
1. Combine salt, pepper and garlic powder in a large mixing bowl.
2. Toss the wings with the seasoning mixture to coat.
3. Preheat griddle to medium heat.
4. Place the wings on the griddle; make sure they are touching so the meat stays moist on the bone while grilling.
5. Flip wings every 5 minutes, for a total of 20 minutes of cooking.
6. Heat the butter, buffalo sauce, vinegar and honey in a saucepan over low heat; whisk to combine well.
7. Add wings to a large mixing bowl, toss the wings with the sauce to coat.
8. Turn griddle up to medium high and place wings back on the griddle until the skins crisp; about 1 to 2 minutes per side.
9. Add wings back into the bowl with the sauce and toss to serve.
Nutrition Info: Calories:410, Sodium: 950 mg, Dietary Fiber: 0.2 g, Fat: 21.3g, Carbs: 2.7g, Protein: 49.4g.

149.Chicken "steaks"

Servings: 4
Cooking Time: 8 Minutes
Ingredients:

- 2 whole boneless chicken breasts (each 12 to 16 ounces), or 4 half chicken breasts (each half 6 to 8 ounces)
- Coarse salt (kosher or sea) and freshly ground black pepper
- ¼ cup white wine vinegar or red wine vinegar
- ½ sweet onion, finely diced (about ½ cup)
- 3 cloves garlic, coarsely chopped
- 1 teaspoon dried oregano
- ½ teaspoon ground cumin
- ¾ cup extra-virgin olive oil
- ⅓ cup chopped fresh flat-leaf parsley

Directions:
1. Preparing the Ingredients
2. If using whole breasts, cut each breast in half. Remove the tenders from the chicken breasts, place a breast half between 2 pieces of plastic wrap and gently pound it to a thickness of ½ inch using a meat pounder, the side of a heavy cleaver, a rolling pin, or the bottom of a heavy saucepan. Repeat with the remaining breast halves. Place the chicken breasts in a large baking dish and season them on both sides with salt and pepper.
3. Place the vinegar, onion, garlic, oregano, and cumin in a nonreactive mixing bowl. Add ½ teaspoon of salt and ¼ teaspoon of pepper and whisk until the salt dissolves. Whisk in the olive oil. Correct the seasoning, adding salt and pepper to taste. The mixture should be highly seasoned. Pour half of this mixture into another nonreactive serving bowl and set aside for use as a sauce. Whisk 2 tablespoons of the parsley into the mixture in the mixing bowl then pour it over the chicken, turning the breasts to coat on both sides. Let the chicken breasts marinate in the refrigerator, covered, for at least 2 hours or as long as overnight, turning them a few times so that they marinate evenly.
4. Drain the chicken breasts well and discard the marinade.
5. Turn control knob to the high position, when the griddle is hot, place the chicken breasts and cook for 5 Minutes. Use the poke test to check for doneness; the chicken should feel firm when pressed. Or insert an instant-read meat thermometer into the breast through one end: The internal temperature should be about 160°F. You may need to cook the chicken breasts in more than one batch; cover the grilled chicken with aluminum foil to keep warm until ready to serve.
6. Whisk the remaining parsley into the reserved bowl of vinegar mixture. Spoon half of it over the chicken breasts and serve the remainder on the side.

150.Zucchini Turkey Patties

Servings: 5

Cooking Time: 10 Minutes
Ingredients:
- 1 lb ground turkey
- 1/4 cup breadcrumbs
- 6 oz zucchini, grated and squeezed out all liquid
- 1 tbsp onion, grated
- 1 garlic clove, grated
- Pepper
- Salt

Directions:
1. Add ground turkey and remaining ingredients into the bowl and mix until well combined.
2. Preheat the griddle to medium heat.
3. Spray griddle top with cooking spray.
4. Make patties from mixture and place onto the hot griddle top and cook until patties are golden brown from both sides.
5. Serve and enjoy.
Nutrition Info: (Per Serving): Calories 190 ;Fat 10 g ;Carbohydrates 1.8 g ;Sugar 0.7 g ;Protein 25 g ;Cholesterol 93 mg

151.Chicken Bbq With Sweet And Sour Sauce

Servings: 6
Cooking Time: 40 Minutes
Ingredients:
- ¼ cup minced garlic
- ¼ cup tomato paste
- ¾ cup minced onion
- ¾ cup sugar
- 1 cup soy sauce
- 1 cup water
- 1 cup white vinegar
- 6 chicken drumsticks
- Salt and pepper to taste

Directions:
1. 1 Preparing the Ingredients. Place all Ingredients in a Ziploc bag
2. Allow to marinate for at least 2 hours in the fridge.
3. 2 Bring the griddle grill to high heat. When the griddle is hot, grill the chicken for 40 Minutes.
4. Flip the chicken every 10 Minutes for even grilling.
5. Meanwhile, pour the marinade in a saucepan and heat over medium flame until the sauce thickens.
6. Before serving the chicken, brush with the glaze.
Nutrition Info: (Per Serving): CALORIES: 4607; FAT: 19.7G; PROTEIN:27.8G; SUGAR:3G

152.Caesar Marinated Grilled Chicken

Servings: 3
Cooking Time: 24 Minutes
Ingredients:
- ¼ cup crouton
- 1 teaspoon lemon zest. Form into ovals, skewer and grill.
- 1/2 cup Parmesan
- 1/4 cup breadcrumbs
- 1-pound ground chicken
- 2 tablespoons Caesar dressing and more for drizzling
- 2-4 romaine leaves

Directions:
1. Preparing the Ingredients. In a shallow dish, mix well chicken, 2 tablespoons Caesar dressing, parmesan, and breadcrumbs. Mix well with hands. Form into 1-inch oval patties.
2. Thread chicken pieces in skewers. Bring the griddle grill to high heat. When the griddle is hot, put the skewers and cook for 12 Minutes. Halfway through cooking time, turnover skewers. Serve and enjoy on a bed of lettuce and sprinkle with croutons and extra dressing.

Nutrition Info: (Per Serving): CALORIES: 339; FAT: 18.9G; PROTEIN:32.6G; SUGAR:1G

153.Lemony Chicken Paillards With Asparagus And Feta

Servings: 4
Cooking Time: 6 Minutes
Ingredients:
- 1 pound thin asparagus
- 1 tablespoon good-quality olive oil, plus more for brushing
- Salt and pepper
- 1½ pounds boneless, skinless chicken breasts, cut and pounded into paillards
- ½ cup crumbled feta cheese
- Lemon wedges for serving

Directions:
1. Preparing the Ingredients
2. Cut off the bottoms of the asparagus, then toss the spears with 1 tablespoon oil and sprinkle with salt. Put them on the griddle grill and cook, turning once, until browned and crisp-tender, 3 to 5 Minutes. Transfer to a plate.
3. Brush the paillards with oil and sprinkle with salt and pepper on both sides. Put them on the griddle grill and cook, turning once, until the chicken is no longer pink in the center, 2 to 3 Minutes per side. (Nick with a small knife and peek inside.) Transfer to individual plates, top with the asparagus, sprinkle with feta, and serve with the lemon wedges.

154.Teriyaki Chicken And Veggie Rice Bowls

Servings: 4
Cooking Time: 20 Minutes
Ingredients:
- 1 bag brown rice
- For the skewers:
- 2 boneless skinless chicken breasts, cubed
- 1 red onion, quartered
- 1 red pepper, cut into cube slices
- 1 green pepper, cut into cube slices
- 1/2 pineapple, cut into cubes
- For the marinade:
- 1/4 cup light soy sauce
- 1/4 cup sesame oil
- 1 tablespoon ginger, fresh grated
- 1 garlic clove, crushed
- 1/2 lime, juiced

Directions:
1. Whisk the marinade ingredients together in a small mixing bowl.
2. Add chicken and marinade to a resealable plastic bag, seal and toss well to coat.
3. Refrigerate for one hour or overnight.
4. Prepare rice as instructed on the bag.
5. Preheat the griddle to medium-high heat.
6. Thread the chicken and the cubed veggies onto 8 metal skewers and cook for 8 minutes on each side until seared and cooked through.
7. Portion rice out into bowls and top with two skewers each, and enjoy!

Nutrition Info: Calories: 477, Sodium:362 mg, Dietary Fiber: 3.8 g, Fat: 20.6g, Carbs:48.1g, Protein: 26.1g.

155.Chicken Portobello Panini

Servings: 4
Cooking Time: 5 Minutes
Ingredients:
- 1 tbsp. olive oil
- 1 tbsp. red wine vinegar
- 1/2 tsp. Italian Seasoning Mix
- 1/2 tsp. salt
- 1/4 tsp. coarsely ground black pepper
- 1 garlic clove, pressed
- 2 large Portobello mushroom caps
- 2 slices (1/2" thick) large white onion
- 1 cup (4 ounces) grated Provolone cheese
- 2 plum tomatoes, sliced
- 8 slices (3/4" thick) Italian bread
- 1 cup shredded roasted chicken

Directions:
1. Preheat the griddle grill on medium heat for 5 minutes. Then place the onions and the mushrooms in the grill. Allow them to cook for about 4 to 6 minutes, making sure to flip halfway through. Cut the onions in half and the mushrooms into thin slices.
2. Brush what's going to be the outside of the bread with olive oil. Top half the pieces of bread with a layer cheese, then, chicken, then mushrooms, then onions, then tomatoes, and a second layer of cheese. Top with another piece of bread making sure the olive oil side is on the outside.
3. Preheat the Griddle Grill to Medium-High.
4. Cook the sandwiches for 5 minutes, and make sure to flip halfway through. The bread should be brown, and the cheese should be melted.
Nutrition Info: (Per serving):Calories 252, Fat 10.3g, carbs 5.5g, protein 8g

156.Pesto Chicken Breasts

Servings: 6
Cooking Time: 10 Minutes
Ingredients:
- 1 3/4 lbs chicken breasts, skinless, boneless, and slice
- 1/2 cup mozzarella cheese, shredded
- 1/4 cup basil pesto

Directions:
1. Add chicken and pesto in a bowl and mix well, cover and place in the refrigerator for 2-3 hours.
2. Preheat the griddle to high heat.
3. Spray griddle top with cooking spray.
4. Place marinated chicken on hot griddle top and cook until chicken is completely done.
5. Sprinkle cheese over chicken and serve.
Nutrition Info: (Per Serving): Calories 305 ;Fat 14 g ;Carbohydrates 0.8 g ;Sugar 0.7 g ;Protein 40 g ;Cholesterol 122 mg

157.Chicken Wings With Sweet Red Chili And Peach Glaze

Servings: 4
Cooking Time: 30 Minutes
Ingredients:
- 1 (12 oz.) jar peach preserves
- 1 cup sweet red chili sauce
- 1 teaspoon lime juice
- 1 tablespoon fresh cilantro, minced
- 1 (2-1/2 lb.) bag chicken wing sections
- Non-stick cooking spray

Directions:

1. Mix preserves, red chili sauce, lime juice and cilantro in mixing bowl. Divide in half, and place one half aside for serving.
2. Preheat griddle to medium heat and spray with non-stick cooking spray.
3. Cook wings for 25 minutes turning several times until juices run clear.
4. Remove wings from griddle, toss in a bowl to coat wings with remaining glaze.
5. Return wings to griddle and cook for an additional 3 to 5 minutes turning once.
6. Serve warm with your favorite dips and side dishes!
Nutrition Info: Calories: 790, Sodium: 643 mg, Dietary Fiber: 1 g, Fat: 16.9 g, Carbs:87.5g, Protein: 66g.

158.Bone-in Chicken Thighs With Caramelized Fish Sauce

Servings: 4
Cooking Time: 55 Minutes
Ingredients:
- 3 pounds bone-in, skin-on chicken thighs
- Salt and pepper
- ¼ cup fish sauce
- 2 tablespoons turbinado sugar
- 1 tablespoon minced garlic
- 3 dried red chiles

Directions:
1. Preparing the Ingredients.
2. Trim excess fat and skin from the chicken without exposing the meat. Sprinkle with salt and pepper on both sides. Turn control knob to the high position, when the griddle is hot, put the thighs on the griddle grill, skin side up, and cook for about 20 Minutes, then turn the pieces and rotate them 180 degrees for even browning. Cook until the meat is no longer pink at the bone, 40 to 55 Minutes total, depending on the size of the pieces.
3. While the thighs cook, put the fish sauce, sugar, garlic, and chiles in a small saucepan over low heat. Stir until the sugar dissolves completely. Let cool a few Minutes before pouring into a large heatproof bowl; remove the chiles. When the thighs are done, transfer them to the bowl and toss to coat evenly with the glaze, using tongs. Turn the heat to medium. Remove the thighs from the glaze, let any excess glaze drip off, then arrange the thighs skin side up on the griddle. Cook, turning once, until crisp and brown, 1 to 3 Minutes per side; move the thighs away from the flames if the glaze starts to burn. Transfer to a platter and serve.

159.Italian-style Sweet Pork Sausage With Fennel Seeds

Servings: 8
Cooking Time: 10 Minutes
Ingredients:
- 2½ pounds fatty boneless pork shoulder, cut into 1-inch cubes
- 3 cloves garlic, minced
- 1 tablespoon fennel seeds
- 1 teaspoon salt
- 1 teaspoon black pepper
- Sausage casings (optional)

Directions:
1. Preparing the Ingredients
2. Working in batches if necessary, put the meat in a food processor and pulse until coarsely ground—finer than chopped, but not much. Take your time and be careful not to pulverize the meat. As you finish each batch, transfer it to a bowl. Add the garlic, fennel seeds, salt, and pepper and work the mixture gently with your hands to incorporate them into the meat; add a little water if the mixture seems dry and crumbly. Cook up a spoonful in a small skillet to taste it; adjust the seasoning. Shape into 8 or more patties, or stuff into casings if you prefer. (You can freeze some or all of them, wrapped well, for up to several months.)
3. Bring the griddle grill to high heat. When the griddle is hot, put the sausages on the griddle, and cook until they release from the grates easily, 5 to 10 Minutes, then turn and cook the other side until the sausages are no longer pink in the center; the internal temperature should be 160°F (check with an instant-read thermometer, or nick with a small knife and peek inside). Transfer to a platter and serve.

160.Bacon Chipotle Chicken Panini

Servings: 1
Cooking Time: 5 Minutes
Ingredients:
- 2 Slices Sourdough Bread
- 1/4 Cup Caesar Salad Dressing
- 1 Cooked Chicken Breast, Diced
- 1/2 Cup Shredded Cheddar Cheese
- 1 Tbsp. Bacon Bits
- 1-1/2 Tsps. Chipotle Chili Powder, Or To Taste
- 2 Tbsps. Softened Butter

Directions:
1. Preheat the Griddle Grill to Medium-High with unit closed.
2. Spread the salad dressing on one side of both pieces of bread. Then top the dressing side of one piece of bread with chicken, then cheese, then bacon, and finally chipotle chili powder.

3. Place the other piece of bread with the dressing side down on top. Butter the other side of both pieces of bread.
4. Cook the Panini for 5 minutes, checking halfway through. The bread should be brown, and the cheese should be melted.

Nutrition Info: (Per serving):Calories 407; Fat13 g; Carbs 4 g; Protein 10g

161.Fiery Italian Chicken Skewers

Servings: 2 -4
Cooking Time: 20 Minutes
Ingredients:
- 10 boneless, skinless chicken thighs, cut into chunks
- 1 large red onion, cut into wedges
- 1 large red pepper, stemmed, seeded, and cut into chunks
- For the marinade:
- 1/3 cup toasted pine nuts
- 1 1/2 cups sliced roasted red peppers
- 5 hot cherry peppers, stemmed and seeded, or to taste
- 1 cup packed fresh basil leaves, plus more to serve
- 4 cloves garlic, peeled
- 1/4 cup grated Parmesan cheese
- 1 tablespoon paprika
- extra virgin olive oil, as needed

Directions:
1. Combine the toasted pine nuts, roasted red peppers, hot cherry peppers, basil, garlic, Parmesan, and paprika in a food processor or blender and process until well-combined.
2. Add in olive oil until the pesto reaches a thin consistency in order to coat the chicken as a marinade.
3. Transfer half of the pesto to a large sealable plastic bag, and reserve the other half for serving.
4. Add the chicken thigh chunks to the bag of pesto, seal, and massage the bag to coat the chicken.
5. Refrigerate for 1 hour.
6. Preheat griddle to medium-high heat and brush with olive oil.
7. Thread the chicken cubes, red onion, and red pepper onto metal skewers.
8. Brush the chicken with the reserved pesto.
9. Cook until the chicken reaches an internal temperature of 165°F; about 5 minutes per side. Serve warm with your favorite salad or vegetables!

Nutrition Info: Calories: 945, Sodium: 798 mg, Dietary Fiber: 3.2 g, Fat: 46.7 g, Carbs: 14.7g, Protein: 112.2g.

162. Jerk Chicken

Servings: 4
Cooking Time: 40 Minutes
Ingredients:
- 4 scallions, cut into chunks
- 1 or 2 habanero or Scotch bonnet chiles, or to taste, stemmed (remove the seeds and pith if you want it a bit milder)
- 3 cloves garlic, peeled
- 1 small shallot, peeled
- 1 1-inch piece fresh ginger, peeled and sliced
- 2 tablespoons good-quality vegetable oil
- 2 tablespoons fresh lime juice
- 1 tablespoon brown sugar
- 1 tablespoon fresh thyme leaves
- 1 teaspoon ground allspice
- 1 teaspoon salt
- 1 teaspoon black pepper
- ½ teaspoon freshly grated nutmeg
- 3 pounds bone-in, skin-on chicken thighs, drumsticks, or a mix

Directions:
1. Preparing the Ingredients
2. 1 Put the scallions, chiles, garlic, shallot, ginger, oil, lime juice, sugar, thyme, allspice, salt, pepper, and nutmeg in a blender or food processor and purée to a rough paste. Trim excess skin and fat from the chicken without exposing the meat. Pat the chicken dry with paper towels, then rub the jerk paste all over the pieces. Let the chicken sit at room temperature.
3. 2 Turn control knob to the medium position, when the griddle is hot, put the chicken on the griddle grill, and cook until the meat is no longer pink at the bone, 40 Minutes total, depending on the size of the pieces. (Nick with a small knife and peek inside.)
4. Transfer to a platter and serve.

163. Chicken Salad With Mango And Fresh Herbs

Servings: 4
Cooking Time: 8 Minutes
Ingredients:
- 1½ pounds boneless, skinless chicken breasts
- ¼ cup olive oil, plus more for brushing
- Salt and pepper
- Grated zest of 1 lime
- 2 tablespoons fresh lime juice
- 1 head Boston lettuce, torn into pieces
- ½ cup whole fresh mint leaves
- 1 ripe mango, peeled, pitted, and cut into 1-inch pieces

Directions:
1. Preparing the Ingredients
2. 1 Brush with oil and sprinkle with salt and pepper on both sides.
3. Turn control knob to the high position, when the griddle is hot, place the chicken on the griddle grill and cook for 8 Minutes. Transfer the chicken to a plate and let rest while you put the rest of the salad together.
4. 2 Make the dressing: Put the ¼ cup oil in a small bowl with the lime zest and juice and a pinch of salt. Whisk until the dressing thickens; taste and adjust the seasoning.
5. Put the lettuce and mint in a salad bowl and toss to mix. Cut the chicken across the grain into ½-inch slices and put over the greens. Top with the mango pieces, then drizzle with the dressing and serve (or toss before serving if you like).

164. Curried Chicken Kebabs

Servings: 4
Cooking Time: 10 Minutes
Ingredients:
- 1 1/2 lbs chicken breasts, boneless & cut into 1-inch pieces
- 1/2 cup soy sauce
- 1 tbsp olive oil
- 1 tbsp curry powder
- 1 tbsp brown sugar
- 2 tbsp peanut butter

Directions:
1. Add chicken in a large zip-lock bag.
2. In a small, bowl mix soy sauce, olive oil, curry powder, brown sugar, and peanut butter and pour over chicken.
3. Seal bag and shake until chicken is well coated and place in the refrigerator for overnight.
4. Thread marinated chicken onto skewers.
5. Preheat the griddle to high heat.
6. Spray griddle top with cooking spray.
7. Place chicken skewers onto the hot griddle top and cook for 12-15 minutes. Turn frequently.
8. Serve and enjoy.
Nutrition Info: (Per Serving): Calories 430 ;Fat 20 g ;Carbohydrates 7 g ;Sugar 3.5 g ;Protein 53 g ;Cholesterol 151 mg

165. Yellow Curry Chicken Wings

Servings: 6
Cooking Time: 30 Minutes To 1 Hour
Ingredients:
- 2 lbs. chicken wings
- For the marinade:

- 1/2 cup Greek yogurt, plain
- 1 tablespoon mild yellow curry powder
- 1 tablespoon olive oil
- ½ teaspoon sea salt
- ½ teaspoon black pepper
- 1 teaspoon red chili flakes

Directions:
1. Rinse and pat wings dry with paper towels.
2. Whisk marinade ingredients together in a large mixing bowl until well-combined.
3. Add wings to bowl and toss to coat.
4. Cover bowl with plastic wrap and chill in the refrigerator for 30 minutes.
5. Prepare one side of the griddle for medium heat and the other side on medium-high.
6. Working in batches, grill wings over medium heat, turning occasionally, until skin starts to brown; about 12 minutes.
7. Move wings to medium-high area of griddle for 5 minutes on each side to char until cooked through; meat thermometer should register 165°F when touching the bone.
8. Transfer wings to a platter and serve warm.

Nutrition Info: Calories: 324, Sodium:292 mg, Dietary Fiber: 0.4 g, Fat: 14g, Carbs:1.4g, Protein: 45.6g.

166.Classic Bbq Chicken

Servings: 4-6
Cooking Time: 1 Hour 45 Minutes
Ingredients:
- 4 pounds of your favorite chicken, including legs, thighs, wings, and breasts, skin-on
- Salt
- Olive oil
- 1 cup barbecue sauce, like Hickory Mesquite or homemade

Directions:
1. Rub the chicken with olive oil and salt.
2. Preheat the griddle to high heat.
3. Sear chicken skin side down on the grill for 5-10 minutes.
4. Turn the griddle down to medium low heat, tent with foil and cook for 30 minutes.
5. Turn chicken and baste with barbecue sauce.
6. Cover the chicken again and allow to cook for another 20 minutes.
7. Baste, cover and cook again for 30 minutes; repeat basting and turning during this time.
8. The chicken is done when the internal temperature of the chicken pieces are 165°F and juices run clear.
9. Baste with more barbecue sauce to serve!

Nutrition Info: Calories: 539, Sodium: 684 mg, Dietary Fiber: 0.3 g, Fat: 11.6 g, Carbs: 15.1 g, Protein: 87.6 g.

167.Simple Chicken Fajita

Servings: 4
Cooking Time: 15 Minutes
Ingredients:
- 1 lb chicken breast, boneless, skinless & sliced
- 2 tsp olive oil
- 1 onion, sliced
- 2 bell peppers, sliced
- 1/8 tsp cayenne
- 1 tsp cumin
- 2 tsp chili powder
- Pepper
- Salt

Directions:
1. Add chicken, onion, and sliced bell peppers into the bowl.
2. Add cayenne, cumin, chili powder, oil, pepper, and salt and toss well.
3. Preheat the griddle to medium heat.
4. Add chicken mixture onto the hot griddle top and cook until vegetables are tender and chicken is cooked.
5. Serve and enjoy.

Nutrition Info: (Per Serving): Calories 185 ;Fat 5 g ;Carbohydrates 8.1 g ;Sugar 4.3 g ;Protein 25.2 g ;Cholesterol 73 mg

168.Hasselback Stuffed Chicken

Servings: 4
Cooking Time: 30 Minutes
Ingredients:
- 4 boneless, skinless chicken breasts
- 2 tablespoons olive oil
- 2 tablespoons taco seasoning
- 1/2 red, yellow and green pepper, very thinly sliced
- 1 small red onion, very thinly sliced
- 1/2 cup Mexican shredded cheese
- Guacamole, for serving
- Sour cream, for serving
- Salsa, for serving

Directions:
1. Preheat griddle to med-high.
2. Cut thin horizontal cuts across each chicken breast; like you would hasselback potatoes.
3. Rub chicken evenly with olive oil and taco seasoning.

4. Add a mixture of bell peppers and red onions to each cut, and place the breasts on the griddle.
5. Cook chicken for 15 minutes.
6. Remove and top with cheese.
7. Tent loosely with foil and cook another 5 minutes, until cheese is melted.
8. Remove from griddle and top with guacamole, sour cream and salsa. Serve alongside your favorite side dishes!
Nutrition Info: Calories:643 , Sodium:1549 mg, Dietary Fiber: 3.8 g, Fat: 18.6g, Carbs: 26.3g, Protein: 93.3g.

169.Tasty Chicken Fritters

Servings: 4
Cooking Time: 10 Minutes
Ingredients:
- 1 lb ground chicken
- 1 tsp onion powder
- 1 tsp garlic powder
- 1/2 cup parmesan cheese, shredded
- 1 tbsp dill, chopped
- 1/2 cup breadcrumbs
- Pepper
- Salt

Directions:
1. Preheat the griddle to medium-low heat.
2. Spray griddle top with cooking spray.
3. Add all ingredients into the mixing bowl and mix until well combined.
4. Make patties from chicken mixture and place onto the hot griddle top and cook until golden brown from both sides.
5. Serve and enjoy.
Nutrition Info: (Per Serving): Calories 310 ;Fat 11 g ;Carbohydrates 12 g ;Sugar 1.3 g ;Protein 38 g ;Cholesterol 109 mg

170.Honey Jalapeno Chicken

Servings: 4
Cooking Time: 20 Minutes
Ingredients:
- 1-1/2 lbs. Chicken thighs, skinless and boneless.
- 1 tsp. Garlic, crushed.
- 1 Jalapeno pepper, minced.
- 3 tbsps. Fresh lime juice
- 3 tbsps. Honey
- 3 tbsps. Olive oil
- 1 tsp. Kosher salt

Directions:

1. Add chicken and remaining ingredients into the zip-lock bag. Seal bag and place in the refrigerator overnight.
2. Heat the griddle grill to a medium-high heat. Spray grill with cooking spray.
3. Remove chicken from the marinade and place on a hot grill and cook for 8-10 minutes on each side. Serve.
Nutrition Info: (Per serving):Calories 415, Carbs 14g, Fat 19g, Protein 43g

171.Balsamic-rosemary Chicken Breasts

Servings: 4
Cooking Time: 6 Minutes
Ingredients:
- ½ cup balsamic vinegar
- 2 tablespoons olive oil
- 2 rosemary sprigs, coarsely chopped
- 2 pounds boneless, skinless chicken breasts, pounded to ½-inch thickness

Directions:
1. Preparing the Ingredients
2. Combine the balsamic vinegar, olive oil, and rosemary in a shallow baking dish. Add the chicken breasts and turn to coat. Cover with plastic wrap and refrigerate for at least 30 Minutes or overnight.
3. Bring the griddle grill to high heat. When the griddle is hot, place the s chicken breasts on the Griddle and cook for 6 Minutes until they have taken on grill marks and are cooked through.
Nutrition Info: (Per Serving): CALORIES: 299; FAT: G; PROTEIN:52G;

172.Chicken Fried Rice

Servings: 4
Cooking Time: 20 Minutes
Ingredients:
- 2 boneless, skinless chicken breasts, cut into small pieces
- 4 cups long grain rice, cooked and allowed to air dry
- 1/3 cup soy sauce
- 1 yellow onion, finely chopped
- 4 cloves garlic, finely chopped
- 1 cups petite peas
- 2 carrots sliced into thin rounds
- 1/2 cup corn kernels
- 1/4 cup vegetable oil
- 2 tablespoons butter

Directions:
1. Preheat griddle to medium-high.
2. Add the vegetable oil to the griddle.

3. When the oil is shimmering, add the onion, carrot, peas, and corn.
4. Cook for several minutes, until lightly charred.
5. Add the chicken and cook until just browned.
6. Add the rice, soy sauce, garlic, and butter.
7. Toss until the rice is tender and the vegetables are just softened.
8. Serve immediately.

Nutrition Info: Calories: 485, Sodium: 1527 mg, Dietary Fiber: 4.7g, Fat: 20.8g, Carbs: 60.9g Protein: 13.4g

173.Penne With Grilled Chicken, Portobellos, And Walnuts

Servings: 5
Cooking Time: 11 Minutes
Ingredients:
- 5 portobello mushrooms, stemmed
- 1 cup olive oil
- ½ teaspoon salt
- ½ teaspoon freshly ground black pepper
- 1 pound dried penne
- 2 pounds boneless, skinless chicken
- breasts, pounded to ½-inch thickness
- 1 cup walnut pieces
- ½ cup grated Parmesan cheese, preferably freshly grated
- ¼ cup chopped fresh basil or parsley leaves
- 2 garlic cloves, minced

Directions:
1. Preparing the Ingredients
2. Bring a medium pot of salted water to a boil, then reduce to a simmer. Brush the portobellos lightly with a couple of tablespoons of the olive oil and season with ¼ teaspoon of the salt and ¼ teaspoon of the pepper.
3. Turn control knob to the high position, when the griddle is hot, place the mushrooms, gill-side down, on the griddle, and grill for 8 Minutes, until the mushrooms are tender.
4. Transfer to a cutting board; keep the griddle on high. Bring the water up to a full boil, add the penne, and cook.
5. Sprinkle the chicken with the remaining ¼ teaspoon salt and ¼ teaspoon pepper. Grill for about 3 Minutes. Transfer to the cutting board with the mushrooms.
6. Cut the cooked breasts in half lengthwise and then cut them into ½-inch strips. Slice the portobello caps into pieces approximately the same size.
7. Drain the penne and transfer to a serving bowl. Add the remaining olive oil (about ¼ cup), the mushrooms, chicken, walnuts, Parmesan, basil, and garlic. Toss gently to combine and serve immediately.

Nutrition Info: (Per Serving): CALORIES: 510; FAT: 11G; PROTEIN:41G

174.Spicy Chicken Breasts

Servings: 4
Cooking Time: 15 Minutes
Ingredients:
- Chicken breasts – 4, skinless & boneless.
- Red pepper flakes – 1 tbsp.
- Chili powder – 1 tbsp.
- Brown sugar – 6 tbsps.
- BBQ sauce – 6 tbsps.
- Pineapple juice – 1 cup.

Directions:
1. Add chicken breasts into the zip-lock bag.
2. Mix together pineapple juice, BBQ sauce, brown sugar, chili powder, and red pepper flakes and pour over chicken breasts. Seal zip-lock bag and place in the refrigerator overnight.
3. Heat the griddle grill to a medium-high heat.
4. Place marinated chicken breasts on the hot grill and cook for 12-15 minutes or until done. Serve.

Nutrition Info: (Per serving):Calories 407, Carbs 31.6g, Fat 11.5g, Protein 42.9g

175.Grilled Chicken Fajitas

Servings: 6
Cooking Time: 6 Minutes
Ingredients:
- CHICKEN
- ¼ cup olive oil, divided
- juice from 1 lime
- 3 large boneless skinless chicken breasts, butterflied
- 1 each red, yellow, and orange peppers
- 1 medium Vidalia onion
- a pinch of salt
- 12 small soft flour tortillas
- SEASONING
- 1½ Tbsp. chili powder
- 2 tsp. ground cumin
- 2 tsp. kosher salt
- 2 tsp. smoked paprika
- 1 tsp. ground cinnamon
- 1 tsp. onion powder
- 1 tsp. garlic powder
- 1 tsp. cayenne pepper
- ½ tsp. white sugar
- zest from 1 lime

Directions:
1. Preparing the Ingredients

2. Combine all the seasoning ingredients into small bowl and whisk together.

3. Whisk 2 tablespoons olive oil and the lime juice together in medium mixing bowl. Add butterflied chicken breasts. Toss to evenly coat.

4. Evenly sprinkle seasoning on both sides of chicken, ensuring uniform coverage.

5. Thinly slice peppers and onion.

6. In a large mixing bowl, toss sliced vegetables with remaining 2 tablespoons of olive oil and a pinch of salt.

7. Bring the griddle grill to high heat. When the griddle is hot, place the vegetables and cook for 4 Minutes.

8. As veggies near completion, place seasoned chicken on the griddle, and cook for 4 Minutes.

9. Remove both meat and vegetables from the grill, slice chicken into thin strips, and keep warm.

10. Toss flour tortillas on grill for 15 to 30 seconds per side, just to warm them up and slightly toast them. Don't cook them to the point that they are no longer flexible.

11. Serve hot with toppings of your choice: cheese, fresh limes, sour cream, cilantro, and so on.

176.Tandoori Chicken

Servings: 4
Cooking Time: 45 Minutes
Ingredients:
- 1 cup yogurt
- ¼ cup fresh lemon juice
- 1 tablespoon minced garlic
- 1 tablespoon minced fresh ginger
- 1 tablespoon ground cumin
- 1 tablespoon ground coriander
- 2 teaspoons smoked paprika (pimentón)
- 2 teaspoons salt
- 1 whole chicken (3–4 pounds), cut into pieces, or 3 pounds bone-in, skin-on
- chicken parts
- 1 medium onion, cut into wedges
- Good-quality olive oil for brushing
- 1 lemon, halved

Directions:
1. Preparing the Ingredients
2. Whisk the yogurt, lemon juice, garlic, ginger, cumin, coriander, paprika, and salt together in a large bowl to combine. Trim excess fat and skin from the chicken without exposing the meat. Add the chicken pieces to the marinade, turning to coat them completely. Cover with plastic wrap and refrigerate for 2 to 4 hours. If you're using bamboo or wooden skewers, soak them in water for 30 Minutes.

3. Thread the onion wedges onto 2 skewers, then brush with oil. Remove the chicken from the marinade, letting any excess drip off.

4. Turn control knob to the high position, when the griddle is hot, put the chicken on the griddle, skin side up, and cook, turning the pieces and rotating them 180 degrees for even browning after 15 to 20 Minutes (breasts) and 20 to 25 Minutes (dark meat). Cook the chicken until the meat is no longer pink at the bone; depending on the size of the pieces, this can take 25 to 40 Minutes total for the breasts and 40 to 50 Minutes for the dark meat. (Nick with a small knife and peek inside.)

5. Put the lemon halves cut side down on the grill grate. As the chicken and onions char, transfer them to a platter, squeeze the lemon halves over all, and serve.

177.Tasty Chicken Bites

Servings: 2
Cooking Time: 10 Minutes
Ingredients:
- 1 lb chicken breasts, skinless, boneless and cut into cubes
- 2 tbsp fresh lemon juice
- 1 tbsp fresh oregano, chopped
- 2 tbsp olive oil
- 1/8 tsp cayenne pepper

Directions:
1. Place chicken in a bowl. Add reaming ingredients over chicken and mix well. Place chicken in the refrigerator for 1 hour.
2. Preheat the griddle to medium heat.
3. Spray griddle top with cooking spray.
4. Thread marinated chicken cubes onto the skewers.
5. Place skewers onto the hot griddle top and cook until chicken is completely done.
6. Serve and enjoy.

Nutrition Info: (Per Serving): Calories 560 ;Fat 31 g ;Carbohydrates 2 g ;Sugar 0.4 g ;Protein 66 g ;Cholesterol 202 mg

178.Chipotle Adobe Chicken

Servings: 4 - 6
Cooking Time: 20 Minutes
Ingredients:
- 2 lbs chicken thighs or breasts (boneless, skinless)
- For the marinade:
- ¼ cup olive oil
- 2 chipotle peppers, in adobo sauce, plus 1 teaspoon adobo sauce from the can

- 1 tablespoon garlic, minced
- 1 shallot, finely chopped
- 1 ½ tablespoons cumin
- 1 tablespoon cilantro, super-finely chopped or dried
- 2 teaspoons chili powder
- 1 teaspoon dried oregano
- 1/2 teaspoon salt
- Fresh limes, garnish
- Cilantro, garnish

Directions:
1. Preheat griddle to medium-high.
2. Add marinade ingredients to a food processor or blender and pulse into a paste.
3. Add the chicken and marinade to a sealable plastic bag and massage to coat well.
4. Place in the refrigerator for 1 hour to 24 hours before cooking.
5. Sear chicken for 7 minutes, turn and cook and additional 7 minutes.
6. Turn heat to low and continue to cook until chicken has reached an internal temperature of 165°F.
7. Remove chicken from griddle and allow to rest 5 to 10 minutes before serving.
8. Garnish with a squeeze of fresh lime and a sprinkle of cilantro to serve.

Nutrition Info: Calories: 561, Sodium: 431 mg, Dietary Fiber: 0.3 g, Fat: 23.8 g, Carbs: 18.7 g, Protein: 65.9 g.

179.Chicken Breast

Servings: 5
Cooking Time: 8 Minutes
Ingredients:
- boneless, skinless chicken breasts, leveled out to a similar thickness
- olive oil
- salt and pepper to taste

Directions:
1. Preparing the Ingredients
2. Brush the chicken breasts with the olive oil until they are coated liberally.
3. Add salt and pepper to taste, and let the breasts relax at room temperature for about 10 Minutes.
4. Turn control knob to the medium position, when the griddle is hot, place the chicken breasts on the griddle grill and cook for 5 Minutes.
5. Remove the breasts from the griddle and let them relax for several Minutes to allow the juices to redistribute.
6. Turn the griddle grill to medium heat.
7. Return the breasts to the grill, and cook them until the internal temperature is 160 degrees (they

will continue to cook after you remove them from the heat until they are over 165 degrees).
8. Let the breasts relax for 5–10 Minutes before cutting and serving.

180.Zesty Basil Crusted Chicken

Servings: 4
Cooking Time: 5 Minutes
Ingredients:
- Salt and pepper for taste
- 1 pound boneless, skinless chicken meat, cut into bite-sized pieces
- 1 red bell pepper, washed and diced
- 8 ounces mushrooms, cleaned and sliced
- 2 cups zucchini or other summer squash (washed, stemmed and sliced)
- 3 garlic cloves (minced or pressed)
- 8 ounces fresh basil (chopped)

Directions:
1. Preheat the Griddle Grill to High.
2. Season the chicken with salt and pepper for taste.
3. Add the chicken to the griddle, cooking on both sides until brown.
4. Pour in the rest of the ingredients and cook for 3 minutes.

Nutrition Info: (Per serving):Calories 550, Fat 33g, Carbs 9g, Protein Fat 16g

181.Chicken Veggie Stir Fry

Servings: 2
Cooking Time: 10 Minutes
Ingredients:
- 6 oz chicken breast, boneless and cut into cubes
- 1/4 onion, sliced
- 1/2 bell pepper, chopped
- 1/2 zucchini, chopped
- 1 tbsp olive oil
- 1/4 tsp dried thyme
- 1/2 tsp garlic powder
- 1 tsp dried oregano

Directions:
1. Add all ingredients into the large bowl and toss well.
2. Preheat the griddle to medium heat.
3. Transfer chicken mixture onto the hot griddle top and cook until vegetables are tender and chicken is cooked.
4. Serve and enjoy.

Nutrition Info: (Per Serving): Calories 186 ;Fat 8 g ;Carbohydrates 5 g ;Sugar 4 g ;Protein 20 g ;Cholesterol 0 mg

182. Lemon Herb Chicken

Servings: 4
Cooking Time: 12 Minutes
Ingredients:
- 4 chicken breasts, skinless and boneless
- 1/4 tsp garlic powder
- 1/2 tsp cumin
- 1/2 tsp dried oregano
- 1/2 tsp dried basil
- 1 tbsp olive oil
- 1 tbsp fresh lemon juice
- 1/2 tsp granulated sugar
- Pepper
- Salt

Directions:
1. In a small bowl, mix basil, oregano, cumin, garlic powder, and sugar.
2. Brush chicken breasts with oil from both sides and season with dry seasoning mix.
3. Preheat the griddle to high heat.
4. Spray griddle top with cooking spray.
5. Place chicken on hot griddle top and cook for 5-6 minutes.
6. Turn chicken to other side and cook for 5-6 minutes more.
7. Transfer chicken to the serving plate and drizzle with lemon juice.
8. Serve and enjoy.

Nutrition Info: (Per Serving): Calories 310 ;Fat 14 g ;Carbohydrates 1 g ;Sugar 0.6 g ;Protein 42 g ;Cholesterol 130 mg

183. Sweet Thai Cilantro Chili Chicken Quarters

Servings: 5
Cooking Time: 5 Minutes
Ingredients:
- 4 chicken leg quarters, lightly coated with olive oil
- 1 cup and 1 tsp. water
- ¾ cup rice vinegar
- ½ cup white sugar
- 3 Tbsp. freshly chopped cilantro
- 2 Tbsp. freshly minced ginger root
- 2 tsp. freshly minced garlic
- 2 Tbsp. crushed red pepper flakes
- 2 Tbsp. ketchup
- 2 Tbsp. cornstarch
- 2 Tbsp. fresh basil chiffonade ("chiffonade" is fancy for "thinly sliced")

Directions:

1. Preparing the Ingredients
2. 1 In a medium-sized saucepan, bring 1 cup water and the vinegar to a boil over high heat.
3. Stir in sugar, cilantro, ginger, garlic, red pepper flakes, and ketchup; simmer for 5 Minutes.
4. In small mixing bowl, mix together 1 teaspoon warm water and 2 tablespoons cornstarch. Use a fork for mixing this, and what you'll end up with will resemble white school glue.
5. Slowly whisk the cornstarch mixture into the simmering sauce, and continue mixing until sauce thickens. Set aside.
6. 2 Bring the griddle grill to high heat. When the griddle is hot, place the chicken quarters skin side down and cook for 8 Minutes.
7. At 155°F internal temperature, glaze chicken with sauce and allow to finish cooking to an internal temperature of 165°F. Plate, garnish with basil, and serve.

184. Seared Spicy Citrus Chicken

Servings: 4
Cooking Time: 20 Minutes
Ingredients:
- 2 lbs. boneless, skinless chicken thighs
- For the marinade:
- 1/4 cup fresh lime juice
- 2 teaspoon lime zest
- 1/4 cup honey
- 2 tablespoons olive oil
- 1 tablespoon balsamic vinegar
- 1/2 teaspoon sea salt
- 1/2 teaspoon black pepper
- 2 garlic cloves, minced
- 1/4 teaspoon onion powder

Directions:
1. Whisk together marinade ingredients in a large mixing bowl; reserve 2 tablespoons of the marinade for basting.
2. Add chicken and marinade to a sealable plastic bag and marinate 8 hours or overnight in the refrigerator.
3. Preheat griddle to medium high heat and brush lightly with olive oil.
4. Place chicken on griddle and cook 8 minutes per side.
5. Baste each side of chicken with reserved marinade during the last few minutes of cooking; chicken is done when the internal temperature reaches 165°F.
6. Plate chicken, tent with foil, and allow to rest for 5 minutes.
7. Serve and enjoy!

Nutrition Info: Calories: 381, Sodium: 337mg, Dietary Fiber: 1.1 g, Fat: 20.2 g, Carbs: 4.7 g, Protein: 44.7 g.

185.Korean Grilled Chicken Wings With Scallion

Servings: 6
Cooking Time: 30 Minutes To 1 Hour
Ingredients:
* 2 pounds chicken wings (flats and drumettes attached or separated)
* For the marinade:
* 1 tablespoon olive oil
* 1 teaspoon sea salt, plus more
* 1/2 teaspoon black pepper
* 1/2 cup gochujang, Korean hot pepper paste
* 1 scallion, thinly sliced, for garnish
Directions:
1. Rinse and pat wings dry with paper towels.
2. Whisk marinade ingredients together in a large mixing bowl until well-combined.
3. Add wings to bowl and toss to coat.
4. Cover bowl with plastic wrap and chill in the refrigerator for 30 minutes.
5. Prepare one side of the griddle for medium heat and the other side on medium-high.
6. Working in batches, cook wings over medium heat, turning occasionally, until skin starts to brown; about 12 minutes.
7. Move wings to medium-high area of griddle for 5 minutes on each side to sear until cooked through; meat thermometer should register 165°F when touching the bone.
8. Transfer wings to a platter, garnish with scallions, and serve warm with your favorite dipping sauces.
Nutrition Info: Calories: 312, Sodium:476 mg, Dietary Fiber: 0.4 g, Fat: 13.5g, Carbs:1.1g, Protein: 43.9g.

186.Chicken Thighs With Ginger-sesame Glaze

Servings: 4 - 8
Cooking Time: 20 Minutes
Ingredients:
* 8 boneless, skinless chicken thighs
* For the glaze:
* 3 tablespoons dark brown sugar
* 2 1/2 tablespoons soy sauce
* 1 tablespoon fresh garlic, minced
* 2 teaspoons sesame seeds
* 1 teaspoon fresh ginger, minced

* 1 teaspoon sambal oelek
* 1/3 cup scallions, thinly sliced
* Non-stick cooking spray
Directions:
1. Combine glaze ingredients in a large mixing bowl; separate and reserve half for serving.
2. Add chicken to bowl and toss to coat well.
3. Preheat the griddle to medium-high heat.
4. Coat with cooking spray.
5. Cook chicken for 6 minutes on each side or until done.
6. Transfer chicken to plates and drizzle with remaining glaze to serve.
Nutrition Info: Calories: 301, Sodium: 413 mg, Dietary Fiber: 0.3 g, Fat: 11.2g, Carbs: 4.7g, Protein: 42.9g.

187.Double-stuffed Bone-in Chicken Breasts

Servings: 4
Cooking Time: 20 Minutes
Ingredients:
* 1 lemon
* 6 tablespoons (¾ stick) butter, softened
* 1–2 tablespoons any chopped fresh herb
* Salt and pepper
* 3 bone-in, skin-on chicken breast halves (1¾ to 2 pounds total)
Directions:
1. Preparing the Ingredients
2. 1 Finely grate the zest of the lemon, then cut the lemon into thin slices. Mash the butter, zest, and herb together in a small bowl with some salt and pepper. Taste and adjust the seasoning.
3. Working with the skin side up, cut a slit into the thickest part of the breast with the tip of a small sharp knife. Keeping the opening slit just large enough for your finger (this will help the filling stay in the pocket), work the knife back and forth to create as big a pocket as possible inside the breast; be careful not to cut through to the other side. Divide the compound butter evenly between the breasts, pushing it into the slit and massaging it to fill the pocket.
4. Still using your fingers, separate the skin from the meat on one edge so you can work 2 lemon slices underneath to cover as much of the breast as possible. Sprinkle the breasts with salt and pepper and refrigerate. (You can make these to this point up to several hours ahead.)
5. 2 Bring the griddle grill to high heat, when the griddle is hot, put the chicken skin side up and cook until firm when pressed and browned on top, 15 to 20 Minutes. Turn to crisp the skin; cook for another 5 Minutes. If the chicken is still pink at the bone at the

thickest point, turn skin side up again to finish cooking. (Nick with a small knife and peek inside.) Transfer the chicken to a platter and let rest for 5 Minutes.

188.Tasty Turkey Patties

Servings: 2
Cooking Time: 15 Minutes
Ingredients:
- 8 oz ground turkey breast
- 2 tsp fresh oregano, chopped
- 2 garlic cloves, minced
- 1/2 tsp red pepper, crushed
- 1/4 tsp salt

Directions:
1. Preheat the griddle to medium heat.
2. Add ground turkey and remaining ingredients into the bowl and mix until well combined.
3. Spray griddle top with cooking spray.
4. Make 2 patties from the mixture and place onto the hot griddle top and cook until golden brown from both sides.
5. Serve and enjoy.
Nutrition Info: (Per Serving): Calories 325 ;Fat 19 g ;Carbohydrates 4 g ;Sugar 1.6 g ;Protein 33 g ;Cholesterol 84 mg

189.Chicken & Broccoli Stir Fry

Servings: 4
Cooking Time: 15 Minutes
Ingredients:
- 1 lb chicken breast, skinless, boneless, and cut into chunks
- 1 tbsp soy sauce
- 1 tbsp ginger, minced
- 1/2 tsp garlic powder
- 1 tbsp olive oil
- 1/2 onion, sliced
- 2 cups broccoli florets
- 2 tsp hot sauce
- 2 tsp vinegar
- 1 tsp sesame oil
- Pepper
- Salt

Directions:
1. Add all ingredients into the large mixing bowl and toss well.
2. Preheat the griddle to medium heat.
3. Spray griddle top with cooking spray.
4. Transfer chicken and broccoli mixture onto the hot griddle top and cook until broccoli is tender and chicken is cooked.
5. Serve and enjoy.

190.Salsa Verde Marinated Chicken

Servings: 6
Cooking Time: 4 Hours 50 Minutes
Ingredients:
- 6 boneless, skinless chicken breasts
- 1 tablespoon olive oil
- 1 teaspoon sea salt
- 1 teaspoon chili powder
- 1 teaspoon ground cumin
- 1 teaspoon garlic powder
- For the salsa verde marinade:
- 3 teaspoons garlic, minced
- 1 small onion, chopped
- 6 tomatillos, husked, rinsed and chopped
- 1 medium jalapeño pepper, cut in half, seeded
- ¼ cup fresh cilantro, chopped
- ½ teaspoon sugar or sugar substitute

Directions:
1. Add salsa verde marinade ingredients to a food processor and pulse until smooth.
2. Mix sea salt, chili powder, cumin, and garlic powder together in a small mixing bowl. Season chicken breasts with olive oil and seasoning mix, and lay in glass baking dish.
3. Spread a tablespoon of salsa verde marinade over each chicken breast to cover; reserve remaining salsa for serving.
4. Cover dish with plastic wrap and refrigerate for 4 hours.
5. Preheat griddle to medium-high and brush with olive oil.
6. Add chicken to griddle and cook 7 minutes per side or until juices run clear and a meat thermometer reads 165°F.
7. Serve each with additional salsa verde and enjoy!
Nutrition Info: Calories: 321, Sodium: 444 mg, Dietary Fiber: 1.3 g, Fat: 13.7 g, Carbs: 4.8 g, Protein: 43 g.

191.Buffalo Chicken Panini

Servings: 4
Cooking Time: 4 Minutes
Ingredients:
- 2 cups shredded cooked chicken
- 1 large sweet onion, sliced
- 8 slices seedless rye
- 1/4 lb. thinly sliced Swiss cheese, about 8 slices
- 1/4 cup blue cheese dressing
- 1 cup mayonnaise
- 1 cup buffalo hot sauce
- 2 tbsps. unsalted butter
- blue cheese dressing

Directions:
1. Melt the butter in a large skillet on medium heat. Add the onions and cook for about 20 minutes.
2. Mix the buffalo sauce and mayonnaise in a medium bowl and toss with the chicken.
3. Put a slice of cheese on a piece of bread then the chicken, the onions and top with another slice of cheese and top with another piece of bread. Repeat the process with the remaining sandwiches. Spread the butter on the top and bottom of the sandwich
4. Preheat the Griddle Grill to Medium-High with unit closed.
5. Cook the sandwiches for 4 minutes, and make sure to check halfway through. The bread should be brown, and the cheese should be melted. Serve the sandwiches with a side of the blue cheese dressing.
Nutrition Info: (Per serving):Calories 387 Fat 11.3g, protein 9g, carbs 7g

192.Grilled Chicken With Salsa Criolla

Servings: 5
Cooking Time: 6 Minutes
Ingredients:
- 8 chicken thighs, with skin and bones (about 2 pounds total)
- 1 tablespoon extra-virgin olive oil
- Coarse salt (kosher or sea) and freshly ground or cracked black peppercorns
- About 1 tablespoon dried oregano
- SALSA CRIOLLA
- 1 luscious ripe red tomato, seeded (but not peeled) and cut into ¼-inch dice
- 1 small or ½ large red bell pepper, seeded and cut into ¼-inch dice
- 1 small or ½ medium-size onion, cut into ¼-inch dice
- 1 tablespoon finely chopped fresh flat-leaf parsley
- ¼ cup extra-virgin olive oil
- 2 tablespoons red wine vinegar
- Coarse salt (kosher or sea) and freshly ground black pepper
Directions:
1. Preparing the Ingredients
2. Rinse the thighs under cold running water, then drain and blot dry with paper towels. Place a thigh on a work surface skin side down. Using a sharp paring knife, cut along the length of the thigh bone. Cut the meat away from one end of the bone, then pull or scrape the meat from the bone. Cut the meat away from the other end of the bone. Repeat with the remaining thighs. Discard the bones or set them aside for making stock or another use.
3. Lightly brush the chicken thighs all over with olive oil, then season them generously with salt, pepper, and oregano
4. Bring the griddle grill to high heat. When the griddle is hot, place the chicken thighs on the griddle, and cook for 6 Minutes.
5. Use the poke test to check for doneness; the chicken should feel firm when pressed.
6. Place the tomato, bell pepper, onion, parsley, olive oil, and vinegar in an attractive nonreactive serving bowl and toss to mix. Season with salt and pepper to taste. The sauce can be made several hours ahead.
7. Transfer the chicken thighs to a platter or plates and serve at once with the Salsa Criolla on top or on the side.

193.Honey-mustard Chicken Tenders

Servings: 4
Cooking Time: 3 Minutes
Ingredients:
- ½ cup Dijon mustard
- 2 tablespoons honey
- 2 tablespoons olive oil
- 1 teaspoon freshly ground black pepper
- 2 pounds chicken tenders
- ½ cup walnuts
Directions:
1. Preparing the Ingredients
2. Whisk together the mustard, honey, olive oil, and pepper in a medium bowl. Add the chicken and toss to coat.
3. Finely grind the walnuts by pulsing them in a food processor or putting them in a heavy-duty plastic bag and pounding them with a rolling pin or heavy skillet.
4. Toss the chicken tenders in the ground walnuts to coat them lightly.
5. Bring the griddle grill to high heat. When the griddle is hot, grill the chicken tenders for about 3 Minutes, until they have taken on grill marks and are cooked through. Serve hot, at room temperature, or refrigerate and serve cold.
Nutrition Info: (Per Serving): CALORIES: 444; FAT: 20G; PROTEIN:5G

BEEF, PORK AND LAMB RECIPES

194.Grilled Pork Chops With Herb Apple Compote

Servings: 4
Cooking Time: 20 Minutes
Ingredients:
- 4, bone-in pork chops
- 2 honeycrisp apples, peeled, cored and chopped
- 1/3 cup orange juice
- 1 teaspoon chopped fresh rosemary
- 1 teaspoon chopped fresh sage
- Sea salt
- Black pepper

Directions:
1. Add the apples, herbs and orange juice to a saucepan and simmer over medium heat until the apples are tender and the juices are thickened to a thin syrup, about 10 to 12 minutes.
2. Season pork chops with salt and pepper.
3. Place on the griddle and cook until the pork chop releases from the griddle, about 4 minutes.
4. Flip and cook on the other side for 3 minutes.
5. Transfer to a cutting board and tent with foil.
6. Top with apple compote and serve!

Nutrition Info: Calories: 284, Sodium: 173 mg, Dietary Fiber: 1g, Fat: 20g, Carbs:7.2g Protein: 18.2g

195.Pork Loin Roast

Servings: 4
Cooking Time: 45 Minutes
Ingredients:
- 1 (3 lbs.) Pork Top Loin Roast
- Kosher Salt
- Black Pepper To Taste
- Orange Marmalade

Directions:
1. Remove any silver skin and excess fat from the loin. Trim the loin to be even in thickness throughout.
2. Coat the loin with Kosher salt liberally, place in a resealable bag, and refrigerate for at least 3 hours or overnight. This will dry brine the roast and keep it moist while it cooks.
3. Rinse the excess salt off the roast, pat it dry, and season it with black pepper.
4. Turn the Griddle grill on to high, and spray it with spray oil.
5. Cook the loin on high for several minutes per side until it pulls cleanly from the grill.
6. Remove the loin from the grill and allow it to relax for several minutes to allow the juices to redistribute.
7. Turn the grill down to medium, and return the loin to the grill. Cook for about 30 minutes, turning

occasionally, until the internal temperature reaches 145 degrees.
8. Glaze the outside of the loin with the marmalade, and let it relax for at least 10 minutes before slicing and serving.

Nutrition Info: (Per serving):calories 163; fats 7.5g; carbs 48g; Protein 19g

196.Lumberjack Steak And Potatoes

Servings: 4
Cooking Time: 22 Minutes
Ingredients:
- 1 lb. Boneless beef sirloin steak, cut into 4 serving pieces
- 3/4 tsp. Seasoned salt
- 1/2 tsp. Garlic-pepper blend
- 1-1/2 cups frozen stir-fry vegetables
- 1 bag refrigerated home-style potato slices
- 4 oz. or 1/2 cup shredded American-cheddar cheese blend

Directions:
1. Preheat Griddle Grill to Sear with the unit closed.
2. Place the steak onto a griddle and sprinkle with the seasoned salt and garlic pepper.
3. Cook on medium heat for 3 minutes on each side.
4. Remove steak from griddle and add vegetables, cooking for 3 minutes.
5. Pour in potatoes and cook for 10 minutes.
6. When done, pour in the steak and mix together before serving.

Nutrition Info: (Per serving):Calories 700.2kcal, fat 40g, Carbs 51.8 g, Protein70.1 g

197.Pork Chimichurri

Servings: 4
Cooking Time: 10 Minutes
Ingredients:
- CHIMI CHURRI SAUCE
- 1 large red onion, cut into ½-inch slices
- 2 red bell peppers, cored, seeded, and cut into 1-inch strips
- 2 yellow bell peppers, cored, seeded, and cut into 1-inch strips
- 3 tablespoons olive oil
- 2 tablespoons white wine vinegar
- Juice of 1 lime
- 1 teaspoon Worcestershire sauce
- ½ teaspoon red pepper flakes
- 2 tablespoons chopped fresh parsley leaves
- PORK
- 2 pounds pork tenderloin

- 1 tablespoon olive oil
- ¼ teaspoon salt
- ½ teaspoon freshly ground black pepper

Directions:
1. Preparing the Ingredients
2. Toss the onion slices and bell pepper strips in 2 tablespoons of the olive oil to coat them lightly. Bring the griddle grill to high heat. When the griddle is hot, grill the onion and peppers for about 6 Minutes, until soft and charred.
3. Finely chop the peppers and onion in a food processor or by hand using a large sharp knife. Transfer to a medium bowl. Stir in the remaining tablespoon olive oil, the vinegar, lime juice, Worcestershire sauce, and red pepper flakes. (The sauce can be covered with plastic wrap and refrigerated for up to 2 days. Bring to room temperature before serving.) Stir in the parsley just before serving.
4. Cut the pork tenderloin into 8 medallions, each about 1 inch thick, and then pound them to a ½-inch thickness. Rub the pork cutlets with the olive oil and season with the salt and pepper. Grill for about 3 Minutes, until the cutlets have taken on grill marks and are firm to the touch. Serve each person 2 cutlets with the sauce heaped on top.

Nutrition Info: (Per Serving): CALORIES: 446; FAT: 22G; PROTEIN:49G

198.Sweet And Salty Lemongrass Pork Chops

Servings: 4
Cooking Time: 5 Minutes
Ingredients:
- ¼ cup sugar
- ¼ cup oyster sauce
- ¼ cup soy sauce
- 1 teaspoon freshly ground black pepper
- 2 stalks lemongrass, or 2 strips of lemon zest
- 4 cloves garlic, peeled and gently crushed with the side of a cleaver
- 4 boneless pork loin chops (each ¼ to ½ inch thick, and about 1½ pounds total

Directions:
1. Preparing the Ingredients
2. Place the sugar, oyster sauce, soy sauce, and pepper in a large shallow mixing bowl and whisk until the sugar dissolves.
3. Trim the lemongrass, removing the root ends and flexible green stalks. You should be left with a cream-colored core that is 3 to 4 inches long. Cut this into 1-inch pieces and gently crush them with the side of a cleaver to release the aroma. Stir the lemongrass and garlic into the marinade.

4. Add the pork chops to the marinade, turning to coat both sides. Cover the bowl with plastic wrap and let the pork chops marinate in the refrigerator for at least 2 hours or as long as overnight, turning them several times; the longer the chops marinate, the richer the flavor will be. You can also marinate the chops in a resealable plastic bag.
5. Bring the griddle grill to high heat. When the griddle is hot, place the pork chops on the hot griddle. The chops will be done after cooking 2 to 4 Minutes.
6. To test for doneness, use the poke method; the meat should be firm but gently yielding.
7. Transfer the pork chops to a platter or plates and serve at once.

199.Mexican Steak Salad

Servings: 2
Cooking Time: 10 Minutes
Ingredients:
- Steak marinade:
- 2 tablespoons olive oil
- 3 garlic cloves, minced
- 2 teaspoons chili powder
- 1 teaspoon ground cumin
- 1 teaspoon kosher salt
- 1 teaspoon freshly ground pepper
- 1 1/2 pounds skirt or flap steak, cut into 4-inch lengths
- ½ cup lager beer
- Salad:
- 12 ounces romaine hearts, trimmed and chopped
- 1 can black beans, drained and rinsed
- 1 pint cherry tomatoes, halved
- 1 large ripe avocado, pitted, peeled, and cut into chunks
- About 1/3 cup crumbled queso fresco
- Chopped fresh cilantro, for garnish
- Kosher salt
- Dressing:
- ½ cup plain whole milk yogurt
- 1/3 cup chopped fresh cilantro
- Zest of 1 lime
- Juice of 2 limes

Directions:
1. Make marinade, then marinate steak for 4 hours to overnight.
2. Combine salad ingredients in a large bowl; add dressing and mix well. Place salad on separate plates.
3. Preheat griddle to high. Place marinated steak on griddle, reduce heat to medium, tent with foil and cook for 5 minutes.
4. Flip, re-tent, and cook for an additional 5 minutes.

5.   Remove steak from the griddle and slice into 2 inch strips.
6.   Place steak strips on individual salads, and sprinkle with flakey salt and a little black pepper. Garnish with cilantro.
Nutrition Info: Calories:1332, Sodium: 2011 mg, Dietary Fiber: 13.3g, Fat: 65.1g, Carbs:29.4g Protein: 152.3g

200.Peanut Satay Pork

Servings: 5
Cooking Time: 12 Minutes
Ingredients:
- 11 Ozs Pork Fillet, sliced into bite sized strips
- 4 Cloves Garlic, crushed
- 1 Tsp Ginger Powder
- 2 Tsps Chili Paste
- 2 Tbsps Sweet Soy Sauce
- 2 Tbsps Vegetable Oil
- 1 Shallot, finely chopped
- 1 Tsp Ground Coriander
- 3/4 Cup Coconut Milk
- 1/3 Cup Peanuts, ground

Directions:
1.   Preparing the Ingredients.
2.   1 Mix half of the garlic in a dish with the ginger, a tablespoon of sweet soy sauce, and a tablespoon of the oil. Combine the meat into the mixture and leave to marinate for 12 Minutes
3.   2 Bring the griddle grill to high heat. When the griddle is hot, place the marinated meat and roast the meat until brown and done. Turn once while roasting
4.   In the meantime, make the peanut sauce by heating the remaining tablespoon of oil in a saucepan and gently sauté the shallot with the garlic. Add the coriander and fry until fragrant
5.   Mix the coconut milk and the peanuts with the chili paste and remaining soy sauce with the shallot mixture and gently boil for 5 Minutes, while stirring
6.   Drizzle over the cooked meat and serve with rice.

201.Texas-style Brisket

Servings: 6
Cooking Time: 6 Hours 20 Minutes
Ingredients:
- 1 (4 1/2 lb) flat cut beef brisket (about 3 inches thick)
- For the rub:
- 1 tablespoon sea salt
- 1 tablespoon dark brown sugar
- 2 teaspoons smoked paprika
- 2 teaspoons chili powder
- 1 teaspoon garlic powder
- 1 teaspoon onion powder
- 1 teaspoon ground black pepper
- 1 teaspoon mesquite liquid smoke, like Colgin

Directions:
1.   Combine the rub ingredients in a small mixing bowl.
2.   Rinse and pat brisket dry and rub with coffee mix.
3.   Preheat the griddle for two zone cooking; heat one side to high and leaving one side with low heat.
4.   Sear on high heat side for 3 - 5 minutes on each side or until nicely charred.
5.   Move to low heat side, tent with foil, and cook for 6 hours or until a meat thermometer registers 195°F.
6.   Remove from griddle. Let stand, covered, 30 minutes.
7.   Cut brisket across grain into thin slices and serve.
Nutrition Info: Calories:591, Sodium: 3953 mg, Dietary Fiber: 0.7g, Fat: 42.8g, Carbs: 3.2g Protein: 45.9g

202.Korean-style Short Ribs

Servings: 4
Cooking Time: 5 Minutes
Ingredients:
- 1 small onion, quartered
- ½ Asian or regular pear, peeled, cored, and quartered
- 6 cloves garlic, peeled
- ½ cup soy sauce
- ¼ cup sugar
- 2 tablespoons rice wine or sake
- 1 tablespoon sesame oil
- 2½ pounds flanken-cut bone-in short ribs, or 2 pounds boneless short ribs, each cut into a single thin strip
- 1 head Boston lettuce, pulled apart into leaves
- 12 or so fresh perilla leaves (optional)
- 1 or 2 hot green chiles (like jalapeño), thinly sliced
- Gochujang for serving
- 2 tablespoons toasted sesame seeds
- 3 scallions, trimmed and chopped

Directions:
1.   Preparing the Ingredients
2.   1 Put the onion, pear, garlic, soy sauce, sugar, rice wine, and sesame oil in a blender or food processor and purée. Put the short ribs in a large baking dish or rimmed baking sheet. Pour the marinade over them, turning them several times to completely coat. Let sit at room temperature while

you prepare the griddle. Or cover and refrigerate for several hours or overnight, turning the beef several times.
3.   Put the lettuce, perilla leaves if you're using them, and sliced chiles on a large platter, leaving room for the grilled short ribs. Put some gochujang in a small bowl.
4.   Remove the beef from the marinade, scraping any solids from the purée off the strips.
5.   2 Turn control knob to the high position, when the griddle is hot, add cooking oil, and when it begins to shimmer put the strips on the griddle, and cook for 5 Minutes.
6.   Transfer to a cutting board and slice into pieces. Put on the platter, garnish with the sesame seeds and scallions, and serve family style.

203.Parmesan Garlic Beef

Servings: 4
Cooking Time: 10 Minutes
Ingredients:
- 2 Lbs. Sirloin Beef, Cut Into 1-Inch Cubes
- 6 Garlic Cloves, Finely Minced
- 1/4 Cup Olive Oil
- Sea Salt To Taste
- 1/4 Cup Grated Parmesan

Directions:
1.   Mix the ingredients together and place them in a covered bowl or bag in the fridge for 3 hours to overnight.
2.   Place the beef chunks onto skewers.
3.   Heat the griddle grill to high, and grill for about 3 minutes per side, sprinkling each side with parmesan. Grill for a few minutes more until it's done to the point you like it.
4.   Let the meat relax for several minutes before serving.
Nutrition Info: (Per serving): Calories: 175.2, Carbs: 75g, Fats: 4g, Protein: 30.7g

204.Greek Lamb Patties

Servings: 4
Cooking Time: 8 Minutes
Ingredients:
- 1 lb ground lamb
- 5 basil leaves, minced
- 10 mint leaves, minced
- 1/4 cup fresh parsley, chopped
- 1 tsp dried oregano
- 1 cup feta cheese, crumbled
- 1 tbsp garlic, minced
- 1 jalapeno pepper, minced

- 1/4 tsp pepper
- 1/2 tsp kosher salt

Directions:
1.   Add all ingredients into the mixing bowl and mix until well combined.
2.   Preheat the griddle to high heat.
3.   Spray griddle top with cooking spray.
4.   Make four equal shape patties from meat mixture and place onto the hot griddle top and cook for 4 minutes on each side.
5.   Serve and enjoy.
Nutrition Info: (Per Serving): Calories 317 ;Fat 16.4 g ;Carbohydrates 3 g ;Sugar 1.7 g ;Protein 37.5 g ;Cholesterol 135 mg

205.Boston Strip Steak And Blue Cheese Butter

Servings: 3
Cooking Time: 5 Minutes
Ingredients:
- 2 tsp. olive oil
- 1 large Vidalia onion, sliced
- 1 tsp. Worcestershire sauce
- 2 to 4 (8-oz.) Boston strip steaks
- ½ tsp. sea salt per steak
- 1 Tbsp. roasted garlic and blue cheese butter per steak

Directions:
1.   Preparing the Ingredients
2.   Turn control knob to the high position. Add cooking oil and when it begins to shimmer, sauté onions, adding Worcestershire sauce after onions have cooked for 5 Minutes.
3.   Prepare each steak by sprinkling each with ½ teaspoon of sea salt.
4.   Place steaks on hot griddle. Grill for 2 Minutes, rotate 90 degrees, and grill for an additional 2 Minutes.
5.   Flip steak and repeat, removing from grill when internal temperature reaches 125°F
6.   Serve over sautéed onions, and top with 1 tablespoon of roasted garlic and blue cheese butter.

206.Easy Pork Kabab

Servings: 6
Cooking Time: 8 Minutes
Ingredients:
- 2 lbs pork tenderloin, cut into 1-inch cubes
- 3 tbsp fresh parsley, chopped
- 1 tbsp garlic, chopped
- 1 onion, chopped
- 1/2 cup olive oil

- 1/2 cup vinegar
- Pepper
- Salt

Directions:

1. In a large zip-lock bag, mix vinegar, parsley, garlic, onion, and oil.
2. Add meat to bag and marinate in the refrigerator for overnight.
3. Thread marinated meat onto skewers. Season with pepper and salt.
4. Preheat the griddle to high heat.
5. Spray griddle top with cooking spray.
6. Place meat skewers onto the hot griddle top and cook for 3-4 minutes on each side.
7. Serve and enjoy.

Nutrition Info: (Per Serving): Calories 375 ;Fat 22 g ;Carbohydrates 2.5 g ;Sugar 1 g ;Protein 40 g ;Cholesterol 110 mg

207.Herb Beef Skewers

Servings: 4
Cooking Time: 8 Minutes
Ingredients:

- 2 lbs beef sirloin, cut into cubes
- 2 tsp fresh thyme, minced
- 1 tbsp fresh parsley, minced
- 1 tbsp lemon zest
- 4 garlic cloves, minced
- 2 tbsp fresh lemon juice
- 1/4 cup olive oil
- 2 tsp dried oregano
- 2 tsp fresh rosemary, minced
- Pepper
- Salt

Directions:

1. Add all ingredients except meat in a mixing bowl and stir everything well.
2. Add meat to the bowl and coat well with marinade.
3. Place in refrigerator for overnight.
4. Preheat the griddle to high heat.
5. Spray griddle top with cooking spray.
6. Slide marinated meat onto the skewers.
7. Place skewers onto the hot griddle top and cook for 6-8 minutes. Turn after every 2 minutes.
8. Serve and enjoy.

Nutrition Info: (Per Serving): Calories 543 ;Fat 27 g ;Carbohydrates 2.7 g ;Sugar 0.3 g ;Protein 69.3 g ;Cholesterol 203 mg

208.Tender Steak With Pineapple Rice

Servings: 4

Cooking Time: 10 Minutes
Ingredients:

- 4 (4-ounce) beef fillets
- ¼ cup soy sauce
- ½ teaspoon black pepper
- ½ teaspoon garlic powder
- 1 (8-ounce) can pineapple chunks, in juice, drained
- 2 scallions, thin sliced
- 2 (8.8-ounce) packages pre-cooked brown rice, like Uncle Ben's
- 7/8 teaspoon kosher salt
- Olive oil, for brushing

Directions:

1. Combine soy sauce, pepper, garlic powder, and beef in a large sealable plastic bag.
2. Seal and massage sauce into beef; let stand at room temperature for 7 minutes, turning bag occasionally.
3. Preheat griddle to medium-high heat and brush with olive oil.
4. Add pineapple and green onions to grill and cook 5 minutes or until well charred, turning to char evenly.
5. Remove pineapple mix and brush with additional olive oil.
6. Add steaks and cook 3 minutes on each side, for rare, or until desired temperature is reached.
7. Cook rice according to package instructions.
8. Add rice, pineapple, onions, and salt to a bowl and stir gently to combine.
9. Plate steaks with pineapple rice and serve!

Nutrition Info: Calories: 369, Sodium: 1408 mg, Dietary Fiber: 2.1g, Fat: 12.4g, Carbs: 37g Protein: 27.9g

209.Honey Soy Pork Chops

Servings: 6
Cooking Time: 25 Minutes
Ingredients:

- 6 (4 ounce) boneless pork chops
- 1/4 cup organic honey
- 1 to 2 tablespoons low sodium soy sauce
- 2 tablespoons olive oil
- 1 tablespoon rice mirin

Directions:

1. Combine honey, soy sauce, oil, and white vinegar and whisk until well-combined. Add sauce and pork chops to a large sealable plastic bag and marinate for 1 hour.
2. Preheat the griddle to medium-high heat and cook for 4 to 5 minutes, or until the pork chop easily releases from the griddle.

3. Flip and continue to cook for 5 additional minutes, or until internal temperature reaches 145°F.
4. Serve and enjoy!
Nutrition Info: Calories: 251, Sodium: 187mg, Dietary Fiber: 0.1g, Fat: 8.7g, Carbs: 13.1g Protein: 29.9g

210.Flash-marinated Skirt Steak

Servings: 4
Cooking Time: 45 Minutes
Ingredients:
- 2 (8 ounce) skirt steaks
- For the marinade:
- 2 tablespoons balsamic vinegar
- 2 teaspoons olive oil, more for brushing
- 2 garlic cloves, minced
- Sea salt, to taste
- Black pepper, to taste

Directions:
1. Combine marinade ingredients in a sealable plastic bag, add steaks, seal bag, turn to coat; let stand at room temperature for 30 minutes.
2. Preheat griddle to medium-high heat.
3. Remove steaks and discard marinade, place on griddle and cook about 3 minutes per side. Transfer steaks to cutting board and rest for 5 Minutes.
4. Cut across the grain into slices and serve with your favorite sides.
Nutrition Info: Calories: 256, Sodium: 204 mg, Dietary Fiber: 0g, Fat: 13.8g, Carbs: 0.6g Protein: 30.3g

211.Grill Pork Quesadilla

Servings: 2
Cooking Time: 12 Minutes
Ingredients:
- Two 6-inch corn or flour tortilla shells
- 1 medium-sized pork shoulder, approximately 4 ounces, sliced
- ½ medium-sized white onion, sliced
- ½ medium-sized red pepper, sliced
- ½ medium sized green pepper, sliced
- ½ medium sized yellow pepper, sliced
- ¼ cup of shredded pepper-jack cheese
- ¼ cup of shredded mozzarella cheese

Directions:
1. Preparing the Ingredients.
2. Bring the griddle grill to high heat. When the griddle is hot, grill the pork, onion, and peppers in foil in the griddle grill, allowing the moisture from the vegetables and the juice from the pork mingle together. Remove pork and vegetables. While they're cooling, sprinkle half the shredded cheese over one of the tortillas, then cover with the pieces of pork, onions, and peppers, and then layer on the rest of the shredded cheese. Top with the second tortilla. Place directly on hot surface of the griddle.
3. Set the temperature to MED. After 6 Minutes, flip the tortillas onto the other side with a spatula; the cheese should be melted enough that it won't fall apart, but be careful anyway not to spill any toppings.
4. Reset to HIGH for another 6 Minutes.
5. After 6 Minutes, the tortillas should be browned and crisp, and the pork, onion, peppers and cheese will be crispy and hot and delicious. Remove with tongs and let sit on a serving plate to cool for a few Minutes before slicing.

212.Easy Pork Chops

Servings: 4
Cooking Time: 12 Minutes
Ingredients:
- 8 oz pork chops, boneless
- 1 tsp smoked paprika
- 1 tsp olive oil
- 1 tsp onion powder
- Pepper
- Salt

Directions:
1. Brush pork chops with oil.
2. Mix together remaining ingredients and rub over pork chops.
3. Preheat the griddle to high heat.
4. Place pork chops onto the hot griddle top and cook pork chops from both sides until completely done.
5. Serve and enjoy.
Nutrition Info: (Per Serving): Calories 195 ;Fat 15 g ;Carbohydrates 0.8 g ;Sugar 0.3 g ;Protein 13 g ;Cholesterol 49 mg

213.Moroccan Lamb Kabobs

Servings: 4
Cooking Time: 10 Minutes
Ingredients:
- 2 Lbs. Lamb, Cut Into 1/8-Inch Strips
- 6 Garlic Cloves, Minced
- 1/2 Cup Olive Oil
- 1 Tbsp. Coriander
- 2 Tsp. Cumin
- Zest And Juice Of 2 Lemons
- 2 Tbsp. Fresh Mint, Chopped
- 3 Tsp. Salt
- 2 Tsp. Black Pepper

- Apricot Jam

Directions:
1. Mix all of the ingredients except for the apricot jam together, and place in the refrigerator for several hours to overnight.
2. Put all the lamb pieces onto skewers, leaving space between the pieces.
3. Heat the griddle grill to high, and grill the skewers for 3–4 minutes per side until cooked through.
4. Brush the apricot jam on the lamb, and grill for less than 1 minute on each side to set the glaze.
5. Let the meat relax for 5 minutes before serving.

Nutrition Info: (Per serving): Calories: 149, Carbs: 3g, Fats: 9g, Protein: 12g

214. Steak Kababs

Servings: 4
Cooking Time: 15 Minutes
Ingredients:
- 1 lb beef sirloin, cut into 1-inch pieces
- 1 green bell pepper, cut into 1-inch pieces
- 1 cup mushrooms
- 1 tbsp fresh parsley, chopped
- 1 tsp garlic, minced
- 2 tsp olive oil
- 1 onion, cut into 1-inch pieces
- 3 tbsp butter
- Pepper
- Salt

Directions:
1. Preheat the griddle to medium-low heat.
2. Thread the beef, bell pepper, mushrooms, and onion onto the skewers.
3. Brush meat and vegetables with olive oil and season with pepper and salt.
4. Place skewers onto the hot griddle top and cook for 4-5 minutes per side.
5. Melt butter in a pan over medium-low heat.
6. Add garlic and sauté for a minute.
7. Remove pan from heat and stir in parsley, pepper, and salt.
8. Brush butter mixture all over kababs.
9. Serve and enjoy.

Nutrition Info: (Per Serving): Calories 302 ;Fat 20 g ;Carbohydrates 5 g ;Sugar 0 g ;Protein 25 g ;Cholesterol 0 mg

215. Filipino-style Pork Skewers

Servings: 4
Cooking Time: 20 Minutes
Ingredients:
- 2 pounds boneless pork shoulder

- ½ cup ginger beer
- 2 tablespoons soy sauce
- 2 tablespoons ketchup
- 2 tablespoons brown sugar
- 1 tablespoon minced garlic
- 1 tablespoon fresh lime juice
- Salt and pepper

Directions:
1. Preparing the Ingredients.
2. Trim the pork of excess fat and cut into 1-to 1½-inch pieces.
3. Put the ginger beer, soy sauce, ketchup, sugar, garlic, lime juice, and some salt and pepper in a large bowl and whisk to combine. Add the pork and stir to coat. Let sit at room temperature while you prepare the fire or up to 1 hour. Or refrigerate up to overnight.
4. If you're using bamboo or wooden skewers, soak them in water for 30 Minutes.
5. Skewer the pork; you can push the pieces close together. Bring the griddle grill to high heat. When the griddle is hot, put the skewers on the griddle, and cook until crusty brown and no longer pink in the center; turn the skewers. Total cooking time will be about 20 Minutes. Transfer the skewers to a platter and serve.

216. Sheboygan-style Bratwursts

Servings: 4
Cooking Time: 20 Minutes
Ingredients:
- 4 or 8 fresh bratwursts
- 4 hard rolls
- Coarse brown mustard for serving
- Ketchup for serving
- Thinly sliced onion for serving
- Dill pickle slices for serving

Directions:
1. Preparing the Ingredients.
2. 1 Bring the griddle grill to high heat. When the griddle is hot, put the brats on the griddle grill, and cook for for 20 Minutes.
3. Transfer the brats to a platter. Split the rolls and put 1 or 2 bratwurst in each. Serve, passing the condiments at the table.

217. Ham Steak With Spicy Pineapple Glaze

Servings: 6
Cooking Time: 15 Minutes
Ingredients:
- ¼ cup pineapple preserves

- 2 tablespoons brown sugar
- 1 tablespoon hot sauce, or to taste
- 1 or 2 center-cut bone-in ham steaks (1–1½ inches thick; about 2 pounds)

Directions:
1. Preparing the Ingredients.
2. To make the glaze, stir the preserves, brown sugar, and hot sauce together in a small bowl.
3. Bring the griddle grill to high heat. When the griddle is hot, put the ham steak(s) on the griddle, and cook for 10 Minutes. Brush the top with the glaze and turn again; brush the top with glaze as well. Cook until the glaze on the bottom starts to brown (this will only take a minute or 2). Brush the top with glaze again and cook until the other side starts to brown. Continue building up the glaze until the steak is hot throughout and browned and crusted on both sides.
4. Transfer to a cutting board, slice, and serve.

218.Pork Chops With Potatoes

Servings: 4
Cooking Time: 15 Minutes
Ingredients:
- 4 pork chops, boneless
- 1 oz ranch seasoning, homemade
- 2 1/2 lbs potatoes, cut into bite-size pieces
- 1/4 tsp pepper
- 1/4 tsp ground oregano
- 1 tsp dried parsley
- 3 tbsp olive oil

Directions:
1. Preheat the griddle to high heat.
2. Spray griddle top with cooking spray.
3. In a small bowl, mix together ranch seasoning mix, oregano, parsley, oil, and pepper.
4. Add potatoes and 1 1/2 tbsp seasoning mixture to the bowl and toss well.
5. Place potatoes onto the hot griddle top.
6. Season pork chops with remaining seasoning and place onto the griddle top along with potatoes.
7. Cook potatoes and pork chops until potatoes are tender and pork chops are completely cooked.
8. Serve and enjoy.
Nutrition Info: (Per Serving): Calories 542 ;Fat 30.7 g ;Carbohydrates 44.7 g ;Sugar 3.3 g ;Protein 22.8 g ;Cholesterol 69 mg

219.Thick-cut Pork Chops With Quick Orange-sage Drizzle

Servings: 4
Cooking Time: 15 Minutes
Ingredients:

- 4 boneless loin pork chops (1–2 inches thick each)
- Salt and pepper
- 4 tablespoons (½ stick) butter
- 1 tablespoon minced shallot
- 2 tablespoons fresh orange juice
- 1 tablespoon grated orange zest
- 3 teaspoons minced fresh sage

Directions:
1. Preparing the Ingredients
2. Pat the chops dry with paper towels and sprinkle with salt and pepper on all sides.
3. Bring the griddle grill to high heat. When the griddle is hot, put the chops on the griddle, and cook until the internal temperature reaches 135° to 140°F, 15 to 20 Minutes.
4. Transfer the chops to a platter and let rest until the internal temperature rises to 145°F. While the chops rest, melt the butter in a small saucepan over medium-low heat; you can also do this on the grill, if you prefer. Add the shallot and cook until it softens, 1 to 2 Minutes. Add 2 tablespoons water and the orange juice and let bubble for a minute or 2. Stir in the orange zest and sage and season with salt and pepper. Drizzle over the pork chops and serve.

220.Molasses Bbq Pork Chops

Servings: 4
Cooking Time: 4 Minutes
Ingredients:
- MOLASSES BARBECUE SAUCE
- 2 tablespoons molasses
- 2 tablespoons ketchup
- 1 tablespoon cider vinegar
- 1 teaspoon light brown sugar
- ¼ teaspoon salt
- Pinch of ground cloves
- Pinch of sweet paprika
- PORK
- 4 (6-ounce) boneless center-cut pork
- chops, pounded to ½-inch thickness

Directions:
1. Preparing the Ingredients
2. Whisk together the molasses, ketchup, vinegar, brown sugar, salt, cloves, and paprika in a small bowl. (The sauce can be covered with plastic wrap and refrigerated for up to 3 days.)
3. Pour the sauce into a shallow baking dish. Add the chops and turn to coat. Bring the griddle grill to high heat. When the griddle is hot, grill the chops for about 4 Minutes, until they have taken on grill marks and are firm to the touch. Serve immediately.
Nutrition Info: (Per Serving): CALORIES: 283; FAT: 4G; PROTEIN:37G

221.Pork Cutlet Rolls

Servings: 4
Cooking Time: 15 Minutes
Ingredients:
- 4 Pork Cutlets
- 4 Sundried Tomatoes in oil
- 2 Tbsps Parsley, finely chopped
- 1 Green Onion, finely chopped
- Black Pepper to taste
- 2 Tsps Paprika
- 1/2 Tbsp Olive Oil
- String for Rolled Meat

Directions:
1. Preparing the Ingredients.
2. Finely chop the tomatoes and mix with the parsley and green onion. Add salt and pepper to taste
3. Spread out the cutlets and coat them with the tomato mixture. Roll up the cutlets and secure intact with the string
4. Rub the rolls with salt, pepper, and paprika powder and thinly coat them with olive oil
5. Bring the griddle grill to high heat. When the griddle is hot, put the cutlet rolls and cook for 15 Minutes. Roast until nicely brown and done.
6. Serve with tomato sauce.

222.Glazed Country Ribs

Servings: 6
Cooking Time: 4 Hours
Ingredients:
- 3 pounds country-style pork ribs
- 1 cup low-sugar ketchup
- ½ cup water
- ¼ cup onion, finely chopped
- ¼ cup cider vinegar or wine vinegar
- ¼ cup light molasses
- 2 tablespoons Worcestershire sauce
- 2 teaspoons chili powder
- 2 cloves garlic, minced

Directions:
1. Combine ketchup, water, onion, vinegar, molasses, Worcestershire sauce, chili powder, and garlic in a saucepan and bring to boil; reduce heat. Simmer, uncovered, for 10 to 15 minutes or until desired thickness is reached, stirring often.
2. Trim fat from ribs.
3. Preheat griddle to medium-high.
4. Place ribs, bone-side down, on griddle and cook for 1-1/2 to 2 hours or until tender, brushing occasionally with sauce during the last 10 minutes of cooking.

5. Serve with remaining sauce and enjoy!
Nutrition Info: Calories: 404, Sodium: 733 mg, Dietary Fiber: 0.4g, Fat: 8.1g, Carbs:15.2g Protein: 60.4g

223.Pork Chops

Servings: 5
Cooking Time: 8 Minutes
Ingredients:
- pork chops, cut 1 inch thick
- salt and pepper to taste

Directions:
1. Preparing the Ingredients
2. Salt and pepper the outside of the pork chops evenly on both sides.
3. Let the pork chops relax at room temperature for 10 Minutes.
4. Bring the griddle grill to high heat. When the griddle is hot, place the pork chops on the hot griddle and cook them for 6 Minutes.
5. Remove the pork chops and set them to the side to relax at room temperature for several Minutes. This will allow the juice to redistribute and allow for even cooking. Turn the griddle grill down to medium.
6. Return the pork chops to the grill, rotating the grill marks, and grill them for several Minutes per side. The internal temperature should be 145 degrees.
7. Remove the pork chops from the grill, and let them relax for 5–7 Minutes before slicing to serve.

224.Grilled Flank Steak With Jalapeño Chimichurri

Servings: 4
Cooking Time: 3 Minutes
Ingredients:
- MEAT
- 1 flank steak, roughly 1.5 to 2 lb. trimmed
- olive oil (enough for a light coat)
- 1 Tbsp. salt, preferably hickory smoked salt, but sea salt works well also
- CHIMICHURRI SAUCE
- 3 cloves garlic, finely minced
- 1 shallot, finely chopped
- 1 red jalapeño, seeded and finely chopped
- 2 Tbsp. finely chopped chives
- ¾ cup finely chopped fresh cilantro
- ¾ cup finely chopped fresh flat-leaf parsley
- ¾ cup extra-virgin olive oil
- 1½ Tbsp. red wine vinegar
- 3 tsp. kosher salt (or to taste)
- 1 tsp. lemon juice

Directions:
1. Preparing the Ingredients
2. Add garlic, shallot, jalapeño, chives, cilantro, and parsley to a bowl. Toss gently until combined.
3. In the same bowl, whisk in olive oil, red wine vinegar, salt, and lemon juice. Set aside.
4. Pat steak dry of any moisture and lightly coat with olive oil. Lightly season meat with salt. Because you're using this incredible chimichurri, you don't want to overdo the seasoning on the meat.
5. Turn control knob to the high position, butter the grill surface, when the griddle is hot, place meat and let it cook 3 Minutes per side. This will produce a perfect char and a medium-rare center that suits the cut of meat best. More than medium-rare and this cut tends to get a bit tough. Don't move the steak once it's on the grate until you're ready to turn it.
6. Remove from grill and let rest 5 Minutes.
7. Slice and serve with chimichurri.

225.Coffee Crusted Skirt Steak

Servings: 8
Cooking Time: 20 Minutes
Ingredients:
- 1/4 cup coffee beans, finely ground
- 1/4 cup dark brown sugar, firmly packed
- 1 1/2 teaspoon sea salt
- 1/8 teaspoon ground cinnamon
- Pinch cayenne pepper
- 2 1/2 lb. skirt steak, cut into 4 pieces
- 1 tablespoon olive oil

Directions:
1. Heat griddle to high.
2. Combine coffee, brown sugar, salt, cinnamon, and cayenne pepper in a bowl to make rub.
3. Remove steak from refrigerator and let come to room temperature, about 15 minutes. Rub steak with oil, and sprinkle with spice rub. Massage spice rub into meat.
4. Sear until charred and medium-rare, 2 to 4 minutes per side. Transfer to a cutting board, cover with foil and let rest 5 minutes before thinly slicing against the grain.
Nutrition Info: Calories:324, Sodium: 461 mg, Dietary Fiber: 0.1g, Fat: 16g, Carbs: 4.6g Protein: 37.9g

226.Lemon Pepper London Broil

Servings: 4
Cooking Time: 10 Minutes
Ingredients:
- 1 flank steak or piece of sirloin or top or bottom round steak (1½ to 1¾ pounds)
- 1 tablespoon cracked black peppercorns
- 2 teaspoons finely grated lemon zest
- 3 cloves garlic, coarsely chopped
- 1 shallot, coarsely chopped
- 3 tablespoons soy sauce
- 1 tablespoon Dijon mustard
- 1 tablespoon fresh lemon juice
- 2 tablespoons vegetable oil

Directions:
1. Preparing the Ingredients
2. If using flank steak, score it on both sides in a crosshatch pattern, making shallow cuts on the diagonal no deeper than ⅛ inch and about ¼ inch apart. This will keep the flank steak from curling as it cooks; you don't have to score sirloin or top or bottom round.
3. Place the peppercorns, lemon zest, garlic, and shallot in a food processor and process to a coarse paste. Add the soy sauce, mustard, lemon juice, and 1 tablespoon of the oil. Spread half of the soy sauce mixture in the bottom of a baking dish just large enough to hold the beef. Place the meat on top and spread the remaining soy sauce mixture over it. Let the meat marinate for at least 4 hours or as long as overnight. You can also marinate the beef in a resealable plastic bag.
4. When ready to cook, drain the meat, scraping off most of the marinade with a rubber spatula. (Scraping off the marinade will help the steak to sear better and makes less of a mess on the grill.) Drizzle the remaining 1 tablespoon of oil over the beef on both sides, spreading it over the meat with your fingertips.
5. Turn control knob to the high position, butter the grill surface, when the griddle is hot, place the beef. A thick slab of sirloin or round steak will be cooked to medium-rare after 7 to 10 Minutes; flank steak will be cooked to medium after 3 to 5 Minutes.
6. To test for doneness, use the poke method; when cooked to medium-rare the meat should be gently yielding.
7. Transfer the meat to a cutting board and let rest for 3 Minutes. To serve, thinly slice the meat against the grain on a sharp diagonal. Fan out the slices on a platter or plate and serve at once.

227.Habanero-marinated Pork Chops

Servings: 4
Cooking Time: 13 Minutes
Ingredients:
- 4 ½-inch-thick bone-in pork chops
- 3 tablespoons olive oil, plus more for grill
- Kosher salt and freshly ground black pepper
- For the marinade:

- 1 habanero chili, seeded, chopped fine
- 2 garlic cloves, minced
- ½ cup fresh orange juice
- 2 tablespoons brown sugar
- 1 tablespoon apple cider vinegar

Directions:
1. Combine marinade ingredients in a large sealable plastic bag.
2. Pierce pork chops all over with a fork and add to bag, seal, and turn to coat.
3. Marinate at room temperature, turning occasionally, for 30 minutes.
4. Prepare griddle for medium-high heat.
5. Brush the griddle with oil.
6. Remove pork chops from marinade and pat dry.
7. Sear for 8 minutes, turning occasionally, until charred and cooked through.
8. Transfer to a plate and let rest 5 minutes.
9. Serve with your favorite sides.

Nutrition Info: Calories: 490 Sodium: 171 mg, Dietary Fiber: 1.1g, Fat: 39.2g, Carbs: 10.9g Protein: 23.3g

- 1 small onion, roughly chopped
- 1 apple, roughly chopped
- ¼ cup salt
- ¼ cup light brown sugar
- 3 whole peppercorns
- 3 fresh thyme sprigs or ½ teaspoon dried thyme
- 4 (6-ounce) boneless center-cut pork chops, pounded to ½-inch thickness

Directions:
1. Preparing the Ingredients
2. Combine all of the ingredients except the pork chops in a bowl large enough to hold all of the chops. Stir until the salt and brown sugar dissolve. Add the chops to the brine. Cover with plastic wrap and refrigerate overnight or for up to 24 hours.
3. Bring the griddle grill to high heat. When the griddle is hot, grill the pork chops for about 3 Minutes, until the meat has taken on grill marks and is firm to the touch.
4. Serve immediately.

Nutrition Info: (Per Serving): CALORIES: 244; FAT: 12G; PROTEIN:32G

228.Basic Juicy Ny Strip Steak

Servings: 1
Cooking Time: 8 Minutes
Ingredients:
- 1 (8 ounce) NY strip steak
- Olive oil
- Sea salt
- Fresh ground black pepper

Directions:
1. Remove the steak from the refrigerator and let it come to room temperature, about 30 to 45 minutes.
2. Preheat griddle to medium-high heat and brush with olive oil.
3. Season the steak on all sides with salt and pepper.
4. Cook steak about 4 to 5 minutes.
5. Flip and cook about 4 minutes more for medium rare steak; between 125°F and 130°F on a meat thermometer.
6. Transfer the steak to a plate and let it rest for 5 minutes before serving.

Nutrition Info: Calories:1560, Sodium: 8468 mg, Dietary Fiber: 0.g, Fat: 86g, Carbs: 0.1g Protein: 184g

230.Beef Bulgogi

Servings: 4
Cooking Time: 30 Minutes
Ingredients:
- 2 lbs. flank steak
- 1/2 cup soy sauce
- 1/2 cup brown sugar
- 2 Tbsp. chopped green onion
- 4 cloves garlic, minced
- 2 Tbsps. sesame seeds
- 2 Tbsps. sesame oil
- 2 tsps. black pepper

Directions:
1. Mix all of the ingredients together in a bowl or bag and refrigerate for several hours to overnight.
2. Heat the griddle grill to high, and grill the steak for several minutes per side until it is at your preferred doneness.
3. Let rest for several minutes before slicing and serving.

Nutrition Info: (Per serving): Calories: 339kcal, Carbs: 7g, Fats: 17g, Protein: 35g

229.Apple Cider Pork Chops

Servings: 4
Cooking Time: 3 Minutes
Ingredients:
- 2 cups water
- 1 cup apple cider

231.Adana Kebabs

Servings: 4
Cooking Time: 15 Minutes
Ingredients:
- 1½ pounds ground lamb shoulder or leg
- ½ cup minced red bell pepper

- ½ cup minced onion
- 2 tablespoons ground sumac
- 4 teaspoons ground cumin
- 2 teaspoons ground coriander
- 2 teaspoons red chile flakes or Aleppo pepper
- Salt

Directions:
1. Preparing the Ingredients.
2. 1 Put the lamb, bell pepper, onion, sumac, cumin, coriander, red pepper, and some salt in a large bowl and work everything together with your hands until combined. Pinch off golf ball–sized pieces of the mixture and with one hand, squeeze them into sausages 3 to 3½ inches long and about 1 inch thick. Put them on a platter without touching, cover with plastic wrap, and refrigerate for up to 12 hours.
3. 2 Turn control knob to the high position. Oil the griddle and allow it to heat until the oil is shimmering but not smoking. Put the sausages on the griddle, and cook for 7 Minutes per side until crusty and just cooked through. (Nick with a small knife and peek inside). Transfer to a clean platter and serve.

232.Cuban Pork Chops

Servings: 4
Cooking Time: 1 Hour 30 Minutes
Ingredients:
- 4 pork chops
- 4 cloves garlic, smashed
- 2 tablespoons olive oil
- 1/3 cup lime juice
- 1/4 cup water
- 1 teaspoon ground cumin
- Salt and black pepper

Directions:
1. Set your griddle to medium. Salt the pork chops on both side and cook the chops until lightly browned.
2. Combine the water, garlic, and lime juice in a bowl and whisk until even.
3. Continue cooking the pork chops while basting them with the lime juice mixture.
4. When the pork chops have finished cooking, remove from the griddle and top with additional sauce and black pepper before serving.

Nutrition Info: Calories: 323, Sodium: 58 mg, Dietary Fiber: 0.1g, Fat: 27g, Carbs:1.5g Protein: 18.3g

233.Balsamic Glazed Pork Chops

Servings: 4
Cooking Time: 20 Minutes
Ingredients:

- ¾ cup balsamic vinegar
- 1 ½ tablespoons sugar
- 1 tablespoon butter
- 3 tablespoons olive oil
- tablespoons salt
- 3 pork rib chops

Directions:
1. Preparing the Ingredients.
2. Place all ingredients in bowl and allow the meat to marinate in the fridge for at least 2 hours.
3. Bring the griddle grill to high heat. When the griddle is hot, grill the pork chops for 20 Minutes making sure to flip the meat every 10 Minutes for even grilling.
4. Meanwhile, pour the balsamic vinegar on a saucepan and allow to simmer for at least 10 Minutes until the sauce thickens.
5. Brush the meat with the glaze before serving.

Nutrition Info: (Per Serving): CALORIES: 274; FAT: 18G; PROTEIN:17G

234.Carne Asada

Servings: 4
Cooking Time: 15 Minutes
Ingredients:
- 1 lb. hanger steak or shirt steak
- 1/4 cup olive oil
- 1 lime, juiced
- 1 orange, juiced
- 1 garlic clove, finely chopped
- 1/2 teaspoon cumin
- 1/4 teaspoon salt
- 1/4 teaspoon ground pepper
- handful of fresh cilantro, chopped

Directions:
1. Combine all of the ingredients in a large sealable plastic bag. Marinate in the refrigerator for 1 to 2 hours.
2. Preheat to medium/high heat, cook for 3 minutes on each side or until just cooked through.
3. Transfer to cutting board to rest for 10 minutes.
4. Slice against the grain and serve.

Nutrition Info: Calories: 363, Sodium: 200mg, Dietary Fiber: 1.7g, Fat: 18.4g, Carbs: 7.7g Protein: 41.6g

235.Madeira-style Beef Skewers

Servings: 6
Cooking Time: 10 Minutes
Ingredients:
- 1½ to 2 pounds boneless beef steak
- 6 cloves garlic, peeled

- 1 tablespoon sea salt
- 2 tablespoons good-quality olive oil
- 30–35 bay leaves (preferably fresh)

Directions:
1. Preparing the Ingredients
2. 1 Trim any excess fat from the steak, then cut it into 1-to 1½-inch chunks. Put in a large bowl.
3. With a mortar and pestle or in a blender or mini food processor, mash or process the garlic and salt to a paste, then stir in the oil. Pour over the beef and work into the meat with your hands until the chunks are completely coated. (You can do this up to several hours in advance; if more than an hour, cover and refrigerate until you're ready to grill.)
4. 2 If you're using bamboo or wooden skewers, soak them in water for 30 Minutes
5. Thread the beef onto skewers, alternating the chunks with bay leaves; if any leaves break, wedge them between meat chunks.
6. Turn control knob to the high position, when the griddle is hot, add cooking oil, and when it begins to shimmer, add the skewers to the Griddle, and cook 5 Minutes. Flip and sear for an additional 3 Minutes, based on your desired doneness. Transfer to a platter and serve.

236.High-low Strip Steak

Servings: 2
Cooking Time: 15 Minutes
Ingredients:
- 2 (1-pound) New York strip steaks, trimmed
- For the rub:
- 1 bunch thyme sprigs
- 1 bunch rosemary sprigs
- 1 bunch sage sprigs
- 1 1/2 teaspoons black pepper, divided
- 3/4 teaspoon sea salt, divided
- 1/2 teaspoon garlic powder
- 2 tablespoons chopped fresh flat-leaf parsley
- 2 tablespoons extra-virgin olive oil

Directions:
1. Preheat griddle to high heat.
2. Combine rub ingredients in a small mixing bowl and rub steaks with spice mixture; let rest 10 minutes.
3. Place steaks on grill and cook 1 minute per side.
4. Turn griddle down to medium heat.
5. Turn steaks and grill 3 additional minutes per side; or until thermometer registers 135°F for medium rare.
6. Remove steaks to a platter.
7. Let rest 5 minutes. Cut steaks across grain into thin slices.

Nutrition Info: Calories: 347, Sodium: 831 mg, Dietary Fiber: 1.9g, Fat: 20.4g, Carbs:3.7g Protein: 38.7g

237.Italian "cheese Steak"

Servings: 4
Cooking Time: 6 Minutes
Ingredients:
- 2 pieces thinly sliced beef top or bottom round, or sirloin (each 6 ounces and about 8 inches long, 4 inches wide, and just shy of ¼ inch thick)
- Coarse salt (kosher or sea) and freshly ground black pepper
- 2 ounces thinly sliced imported Italian Fontina cheese
- 2 slices prosciutto (about 1½ ounces in all)
- 3 tablespoons freshly grated Parmesan cheese
- YOU'LL ALSO NEED:
- Wooden toothpicks

Directions:
1. Preparing the Ingredients
2. Place a steak on a work surface with a long edge toward you. Using a sharp knife and making a cut that is perpendicular to the long edge, score the steak down the middle by cutting about halfway through the meat (this will enable you to fold the steak closed like a book). Repeat with the remaining steak. Season the steaks on both sides with salt and pepper.
3. Place a steak on the work surface, cut side down. Arrange half of the slices of Fontina on top of one half of the steak so that they are parallel to the cut. Top the Fontina with a slice of prosciutto, then sprinkle 1½ tablespoons of the Parmesan over it. Folding the steak along the cut edge, cover the cheese and prosciutto with the bare half of the steak. Secure the open end with toothpicks. Repeat with the remaining steak, Fontina, prosciutto, and Parmesan. The steaks can be prepared up to this stage several hours ahead and refrigerated, covered.
4. Turn control knob to the high position, when the griddle is hot, place the stuffed steaks on the hot grill. The steaks will be done after cooking 4 to 6 Minutes until the cheese is melted and the steaks are nicely browned on the outside and cooked through.
5. Transfer the stuffed steaks to a platter or plates. Remove and discard the toothpicks, then serve the steaks at once.

238.Cold Soba With Beef And Cucumber

Servings: 4
Cooking Time: 3 Minutes
Ingredients:
- SOBA

- 8 ounces soba noodles
- 1 tablespoon sesame oil
- STEAK AND DRESSING
- ¾ cup rice vinegar
- 1 tablespoon Asian sesame oil
- 3 garlic cloves, minced
- 1 jalapeño pepper, seeded and minced
- ½ teaspoon salt
- 1 pound flank steak, about 1 inch thick
- 3 tablespoons fresh lime juice (from 2
- limes)
- SALAD
- 1largeseedless cucumber, halved lengthwise and thinly sliced
- 1 ripe mango, halved and thinly sliced
- 1 cup chopped fresh basil leaves
- 1 cup chopped fresh mint leaves
- ½ cup unsalted roasted cashews, chopped
- 1 scallion, chopped

Directions:
1. Preparing the Ingredients
2. Bring a medium saucepan of water to a boil. Add the soba and cook for about 3 to 5 Minutes until it is al dente-soft with just a little firmness left. Drain, rinse with cold water, and transfer to a medium serving bowl. Toss with the sesame oil, cover with plastic wrap, and refrigerate for at least 2 hours or overnight.
3. Combine the rice vinegar, sesame oil, garlic, jalapeño, and salt in a shallow baking dish. Add the steak, turning to coat. Cover with plastic wrap and refrigerate for at least 2 hours or overnight.
4. Remove the steak from the marinade, and reserve the marinade in a small saucepan.
5. Turn control knob to the high position. Oil the griddle and allow it to heat until the oil is shimmering but not smoking. Grill the steak for about 3 Minutes per side for medium-rare. It should have grill marks and feel fairly firm to the touch. Let the steak rest on a cutting board for about 5 Minutes.
6. Bring the marinade to a boil, cook for 1 minute, then remove from the heat. Pour into a small bowl, stir in the lime juice, and refrigerate the dressing to cool while you prepare the salad.
7. Seedless cucumbers are available in supermarkets, but you can easily remove the seeds from the standard variety: after peeling, cut the cucumber in half lengthwise. Use a teaspoon to scoop out the middle core of seeds.
8. Add the dressing to the soba noodles and toss thoroughly. Add the cucumber, mango, basil, and mint and toss gently to combine.
9. Thinly slice the steak across the grain and arrange over the noodles. Sprinkle the cashews and chopped scallion over the top. Serve immediately.

Nutrition Info: (Per Serving): CALORIES:577; FAT: 25G; PROTEIN:32G

239.Greek Flank Steak Gyros

Servings: 4
Cooking Time: 20 Minutes
Ingredients:
- 1 pound flank steak
- 1 white onion, thinly sliced
- 1 roma tomato, thinly sliced
- 1 cucumber, peeled and thinly sliced
- 1/4 cup crumbled feta cheese
- 4 6-inch pita pockets
- For the marinade:
- 1/4 cup olive oil, plus more for brushing
- 1 teaspoon dried oregano
- 1 teaspoon balsamic vinegar
- 1 teaspoon garlic powder
- Sea salt and freshly ground pepper, to taste
- For the sauce:
- 1 cup plain yogurt
- 2 tablespoons fresh dill (can use dried), chopped
- 1 teaspoon garlic, minced
- 2 tablespoons lemon juice

Directions:
1. Cut the flank steak into thin strips against the grain. Add the marinade ingredients to a large sealable plastic bag, add the sliced meat, seal, and turn to coat.
2. Place in the refrigerator to marinate for 2 hours or overnight.
3. Preheat the griddle to medium-high heat, and an oven to 250°F.
4. Combine the sauce ingredients in small mixing bowl and set aside.
5. Spritz the pitas with a little water, wrap in foil and place in the oven to warm.
6. Brush griddle with olive oil.
7. Add meat to grill and discard marinade. Cook until brown and cooked through, about 5 minutes.
8. Remove the pitas from the oven, and cut in half.
9. Arrange the pitas on plates and stuff with cucumber, tomato, onions, and beef.
10. Spoon some yogurt sauce over the meat and top with feta and serve.

Nutrition Info: Calories:901, Sodium: 1221 mg, Dietary Fiber: 5.7g, Fat: 27.2g, Carbs:107.8g Protein: 53.5g

240.Grilled Stuffed Pork Tenderloin

Servings: 4
Cooking Time: 30 Minutes

Ingredients:
- 1½ Tbsp. olive oil, plus a drizzle
- ½ medium Vidalia onion, finely chopped
- 1 tsp. Worcestershire sauce
- 6 oz. chopped baby bella mushrooms
- 2 cloves garlic, minced
- 2 tsp. minced rosemary
- 4 fresh sage leaves, chopped
- ½ tsp. celery salt
- ½ tsp. fresh black pepper
- ¼ cup chopped flat-leaf parsley
- 2 cups fresh spinach leaves, stems removed
- 2 tsp. Dijon mustard
- 1 pork tenderloin, 1½ to 2 lb.
- 4 slices pancetta
- 4 slices provolone cheese
- 2 tsp. rosemary salt

Directions:
1. Preparing the Ingredients
2. In a medium skillet, heat olive oil over medium heat. Add onion and cook for 1 minute before adding Worcestershire sauce, mushrooms, garlic, rosemary, sage, celery salt, and black pepper. Constantly mixing with wooden spoon, cook down till mushrooms are soft (5–7 Minutes).
3. Add parsley and spinach. Continue to mix with wooden spoon. Cook until spinach starts to wilt. Stir in mustard and cook for additional 1 minute. Remove from heat, set aside, and allow to cool while you prep the pork.
4. Place pork tenderloin on cutting board, and with your knife parallel to the cutting surface, roll cut the tenderloin so it's about ½-inch thick when unrolled.
5. Once pork has been roll cut, lay pancetta on top, followed by provolone cheese and spinach mixture. Leave about a 1-inch border around the edge of the loin.
6. Roll tenderloin back up and truss together with butcher's twine. (If you're not sure how to truss, just tie the roll up using a simple square knot every 2 inches, but trussing is super easy.
7. Drizzle outside of roll with a very thin coat of olive oil and sprinkle with rosemary salt.
8. Bring the griddle grill to high heat. When the griddle is hot, place the pork on the griddle grill and cook for 11 Minutes. After 11 Minutes, flip the pork, and cook for an additional 11 Minutes.
9. Remove from grill, slice, and serve.

241.Moroccan Spiced Pork Tenderloin With Creamy Harissa Sauce

Servings: 6
Cooking Time: 20 Minutes

Ingredients:
- 2 (1 lb.) pork tenderloins
- 1 teaspoon ground cinnamon
- 1 teaspoon ground cilantro
- 1 teaspoon ground cumin
- 1 teaspoon paprika
- 1 teaspoon sea salt
- 2 tablespoons olive oil
- For Creamy Harissa Sauce:
- 1 cup Greek yogurt (8 ounces)
- 1 tablespoon fresh lemon juice
- 1 tablespoon extra-virgin olive oil
- 1 teaspoon harissa sauce
- 1 clove garlic, minced
- Kosher salt and cracked black pepper

Directions:
1. Combine harissa ingredients in a small mixing bowl and set aside.
2. Combine the cinnamon, coriander, cumin, paprika, salt and olive oil.
3. Rub the seasonings evenly over the pork tenderloins; cover and refrigerate for 30 minutes.
4. Preheat griddle to high heat and cook tenderloins until browned; about 8 to 10 minutes.
5. Turn and cook an additional 8 to 10 minutes. Transfer the tenderloins to a cutting board, tent with foil and rest for 10 minutes.
6. Slice and serve with creamy harissa sauce.

Nutrition Info: Calories: 376, Sodium: 458mg, Dietary Fiber: 0.4g, Fat: 17.9g, Carbs: 2.6g Protein: 48.7g

242.Beef Stir Fry

Servings: 4
Cooking Time: 10 Minutes
Ingredients:
- 1 lb steak, sliced
- 4 tbsp coconut oil
- 1/2 lb broccoli, cut into florets
- 1 tsp fish sauce
- 1 tsp sesame oil
- For marinade:
- 4 tbsp coconut aminos
- 2 garlic cloves, chopped
- 1 tsp ginger, grated

Directions:
1. Add sliced meat to a zip-lock bag with garlic, ginger, and coconut aminos and let marinate for 1 hour.
2. Blanch broccoli in boiling water for 2 minutes. Drain well.
3. Drain marinated meat.
4. Preheat the griddle to high heat.
5. Spray griddle top with cooking spray.

6. Add marinated meat onto the hot griddle top and cook for 1-3 minutes or until browned.
7. Add broccoli and stir fry for 3 minutes.
8. Add fish sauce and sesame oil and stir well.
9. Serve and enjoy.

Nutrition Info: (Per Serving): Calories 375 ;Fat 20 g ;Saturated fat 14 g ;Carbohydrates 4 g ;Sugar 1.1 g ;Protein 42.8 g ;Cholesterol 102 mg

243.Marinated London Broil

Servings: 4
Cooking Time: 4 Minutes
Ingredients:
- 2-lb. London broil
- MARINADE
- ½ cup soy sauce
- 2 Tbsp. balsamic vinegar
- 2 Tbsp. Dijon mustard
- 4 cloves garlic, minced
- 2 Tbsp. olive oil
- 3 sprigs fresh rosemary
- 1 tsp. coarsely ground black pepper

Directions:
1. Preparing the Ingredients
2. Combine all marinade ingredients in mixing bowl and whisk together.
3. Using a sharp knife, cut a diamond, or crosshatch, pattern into each side of the meat, only cutting about ¼ inch deep. This will allow the marinade to penetrate the meat deeper in a shorter amount of time.
4. Place meat in sealable plastic bag and cover with marinade. Place in refrigerator for 2 hours. After 2 hours, remove from refrigerator and allow to come up to room temperature for 1 hour.
5. Remove meat from marinade and pat dry with paper towel.
6. Turn control knob to the high position. Oil the griddle and allow it to heat until the oil is shimmering but not smoking. Let cook for 2 Minutes, rotate 90 degrees, and allow to cook for another 2 Minutes.
7. Flip meat and repeat.
8. Remove from grill when internal temperature reaches 125°F. Tent with foil and let rest for 5 Minutes before slicing.
9. Serve with chipotle aioli.

244.Spare Ribs With Sweet Ancho-cumin Rub

Servings: 6
Cooking Time: 120 Minutes
Ingredients:
- 1 tablespoon sugar
- 2 teaspoons salt
- 2 teaspoons black pepper
- 2 teaspoons ground cumin
- 2 teaspoons ancho chile powder
- 2 teaspoons paprika
- About 4 pounds spare ribs

Directions:
1. Preparing the Ingredients
2. To make the rub, stir the sugar, salt, pepper, cumin, ancho powder, and paprika together in a small bowl. Rub into the ribs on both sides. (You can do this up to several hours ahead of cooking.)
3. Bring the griddle grill to medium heat. When the griddle is hot, put the ribs, meaty side up in the and cook for 120 Minutes.
4. Every half hour, turn. Cook until the meat is tender enough that you can easily cut between the ribs, 2 hours total.,
5. Transfer to a cutting board and let rest until cool enough to handle, then cut between the ribs, put on a platter, and serve.

245.Skirt Steak With Horseradish Cream

Servings: 4
Cooking Time: 4 Minutes
Ingredients:
- HORSERADISH CREAM
- 2 tablespoons prepared white horseradish
- ¼ cup light sour cream
- Stir together the horseradish and the sour cream in a small bowl. (The horseradish sauce can be covered with plastic wrap and refrigerated overnight.)
- SKIRT STEAK
- 1½ pounds skirt steak, about I inch thick
- 2 tablespoons olive oil
- ¼ teaspoon salt
- ¼ teaspoon freshly ground black pepper
- 2 scallions, white part only, chopped

Directions:
1. Preparing the Ingredients
2. Rub the steak on both sides with the olive oil and season with the salt and pepper.
3. Turn control knob to the high position, when the griddle is hot, add cooking oil, and when it begins to shimmer, grill the steak for about 4 Minutes. Flip and sear for an additional 1 to 3 Minutes, based on your desired doneness.
4. Let the steak rest on a cutting board for about 5 Minutes before slicing, thinly, across the grain. Serve hot or at room temperature, topped with the horseradish cream and scallions.

Nutrition Info: (Per Serving): CALORIES:395; FAT: 28G; PROTEIN:36G

246.Easy Lemon Pepper Pork Chops

Servings: 4
Cooking Time: 12 Minutes
Ingredients:
- 4 pork chops, boneless
- 1 tsp lemon pepper seasoning
- Salt

Directions:
1. Preheat the griddle to high heat.
2. Spray griddle top with cooking spray.
3. Season pork chops with lemon pepper seasoning, and salt and place onto the hot griddle top and cook for 5-7 minutes per side.
4. Serve and enjoy.

Nutrition Info: (Per Serving): Calories 257 ;Fat 20 g ;Carbohydrates 0.3 g ;Sugar 0 g ;Protein 18 g ;Cholesterol 69 mg

247.Grilled Beef Or Calf's Liver

Servings: 4
Cooking Time: 8 Minutes
Ingredients:
- 1–1½ pounds beef or calf's liver
- Salt and pepper
- Lemon wedges for serving

Directions:
1. Preparing the Ingredients
2. Slice the liver lengthwise into slices about ½ inch thick. Pat the slices dry with paper towels, then sprinkle with salt and pepper on both sides.
3. Turn control knob to the high position, when the griddle is hot, put the liver on the griddle and cook for 8 Minutes.
4. Transfer to a platter, let rest for 5 Minutes, then cut across into slices and serve with lemon wedges.

248.Beef And Broccoli

Servings: 4
Cooking Time: 12 Minutes
Ingredients:
- 1 minced garlic clove
- 1 sliced ginger root
- 1 tbsp. olive oil
- 1 tsp. almond flour
- 1 tsp. sweetener of choice
- 1 tsp. low-sodium soy sauce
- 1/3 C. sherry
- 2 tsp. sesame oil
- 1/3 C. oyster sauce
- 1 pounds of broccoli
- ¾ pound round steak

Directions:
1. Preparing the Ingredients.
2. Remove stems from broccoli and slice into florets. Slice steak into thin strips.
3. Combine sweetener, soy sauce, sherry, almond flour, sesame oil, and oyster sauce together, stirring till sweetener dissolves.
4. Put strips of steak into the mixture and allow to marinate 45 Minutes to 2 hours.
5. Turn control knob to the high position, when the griddle is hot, add broccoli and marinated steak. Place garlic, ginger, and olive oil on top and cook 12 Minutes at 400 degrees. Serve with cauliflower rice!

Nutrition Info: (Per Serving): CALORIES: 384; FAT: 16G; PROTEIN:19G

249.Thick Stacked Sizzling Burgers On The Griddle

Servings: 6
Cooking Time: 8 Minutes
Ingredients:
- 1-1/2 pounds ground beef, 80% to 85% lean
- 6 hamburger buns
- 1/4 stick butter (use oil as substitute if desired)
- Pinch salt
- Pinch fresh black pepper
- 6 slices cheese
- Burger toppings:
- 2 sliced tomatoes,
- 1/4 onion (sliced)
- 2 pickles
- 3 tbsp. Ketchup
- 2 tbsp. Mustard
- 6 lettuce leaves

Directions:
1. Preheat Griddle Grill to Sear with the unit closed.
2. Shape ground beef into 6 big and chunky patties, then melt butter on griddle over medium heat. Lightly butter the buns, then toasting them to your desired liking. Move the buns to a clean plate. Then, using the same pan, cook the patties for several minutes. Add a pinch of salt and pepper to each and continue to cook for 3 to 4 min.
3. Flip the burgers and repeat the process, adding a little more salt and pepper than before. Cook for another several minutes or until cooked to your desired liking.

Nutrition Info: (Per serving):calories 980; fats 43g; Carbs 13.3 g; protein 9g

250.Pineapple Bacon Pork Chops

Servings: 6
Cooking Time: 1 Hour
Ingredients:
- 1 large whole pineapple
- 6 pork chops
- 12 slices thick-cut bacon
- Toothpicks, soaked in water
- For the glaze:
- ¼ cup honey
- ⅛ teaspoon cayenne pepper

Directions:
1. Turn both burners to medium-high heat; after about 15 minutes, turn off one of the middle burners and turn the remaining burners down to medium.
2. Slice off the top and bottom of the pineapple, and peel the pineapple, cutting the skin off in strips.
3. Cut pineapple flesh into six quarters.
4. Wrap each pineapple section with a bacon slice; secure each end with a toothpick.
5. Brush quarters with honey and sprinkle with cayenne pepper.
6. Put the quarters on the griddle, flipping when bacon is cooked so that both sides are evenly grilled.
7. While pineapple quarters are cooking, coat pork chops with honey and cayenne pepper. Set on griddle.
8. Tent with foil and cook for 20 minutes. Flip, and continue cooking an additional 10 to 20 minutes or until chops are fully cooked.
9. Serve each chop with a pineapple quarter on the side.
Nutrition Info: Calories: 380 Sodium: 852 mg, Dietary Fiber: 0.5g, Fat: 23.5g, Carbs: 18.2g Protein: 25.8g

251.Balsamic-marinated Whole Beef Tenderloin With Herbs

Servings: 10
Cooking Time: 25 Minutes
Ingredients:
- ½ cup good-quality olive oil
- ¼ cup roughly chopped fresh parsley
- 2 tablespoons balsamic or sherry vinegar
- 1 tablespoon coarsely ground or cracked black peppercorns
- 1 teaspoon fresh thyme leaves, several thyme sprigs, or ½ teaspoon dried thyme
- 1 bay leaf
- 4 cloves garlic, lightly smashed
- 1 beef tenderloin (5–6 pounds), trimmed of fat and silverskin
- Salt and pepper

Directions:
1. Preparing the Ingredients

2. Combine the oil, parsley, vinegar, peppercorns, thyme, bay leaf, and garlic in a large bowl and whisk. Pat the tenderloin dry with paper towels, then put it in the bowl and turn to coat completely with the marinade. Marinate the roast for up to an hour at room temperature, turning it every 15 Minutes or so. Or cover and refrigerate it for several hours or overnight, turning it occasionally.
3. Remove the tenderloin from the marinade.
4. Turn control knob to the high position, when the griddle is hot, add cooking oil and when it begins to shimmer place it on the griddle and cook for 12 Minutes. Flip and sear for an additional 10 Minutes, based on your desired doneness.
5. Transfer to a cutting board and let rest 5 to 10 Minutes, checking the internal temperature. (Or nick with a small knife and peek inside.) Cut the roast into ½-inch or thicker slices, transfer to a platter, pour over any accumulated juices, and serve.

252.Rosemary Dijon Pork Chops

Servings: 4
Cooking Time: 10 Minutes
Ingredients:
- 4 pork chops, boneless
- 2 tbsp fresh rosemary, chopped
- 1/4 cup Dijon mustard
- 1/4 cup coconut aminos
- 2 tbsp olive oil
- 1/2 tsp salt

Directions:
1. In a bowl, mix together rosemary, coconut aminos, olive oil, Dijon mustard, and salt.
2. Add pork chops to the bowl and coat well.
3. Cover and place in the refrigerator for 1 hour.
4. Preheat the griddle to high heat.
5. Spray griddle top with cooking spray.
6. Place marinated pork chops onto the hot griddle top and cook for 5 minutes on each side.
7. Serve and enjoy.
Nutrition Info: (Per Serving): Calories 332 ;Fat 27.8 g ;Carbohydrates 1.9 g ;Sugar 0.1 g ;Protein 18.7 g ;Cholesterol 69 mg

253.Garlic Putter Pork Chops

Servings: 4
Cooking Time: 15 Minutes
Ingredients:
- 2 tsp. parsley
- 2 tsp. grated garlic cloves
- 1 tbsp. coconut oil
- 1 tbsp. coconut butter
- 4 pork chops

Directions:
1.   Preparing the Ingredients.
2.   Mix butter, coconut oil, and all seasoning together. Then rub seasoning mixture over all sides of pork chops. Place in foil, seal, and chill for 1 hour.
3.   Bring the griddle grill to high heat. When the griddle is hot, cook 7 Minutes on one side and 8 Minutes on the other.
4.   Drizzle with olive oil and serve alongside a green salad.
Nutrition Info: (Per Serving): CALORIES: 526; FAT: 23G; PROTEIN:41G; SUGAR:4G

254.Charred Onions And Steak Cube Bbq

Servings: 3
Cooking Time: 40 Minutes
Ingredients:
*   1 cup red onions, cut into wedges
*   1 tablespoon dry mustard
*   1 tablespoon olive oil
*   1-pound boneless beef sirloin, cut into cubes
*   Salt and pepper to taste
Directions:
1.   Preparing the Ingredients.
2.   1 Toss all ingredients in a bowl and mix until everything is coated with the seasonings.
3.   2 Turn control knob to the high position, when the griddle is hot, place on the griddle and cook for 40 Minutes.
4.   Halfway through the cooking time, give a stir to cook evenly.
Nutrition Info: (Per Serving): CALORIES: 260; FAT: 10.7G; PROTEIN:35.5G

255.Griddle Baked Beef Stew

Servings: 8
Cooking Time: 5 Hours
Ingredients:
*   2-1/2 lbs. beef stew meat chunks
*   8 carrots, chopped
*   3 medium white onions, quartered
*   5 medium white potatoes, quartered
*   2 cans Sweet Peas
*   2 bay leaves
*   2 beef bouillon cubes
*   1 tbsp. sugar
*   1 tbsp. salt
*   1/4 tbsp. thyme
*   1 tbsp. black pepper
*   1/4 cup cornstarch
*   1 (28-oz.) can whole tomatoes
*   1 cup water

Directions:
1.   Preheat the griddle to medium high.
2.   Pour all the ingredients in a Skillet and set on the griddle.
3.   Cover and cook for 5 hours, stir once or twice
4.   Serve immediately and enjoy.
Nutrition Info: (Per serving):calories 439kcal, fat 13g, carbs50g, protein30g

256.Dijon Garlic Pork Tenderloin

Servings: 4
Cooking Time: 15 Minutes
Ingredients:
*   1 C. breadcrumbs
*   Pinch of cayenne pepper
*   3 crushed garlic cloves
*   2 tbsp. ground ginger
*   2 tbsp. Dijon mustard
*   2 tbsp. raw honey
*   4 tbsp. water
*   2 tsp. salt
*   1pound pork tenderloin, sliced into 1-inch rounds
Directions:
1.   Preparing the Ingredients.
2.   With pepper and salt, season all sides of tenderloin.
3.   Combine cayenne pepper, garlic, ginger, mustard, honey, and water until smooth.
4.   Dip pork rounds into honey mixture and then into breadcrumbs, ensuring they all get coated well.
5.   Bring the griddle grill to high heat. When the griddle is hot, place coated pork rounds and cook 10 Minutes at 400 degrees. Flip and then cook an additional 5 Minutes until golden in color.
Nutrition Info: (Per Serving): CALORIES: 423; FAT: 18G; PROTEIN:31G; SUGAR:3G

257.Garlic Soy Pork Chops

Servings: 4 - 6
Cooking Time: 1 Hour
Ingredients:
*   4 to 6 pork chops
*   4 cloves garlic, finely chopped
*   1/2 cup olive oil
*   1/2 cup soy sauce
*   1/2 teaspoon garlic powder
*   1/2 teaspoon salt
*   1/2 black pepper
*   1/4 cup butter
Directions:

1. In a large zipperlock bag, combine the garlic, olive oil, soy sauce, and garlic powder. Add the pork chops and make sure the marinade coats the chops. Set aside for 30 minutes.
2. Heat your griddle to medium-high heat. Add 2 tablespoons of olive oil and 2 tablespoons of butter to the griddle.
3. Add the chops to the griddle one at a time, making sure they are not crowded. Add another 2 tablespoons of butter to the griddle and cook the chops for 4 minutes. Cook an additional 4 minutes.
4. Remove the chops from the griddle and spread the remaining butter over them. Serve after resting for 5 minutes.
Nutrition Info: Calories: 398 Sodium: 1484 mg, Dietary Fiber: 0.2g, Fat: 37.7g, Carbs: 2.5g Protein: 13.6g

258.Simply Seared Veal Chops

Servings: 4
Cooking Time: 10 Minutes
Ingredients:
- 4 veal loin or rib chops (about 1 inch thick, 12–16 ounces each)
- Salt and pepper
- Lemon wedges for serving

Directions:
1. Preparing the Ingredients
2. Pat the chops dry with paper towels. Sprinkle with salt and pepper on both sides.
3. Turn control knob to the high position, when the griddle is hot, put the chops on the griddle and cook for 5 Minutes; an instant-read thermometer should register 135°F.
4. Transfer to a platter and let sit about 5 Minutes, flip and sear for an additional 1 to 3 Minutes checking the temperature occasionally. When the chops are ready, serve right away with lemon wedges.

259.Curry Pork Roast In Coconut Sauce

Servings: 6
Cooking Time: 20 Minutes
Ingredients:
- ½ teaspoon curry powder
- ½ teaspoon ground turmeric powder
- 1 can unsweetened coconut milk
- 1 tablespoons sugar
- 2 tablespoons fish sauce
- 2 tablespoons soy sauce
- 3 pounds pork shoulder
- Salt and pepper to taste

Directions:

1. Preparing the Ingredients.
2. Place all Ingredients in bowl and allow the meat to marinate in the fridge for at least 2 hours.
3. Bring the griddle grill to high heat. When the griddle is hot, grill the meat for 20 Minutes making sure to flip the pork every 10 Minutes for even grilling and cook in batches.
4. Meanwhile, pour the marinade in a saucepan and allow to simmer for 10 Minutes until the sauce thickens.
5. Baste the pork with the sauce before serving.
Nutrition Info: (Per Serving): CALORIES: 688; FAT: 52G; PROTEIN:17G

260.Romanian Garlic Steak

Servings: 6
Cooking Time: 10 Minutes
Ingredients:
- 8 cloves garlic, minced
- 1 teaspoon salt
- Juice of 1 lemon
- 1½ to 2 pounds flank steak
- ¼ cup good-quality olive oil

Directions:
1. Preparing the Ingredients
2. To make the marinade, combine half the garlic with the salt and lemon juice in a small bowl.
3. Put the steak in a large shallow baking dish and work the marinade into it on both sides, using your hands to massage it evenly all over the steak. Let sit at room temperature while you prepare the fire. Or cover and refrigerate for several hours or overnight.
4. Whisk the remainder of the garlic and the oil together in another small bowl with a fork, pressing down on the garlic as you work.
5. Remove the steak from the marinade and let any excess drip off.
6. Turn control knob to the high position, when the griddle is hot, add cooking oil and when it begins to shimmer, put the steak on the griddle and cook for 5 Minutes for medium-rare. Flip and sear for an additional 1 to 3 Minutes, based on your desired doneness.
7. Transfer to a cutting board and let rest for 5 to 10 Minutes, checking the internal temperature. (Or nick with a small knife and peek inside.) Slice thinly across the grain, transfer to a platter, pour over any accumulated juices, and serve with the garlic oil on the side to drizzle over.

261.Flank Steak With Garlic And Rosemary

Servings: 4

Cooking Time: 20 Minutes
Ingredients:
- 2 (8 ounce) flank steaks
- For the marinade:
- 1 tablespoon extra virgin olive oil, plus more for brushing
- 2 tablespoons fresh rosemary, chopped
- 4 cloves garlic, minced
- 2 teaspoons sea salt
- 1/4 teaspoon black pepper

Directions:
1. Add marinade ingredients to a food processor or blender and pulse until garlic and rosemary are pulverized.
2. Use a fork to pierce the steaks 10 times on each side.
3. Rub each evenly with the marinade on both sides.
4. Place in a covered dish and refrigerate for at least 1 hour or overnight.
5. Preheat griddle to high and brush with olive oil and preheat to high.
6. Cook steaks for 5 minutes, flip, tent with foil, and cook for about 3-4 minutes more.
7. Transfer meat to rest on a cutting board, cover with aluminum foil, for about 15 minutes.
8. Slice very thin against the grain and serve immediately.

Nutrition Info: Calories: 260, Sodium: 1001 mg, Dietary Fiber: 0.8g, Fat: 13.2g, Carbs:

262.Beef Salad With Fresh Mint

Servings: 4
Cooking Time: 8 Minutes
Ingredients:
- 4 cups torn Boston or romaine lettuce
- leaves, mesclun, or any salad greens
- mixture
- 1 cup torn fresh mint leaves
- ½ small red onion, cut into thin julienne
- 1 cucumber, peeled, seeded if necessary, and cut into thin julienne
- 1 carrot, peeled and cut into thin julienne
- Juice of 2 limes
- 2 tablespoons soy sauce
- 2 tablespoons rice vinegar
- 1 tablespoon sugar
- 1 jalapeño chile, seeded if you like, thinly sliced
- Salt and pepper
- 1½ pounds boneless steak

Directions:
1. Preparing the Ingredients
2. Put the lettuce, mint, onion, cucumber, and carrot in a large bowl. Whisk the lime juice, soy sauce,

vinegar, sugar, jalapeño, and 1 tablespoon water together in a small bowl; the mixture will be thin. Taste and add salt and pepper if you like. (You can prepare the salad and dressing up to several hours in advance; refrigerate both until you're ready to serve; drape a damp kitchen towel over the vegetables to keep them fresh.)
3. Pat the steak dry with paper towels, then sprinkle with salt and pepper on both sides.
4. Turn control knob to the high position, when the griddle is hot, add cooking oil and when it begins to shimmer, place the steak on the griddle and cook for 8 Minutes.
5. Transfer to a cutting board and let rest while you dress the salad; check the temperature of the meat occasionally. (Or nick with a small knife and peek inside.)
6. Transfer 2 tablespoons of the dressing to a medium-sized bowl. Drizzle the rest of the dressing over the salad and toss to coat. Transfer the salad to a platter if you like.
7. Thinly slice the steak across the grain. Put the beef and any accumulated juices in the bowl with the reserved dressing and toss to combine. Scatter the steak slices over the salad, drizzle with the juices, and serve.

263.Paprika Dijon Pork Tenderloin

Servings: 6
Cooking Time: 4 Hours
Ingredients:
- 2 1 lb pork tenderloins
- 2 tablespoons dijon mustard
- 1 1/2 teaspoons smoked paprika
- 1 teaspoon salt
- 2 tablespoons olive oil

Directions:
1. In a small bowl, combine the mustard and paprika.
2. Set your griddle to medium heat.
3. Rub the tenderloins with the mustard mixture, making sure they are evenly coated.
4. Place the tenderloins on the griddle and cook until all sides are well browned and the internal temperature is 135°F.
5. Remove the tenderloins from the griddle and rest 5 minutes before slicing and serving.

Nutrition Info: Calories: 484, Sodium: 755 mg, Dietary Fiber: 4.2g, Fat: 24.7g, Carbs:13.8g Protein: 50.9g

264.Sticky-sweet Pork Shoulder

Servings: 6 - 8

Cooking Time: 8 Minutes
Ingredients:
- 1 (5 lbs.) Boston Butt pork shoulder
- For the marinade:
- 2 tablespoons garlic, minced
- 1 large piece ginger, peeled and chopped
- 1 cup hoisin sauce
- ¾ cup fish sauce
- ⅔ cup honey
- ⅔ cup Shaoxing
- ½ cup chili oil
- ⅓ cup oyster sauce
- ⅓ cup sesame oil
- For the glaze:
- ¾ cup dark brown sugar
- 1 tablespoon light molasses

Directions:
1. Place pork shoulder, fat side down, on a cutting board with a short end facing you. Holding a long sharp knife about 1"–1½" above cutting board, make a shallow cut along the entire length of a long side of shoulder.
2. Continue cutting deeper into meat, lifting and unfurling with your free hand, until it lies flat.
3. Purée marinade in a blender and reserve 1 ½ cups for glaze, cover and refrigerate.
4. Pour remaining marinade in a large sealable plastic bag.
5. Add pork shoulder to bag and marinate in the refrigerator for 8 hours.
6. Preheat griddle to medium heat (with cover closed, thermometer should register 350°). Remove pork from marinade, letting excess drip off.
7. Add glaze ingredients to reserved marinade until sugar is dissolved.
8. Grill pork, for 8 minutes, basting and turning with tongs every minute or so, until thick coated with glaze, lightly charred in spots, and warmed through; an instant-read thermometer inserted into the thickest part should register 145°F.
9. Transfer to a cutting board and slice against the grain, ¼" thick, to serve.
Nutrition Info: Calories: 1286, Sodium: 2875 mg, Dietary Fiber: 1g, Fat: 84.8g, Carbs: 58.3g Protein: 68.7g

265.Roasted Pork Tenderloin

Servings: 4
Cooking Time: 1 Hour
Ingredients:
- 1 (3-pound) pork tenderloin
- 2 tablespoons extra-virgin olive oil
- 2 garlic cloves, minced
- 1 teaspoon dried basil
- 1 teaspoon dried oregano
- 1 teaspoon dried thyme
- Salt
- Pepper

Directions:
1. Preparing the Ingredients.
2. Drizzle the pork tenderloin with the olive oil.
3. Rub the garlic, basil, oregano, thyme, and salt and pepper to taste all over the tenderloin.
4. Bring the griddle grill to high heat. When the griddle is hot, place the tenderloin and cook for 45 Minutes.
5. Use a meat thermometer to test for doneness. Flip the pork tenderloin. Cook for an additional 15 Minutes.
6. Remove the cooked pork and allow it to rest for 10 Minutes before cutting.
Nutrition Info: (Per Serving): CALORIES: 283; FAT: 10G; PROTEIN:48G

266.Herb-crusted Mediterranean Pork Tenderloin

Servings: 4
Cooking Time: 30 Minutes
Ingredients:
- 1 pound pork tenderloin
- 1 tablespoon olive oil
- 2 teaspoons dried oregano
- 3/4 teaspoon lemon pepper
- 1 teaspoon garlic powder
- ¼ cup parmesan cheese, grated
- 3 tablespoons olive tapenade

Directions:
1. Place pork on a large piece of plastic wrap.
2. Rub tenderloin with oil, and sprinkle oregano, garlic powder, and lemon pepper evenly over entire tenderloin.
3. Wrap tightly in the plastic wrap and refrigerate for 2 hours.
4. Preheat griddle to medium-high heat.
5. Transfer pork to cutting board, remove plastic wrap, and make a lengthwise cut through center of tenderloin, opening meat so it lies flat, but do not cut all the way through.
6. Combine tapenade and parmesan in a small mixing bowl; rub into the center of the tenderloin and fold meat back together.
7. Tie together with twine in 2-inch intervals.
8. Sear tenderloin for 20 minutes, turning tenderloin once during grilling, or until internal temperature reaches 145°F.
9. Transfer tenderloin to cutting board.
10. Tent with foil; let rest for 10 minutes.

11. Remove string and cut into 1/4-inch-thick slices and serve.
Nutrition Info: Calories: 413 Sodium: 1279 mg, Dietary Fiber: 0.5g, Fat: 30.5g, Carbs: 2.4g Protein: 31.4g

267.Pomegranate-honey Pork Tenderloin

Servings: 4
Cooking Time: 20 Minutes
Ingredients:
- Salt and pepper
- 2 tablespoons honey
- 1 tablespoon pomegranate molasses
- 2 teaspoons soy sauce
- 1 teaspoon sugar
- Juice of ½ lime

Directions:
1. Preparing the Ingredients
2. Pat the meat dry with paper towels. Sprinkle with salt and pepper on all sides. Whisk the honey, pomegranate molasses, soy sauce, sugar, and lime juice in a small bowl, taste, and adjust the seasoning with salt.
3. Bring the griddle grill to high heat. When the griddle is hot, put the tenderloin on the griddle. Turn the pork, brush the seared side with the glaze, and let the other side for 10 Minutes until the internal temperature at the thickest point is 135° to 140°F.
4. When the pork is done, transfer it to a cutting board, and let rest until the internal temperature rises to 145°F. Cut across into slices and serve.

268.Pork Tenderloin

Servings: 6
Cooking Time: 25 Minutes
Ingredients:
- pork tenderloin
- olive oil
- salt and pepper to taste

Directions:
1. Remove the silver skin and fat from the pork tenderloin and trim to a similar thickness.
2. Brush with olive oil and sprinkle with salt and pepper.
3. Heat up the griddle grill to high, and cook for 3–4 minutes per side or until the meat removes easily from the grill.
4. Remove the tenderloins from the grill and let them relax for several minutes.
5. Turn the griddle grill to medium and return the tenderloins to the grill. Cook for 15–20 minutes or until the temperature is 145 degrees.

6. Remove the tenderloins from the grill, and let them relax for several minutes before serving.
Nutrition Info: (Per serving): Calories: 122, Fat: 3g, Carbs: 8g, Protein: 22g

269.Steak & Mushrooms

Servings: 4
Cooking Time: 15 Minutes
Ingredients:
- 1 lb steaks, cut into 1-inch cubes
- 8 oz mushrooms, halved
- 1/2 tsp garlic powder
- 1 tsp Worcestershire sauce
- 2 tbsp olive oil
- Pepper
- Salt

Directions:
1. Add steak cubes and remaining ingredients into the bowl and toss well.
2. Preheat the griddle to high heat.
3. Transfer meat mixture onto the hot griddle top and stir fry until meat is completely cooked.
4. Serve and enjoy.
Nutrition Info: (Per Serving): Calories 300 ;Fat 12 g ;Carbohydrates 2.4 g ;Sugar 1.3 g ;Protein 42.8 g ;Cholesterol 102 mg

270.Caprese Grilled Filet Mignon

Servings: 4
Cooking Time: 10 Minutes
Ingredients:
- 4 (6 ounce) filets
- 1 teaspoon garlic salt
- Italian Olive oil
- 2 roma tomatoes, sliced
- 4 ounces fresh buffalo mozzarella, cut into four slices
- 8 fresh basil leaves
- Balsamic vinegar glaze, for drizzling
- Sea salt, for seasoning
- Fresh ground pepper

Directions:
1. Lightly brush each filet, on all sides, with olive oil and rub with garlic salt.
2. Preheat griddle to high. Place steaks on griddle, reduce heat to medium, tent with foil and cook for 5 minutes.
3. Flip, re-tent, and cook for an additional 5 minutes; during the last 2 minutes of grilling top each with a slice of mozzarella.
4. Remove steaks from the griddle and top each with a few tomato slices, 2 basil leafs.

5. Drizzle with balsamic, sprinkle with sea salt and black pepper and serve.
Nutrition Info: Calories: 406, Sodium: 688 mg, Dietary Fiber: 0.8g, Fat: 21.8g, Carbs: 7.2g Protein: 45.1g

271.Ranch Pork Chops

Servings: 6
Cooking Time: 15 Minutes
Ingredients:
- 6 pork chops, boneless
- 2 tbsp ranch seasoning, homemade
- 1/4 cup olive oil
- 1 tsp dried parsley
- Pepper
- Salt

Directions:
1. Preheat the griddle to high heat.
2. Spray griddle top with cooking spray.
3. Season pork chops with pepper and salt and place onto the hot griddle top.
4. Mix together olive oil, parsley, and ranch seasoning.
5. Spoon oil mixtures over pork chops and cook pork chops for 5-7 minutes per side.
6. Serve and enjoy.
Nutrition Info: (Per Serving): Calories 328 ;Fat 28.3 g ;Carbohydrates 0 g ;Sugar 0 g ;Protein 18 g ;Cholesterol 69 mg

272.Filets Mignons With Gaucho Seasonings

Servings: 4
Cooking Time: 10 Minutes
Ingredients:
- 1 clove garlic, minced
- Coarse salt (kosher or sea) and freshly ground black pepper
- 1 tablespoon dried oregano
- 1 teaspoon dried sage
- 2 tablespoons distilled white vinegar or wine vinegar, or more to taste
- 2 tablespoons extra-virgin olive oil
- 2 tablespoons boiling water
- 1½ pounds filet mignon

Directions:

1. Preparing the Ingredients
2. Place the garlic, 1 teaspoon of salt, and ½ teaspoon of pepper in a small, heatproof bowl and mash to a paste with the back of a spoon. Add the oregano and sage and continue mashing until combined. Add the vinegar and whisk to mix. Whisk in the olive oil, followed by the boiling water. Taste for seasoning, adding more salt, pepper, and/or vinegar as necessary; the sauce should be highly seasoned. Season the fillets with salt and pepper.
3. Turn control knob to the high position. Oil the griddle and allow it to heat until the oil is shimmering but not smoking. Add the filets to the Griddle. After 4 Minutes, flip the filets and continue cooking for an additional 4 Minutes, or until the filets' internal temperature reads 125°F on a food thermometer. Remove the filets from the griddle; they will continue to cook (called carry-over cooking) to a food-safe temperature even after you've removed them from the grill.
4. Let the filets rest for a total of 10 Minutes; this allows the natural juices to redistribute into the steak.

273.Pork Baby Back Ribs

Servings: 4
Cooking Time: 2 Hours
Ingredients:
- 2 lbs. baby back ribs
- olive oil
- salt and pepper to taste
- BBQ sauce

Directions:
1. Remove the membrane from the bone side of the ribs. Coat with olive oil and sprinkle with salt and pepper. Let stand for 10 minutes.
2. Heat up the griddle grill to medium, and place the ribs bone side to the heat. Cook for 1.5 hours or until the temperature is 190–195 degrees.
3. Remove the ribs from the grill and let them relax for 30 minutes.
4. Brush the ribs with BBQ sauce, and place on a hot grill for 2–3 minutes to set the sauce before serving.
Nutrition Info: (Per serving):calories 290; fats 20g; carbohydrates 5g; Protein 23g

274.Delicious Beef Kebabs

Servings: 4
Cooking Time: 10 Minutes
Ingredients:
- 1 lb beef chuck ribs, cut into 1-inch pieces
- 1/2 onion, cut into 1-inch pieces
- 1 bell pepper, cut into 1-inch pieces
- 2 tbsp soy sauce
- 1/3 cup sour cream

Directions:
1. Add meat, soy sauce, and sour cream into the bowl and mix well.
2. Cover and place in the refrigerator overnight.
3. Thread marinated meat, onion, and bell peppers pieces onto the skewers.
4. Preheat the griddle to high heat.
5. Spray griddle top with cooking spray.
6. Place skewers onto the hot griddle top and cook until vegetables are tender and meat is completely cooked.
7. Serve and enjoy.

Nutrition Info: (Per Serving): Calories 370 ;Fat 30.2 g ;Carbohydrates 5 g ;Sugar 2.3 g ;Protein 20.6 g ;Cholesterol 84 mg

275.Beef Dill Patties

Servings: 4
Cooking Time: 12 Minutes
Ingredients:
- 1 lb ground beef
- 1/8 tsp dried dill
- 1/2 tsp paprika
- 1/2 tsp dried dill
- 1/2 tsp onion powder
- 1/2 tsp garlic powder
- 2 tsp dried parsley
- Pepper
- Salt

Directions:
1. Add all ingredients into the large bowl and mix until well combined.
2. Preheat the griddle to medium-low heat.
3. Spray griddle top with cooking spray.
4. Make four even shape patties from meat mixture and place onto the hot griddle top and cook until golden brown from both sides.
5. Serve and enjoy.

Nutrition Info: (Per Serving): Calories 215 ;Fat 7.1 g ;Carbohydrates 0.7 g ;Sugar 0.2 g ;Protein 35 g ;Cholesterol 101 mg

276.Spicy Soy Flank Steak

Servings: 4
Cooking Time: 5 Minutes
Ingredients:
- SPICY SOY SAUCE
- 1 tablespoon olive oil
- 1 tablespoon minced garlic
- 1 tablespoon minced fresh ginger
- ½ cup low-sodium soy sauce
- 2 tablespoons dark brown sugar
- ½ teaspoon red pepper flakes
- Heat the olive oil in a small saucepan over medium heat. Add the garlic and ginger and, stirring frequently, cook until the garlic begins to brown, about 2 Minutes. Add the soy sauce, sugar, and red pepper flakes and bring to a simmer. Cook, stirring occasionally, until a thick glaze forms, about 10 Minutes. (The sauce can be cooled, covered, and refrigerated overnight. Reheat before serving.)
- FLANKSTEAK
- 1½ pounds flank steak, about 1 inch thick
- ¼ teaspoon salt
- ½ teaspoon freshly ground black pepper
- 1 lime, cut into wedges

Directions:
1. Preparing the Ingredients
2. Pour half of the spicy soy sauce into a small bowl to use as a glaze. Put the remaining sauce aside.
3. Season the steak on both sides with the salt and pepper. Brush both sides of the steak with some of the sauce from the small bowl.
4. Turn control knob to the high position, when the griddle is hot, add cooking oil, and when it begins to shimmer, grill the steak for 2 Minutes, then brush the top of the steak with the rest of the sauce in the bowl. Grill for about 3 Minutes more for medium-rare. It should have grill marks and feel fairly firm to the touch. Let the steak rest on a cutting board for about 5 Minutes before slicing, thinly, across the grain.
5. Divide the slices among 4 plates and drizzle with a spoonful of the reserved sauce. Squeeze some lime juice over each portion and serve immediately.

Nutrition Info: (Per Serving): CALORIES:350; FAT: 16G; PROTEIN:38G

277.Pork Chops With Greek Oregano

Servings: 4
Cooking Time: 6 Minutes
Ingredients:
- 4 boneless pork loin chops (each about ¼ to ½ inch thick; about 1½ pounds total
- 1 to 2 cloves garlic, minced
- 1 teaspoon coarse salt (kosher or sea), or more to taste
- ¼ cup red wine vinegar, or more to taste
- ½ teaspoon finely grated lemon zest
- 2 tablespoons fresh lemon juice
- 1 cup extra-virgin olive oil (preferably Greek)
- 2 teaspoons dried Greek oregano
- ½ teaspoon cracked black peppercorns

Directions:
1. Preparing the Ingredients
2. Arrange the pork chops in a single layer in a baking dish or roasting pan.
3. Place the garlic and salt in a mixing bowl and mash with the back of a spoon. Add the wine vinegar, lemon zest, and lemon juice and whisk until the salt dissolves. Gradually whisk in the olive oil, oregano, and peppercorns. Taste for seasoning, adding more salt and/or vinegar as necessary; the marinade should be highly seasoned.
4. Pour ½ cup of the marinade over the pork, turning the chops to coat both sides evenly. Pour ¼ cup of the marinade into a small nonreactive bowl and set aside to use for basting. Pour the rest of the marinade into a nonreactive bowl and set aside for serving. Let the chops marinate in the refrigerator, covered, for 1 to 2 hours.
5. Drain the pork chops well and discard the marinade.
6. Bring the griddle grill to high heat. When the griddle is hot, place the pork chops on the hot griddle. The chops will be done after cooking 4 to 6 Minutes. You will need to turn the chops so that you can baste both sides; use the baste sparingly.
7. To test for doneness, use the poke method; the meat should be firm but gently yielding. If desired, rotate each chop a quarter turn after 1½ Minutes to create a handsome crosshatch of grill marks.

8. Stir the ¼ cup of reserved marinade with a fork to recombine and use it to baste the chops as they grill (apply it only to cooked meat, not raw, to avoid cross-contamination).
9. Transfer the pork chops to a platter or plates. Stir the remaining marinade with a fork, spoon it over the chops, and serve at once.

278.Tuscan Pork Chops

Servings: 4
Cooking Time: 15 Minutes
Ingredients:
- 1/4 cup all-purpose flour
- 1 teaspoon salt
- 3/4 teaspoons seasoned pepper
- 4 (1-inch-thick) boneless pork chops
- 1 tablespoon olive oil
- 3 to 4 garlic cloves
- 1/3 cup balsamic vinegar
- 1/3 cup chicken broth
- 3 plum tomatoes, seeded and diced
- tablespoons capers

Directions:
1. Preparing the Ingredients.
2. 1 Combine flour, salt, and pepper
3. Press pork chops into flour mixture on both sides until evenly covered.
4. 2 Bring the griddle grill to high heat. When the griddle is hot, cook at 360 degrees for 14 Minutes, flipping half way through.
5. While the pork chops cook, warm olive oil in a medium skillet.
6. Add garlic and sauté for 1 minute; then mix in vinegar and chicken broth.
7. Add capers and tomatoes and turn to high heat.
8. Bring the sauce to a boil, stirring regularly, then add pork chops, cooking for one minute.
9. Remove from heat and cover for about 5 Minutes to allow the pork to absorb some of the sauce; serve hot.

Nutrition Info: (Per Serving): CALORIES: 349; FAT: 23G; PROTEIN:20G; FIBER:1.5G

279.Korean Spicy Pork

Servings: 4
Cooking Time: 10 Minutes

Ingredients:

- 2 Lbs. Pork, Cut Into ⅛-Inch Slices
- 1/2 Cup Soy Sauce
- 5 Cloves Garlic, Minced
- 3 Tbsp. Minced Green Onion
- 1 Yellow Onion, Sliced
- 2 Tbsp. Sesame Seeds
- 3 Tsp. Black Pepper
- 1/2 Cup Brown Sugar
- 3 Tbsp. Gochujang (Korean Red Chili Paste)

Directions:

1. Mix all the ingredients together in a covered glass bowl or resealable bag and refrigerate for several hours to overnight.
2. Heat the griddle grill to high, and grill the pork for 2–3 minutes per side until it is cooked through.
3. Serve immediately on rice or lettuce leaves with soy and/or kimchi.

Nutrition Info: (Per serving): Calories: 120, Fats: 5g, Protein: 12g, carbs

280.Spicy Cajun Pork Chops

Servings: 4
Cooking Time: 15 Minutes
Ingredients:

- 4 pork chops
- 1 tablespoon paprika
- 1/2 teaspoon ground cumin
- 1/2 teaspoon dried sage
- 1/2 teaspoon salt
- 1/2 teaspoon black pepper
- 1/2 teaspoon garlic powder
- 1/4 teaspoon cayenne pepper
- 1 tablespoon butter
- 1 tablespoon vegetable oil

Directions:

1. In a medium bowl, combine the paprika, cumin, sage, salt, pepper, garlic, and cayenne pepper.
2. Heat your griddle to medium-high heat and add the butter and oil.
3. Rub the pork chops with a generous amount of the seasoning rub.
4. Place the chops on the griddle and cook for 4 to 5 minutes. Turn the pork chops and continue cooking an additional 4 minutes.
5. Remove the pork chops from the griddle and allow to rest 5 minutes before serving.

Nutrition Info: Calories: 320, Sodium: 368 mg, Dietary Fiber: 0.8g, Fat: 26.5g, Carbs:1.6g Protein: 18.4g

281.Tuscan-style Steak With Crispy Potatoes

Servings: 4
Cooking Time: 35 Minutes
Ingredients:

- 2 bone-in porterhouse steaks
- 1 1/2 lb. small potatoes, like Yukon Gold, scrubbed but skins left on, halved
- 4 tablespoons extra-virgin olive oil, divided
- Sea salt and freshly ground pepper, to taste
- 2 teaspoons red wine, like Sangiovese or Montepulciano
- 1 teaspoon balsamic vinegar
- pinch red pepper flakes
- 3 fresh rosemary sprigs, needles removed (discard stems)

Directions:

1. Add potatoes to a large pot and cover with water, bring to a boil over high heat, then reduce the heat to medium-high and cook until the potatoes are almost tender, about 10 minutes. Drain, add to a medium mixing bowl, coat with 2 tablespoons olive oil, and set aside.
2. Preheat griddle to medium heat.
3. Whisk 2 tablespoons olive oil, rosemary, red wine, vinegar, and pepper flakes; add steaks to marinade and set aside until ready to cook.
4. Sprinkle potatoes with salt and pepper.
5. Add steaks to one side of the griddle and potatoes to the other.
6. Cook steak for 5 minutes, flip and 4 minutes on the other side for medium rare.
7. Add the potatoes to cook for 5 minutes.
8. Transfer steaks to a cutting board and tent with aluminum foil and let rest for 5 minutes while potatoes are cooking.
9. Divide each steak into 2 pieces and divide among 4 dinner plates. Spoon some potatoes around the steak and serve hot!

Nutrition Info: Calories:366, Sodium: 153 mg, Dietary Fiber: 4.5g, Fat: 23.3g, Carbs: 27.3g Protein: 13.4g

282. Breaded Steaks With Parmesan And Garlic

Servings: 2
Cooking Time: 8 Minutes
Ingredients:
- Good-quality vegetable oil for the grates
- 1 cup dry bread crumbs
- ½ cup freshly grated Parmesan cheese
- ¼ cup chopped fresh parsley
- 2 tablespoons minced garlic
- ½ teaspoon salt
- ½ teaspoon black pepper
- 1½ pounds boneless strip, rib-eye, or sirloin steaks (½ to ¾ inch thick)
- 2 tablespoons good-quality olive oil
- Lemon wedges for serving

Directions:
1. Preparing the Ingredients
2. Combine the bread crumbs, Parmesan, parsley, garlic, salt, and pepper on a large plate.
3. Using a meat mallet or rolling pin, pound the steaks to a thickness of ½ inch or less. Brush both sides with the olive oil, then dredge in the bread crumbs, pressing to coat them completely.
4. Turn control knob to the high position, when the griddle is hot, add cooking oil, and when it begins to shimmer put the steaks on the griddle, and cook for 8 Minutes for medium-rare. Flip and sear for an additional 1 to 3 Minutes, based on your desired doneness.
5. Transfer to a cutting board and let rest 5 to 10 Minutes, continuing to check the temperature with an instant-read thermometer. (Or nick with a small knife and peek inside.) Cut into ½- to 1-inch slices, transfer to a platter, pour over any accumulated juices, and serve with lemon wedges.

283. Beef Ribeye Steak

Servings: 4
Cooking Time: 10 Minutes
Ingredients:
- 4 (8-ounce) ribeye steaks
- 1 tablespoon McCormick Grill Mates Montreal Steak Seasoning
- Salt
- Pepper

Directions:
1. Preparing the Ingredients.
2. Season the steaks with the steak seasoning and salt and pepper to taste.
3. Turn control knob to the high position. Oil the griddle and allow it to heat until the oil is shimmering but not smoking. Place 2 steaks in the grill grate. Cook for 4 Minutes and flip the steaks.
4. Cook for an additional 4 to 5 Minutes. Check for doneness to determine how much additional cook time is need. Remove the cooked steaks from the grill, then repeat steps for the remaining 2 steaks. Cool before serving.

Nutrition Info: (Per Serving): CALORIES: 293; FAT: 22G; PROTEIN:23G; FIBER:0G

FISH & SEAFOOD RECIPES

284.Salmon Zucchini Patties

Servings: 6
Cooking Time: 10 Minutes
Ingredients:
- 2 eggs
- 1 1/2 lbs salmon, cooked
- 2 cups zucchini, shredded
- 2 tbsp onion, minced
- 1/4 cup fresh cilantro, chopped
- 1/4 cup olive oil
- 3/4 cup almond flour
- 3 tbsp fresh lime juice
- 2 tbsp jalapeno, minced
- 2 tsp salt

Directions:
1. Add salmon, lime juice, cilantro, zucchini, jalapenos, onion, eggs, and salt into the food processor and process until the mixture is combined.
2. Add almond flour to a shallow dish.
3. Preheat the griddle to high heat. Add oil to griddle.
4. Take 1/4 cup salmon mixture and form patties, coat patties with almond flour then place onto the hot griddle top and cook for 5 minutes per side.
5. Serve and enjoy.

Nutrition Info: (Per Serving): Calories 330 ;Fat 24 g ;Carbohydrates 5 g ;Sugar 1.5 g ;Protein 27.4 g ;Cholesterol 105 mg

285.Honey-lime Tilapia And Corn Foil Pack

Servings: 4
Cooking Time: 10 Minutes
Ingredients:
- 4 fillets tilapia
- 2 tablespoons honey
- 4 limes, thinly sliced
- 2 ears corn, shucked
- 2 tablespoons fresh cilantro leaves
- 1/4 cup olive oil
- Kosher salt
- Freshly ground black pepper

Directions:
1. Preheat griddle to high.
2. Cut 4 squares of foil about 12" long.
3. Top each piece of foil with a piece of tilapia.
4. Brush tilapia with honey and top with lime, corn and cilantro.
5. Drizzle with olive oil and season with sea salt and pepper.
6. Cook until tilapia is cooked through and corn tender, about 15 minutes.

Nutrition Info: Calories: 319, Sodium: 92 mg, Dietary Fiber: 4g, Fat: 14.7g, Carbs: 30.3g Protein: 24g

286."barbecued" Salmon

Servings: 4
Cooking Time: 5 Minutes
Ingredients:
- 4 pieces skinless salmon fillet (each about 6 ounces)
- 2 tablespoons Basic Barbecue Rub
- 2 tablespoons olive oil
- 1 teaspoon liquid smoke
- BARBECUE VINAIGRETTE
- 1 tablespoon red barbecue sauce
- 1 tablespoon fresh lemon juice
- 3 tablespoons olive oil
- 1 tablespoon very finely diced sweet onion
- 1 tablespoon very finely diced seeded tomato
- 1 tablespoon very finely diced green bell pepper
- Coarse salt (kosher or sea) and freshly ground black pepper

Directions:
1. Preparing the Ingredients
2. Run your fingers over the fish fillets, feeling for bones. Using needle-nose pliers or tweezers, pull out any you find. Rinse the fish under cold running water, then blot it dry with paper towels. Sprinkle the barbecue rub all over the fish, patting it on with your fingertips. Let the fish cure at room temperature for 10 Minutes.
3. Place the olive oil and liquid smoke in a small bowl and stir with a fork. Set the basting mixture aside.
4. Bring the griddle grill to high heat. Oil the griddle. Place the fish on the hot griddle grill. The fish will be cooked through after 3 to 5 Minutes (if you prefer it pink in the center, cook it a minute or so less). You will need to turn the fish so that you can baste both sides until it is just cooked through. To test for doneness, press the fish with your finger; it should break into clean flakes. Start basting the fish with the olive oil mixture after 1 minute and baste both sides at least twice.
5. Transfer the fish to a platter or plates. Spoon the Barbecue Vinaigrette on top, if using, and serve at once.
6. BARBECUE VINAIGRETTE
7. Place the barbecue sauce in a small nonreactive bowl. Gradually whisk in 2 tablespoons of water and the lemon juice, olive oil, onion, tomato, and bell pepper. Season with salt and pepper to taste. The

sauce is best made no more than an hour before serving.

287.Shrimp

Servings: 4
Cooking Time: 5 Minutes
Ingredients:
- Large Raw Shrimp, Peeled And Mud Vein Removed
- Olive Oil
- Garlic Salt To Taste
- Fresh Lime Juice

Directions:
1. Preheat the griddle grill to high.
2. Place the shrimp on the skewers through the center in the same direction.
3. Brush with olive oil and sprinkle with garlic salt.
4. Place the skewers on the grill and cook for 2 minutes on each side or until the half toward the heat has turned pink and white.
5. Drizzle with the lime juice, and grill a few seconds per side.
6. Remove from heat and serve immediately.

Nutrition Info: (Per serving):Calories 101, Fat 1.4g, carbs 6g, protein 10g

288.Paprika Garlic Shrimp

Servings: 4
Cooking Time: 5 Minutes
Ingredients:
- 1 lb shrimp, peeled and cleaned
- 5 garlic cloves, chopped
- 2 tbsp olive oil
- 1 tbsp fresh parsley, chopped
- 1 tsp paprika
- 2 tbsp butter
- 1/2 tsp sea salt

Directions:
1. Add shrimp, 1 tbsp oil, garlic, and salt in a large bowl and toss well and place in the refrigerator for 1 hour.
2. Preheat the griddle to high heat.
3. Add remaining oil and butter on the hot griddle top.
4. Once butter is melted then add marinated shrimp and paprika and stir constantly for 2-3 minutes or until shrimp is cooked.
5. Garnish with parsley and serve.

Nutrition Info: (Per Serving): Calories 253 ;Fat 15 g ;Carbohydrates 3.3 g ;Sugar 0.1 g ;Protein 26.2 g ;Cholesterol 254 mg

289.Lump Crab Cakes

Servings: 4
Cooking Time: 15 Minutes
Ingredients:
- 1 lb lump crab meat
- 1/2 cup panko breadcrumbs
- 1/3 cup mayonnaise
- 1 egg, beaten
- 2 tablespoons dijon mustard
- 2 teaspoons Worcestershire sauce
- 1/2 teaspoon paprika
- 1/2 teaspoon salt
- 1/4 teaspoon black pepper
- 3 tablespoons vegetable oil

Directions:
1. Preheat griddle to medium heat.
2. In a large bowl, combine the crab, breadcrumbs, mayo, egg, mustard Worcestershire sauce, paprika, salt and pepper. Mix well to combine.
3. Form the crab mixture into 4 large balls and flatten them slightly.
4. Add the oil to the griddle and cook the crab cakes for approximately 5 minutes per side or until browned and crispy. Serve immediately.

Nutrition Info: Calories: 282, Sodium: 1205 mg, Dietary Fiber: 0.6g, Fat: 27.4g, Carbs: 9.5g Protein: 18.8g

290.Coconut-rum Shrimp And Pineapple Skewers

Servings: 6
Cooking Time: 10 Minutes
Ingredients:
- ½ cup coconut milk
- ¼ cup dark or spiced rum
- ¼ cup fresh lime juice
- 1 teaspoon ras el hanout
- Salt and pepper
- 2 cloves garlic, chopped
- 2 pounds large or jumbo shrimp, peeled (and deveined if you like)
- 1 ripe pineapple, peeled, cored, and cut into 1½-inch cubes
- Lime wedges for serving

Directions:
1. Preparing the Ingredients
2. 1 Stir the coconut milk, rum, lime juice, ras el hanout, and garlic together in a large bowl. Add the shrimp and toss to coat completely. Marinate at room temperature while you prepare the grill, or cover and refrigerate for up to 1 hour.
3. If you're using bamboo or wooden skewers, soak them in water for 30 Minutes.

4.   2 Alternate the shrimp and pineapple cubes on skewers. Discard any remaining marinade. Turn control knob to the high position. Oil the griddle and allow it to heat. Put the skewers on the griddle and cook until the shrimp are opaque all the way through and the pineapple browns in spots10Minutes.Transfer the skewers to a platter and serve with lime wedges.

291.Bacon Wrapped Scallops

Servings: 4
Cooking Time: 4 Minutes
Ingredients:
- 12 large sea scallops, side muscle removed
- 8 slices of bacon
- 1 tablespoon vegetable oil
- 12 toothpicks

Directions:
1.   Heat your griddle to medium heat and cook the bacon until fat has rendered but bacon is still flexible. Remove bacon from the griddle and place on paper towels.
2.   Raise griddle heat to medium-high.
3.   Wrap each scallop with a half slice of bacon and skewer with a toothpick to keep the bacon in place.
4.   Place the scallops on the griddle and cook for 90 seconds per side. They should be lightly browned on both sides.
5.   Remove from the griddle and serve immediately.
Nutrition Info: Calories: 315, Sodium: 1023 mg, Dietary Fiber: 0g, Fat: 20g, Carbs:2.7g Protein: 29.2g

292.Spicy Lemon Butter Shrimp

Servings: 4
Cooking Time: 10 Minutes
Ingredients:
- 1 1/2 lbs shrimp, peeled and deveined
- 3 garlic cloves, minced
- 1 small onion, minced
- 1/2 cup butter
- 1 1/2 tbsp fresh parsley, chopped
- 1 tbsp fresh lemon juice
- 1/4 tsp red pepper flakes
- Pepper
- Salt

Directions:
1.   Preheat the griddle to high heat.
2.   Melt butter on the griddle top.
3.   Add garlic, onion, red chili flakes, pepper, and salt and stir for 2 minutes.
4.   Season shrimp with pepper and salt and thread onto skewers.
5.   Brush shrimp skewers with butter mixture.

6.   Place shrimp skewers on griddle top and cook until shrimp turns to pink, about 3-4 minutes.
7.   Transfer shrimp to the serving plate.
8.   Drizzle lemon juice over shrimp and garnish with parsley.
9.   Serve and enjoy.
Nutrition Info: (Per Serving): Calories 419 ;Fat 25 g ;Carbohydrates 5.2 g ;Sugar 0.9 g ;Protein 39.4 g ;Cholesterol 419 mg

293.Swordfish In Salmoriglio

Servings: 4
Cooking Time: 10 Minutes
Ingredients:
- ½ cup good-quality olive oil
- ¼ cup fresh lemon juice
- 2 tablespoons chopped fresh oregano
- 2 tablespoons chopped fresh parsley
- ¼ teaspoon red chile flakes, or more to taste
- 2 cloves garlic, minced
- Salt
- 1½ pounds 1-inch-thick swordfish steaks

Directions:
1.   Preparing the Ingredients
2.   Whisk the oil and lemon juice in a small bowl until it thickens. Stir in the oregano, parsley, red pepper, garlic, and salt to taste. Transfer 2 tablespoons of the sauce to a small bowl and brush the steaks with it on both sides.
3.   Bring the griddle grill to high heat. Oil the griddle and allow it to heat. Put the steaks and cook until the fish releases easily from the grates, 4 to 5 Minutes. Turn the steaks, and cook until they lose their translucence in the center, 4 to 5 Minutes; at that point, you should be able to insert a skewer or thin knife through the center with no resistance. Transfer the steaks to a platter, pour over the remaining salmoriglio, and serve.

294.Ahi Tuna

Servings: 2
Cooking Time: 13 Minutes
Ingredients:
- Ahi Steaks, Cut About 1.5 Inches Thick
- Soy Sauce
- Brown Sugar
- Toasted Sesame Seeds

Directions:
1.   Preheat the griddle grill to the highest setting.
2.   Drizzle the soy sauce followed by the brown sugar on both sides of the ahi steaks.
3.   Roll the steaks in the sesame seeds.
4.   Spray the grill with spray oil.

5. Grill the ahi steaks for 2–3 minutes per side.
6. Let the steaks relax for 5 minutes.
7. Slice thin and serve. Drizzle with more soy sauce if desired.
Nutrition Info: (Per serving):calories 120kcal, fat 13g, carbs 7g, Protein 6.8g

browned and cooked through. To test for doneness, press the fish with your finger; it should break into clean flakes.
6. Arrange the salmon on a platter or plates. Stir the remaining charmoula to recombine, then spoon it on top of the salmon.

295.Moroccan Salmon

Servings: 4
Cooking Time: 5 Minutes
Ingredients:
- ½ cup fresh cilantro leaves
- ½ cup fresh flat-leaf parsley leaves
- 2 cloves garlic, coarsely chopped
- 1 teaspoon sweet paprika
- ½ teaspoon coarse salt (kosher or sea), or more to taste
- ½ teaspoon freshly ground black pepper
- ½ teaspoon ground coriander
- ½ teaspoon ground cumin
- ½ teaspoon hot red pepper flakes, or more to taste
- 3 tablespoons fresh lemon juice, or more to taste
- ½ cup extra-virgin olive oil
- 4 pieces salmon fillet or salmon steaks (each 6 to 8 ounces)

Directions:
1. Preparing the Ingredients
2. Place the cilantro, parsley, garlic, paprika, salt, black pepper, coriander, cumin, and hot pepper flakes in a food processor and pulse the machine to finely chop. Add the lemon juice and process until a coarse purée forms. With the motor running, add the olive oil in a thin stream. Taste for seasoning, adding more salt, hot pepper flakes, and/or lemon juice as necessary; the charmoula should be highly seasoned.
3. If using salmon fillets, run your fingers over them, feeling for bones. Using needle-nose pliers or tweezers, pull out any you find (you will not need to do this with salmon steaks). Rinse the fish under cold running water, then blot it dry with paper towels. Pour a third of the charmoula over the bottom of a nonreactive baking dish just large enough to hold the salmon in one layer. Arrange the salmon pieces on top. Spoon half of the remaining charmoula over the fish, then set the rest of the charmoula aside. Let the salmon marinate in the refrigerator, covered, for 2 to 4 hours (the longer it marinates, the richer the flavor will be).
4. When ready to cook, drain the salmon and discard the marinade.
5. Bring the griddle grill to high heat. Oil the griddle, when is hot, place the salmon. The salmon will be done after cooking 3 to 5 Minutes until it is

296.Spiced Crab Legs

Servings: 4
Cooking Time: 5 Minutes
Ingredients:
- 4 lbs king crab legs, cooked
- 2 tablespoons chili oil

Directions:
1. Preheat griddle to high.
2. Brush both sides of crab legs with chili oil and place on grill. Tent with foil.
3. Cook 4 to 5 minutes, turning once.
4. Transfer to plates and serve with drawn butter.
Nutrition Info: Calories: 518, Sodium: 4857 mg, Dietary Fiber: 0g, Fat: 13.9g, Carbs: 0g Protein: 87.1g

297.Salmon Lime Burgers

Servings: 2
Cooking Time: 10 Minutes
Ingredients:
- 2 hamburger buns, sliced in half
- 1 tablespoon cilantro, fresh minced
- 1/8 teaspoon fresh ground pepper
- 1/2 lb. Salmon fillets, skinless, cubed
- 1/2 tablespoon grated lime zest
- 1/4 teaspoon sea salt, fine ground
- 1-1/2 garlic cloves, minced
- 1/2 tablespoon Dijon mustard
- 1-1/2 tablespoons shallots, finely chopped
- 1/2 tablespoon honey
- 1/2 tablespoon soy sauce

Directions:
1. Mix all of your ingredients in a mixing bowl, except the hamburger buns.
2. Make 2 burger patties that are 1/2-inch thick with this mixture.
3. Preheat your griddle grill on the medium temperature setting.
4. Once your grill is preheated, place the 2 patties on the grill.
5. Grill your patties for 5 minutes per side. Serve on warm buns and enjoy!
Nutrition Info: (Per serving):Calories 220, Fat: 15g, Protein: 16g, carbs 6g

298.Gremolata Swordfish Skewers

Servings: 4
Cooking Time: 10 Minutes
Ingredients:
- 1 1/2 lb. skinless swordfish fillet
- 2 teaspoons lemon zest
- 3 tablespoons lemon juice
- 1/2 cup finely chopped parsley
- 2 teaspoons garlic, minced
- 3/4 teaspoon sea salt
- 1/4 teaspoon black pepper
- 2 tablespoons extra-virgin olive oil, plus extra for serving
- 1/2 teaspoon red pepper flakes
- 3 lemons, cut into slices

Directions:
1. Preheat griddle to medium-high.
2. Combine lemon zest, parsley, garlic, 1/4 teaspoon of the salt, and pepper in a small bowl with a fork to make gremolata and set aside.
3. Mix swordfish pieces with reserved lemon juice, olive oil, red pepper flakes, and remaining salt.
4. Thread swordfish and lemon slices, alternating each, onto the metal skewers.
5. Grill skewers 8 to 10 minutes, flipping halfway through, or until fish is cooked through.
6. Place skewers on a serving platter and sprinkle with gremolata.
7. Drizzle with olive oil and serve.
Nutrition Info: Calories: 333, Sodium: 554 mg, Dietary Fiber: 0.5g, Fat: 16g, Carbs:1.6g Protein: 43.7g

299.Mussels With Pancetta Aïoli

Servings: 4
Cooking Time: 5 Minutes
Ingredients:
- ¾ cup mayonnaise
- 1 tablespoon minced garlic, or more to taste
- 1 4-ounce slice pancetta, chopped
- Salt and pepper
- 4 pounds mussels
- 8 thick slices Italian bread
- ¼ cup good-quality olive oil

Directions:
1. Preparing the Ingredients
2. 1 Whisk the mayonnaise and garlic together in a small bowl. Put the pancetta in a cold small skillet and turn the heat to low; cook, stirring occasionally, until most of the fat is rendered and the meat turns golden and crisp, about 5 Minutes. Drain on a paper towel, then stir into the mayonnaise along with 1 teaspoon of the rendered fat from the pan. Taste and add more garlic and some salt if you like. Cover and refrigerate until you're ready to serve. (You can make the aïoli up to several days ahead; refrigerate in an airtight container.)
3. Rinse the mussels and pull off any beards. Discard any that are broken or don't close when tapped.
4. Brush both sides of the bread slices with the oil.
5. Bring the griddle grill to high heat. Oil the griddle. Put the bread on the grill and toast, turning once, until it develops grill marks with some charring, 1 to 2 Minutes per side. Remove from the grill and keep warm.
6. Scatter the mussels onto the griddle, spreading them out so they are in a single layer. Cook for 3 Minutes. Transfer the open mussels to a large bowl with tongs. If any have not opened, leave them on the grill, and cook for another minute or 2, checking frequently and removing open mussels until they are all off the grill.
7. 2 Dollop the aïoli over the tops of the mussels and use a large spoon to turn the mussels over to coat them. Serve the mussels drizzled with their juices, either over (or alongside) the bread.

300.Grilled Honey, Garlic, And Ginger Shrimp

Servings: 5
Cooking Time: 5 Minutes
Ingredients:
- 2lb.extra-large shrimp, peeled and
- deveined
- ½ cup olive oil
- 2 cloves fresh garlic, minced
- ½ medium shallot, minced
- ¼ cup honey
- 4 tsp. ground ginger
- 1 tsp. dried dill

Directions:
1. Preparing the Ingredients
2. 1 Heat olive oil over medium heat and add shallot and garlic. Cook for 3–5 Minutes until shallot becomes translucent.
3. Add in remaining ingredients, minus the shrimp, and heat for 2–3 Minutes. Remove sauce from heat, divide in half, and let cool to room temperature.
4. Toss shrimp with half of sauce, coating thoroughly, and place on nonstick grill pan. The grill pan isn't a requirement; you can also use skewers, but you'll need one or the other, because shrimp tend to fall through the grates of a standard grill.
5. 2 Turn control knob to the high position. Oil the griddle and allow it to heat until the oil is shimmering but not smoking, allow shrimp to cook for 3 Minutes.

6. Turn shrimp and baste with remaining sauce, and allow to cook for 5 Minutes.
7. Remove from grill and serve hot.

301. Lemon Garlic Scallops

Servings: 2
Cooking Time: 5 Minutes
Ingredients:
- 1 lb frozen bay scallops, thawed, rinsed & pat dry
- 1 tsp garlic, minced
- 2 tbsp olive oil
- 1 tsp parsley, chopped
- 1 tsp lemon juice
- Pepper
- Salt

Directions:
1. Preheat the griddle to high heat.
2. Add oil to the griddle top.
3. Add garlic and sauté for 30 seconds.
4. Add scallops, lemon juice, pepper, and salt, and sauté until scallops turn opaque.
5. Garnish with parsley and serve.
Nutrition Info: (Per Serving): Calories 123 ;Fat 14 g ;Carbohydrates 0.6 g ;Sugar 0.1 g ;Protein 0.1 g ;Cholesterol 0 mg

302. Tuna With Fresh Tomato-basil Sauce

Servings: 4
Cooking Time: 20 Minutes
Ingredients:
- TOMATO-BASIL SAUCE
- 2 tablespoons olive oil
- 1 small yellow onion, diced
- ¼ teaspoon salt
- ½ pint cherry tomatoes, cut in half
- 2 tablespoons water
- ¼ cup fresh basil leaves, chopped
- TUNA
- 1 tablespoon olive oil
- 4 (6-ounce) tuna steaks, about 1 inch thick

Directions:
1. Preparing the Ingredients
2. In a medium saucepan, heat the olive oil over medium heat. Add the onion and salt. Cook, stirring frequently, until the onion is golden brown, 10 to 15 Minutes. Add the tomatoes and water and cook for approximately 5 to 7 Minutes, until the tomatoes have softened and wrinkled. (The sauce can be cooled, covered, and refrigerated overnight. Reheat before serving.) Stir in the basil just before serving.
3. Bring the griddle grill to high heat. Oil the griddle. Rub the olive oil over the tuna steaks. Grill for about 4 Minutes. To test for doneness, prod on edge of the tuna with a fork. The fish should flake, but the center will still be a bit rosy.
4. Spoon the tuna into 4 shallow bowls and top with the warm tomato-basil sauce.
Nutrition Info: (Per Serving): CALORIES: 289; FAT:12G; PROTEIN:40G; SUGAR:4G

303. Balsamic Salmon

Servings: 6
Cooking Time: 10 Minutes
Ingredients:
- 6 salmon fillets
- 5 tbsp balsamic vinaigrette
- 2 tbsp olive oil
- 1 1/2 tsp garlic powder
- Pepper
- Salt

Directions:
1. In a mixing bowl, add salmon, garlic powder, balsamic vinaigrette, pepper, and salt and mix well. Set aside.
2. Preheat the griddle to high heat.
3. Add oil to the hot griddle top.
4. Place salmon onto the griddle top and cook for 3-5 minutes on each side or until cooked through.
5. Serve and enjoy.
Nutrition Info: (Per Serving): Calories 328 ;Fat 20.7 g ;Carbohydrates 1.4 g ;Sugar 1 g ;Protein 34.7 g ;Cholesterol 78 mg

304. Grilled Salmon

Servings: 2
Cooking Time: 10 Minutes
Ingredients:
- 2 Salmon Fillets
- 1/2 Tsp Lemon Pepper
- 1/2 Tsp Garlic Powder
- Salt and Pepper
- 1/3 Cup Soy Sauce
- 1/3 Cup Sugar
- 1 Tbsp Olive Oil

Directions:
1. 1 Preparing the Ingredients. Season salmon fillets with lemon pepper, garlic powder and salt. In a shallow bowl, add a third cup of water and combine the olive oil, soy sauce and sugar. Place salmon the bowl and immerse in the sauce. Cover with cling film and allow to marinate in the refrigerator for at least an hour.

2.   2 Turn control knob to the high position. Oil the griddle and allow it to heat until the oil is shimmering but not smoking, place salmon and cook for 5 Minutes per side or more until the fish is tender. Serve with lemon wedges

305.Shrimp With Yogurt-herb Sauce

Servings: 4
Cooking Time: 10 Minutes
Ingredients:
- 4 scallions, trimmed and cut into pieces
- 2 cloves garlic, peeled
- 1 small bunch fresh parsley, thick stems removed (thin stems are fine)
- 1 cup yogurt
- Salt and pepper
- 2 pounds large or jumbo shrimp, peeled (and deveined if you like)
- Lemon wedges for serving

Directions:
1.   Preparing the Ingredients
2.   1 Put the scallions, garlic, parsley, and yogurt in a blender or food processor, sprinkle with salt and pepper, and purée until smooth. Transfer to a large bowl, add the shrimp, and toss to coat fully with the marinade. Marinate at room temperature while the grill heats up, or cover and refrigerate for up to several hours.
3.   2 Bring the griddle grill to high heat. Oil the griddle. Put the shrimp and cook until the shrimp are opaque all the way through, 6 to 10 Minutes, depending on their size. Discard any remaining marinade. Transfer to a platter and serve with lemon wedges.

306.Salmon

Servings: 4
Cooking Time: 15 Minutes
Ingredients:
- Boneless Salmon Fillets, Scaled
- Olive Oil
- Sea Salt And Pepper To Taste

Directions:
1.   Preheat the griddle grill to high.
2.   Drizzle the fillets with olive oil and season with sea salt and black pepper.
3.   Place on the griddle grill, and cook for 3 minutes per side.
4.   Turn the grill down to medium and continue grilling for several minutes until the fillet is homogeneous in color and white is beginning to appear on top of the fillet.

5.   Remove from heat, and let it rest for a few minutes before serving.
Nutrition Info: (Per serving):Calories 170kcal, Fat 8g, carbs 15g, Protein 26g

307.Garlic Butter Tilapia

Servings: 6
Cooking Time: 8 Minutes
Ingredients:
- 2 lbs tilapia fillets
- 1 tsp garlic powder
- 1/2 fresh lemon juice
- 1 tbsp butter, melted
- Pepper
- Salt

Directions:
1.   In a small bowl, combine together lemon juice, garlic powder, and butter and microwave for 10 seconds.
2.   Brush both the side of the fish fillet with lemon mixture. Season fillet with pepper and salt.
3.   Preheat the griddle to high heat.
4.   Spray griddle top with cooking spray.
5.   Place fillets on hot griddle top and cook for 4 minutes on each side.
6.   Serve and enjoy.
Nutrition Info: (Per Serving): Calories 143 ;Fat 3 g ;Carbohydrates 0.4 g ;Sugar 0.1 g ;Protein 28.2 g ;Cholesterol 79 mg

308.Spanish Shrimp

Servings: 4
Cooking Time: 3 Minutes
Ingredients:
- 1½ pounds shelled and deveined medium shrimp
- ½ cup olive oil
- 2 garlic cloves, minced
- ½ teaspoon salt
- ½ teaspoon red pepper flakes
- 1 lemon, cut into wedges

Directions:
1.   Preparing the Ingredients
2.   Rinse the shrimp and pat dry with paper towels. Combine the shrimp, olive oil, garlic, salt, and red pepper flakes in a medium bowl. Toss gently to combine. Cover with plastic wrap and then refrigerate for at least 30 Minutes or up to 2 hours.
3.   Bring the griddle grill to high heat, when the griddle is hot, Grill the shrimp for about 3 Minutes, until they are opaque and firm to the touch. Serve the shrimp immediately in 4 small bowls with the lemon wedges.

Nutrition Info: (Per Serving): CALORIES: 305; FAT:17 G; PROTEIN:35G

309.Pesto Pistachio Shrimp

Servings: 4
Cooking Time: 10 Minutes
Ingredients:
- 1-1/2 lb. Uncooked shrimp, peeled and deveined
- 2 tablespoons lemon juice
- 1/4 cup Parmesan cheese, shredded
- 1/4 teaspoon of sea salt
- 1/8 teaspoon black ground pepper
- 1/2 cup olive oil
- 1/2 cup parsley, fresh minced
- 1 garlic clove, peeled
- 1/3 cup pistachios, shelled
- 1/4 teaspoon grated lemon zest
- 3/4 cup arugula, fresh

Directions:
1. Begin by adding the olive oil, lemon zest, garlic clove, pistachios, parsley, arugula and lemon juice to a blender. Blend until smooth.
2. Add your Parmesan cheese, sea salt and pepper, then mix well.
3. Toss in your shrimp and allow to marinate in the fridge for 30 minutes.
4. Thread your shrimp onto skewers.
5. Preheat your griddle grill on the medium temperature setting.
6. Once preheated, add your skewers onto the grill and close lid.
7. Grill for 6 minutes. Rotate the skewers every 2 minutes. Cooking skewers in batches. Serve and enjoy!

Nutrition Info: (Per serving): Calories: 293, Fat: 16g, Carbs: 5.2g, Protein: 34.2g

310.Crisp-skin Salmon With Maple-ginger Glaze

Servings: 6
Cooking Time: 10 Minutes
Ingredients:
- 1 2-pound skin-on salmon fillet
- 1 tablespoon good-quality vegetable oil
- Salt and pepper
- ¼ cup maple syrup
- 1 tablespoon Dijon mustard
- 1 tablespoon minced fresh ginger

Directions:
1. Preparing the Ingredients

2. Pull any remaining pin bones from the salmon. With a sharp knife, score the skin in a crosshatch pattern.
3. Pat the fish dry with paper towels and put it on a large baking sheet. Brush the skin side with the oil, sprinkle with salt and pepper on both sides, and turn it skin side down. Put the maple syrup, mustard, and ginger in a small bowl and stir to combine. Brush the glaze over the top.
4. Bring the griddle grill to high heat, when the griddle is hot, put the salmon skin side down and cook, without turning, until the thickest part is as opaque as you like,10 Minutes; nick with a sharp knife and peek inside to check a couple of times. Transfer the salmon to a cutting board, cut into 4 or 6 pieces, and serve.

311.Whole Fish With Basil-orange Oil

Servings: 4
Cooking Time: 16 Minutes
Ingredients:
- ¼ cup good-quality olive oil, plus more for brushing the fish
- 2 cloves garlic, thinly sliced
- 1 orange
- 2 1½-pound or 4 12- to 16-ounce whole fish, scaled and gutted
- Salt and pepper
- 8–12 large sprigs fresh basil
- 2 tablespoons chopped fresh basil

Directions:
1. Preparing the Ingredients
2. Put the oil and garlic in a small saucepan or skillet over the lowest heat possible. When the garlic begins to sizzle, swirl the oil a bit, then turn the heat off; don't allow the garlic to brown.
3. Grate 2 teaspoons zest from the rind of the orange, then slice the orange thinly, removing any seeds.
4. Pat the fish dry with paper towels. Brush them on both sides with olive oil and sprinkle with salt and pepper on both sides and in the cavity. Divide the orange slices between the fish, overlapping them in the cavities. Put the basil sprigs on top of the orange slices and close the fish.
5. Turn control knob to the high position. Oil the griddle and allow it to heat. Put the fish on the griddle and cook until the skin browns and the fish release easily, 10 to 12 Minutes. Carefully turn the fish, using a second spatula to lower them back down to the grate and cook until a skewer or thin knife inserted at the thickest point easily pierces it all the way through, 4 to 6 Minutes. Transfer the fish to a platter.

6. Heat the oil and garlic over low heat. When the garlic begins to sizzle, stir in the orange zest and chopped basil and remove from the heat.
7. Remove the fillets from both sides of the fish by cutting horizontally between the flesh and the bones with a sharp knife and a spatula. Try to keep them intact, and remove as many bones as possible. Drizzle the warm orange-basil oil over the fillets and serve the carcass alongside if you like.

312.Lime Ginger Salmon

Servings: 5
Cooking Time: 10 Minutes
Ingredients:
- 1 teaspoon onion, finely chopped
- 1/4 teaspoon sea salt
- 1 teaspoon ginger root, fresh minced
- 1 tablespoon rice vinegar
- 1 garlic clove, minced
- 2 teaspoons sugar
- 1/8 cup lime juice
- 1 cucumber, peeled and chopped
- 1/6 cup cilantro, fresh chopped
- 1/4 teaspoon coriander, ground
- 1/4 teaspoon ground pepper
- Salmon:
- 5 (6-ounces) salmon fillets
- 1/4 teaspoon of sea salt
- 1/4 teaspoon freshly ground black pepper
- 1/6 cup ginger root, minced
- 1/2 tablespoon olive oil
- 1/2 tablespoon lime juice

Directions:
1. Begin by blending the first 11 ingredients in a blender until smooth.
2. Season your salmon fillets with olive oil, lime juice, ginger, salt and pepper.
3. Preheat your griddle grill to the medium temperature setting.
4. Once your grill is preheated, place 2 salmon fillets on the grill.
5. Grill it for 4 minutes per side.
6. Cook the remaining fillets in the same manner.
7. Serve salmon fillets with prepared sauce and enjoy!
Nutrition Info: (Per serving): Calories: 457 Fat: 19.1g Carbs; 18.9g Protein: 32.5g

313.Grilled Soy Salmon Fillets

Servings: 4
Cooking Time: 8 Minutes
Ingredients:

- 4 salmon fillets
- 1/4 teaspoon ground black pepper
- 1/2 teaspoon cayenne pepper
- 1/2 teaspoon salt
- 1 teaspoon onion powder
- 1 tablespoon fresh lemon juice
- 1/2 cup soy sauce
- 1/2 cup water
- 1 tablespoon honey
- 2 tablespoons extra-virgin olive oil

Directions:
1. Preparing the Ingredients.
2. 1 Firstly, pat the salmon fillets dry using kitchen towels. Season the salmon with black pepper, cayenne pepper, salt, and onion powder.
3. To make the marinade, combine together the lemon juice, soy sauce, water, honey, and olive oil. Marinate the salmon for at least 2 hours in your refrigerator.
4. 2 Bring the griddle grill to high heat. Oil the griddle. Arrange the fish fillets. Grill for 8 to 9 Minutes, or until salmon fillets are easily flaked with a fork.
5. Serve warm.

314.Seared Sea Scallops With Roasted Garlic And Dill Butter

Servings: 6
Cooking Time: 3 Minutes
Ingredients:
- 12–18 medium-sized scallops
- 1 tsp. kosher salt
- 1 lemon
- 2 Tbsp. roasted garlic and dill butter
- 2 tsp. olive oil

Directions:
1. Preparing the Ingredients
2. Rinse scallops in cold water and dry thoroughly with a paper towel.
3. Season scallops lightly with kosher salt.
4. Slice lemon into ¼-inch thick slices and remove seeds.
5. Melt in the cooking pot butter and olive oil in pan.
6. Gently place the scallops and lemon slices into the oil and butter.
7. Bring the griddle grill to high heat. Oil the griddle, and Sear for 90 seconds on each side. A nice crust will form on both sides of the scallop, with the middle remaining relatively opaque.
8. Serve hot.

315.Halibut Fillets With Spinach And Olives

Servings: 4
Cooking Time: 10 Minutes
Ingredients:
- 4 (6 ounce) halibut fillets
- 1/3 cup olive oil
- 4 cups baby spinach
- 1/4 cup lemon juice
- 2 ounces pitted black olives, halved
- 2 tablespoons flat leaf parsley, chopped
- 2 teaspoons fresh dill, chopped
- Lemon wedges, to serve

Directions:
1. Preheat griddle to medium heat.
2. Toss spinach with lemon juice in a mixing bowl and set aside.
3. Brush fish with olive oil and cook for 3-4 minutes per side, or until cooked through.
4. Remove from heat, cover with foil and let rest for 5 minutes.
5. Add remaining oil and cook spinach for 2 minutes, or until just wilted. Remove from heat.
6. Toss with olives and herbs, then transfer to serving plates with fish, and serve with lemon wedges.

Nutrition Info: Calories: 773, Sodium: 1112 mg, Dietary Fiber: 1.4g, Fat: 36.6g, Carbs: 2.9g Protein: 109.3g

316.Halibut

Servings: 4
Cooking Time: 7 Minutes
Ingredients:
- Halibut Fillets, Cut About 1 Inch Thick
- Olive Oil
- Sea Salt And Pepper
- Fresh Grated Parmesan Cheese
- Fresh Chopped Parsley
- Fresh Lemon Juice

Directions:
1. Brush the halibut fillets with the olive oil and sprinkle with the salt and pepper.
2. Preheat the griddle grill to high.
3. Spray the grill with spray oil, and immediately place the halibut on the heat.
4. Grill for 2 minutes per side.
5. Turn the grill down to medium, and grill for 2 minutes per side.
6. Sprinkle the halibut with the parmesan, and grill an additional minute before removing from the heat.
7. Sprinkle the fillets with parsley and lemon juice, and let it relax for 5 minutes before serving.

Nutrition Info: (Per serving):Calories 223, carbs 10g, Fat 5g, Protein 42g

317.Spicy Grilled Squid

Servings: 4
Cooking Time: 5 Minutes
Ingredients:
- 1 ½ lbs. Squid, prepared
- Olive oil
- For the marinade:
- 2 cloves garlic cloves, minced
- ½ teaspoon ginger, minced
- 3 tablespoons gochujang
- 3 tablespoons corn syrup
- 1 teaspoon yellow mustard
- 1 teaspoon soy sauce
- 2 teaspoons sesame oil
- 1 teaspoon sesame seeds
- 2 green onions, chopped

Directions:
1. Preheat griddle to medium high heat and brush with olive oil.
2. Add the squid and tentacles to the griddle and cook for 1 minute until the bottom looks firm and opaque.
3. Turn them over and cook for another minute; straighten out the body with tongs if it curls.
4. Baste with sauce on top of the squid and cook 2 additional minutes.
5. Flip and baste the other side, cook 1 minute until the sauce evaporates and the squid turns red and shiny.

Nutrition Info: Calories: 292, Sodium: 466 mg, Dietary Fiber: 2.7g, Fat: 8.6g, Carbs: 25.1g Protein: 27.8g

318.Salmon Skewers

Servings: 4
Cooking Time: 10 Minutes
Ingredients:
- 1 lb salmon fillets, cut into 1-inch cubes
- 2 tbsp soy sauce
- 1 tbsp toasted sesame seeds
- 1 lime zest
- 2 tsp olive oil
- 1 1/2 tbsp maple syrup
- 1 tsp ginger, crushed
- 1 lime juice

Directions:
1. In a bowl, mix together olive oil, soy sauce, lime zest, lime juice, maple syrup, and ginger.

2. Add salmon and stir to coat. Set aside for 10 minutes.
3. Preheat the griddle to high heat.
4. Slide marinated salmon pieces onto the skewers and cook on a hot griddle top for 8-10 minutes or until cooked through.
5. Sprinkle salmon skewers with sesame seeds and serve.

Nutrition Info: (Per Serving): Calories 209 ;Fat 10 g ;Carbohydrates 6.5 g ;Sugar 4.6 g ;Protein 22.9 g ;Cholesterol 50 mg

319.Mexican Shrimp Tacos

Servings: 4
Cooking Time: 10 Minutes
Ingredients:
- 2 lbs. medium shrimp, peeled and deveined
- 8 flour tortillas, warmed
- 1 bag cabbage slaw
- 1 cup salsa
- 1 cup Mexican crema
- For marinade:
- 2 tablespoons olive oil
- 1 tablespoon chili powder
- 1 tablespoon cumin
- 1 tablespoon garlic powder
- 1 tablespoon fresh lime juice
- ¼ teaspoon sea salt
- ⅛ teaspoon fresh ground pepper

Directions:
1. Preheat a griddle to medium-high.
2. Combine oil marinade in a large sealable plastic bag. Add shrimp and toss coat; let marinate in the refrigerator for 30 minutes.
3. Cook shrimp for 3 minutes, on each side, until cooked through.
4. Transfer to a plate.
5. Lay two tortillas on each plate. Evenly divide the shrimp, cabbage slaw, salsa in the middle of each tortilla.
6. Drizzle with Mexican crema and serve.

Nutrition Info: Calories: 400, Sodium: 92 mg, Dietary Fiber: 4g, Fat: 14.7g, Carbs: 30.3g Protein: 24g

320.Shrimp On The Barbie

Servings: 4
Cooking Time: 55 Minutes
Ingredients:
- 3 Lbs. Large Raw Shrimp, Peeled And Deveined
- 1/2 Lb. Butter, Melted
- 3 Cloves Garlic, Minced
- Zest And Juice Of 1 Lemon
- 2 Tsp. Sea Salt
- 2 Tsp. Black Pepper
- 1/4 Cup Grated Parmesan Cheese

Directions:
1. Place the shrimp on skewers.
2. Mix the remaining ingredients together and set in a bowl.
3. Heat the griddle grill to high and grill the shrimp, brushing with the butter mixture, for 2 minutes per side until they are cooked through. They will be solid in color with white and pink tones rather than blue and gray.
4. Serve with grilled summer vegetables, grilled yellow potatoes, or grilled corn (elote).

Nutrition Info: (Per serving):Calories 325, Fat 20g, carbs 8g, protein 13.7g

321.Greek Salmon Fillets

Servings: 2
Cooking Time: 6 Minutes
Ingredients:
- 2 salmon fillets
- 1 tbsp fresh basil, minced
- 1 tbsp butter, melted
- 1 tbsp fresh lemon juice
- 1/8 tsp salt

Directions:
1. Preheat the griddle to high heat.
2. In a small bowl, mix together lemon juice, basil, butter, and salt.
3. Brush salmon fillets with lemon mixture and place them on the hot griddle top.
4. Cook salmon for 2-3 minutes. Flip salmon and cook for 2-3 minutes more.
5. Serve and enjoy.

Nutrition Info: (Per Serving): Calories 290 ;Fat 16.8 g ;Carbohydrates 0.3 g ;Sugar 0.2 g ;Protein 34.7 g ;Cholesterol 46 mg

322.Scallops

Servings: 4
Cooking Time: 10 Minutes
Ingredients:
- Large Fresh Bay Scallops
- Real Butter, Melted
- Sea Salt And Pepper To Taste

Directions:
1. Preheat the griddle grill to high.
2. Melt the butter, and set it aside so that it is ready for later.
3. Season the scallops with salt and pepper.

4. Spray the grill with spray oil, and immediately place the scallops on the heat. Brush the tops with butter.
5. Grill for 3–4 minutes per side, brushing with the butter again after flipping. The scallops are ready to turn when they pull away easily from the grill.
6. Brush the scallops again with the butter, and grill for an additional thirty seconds per side.
7. Let the scallops relax for 5 minutes before serving.
Nutrition Info: (Per serving):Calories 1070, Carbs 240g, Fat 89g, Protein 77g

323.Italian Shrimp

Servings: 4
Cooking Time: 5 Minutes
Ingredients:
- 1 lb shrimp, deveined
- 1 tsp Italian seasoning
- 1 tsp paprika
- 1 1/2 tsp garlic, minced
- 1 stick butter
- 1 fresh lemon juice
- 1/4 tsp pepper
- 1/2 tsp salt
Directions:
1. Preheat the griddle to high heat.
2. Melt butter on the hot griddle top.
3. Add garlic and cook for 30 seconds.
4. Toss shrimp with paprika, Italian seasoning, pepper, and salt.
5. Add shrimp into the pan and cook for 2-3 minutes per side.
6. Drizzle lemon juice over shrimp.
7. Stir and serve.
Nutrition Info: (Per Serving): Calories 346 ;Fat 25 g ;Carbohydrates 2.6 g ;Sugar 0.2 g ;Protein 26.2 g ;Cholesterol 300 mg

324.Scallops With Lemony Salsa Verde

Servings: 2
Cooking Time: 5 Minutes
Ingredients:
- 1 tablespoon olive oil, plus more for grilling
- 12 large sea scallops, side muscle removed
- Sea salt, for seasoning
- For the Lemony Salsa Verde:
- ½ lemon, with peel, seeded and chopped
- 5 tomatillos, peeled and pulsed in a blender
- 1 small shallot, finely chopped
- 1 garlic clove, finely chopped
- ¼ cup olive oil

- ¾ cup finely chopped fresh parsley
- ½ cup finely chopped fresh cilantro
- ¼ cup chopped fresh chives
- ¼ teaspoon sea salt
- ¼ teaspoon black pepper
Directions:
1. Toss Lemony Salsa ingredients in a small mixing bowl and set aside.
2. Preheat griddle for medium-high and brush with olive oil.
3. Toss scallops with 1 tablespoon olive oil on a baking sheet and season with salt.
4. Add scallops to griddle, turning once after 45 seconds to 1 minute. Cook an additional 1 minute before removing from the griddle.
5. Serve scallops topped with Lemony Salsa Verde.
Nutrition Info: Calories: 267, Sodium: 541mg, Dietary Fiber: 3.1g, Fat: 9.6g, Carbs: 13.9g Protein: 32.4g

325.Blackened Salmon

Servings: 5
Cooking Time: 10 Minutes
Ingredients:
- 1 1/4 lbs salmon fillets
- 2 tbsp blackened seasoning
- 2 tbsp butter
Directions:
1. Season salmon fillets with blackened seasoning.
2. Preheat the griddle to high heat.
3. Melt butter on the griddle top.
4. Place salmon fillets onto the hot griddle top and cook for 4-5 minutes.
5. Turn salmon and cook for 4-5 minutes more.
6. Serve and enjoy.
Nutrition Info: (Per Serving): Calories 190 ;Fat 11 g ;Carbohydrates 0 g ;Sugar 0 g ;Protein 21.1 g ;Cholesterol 62 mg

326.Salt-and-pepper Fish Fillets Or Steaks

Servings: 4
Cooking Time: 11 Minutes
Ingredients:
- 1½ pounds fish fillets or steaks
- Good-quality olive oil for brushing the fish
- Salt and pepper
- Lemon wedges for serving
Directions:
1. Preparing the Ingredients
2. Pat the fillets or steaks dry with paper towels, then brush them with oil and season with salt and pepper on both sides.

3. Bring the griddle grill to high heat. Oil the griddle and allow it to heat. Put the fish skin side down (if it has skin) on the griddle, and cook until the bottoms brown and release easily, 5 to 7 Minutes. Carefully turn the fillets or steaks over, using a second spatula to keep them from breaking apart. Close the lid and cook until a skewer or thin knife inserted at the thickest point of the fish easily pierces it all the way through, 2 to 4 Minutes, depending on the fish and the thickness. Transfer to a platter and serve with lemon wedges.

327.Greek Salmon

Servings: 2
Cooking Time: 6 Minutes
Ingredients:
- 12 oz salmon, cut into two pieces
- 1 tsp Greek seasoning
- 1 tbsp olive oil
- 1/2 tsp lemon zest
- 1 garlic clove, minced
- Pepper
- Salt

Directions:
1. In a large bowl, mix olive oil, lemon zest, garlic, pepper, salt, and greek seasoning.
2. Add salmon in a bowl and coat well with marinade and set aside for 15 minutes.
3. Preheat the griddle to high heat.
4. Place marinated salmon on hot griddle top and cook for 2-3 minutes.
5. Turn salmon to the other side and cook for 2-3 minutes more.
6. Serve and enjoy.
Nutrition Info: (Per Serving): Calories 290 ;Fat 17.6 g ;Carbohydrates 1.4 g ;Sugar 0.1 g ;Protein 33.2 g ;Cholesterol 75 mg

328.Seafood Salad With Caper-shallot Vinaigrette

Servings: 5
Cooking Time: 30 Minutes
Ingredients:
- 1 pound firm white fish fillets
- 8 ounces sea scallops, trimmed of any tough connective tissue
- 8 ounces large shrimp, peeled
- ½ cup good-quality olive oil
- Salt and pepper
- 1 tablespoon white wine vinegar
- 1 tablespoon capers, drained and chopped
- 1 small shallot, minced

- 1 cup packed fresh parsley leaves, chopped
- Lemon wedges for serving

Directions:
1. Preparing the Ingredients
2. Pat the fish, scallops, and shrimp dry with paper towels, then coat with ¼ cup of the olive oil and sprinkle with salt and pepper.
3. Put the remaining ¼ cup oil, the vinegar, capers, and shallot in a small bowl; whisk to combine. Taste and add salt and pepper if you like.
4. Bring the griddle grill to high heat. Oil the griddle and allow it to heat until the oil is shimmering but not smoking. Put the scallops and cook for 10 Minutes until they're golden brown in spots. You want a good sear on the outside, with the center of the scallop still ever so slightly translucent. Transfer to a large serving bowl.
5. Put the shrimp on the griddle, and cook, turning once, until opaque all the way through, 10 Minutes. Transfer to the bowl.
6. Put the fish on the grill (skin side down, if it has skin), and cook until the bottoms brown and release easily, 6 to 7 Minutes. Carefully turn the fillets, using a second spatula to keep them from breaking apart. Cook until a skewer or sharp knife inserted at the thickest point of a fillet easily pierces it all the way through, 2 to 4 Minutes, depending on the thickness. Transfer to the bowl.
7. Add the parsley to the seafood and drizzle the vinaigrette over the top. Very gently toss the salad together, breaking the fish into bite-sized pieces as you do. Serve with the lemon wedges.

329.Grilled Prawns With Roasted Garlic And Dill Butter

Servings: 4
Cooking Time: 3 Minutes
Ingredients:
- 6 to 8 giant prawns
- 2 Tbsp. olive oil
- 1 tsp. sea salt
- 2 lemons, cut in half
- roasted garlic and dill butter

Directions:
1. Preparing the Ingredients
2. Using a sharp knife, slice prawns in half lengthwise from head to tail. Pull meat from shell, leaving the tail attached, and remove vein.
3. Rinse the prawn halves under cold water to remove the organs and internals from the head area.
4. Tuck meat back into shell and drizzle prawn halves with olive oil and sea salt.
5. Bring the griddle grill to high heat. Oil the griddle and allow it to heat. Place lemon halves, cut

side down, over direct heat, and grill till evenly charred.

6.   Place prawns over direct heat, meat side down, and grill for 2 to 3 Minutes, depending on the size of the prawns.

7.   Flip prawns to meat side up and top with garlic and dill butter. Cook an additional 3 Minutes, allowing the butter to melt on and around the meat inside the shell.

8.   Remove from grill and serve with charred lemon.

330. Spiced Snapper With Mango And Red Onion Salad

Servings: 4
Cooking Time: 20 Minutes
Ingredients:
- 2 red snappers, cleaned
- Sea salt
- ⅓ cup tandoori spice
- Olive oil, plus more for grill
- Extra-virgin olive oil, for drizzling
- Lime wedges, for serving
- For the salsa:
- 1 ripe but firm mango, peeled and chopped
- 1 small red onion, thinly sliced
- 1 bunch cilantro, coarsely chopped
- 3 tablespoons fresh lime juice

Directions:
1.   Toss mango, onion, cilantro, lime juice, and a big pinch of salt in a medium mixing bowl; drizzle with a bit of olive oil and toss again to coat.

2.   Place snapper on a cutting board and pat dry with paper towels. Cut slashes crosswise on a diagonal along the body every 2" on both sides, with a sharp knife, cutting all the way down to the bones.

3.   Season fish generously inside and out with salt. Coat fish with tandoori spice.

4.   Preheat griddle medium-high heat and brush with oil.

5.   Grill fish for 10 minutes, undisturbed, until skin is puffed and charred.

6.   Flip and grill fish until the other side is lightly charred and skin is puffed, about 8 to 12 minutes.

7.   Transfer to a platter.

8.   Top with mango salad and serve with lime wedges.

Nutrition Info: Calories: 211 Sodium: 170 mg, Dietary Fiber: 2.5g, Fat: 5.4g, Carbs: 18.9g Protein: 23.6g

331. Healthy Salmon Patties

Servings: 2

Cooking Time: 10 Minutes
Ingredients:
- 6 oz can salmon, drained, remove bones, and pat dry
- 2 tbsp mayonnaise
- 1/2 cup almond flour
- 1/4 tsp thyme
- 1 egg, lightly beaten
- 2 tbsp olive oil
- Pepper
- Salt

Directions:
1.   Add salmon, thyme, egg, mayonnaise, almond flour, pepper, and salt into the mixing bowl and mix until well combined.

2.   Preheat the griddle to high heat.

3.   Add oil to the griddle top.

4.   Make small patties from salmon mixture and place onto the hot griddle top and cook for 5-6 minutes.

5.   Turn patties and cook for 3-4 minutes more.

6.   Serve and enjoy.

Nutrition Info: (Per Serving): Calories 530 ;Fat 41 g ;Carbohydrates 9.8 g ;Sugar 1.1 g ;Protein 30.6 g ;Cholesterol 146 mg

332. Tasty Shrimp Skewers

Servings: 6
Cooking Time: 7 Minutes
Ingredients:
- 1 1/2 lbs shrimp, peeled and deveined
- 1 tbsp dried oregano
- 2 tsp garlic paste
- 2 lemon juice
- 1/4 cup olive oil
- 1 tsp paprika
- Pepper
- Salt

Directions:
1.   Add all ingredients into the mixing bowl and mix well and place in the refrigerator for 1 hour.

2.   Remove marinated shrimp from refrigerator and thread onto the skewers.

3.   Preheat the griddle to high heat.

4.   Place skewers onto the griddle top and cook for 5-7 minutes.

5.   Serve and enjoy.

Nutrition Info: (Per Serving): Calories 212 ;Fat 10.5 g ;Carbohydrates 2.7 g ;Sugar 0.1 g ;Protein 26 g ;Cholesterol 239 mg

333.Lemon Garlic Shrimp

Servings: 4
Cooking Time: 15 Minutes
Ingredients:
- 1 1/2 lbs shrimp, peeled and deveined
- 1 tbsp garlic, minced
- 1/4 cup butter
- 1/4 cup fresh parsley, chopped
- 1/4 cup fresh lemon juice
- Pepper
- Salt

Directions:
1. Preheat the griddle to high heat.
2. Melt butter on the griddle top.
3. Add garlic and sauté for 30 seconds.
4. Add shrimp and season with pepper and salt and cook for 4-5 minutes or until it turns to pink.
5. Add lemon juice and parsley and stir well and cook for 2 minutes.
6. Serve and enjoy.

Nutrition Info: (Per Serving): Calories 312 ;Fat 14.6 g ;Carbohydrates 3.9 g ;Sugar 0.4 g ;Protein 39.2 g ;Cholesterol 389 mg

334.Pop-open Clams With Horseradish-tabasco Sauce

Servings: 4
Cooking Time: 10 Minutes
Ingredients:
- 2 dozen littleneck clams, scrubbed
- 4 tablespoons unsalted butter, softened
- 2 tablespoons horseradish, drained
- 1 tablespoon hot sauce, like Tabasco
- 1/4 teaspoon lemon zest, finely grated
- 1 tablespoon fresh lemon juice
- 1/4 teaspoon smoked paprika
- Sea salt

Directions:
1. Preheat the griddle to high.
2. Blend the butter with the horseradish, hot sauce, lemon zest, lemon juice, paprika, and pinch of salt.
3. Arrange the clams over high heat and grill until they pop open, about 25 seconds.
4. Carefully turn the clams over using tongs, so the meat side is down.
5. Grill for about 20 seconds longer, until the clam juices start to simmer.
6. Transfer the clams to a serving bowl.
7. Top each with about 1/2 teaspoon of the sauce and serve.

Nutrition Info: Calories: 191, Sodium: 382 mg, Dietary Fiber: 0.3g, Fat: 12.7g, Carbs: 4g Protein: 14.8g

335.Salmon Fillets With Basil Butter & Broccolini

Servings: 2
Cooking Time: 12 Minutes
Ingredients:
- 2 (6 ounce) salmon fillets, skin removed
- 2 tablespoons butter, unsalted
- 2 basil leaves, minced
- 1 garlic clove, minced
- 6 ounces broccolini
- 2 teaspoons olive oil
- Sea salt, to taste

Directions:
1. Blend butter, basil, and garlic together until well-incorporated. Form into a ball and place in refrigerator until ready to serve.
2. Preheat griddle to medium-high heat.
3. Season both sides of the salmon fillets with salt and set aside.
4. Add broccolini, a pinch of salt, and olive oil to a bowl, toss to coat, and set aside.
5. Brush griddle with olive oil, and cook salmon, skin side down, for 12 minutes. Turn the salmon and cook for an additional 4 minutes. Remove from the griddle and allow to rest while the broccolini cooks.
6. Add the broccolini to the griddle, turning occasionally, until slightly charred, about 6 minutes.
7. Top each salmon fillet with a slice of basil butter and serve with a side of broccolini.

Nutrition Info: Calories: 398, Sodium: 303 mg, Dietary Fiber: 2.2g, Fat: 26.7g, Carbs: 6.2g Protein: 35.6g

336.Hibachi Salmon

Servings: 4
Cooking Time: 10 Minutes
Ingredients:
- 2 lbs. salmon fillets
- 1/2 cup teriyaki sauce
- 1 tsp. fresh grated ginger
- 2 cloves garlic
- 1/4 cup brown sugar
- 2 tsp. black pepper
- 1 Tbsp. maple syrup

Directions:
1. Mix all the ingredients together in a covered glass bowl or resealable bag, and refrigerate for several hours to overnight.
2. Heat the griddle grill to high, and grill the salmon fillets for 3–4 minutes per side until cooked

through. Salmon should be homogeneous in color with white juice between the flakes.

3. Let rest for several minutes before serving.

Nutrition Info: (Per serving):Calories 251, Carbs, 3g, Fat 13g, Protein 30g

337.Lobster Tails With Lime Basil Butter

Servings: 4
Cooking Time: 6 Minutes
Ingredients:
- 4 lobster tails (cut in half lengthwise)
- 3 tablespoons olive oil
- lime wedges (to serve)
- Sea salt, to taste
- For the lime basil butter:
- 1 stick unsalted butter, softened
- 1/2 bunch basil, roughly chopped
- 1 lime, zested and juiced
- 2 cloves garlic, minced
- 1/4 teaspoon red pepper flakes

Directions:
1. Add the butter ingredients to a mixing bowl and combine; set aside until ready to use.
2. Preheat griddle to medium-high heat.
3. Drizzle the lobster tail halves with olive oil and season with salt and pepper.
4. Place the lobster tails, flesh-side down, on the griddle.
5. Allow to cook until opaque, about 3 minutes, flip and cook another 3 minutes.
6. Add a dollop of the lime basil butter during the last minute of cooking.
7. Serve immediately.

Nutrition Info: Calories: 430, Sodium: 926 mg, Dietary Fiber: 0.5g, Fat: 34.7g, Carbs: 2.4g Protein: 28g

338.Summer Shrimp Salad

Servings: 5
Cooking Time: 3 Minutes
Ingredients:
- ½ pint cherry tomatoes
- 3 tablespoons olive oil
- ½ teaspoon salt
- 1 pound medium to thin asparagus, woody stems snapped off and discarded
- 1 pound shelled and deveined medium shrimp
- ¼ teaspoon freshly ground black pepper
- ¼ teaspoon dried thyme
- Grated zest and juice of ½ lemon

Directions:
1. Preparing the Ingredients

2. Quarter the cherry tomatoes and put them in a medium bowl. Add 1 tablespoon of the olive oil and ¼ teaspoon of the salt. Toss gently and set aside.
3. In a medium bowl, pour 1 tablespoon of the olive oil over the asparagus spears and rub gently to coat them.
4. Turn control knob to the high position. Oil the griddle and allow it to heat until the oil is shimmering but not smoking. Grill the asparagus for about 5 Minutes. The thicker ones will still have a bit of crunch to them and the thinner ones will be tender. Transfer to a cutting board; keep the griddle on high. When they are cool enough to handle, cut the spears into 1-inch pieces. Add to the cherry tomatoes.
5. Rinse the shrimp and pat dry with paper towels. Put them in a medium bowl, add the remaining tablespoon olive oil, and toss to coat. Grill the shrimp for about 3 Minutes, until they are opaque and firm to the touch.
6. Add the shrimp to the tomatoes and asparagus. Add the remaining ¼ teaspoon salt, the pepper, thyme, and lemon juice and zest, and toss to combine. Serve warm or at room temperature, or refrigerate and serve chilled.

Nutrition Info: (Per Serving): CALORIES: 240; FAT:13G; PROTEIN:25G

339.Caper Basil Halibut

Servings: 4
Cooking Time: 8 Minutes
Ingredients:
- 24 oz halibut fillets
- 2 garlic cloves, crushed
- 2 tbsp olive oil
- 2 tsp capers, drained
- 3 tbsp fresh basil, sliced
- 2 1/2 tbsp fresh lemon juice

Directions:
1. In a small bowl, whisk together garlic, olive oil, and lemon juice. Stir in 2 tbsp basil.
2. Season garlic mixture with pepper and salt.
3. Season fish fillets with pepper and salt and brush with garlic mixture.
4. Preheat the griddle to high heat.
5. Place fish fillets on hot griddle and cook for 4 minutes on each side.
6. Transfer fish fillets on serving plate and top with remaining garlic mixture and basil.
7. Serve and enjoy.

Nutrition Info: (Per Serving): Calories 250 ;Fat 10.5 g ;Carbohydrates 0.8 g ;Sugar 0.2 g ;Protein 39.1 g ;Cholesterol 59 mg

340.Crab-stuffed Trout

Servings: 4
Cooking Time: 15 Minutes
Ingredients:
- 12 ounces crabmeat, picked over for shells and cartilage
- 1 cup chopped seeded fresh tomato, drained if necessary
- Grated zest of 1 lemon
- 1 tablespoon good-quality olive oil, plus more for brushing the fish
- 2 scallions, trimmed and chopped
- Salt and pepper
- 4 8- to 10-ounce rainbow trout, cleaned and butterflied
- Lemon wedges for serving

Directions:
1. Preparing the Ingredients
2. Put the crab, tomato, and lemon zest in a medium bowl. Put the oil and scallions in a small skillet over medium heat; cook, stirring occasionally, until softened, 2 to 3 Minutes. Add to the crab, sprinkle with salt and pepper, toss gently, and taste and adjust the seasoning.
3. Pat the trout dry with paper towels. Brush them with oil and sprinkle with salt and pepper on both sides. Divide the crab mixture between the trout, filling their cavities. Pull the two sides closed, pushing the filling in, if needed, to keep it from spilling out.
4. Bring the griddle grill to high heat, Oil the griddle and allow it to heat. Put the trout with the open side of the fish facing you, and cook until the skin browns and the fish release easily, 8 to 10 Minutes. Carefully turn the fish, using a second spatula to lower them back down to the grates. Close the lid and cook until the stuffing is heated through and a skewer or thin knife inserted at the thickest point of a fish easily pierces it all the way through, 4 to 5 Minutes. Transfer the trout to a platter and serve with lemon wedges.

341.Rosemary Salmon

Servings: 4
Cooking Time: 5 Minutes
Ingredients:
- 4 rosemary branches
- 4 pieces skinless salmon fillet (each about 2 inches wide, 3 to 4 inches long, ¾ to 1 inch thick, and 6 ounces)
- 2 tablespoons extra-virgin olive oil
- Coarse salt (kosher or sea) and freshly ground black pepper
- 2 cloves garlic, minced

- 1 teaspoon finely grated lemon zest
- Lemon wedges, for serving

Directions:
1. Preparing the Ingredients
2. Strip the leaves off the bottom 4 inches of each rosemary branch (pull them off between your thumb and forefinger) and very finely chop the leaves; you'll use the chopped rosemary to season the salmon. Run your fingers over the salmon fillets, feeling for bones. Using needle-nose pliers or tweezers, pull out any you find. Rinse the fish under cold running water, then blot it dry with paper towels. Skewer each salmon fillet on the bare part of a rosemary branch through the center of a short side. Place the fish on a large plate and brush on both sides with the olive oil. Generously season the fish on both sides with salt and pepper.
3. Place the chopped rosemary and the garlic and lemon zest in a small bowl and stir to mix. Sprinkle the rosemary mixture over the salmon on all sides, patting it onto the fish with your fingertips. Let the fish stand at room temperature while you preheat the grill.
4. Bring the griddle grill to high heat. Oil the griddle and allow it to heat. Arrange the salmon on the hot grill. It will be done after cooking 3 to 5 Minutes. To test for doneness, press the fish with your finger; it should break into clean flakes.
5. Transfer the salmon to a platter or plates and serve it with lemon wedges on the side.

342.Seared Scallops With Parsley-lemon Stuffing

Servings: 4
Cooking Time: 10 Minutes
Ingredients:
- ½ cup minced fresh parsley
- 2 teaspoons grated lemon zest
- 1 clove garlic, minced
- Salt and pepper
- 1½ pounds sea scallops, trimmed of any tough connective tissue
- Good-quality olive oil for brushing the scallops
- Lemon wedges for serving

Directions:
1. Preparing the Ingredients
2. Stir the parsley, lemon zest, and garlic together in a small bowl and sprinkle with a little salt and pepper if you like.
3. Pat the scallops dry with paper towels. Brush them with oil and season with salt and pepper on both sides. With a small thin knife, make a 1-to 1½-inch-long horizontal slit in the side, going almost all the way through. Jiggle the knife from side to side to

enlarge the pocket without cutting through the side. Using a small spoon with a pointed tip, like a grapefruit spoon, fill each scallop with the stuffing. (You can prepare and refrigerate the scallops up to several hours in advance.)

4.   Bring the griddle grill to high heat. Oil the griddle. Put the scallops on the grill, and cook until they're seared and golden brown in spots, with the centers still ever so slightly translucent, 8 to 10 Minutes. Transfer the scallops to a platter and serve with lemon wedges.

343.Coconut Pineapple Shrimp Skewers

Servings: 4
Cooking Time: 5 Minutes
Ingredients:
*   1-1/2 pounds uncooked jumbo shrimp, peeled and deveined
*   1/2 cup light coconut milk
*   1 tablespoon cilantro, chopped
*   4 teaspoons Tabasco Original Red Sauce
*   2 teaspoons soy sauce
*   1/4 cup freshly squeezed orange juice
*   1/4 cup freshly squeezed lime juice (from about 2 large limes)
*   3/4 pound pineapple, cut into 1 inch chunks
*   Olive oil, for grilling
Directions:
1.   Combine the coconut milk, cilantro, Tabasco sauce, soy sauce, orange juice, lime juice. Add the shrimp and toss to coat.
2.   Cover and place in the refrigerator to marinate for 1 hour.
3.   Thread shrimp and pineapple onto metal skewers, alternating each.
4.   Preheat griddle to medium heat.
5.   Cook 5-6 minutes, flipping once, until shrimp turn opaque pink.
6.   Serve immediately.
Nutrition Info: Calories: 150, Sodium: 190 mg, Dietary Fiber: 1.9g, Fat: 10.8g, Carbs: 14.9g Protein: 1.5g

344.Parmesan Shrimp

Servings: 4
Cooking Time: 6 Minutes
Ingredients:
*   1 lb shrimp, peeled and deveined
*   2 tbsp parmesan cheese, grated
*   1 tbsp fresh lemon juice
*   1 tbsp pine nuts, toasted
*   1 garlic clove

*   1/2 cup basil
*   1 tbsp olive oil
*   Pepper
*   Salt
Directions:
1.   Add basil, lemon juice, cheese, pine nuts, garlic, pepper, and salt in a blender and blend until smooth.
2.   Add shrimp and basil paste in a bowl and mix well.
3.   Place shrimp bowl in the fridge for 20 minutes.
4.   Preheat the griddle to high heat.
5.   Spray griddle top with cooking spray.
6.   Thread marinated shrimp onto skewers and place skewers on the hot griddle top.
7.   Cook shrimp for 3 minutes on each side or until cooked.
8.   Serve and enjoy.
Nutrition Info: (Per Serving): Calories 225 ;Fat 11.2 g ;Carbohydrates 2.2 g ;Sugar 0.2 g ;Protein 27.2 g ;Cholesterol 241 mg

345.Pesto Shrimp

Servings: 4
Cooking Time: 5 Minutes
Ingredients:
*   1 lb shrimp, remove shells and tails
*   1/2 cup basil pesto
*   Pepper
*   Salt
Directions:
1.   Add shrimp, pesto, pepper, and salt into the large bowl and toss well. Set aside for 15 minutes.
2.   Heat grill over medium-high heat.
3.   Thread marinated shrimp onto the skewers and place onto the hot griddle top and cook for 1-2 minutes on each side.
4.   Serve and enjoy.
Nutrition Info: (Per Serving): Calories 270 ;Fat 15 g ;Carbohydrates 3.7 g ;Sugar 2 g ;Protein 28.8 g ;Cholesterol 246 mg

346.Grilled Oysters With Spiced Tequila Butter

Servings: 6
Cooking Time: 25 Minutes
Ingredients:
*   3 dozen medium oysters, scrubbed and shucked
*   Flakey sea salt, for serving
*   For the butter:
*   1/4 teaspoon crushed red pepper
*   7 tablespoons unsalted butter
*   ¼ teaspoon chili oil

- 1 teaspoon dried oregano
- 2 tablespoons freshly squeezed lemon juice
- 2 tablespoons tequila blanco, like Espolon

Directions:
1. Combine butter ingredients in a small mixing bowl until well-incorporated and set aside.
2. Preheat griddle to high.
3. Grill the oysters about 1 to 2 minutes.
4. Sprinkle the oysters with salt flakes.
5. Warm the butter in a microwave for 30 seconds, and spoon the warm tequila butter over the oysters and serve.

Nutrition Info: Calories: 184, Sodium: 300 mg, Dietary Fiber: 0.2g, Fat: 15g, Carbs: 3.8g Protein: 0.2g

347.Seafood Stuffed Sole

Servings: 2
Cooking Time: 14 Minutes
Ingredients:
- 1/4 cup shrimp, cooked, peeled and chopped
- 1 tablespoon lemon juice
- 2 tablespoons butter, melted, divided
- 3/4 cup cherry tomatoes
- 1 tablespoon chicken broth
- 1/2 can (6-ounces) crabmeat, drained
- 1/2 teaspoon parsley, fresh minced
- 1 tablespoon whipped cream cheese
- 1/2 teaspoon grated lemon zest
- 2 tablespoons breadcrumbs
- 1 teaspoon chive, minced
- 2 (6-ounces) sole fish fillets, cut from the side with gutted and cleaned
- 1/4 teaspoon black ground pepper

Directions:
1. Mix your cream cheese, cram, shrimp, garlic, lemon zest, parsley, 2 tablespoons butter and breadcrumbs in a mixing bowl.
2. Stuff each fillet with 1/4 of this mixture and secure the ends with toothpicks.
3. Mix lemon juice, tomatoes, salt and pepper in a different bowl.
4. Place your stuffed fillets in a foil sheet and top with the tomato mixture.
5. Cover and seal the fillets in foil.
6. Preheat your griddle grill on the medium temperature setting.
7. Once your grill is preheated, place 2 sealed fillets on the grill.
8. Grill it for 7 minutes per side. Serve and Enjoy!

Nutrition Info: (Per serving): Calories: 248 Fat: 2.7g Carbs: 31.4g Protein: 24.9g

348.Grilled Salmon With A Mustard And Brown Sugar Crust

Servings: 4
Cooking Time: 5 Minutes
Ingredients:
- 4pieces salmon fillet (each about 6 ounces)
- Coarse salt (kosher or sea) and freshly ground black pepper
- 1 cup firmly packed dark brown sugar
- 3 tablespoons Dijon mustard
- Sweet Mustard and Dill Sauce
- SWEETMUSTARD AND DILL SAUCE
- ⅓cup mayonnaise(preferably Hellmann's)
- ⅓ cup sour cream
- ⅓ cup Dijon or Meaux mustard
- 2 tablespoons chopped fresh dill
- 1 tablespoon brown sugar (dark or light), or more to taste
- Freshly ground black pepper

Directions:
1. Preparing the Ingredients
2. Place the mayonnaise, sour cream, mustard, dill, and brown sugar in a small nonreactive bowl and whisk to mix. Taste for seasoning, adding more brown sugar and pepper to taste. The sauce can be refrigerated, covered, for several days.
3. Run your fingers over the salmon fillets, feeling for bones. Using needle-nose pliers or tweezers, pull out any you find. Rinse the fish under cold running water, then blot it dry with paper towels. Very generously season the salmon on both sides with salt and pepper.
4. Spread the brown sugar out in a large shallow bowl, crumbling it between your fingers or with a fork. Brush or spread each salmon fillet on both sides with the mustard. Dredge both sides of each fillet in the brown sugar, patting it onto the fish with your fingertips. Gently shake off any excess brown sugar; the fish should be fairly thickly crusted.
5. Turn control knob to the high position. Oil the griddle and allow it to heat. Arrange the salmon on the hot Griddle. The salmon will be done after cooking 3 to 5 Minutes until the outside is darkly browned and the fish is cooked through. To test for doneness, press the fish with your finger; it should break into clean flakes.
6. Transfer the salmon to a platter or plates and serve at once.

349.Flavorful Mexican Shrimp

Servings: 4
Cooking Time: 12 Minutes
Ingredients:
- 1 lb shrimp, cleaned

- 3 tbsp fresh parsley, chopped
- 1 tbsp garlic, minced
- 1/4 onion, sliced
- 1/4 tsp paprika
- 1/4 tsp ground cumin
- 2 fresh lime juice
- 2 tbsp olive oil
- 1/4 cup butter
- Pepper
- Salt

Directions:
1. Season shrimp with paprika, cumin, pepper, and salt.
2. Preheat the griddle to high heat.
3. Add oil and butter to the griddle top.
4. Add onion and garlic and sauté for 5 minutes.
5. Add shrimp and cook for 5-8 minutes or until cooked.
6. Add parsley and lime juice.
7. Stir well and serve.

Nutrition Info: (Per Serving): Calories 311 ;Fat 20.5 g ;Carbohydrates 5 g ;Sugar 0.7 g ;Protein 26.4 g ;Cholesterol 269 mg

350.Swordfish

Servings: 4
Cooking Time: 15 Minutes
Ingredients:
- Swordfish Fillets, Cut About 1.5 Inches Thick
- Olive Oil
- Sea Salt And Pepper To Taste

Directions:
1. Preheat the griddle grill to high.
2. Drizzle the fillets with olive oil and season with sea salt and black pepper.
3. Place on the grill and cook for 3 minutes per side.
4. Turn the grill down to medium and continue grilling for 5 minutes per side or until the sides of the swordfish are homogeneous in color.
5. Let the fish relax for 5 minutes before serving.

Nutrition Info: (Per serving): Calories: 132, carbs 8g, Protein: 22 g, Fat: 4 g

351.Lobster With Drawn Butter

Servings: 4
Cooking Time: 10 Minutes
Ingredients:
- ½ pound (2 sticks) butter
- 4 live lobsters (1¼ to 1½ pounds each)
- Salt and pepper
- 4 lemons, halved

Directions:

1. Preparing the Ingredients
2. 1 Melt the butter in a small saucepan over low heat until it foams. Remove the pan from the heat and skim away the foam. Let the pan sit for several Minutes for the milk solids to settle to the bottom. Ladle the clear yellow butterfat into a microwave-safe bowl. (You can clarify the butter up to a day ahead, cover, and refrigerate it.)
3. Bring a large pot of water to a boil and salt it. Fill the sink or a very large bowl with an ice bath.
4. Working in batches if your pot isn't large enough, put the lobsters in the boiling water with tongs. Cover the pot and cook until they turn bright red, about 2 Minutes depending on their size. (The water may not return to a boil.) Transfer the lobsters to the ice bath to stop the cooking, then drain; add more ice and repeat the process with the remaining lobsters if necessary.
5. Split the lobsters in half along the back with a sharp knife, in one fell swoop if you can. If you like, use a spoon to clean out the gills and anything that doesn't look like meat from the torso.
6. 2 Bring the griddle grill to high heat. Oil the griddle. Put the lobsters shell side down on the griddle. Cook, checking every couple of Minutes and turning once, until they're firm and just opaque at the center, 3 to 5 Minutes a side. When you turn the lobsters, put the lemon halves on the grate, cut side down.
7. 3 Heap the lobsters onto a serving platter. Reheat the butter in the microwave, and serve each lobster with a lemon half and a small bowl of drawn butter for dipping.

352.Grilled Popcorn Shrimp

Servings: 5
Cooking Time: 3 Minutes
Ingredients:
- SPICERUB
- 2 teaspoons garlic powder
- 2 teaspoons sweet paprika
- 1 teaspoon onion powder
- 1 teaspoon dried oregano
- 1 teaspoon cayenne pepper
- 1 teaspoon salt
- 1 teaspoon freshly ground black pepper
- 1 teaspoon sugar
- In a large resealable plastic bag, combine the spices and shake to blend them. (The spice mix can be made ahead and kept nearly indefinitely.)
- SHRIMP
- 1½ pounds shelled and deveined small shrimp
- 1 lemon, cut into wedges

Directions:

1. Preparing the Ingredients
2. Add the shrimp to the plastic bag with the spice rub and shake to coat.
3. Turn control knob to the high position. Oil the griddle and allow it to heat until the oil is shimmering but not smoking. Grill the shrimp for about 1 minute per side, until they are opaque and firm to the touch.
4. Serve the shrimp immediately in a bowl garnished with the lemon wedges (and with plenty of napkins).

Nutrition Info: (Per Serving): CALORIES: 193; FAT52G; PROTEIN:35G

353.Spicy Grilled Jumbo Shrimp

Servings: 6
Cooking Time: 8 Minutes
Ingredients:
- 1-1/2 pounds uncooked jumbo shrimp, peeled and deveined
- For the marinade:
- 2 tablespoons fresh parsley
- 1 bay leaf, dried
- 1 teaspoon chili powder
- 1 teaspoon garlic powder
- 1/4 teaspoon cayenne pepper
- 1/4 cup olive oil
- 1/4 teaspoon salt
- 1/8 teaspoon pepper

Directions:
1. Add marinade ingredients to a food processor and process until smooth.
2. Transfer marinade to a large mixing bowl.
3. Fold in shrimp and toss to coat; refrigerate, covered, 30 minutes.
4. Thread shrimp onto metal skewers.
5. Preheat griddle to medium heat.
6. Cook 5-6 minutes, flipping once, until shrimp turn opaque pink.
7. Serve immediately.

Nutrition Info: Calories: 131, Sodium: 980 mg, Dietary Fiber: 0.4g, Fat: 8.5g, Carbs: 1g Protein: 13.7g

SNACKS & DESSERTS

354.Buttermilk Angel Biscuits

Servings: 14 Biscuits
Cooking Time: 15 Minutes
Ingredients:
- 2½ cups all-purpose flour, plus more for kneading
- 2¼ teaspoons (1 package) instant yeast
- 1 teaspoon baking powder
- 1 teaspoon baking soda
- 1 teaspoon salt
- 8 tablespoons (1 stick) butter, melted, plus softened butter for the pans
- 1 cup buttermilk

Directions:
1. Preparing the Ingredients
2. 1 Whisk the flour, yeast, baking powder and soda, and salt together in a large bowl. Stir the melted butter into the buttermilk, then add to the flour and stir it in. With your hands, gather the dough into a ball and transfer to a lightly floured work surface. Knead the dough until smooth, 1 to 2 Minutes, then pat it down to a ½- to ¾-inch thickness. Cut the biscuits using a 2½-inch cutter. Pat the scraps together, flatten again, and cut more biscuits.
3. Coat the insides of two 12-inch cast-iron skillets with softened butter. Put the biscuits in the pans, not touching. Cover with plastic wrap and let rise until doubled, 1 to 1½ hours.
4. 2 Bring the griddle grill to medium-low heat. Oil the griddle and allow it to heat until the oil is shimmering but not smoking. Put the pans on the grill, and bake until the bottoms of the biscuits release easily and are golden brown and the tops have browned in spots, 5 to 7 Minutes per side. The biscuits should be springy to the touch, and a toothpick inserted in the center should come out clean. Transfer the biscuits to a clean dish towel or napkin, wrap loosely, and serve warm.

355.Cripsy Eggplant Bites

Servings: 4
Cooking Time: 10 Minutes
Ingredients:
- 1 eggplant, cut into 1-inch pieces
- 2 tbsp olive oil
- 1/2 tsp Italian seasoning
- 1 tsp paprika
- 1/2 tsp red pepper
- 1 tsp garlic powder

Directions:
1. Add all ingredients into the large bowl and toss well.
2. Preheat the griddle to high heat.
3. Spray griddle top with cooking spray.
4. Transfer eggplant mixture onto the hot griddle top and cook until eggplant pieces are crispy.
5. Serve and enjoy.

Nutrition Info: (Per Serving): Calories 100 ;Fat 7.5 g ;Carbohydrates 8.7 g ;Sugar 4.5 g ;Protein 1.5 g ;Cholesterol 0 mg

356.Grilled Cinnamon S'mores Toast

Servings: 4
Cooking Time: 2 Minutes
Ingredients:
- 1/2 cup sugar
- 1 tbsp. cinnamon
- 4 slices bread 1/4 cup margarine
- 15 baby marshmallows
- 1 (4.4-oz.) chocolate bar

Directions:
1. Combine sugar and cinnamon in a bowl.
2. Spread margarine over one side of each slice of bread. Sprinkle with cinnamon and sugar mixture.
3. Arrange two slices of bread onto the Griddle Grill Pan, margarine side down. Cover each slice with marshmallows and half of the chocolate bar.
4. Top with remaining two slices of bread. Use Grill Press to cook on both sides, 3 minutes per side.
5. Serve alone or with a tall glass of milk!

Nutrition Info: (Per serving):354.3 calories; 20g fat; 5.7 g protein; 54.1 g carbs

357.Stuffed French Toast

Servings: 2
Cooking Time: 6 Minutes
Ingredients:
- 2 loaves of French bread, cut into 1-inch slices
- For the custard
- ¼ cup milk
- 1 egg
- juice of ½ blood orange
- 3 strawberries, stemmed and hulled
- pinch of ground cloves
- ¼ tsp. vanilla
- pinch of sea salt
- For the filling
- ¼ cup mascarpone
- zest of 1 blood orange
- 1 tsp. real maple syrup
- sliced strawberries
- powdered sugar

Directions:

1. Preparing the Ingredients
2. Mix the custard ingredients together in a blender, and set aside in a bowl.
3. Mix the mascarpone, blood orange zest, and maple syrup together in a bowl.
4. Add the mascarpone mixture and the sliced strawberries between two slices of French bread. Dip the outsides of the sandwich in the custard and drip the remaining custard off.
5. Bring the griddle grill to medium-low heat. Oil the griddle and allow it to heat until the oil is shimmering but not smoking. Cook for 5–6 Minutes until the custard is lightly golden brown and the bread is golden.
6. Dust with powdered sugar and enjoy.

358.Pineapple Sundae

Servings: 2
Ingredients:
- ¼ pineapple
- peeled & sliced 2 cups vanilla ice cream
- ¼ cup whipped cream

Directions:
1. Preparing the Ingredients.
2. Let cool before chopping.
3. Grilling
4. Grill the pineapple until tender. Scoop ice cream into 2 serving dishes. Immediately before serving, top with pineapple, whipped cream, and sliced almonds. ¼ cup sliced almonds. You can also make an awesome dessert "salsa" by adding chopped strawberries and fresh mint.

359.Grilled Berry Cobbler

Servings: 2
Cooking Time: 20 Minutes
Ingredients:
- 2 cans (21-ounces) pie filling, raspberry flavor
- vanilla ice cream
- 1 (8-ounces) package of cake mix
- 1/2 cup olive oil
- 1-1/4 cups water

Directions:
1. Mix your cake mix with olive oil and water in a bowl until smooth.
2. Place a foil packet on the working surface along with pie filling.
3. Spread your cake mix on top of the pie filling.
4. Cover your foil packet and seal it.
5. Preheat your indoor grill on the medium temperature setting.
6. Once your grill is preheated, place the foil package on the grill.

7. Close the grill lid and set to "Bake Mode" for 20 minutes.
8. Serve with vanilla ice cream and enjoy!
Nutrition Info: (Per serving): Calories: 319 Fat: 11.9g Carbs: 14.8g Protein: 5g

360.Grilled Peanut Butter Banana Split

Servings: 4
Cooking Time: 10 Minutes
Ingredients:
- 4 ripe bananas
- 1 cup peanut butter baking chips
- 1 cup mini marshmallows
- ¼ cup brown sugar

Directions:
1. Preparing the Ingredients
2. Leaving banana in peel, slice down the length of the banana, but don't cut it in half.
3. Pry apart the bananas and evenly distribute brown sugar inside each banana.
4. On top of the brown sugar, evenly distribute the peanut butter chips.
5. On top of peanut butter chips, place the mini marshmallows.
6. Bring the griddle grill to medium-low heat. Oil the griddle and allow it to heat until the oil is shimmering but not smoking. Place bananas in grill, and cook for 10 Minutes or until peanut better chips have melted and marshmallows are toasted.
7. Remove and serve hot.

361.Butter-rum Pineapple Rings

Servings: 6 To 8
Cooking Time: 8 Minutes
Ingredients:
- 1 pineapple
- 8 tablespoons (1 stick) butter
- 2 tablespoons spiced or dark rum
- 3 tablespoons coconut milk

Directions:
1. Preparing the Ingredients
2. Cut the top and bottom off the pineapple, then remove the peel by standing the pineapple upright and running the knife down from top to bottom, working all around, without taking much of the flesh. Lay the pineapple on its side and cut it across into 1- to 1½-inch rings. Cut the core out of each ring. (An easy way to do this is to use a small cookie cutter or swivel peeler, or with a paring knife.) If not using immediately, put the rings in an airtight container; they will keep in the refrigerator for up to 2 days.
3. Melt the butter in a small saucepan over medium heat. When it foams, add the rum and

coconut milk and bring to a gentle bubble. Cook without boiling, stirring occasionally, until the mixture reduces a bit and gets syrupy, 4 to 5 Minutes. Remove from the heat. Brush the pineapple rings on both sides with the glaze; reserve the remaining glaze.

4.   Bring the griddle grill to medium low heat. Oil the griddle and allow it to heat until the oil is shimmering but not smoking. Put the pineapple rings on the grill, and cook, turning once, until they develop grill marks and are heated all the way through, 4 Minutes per side, Transfer to a plate and serve drizzled with the remaining glaze.

362.Pineapple–star Fruit Skewers With Orange-clove Syrup

Servings: 4
Cooking Time: 16 Minutes
Ingredients:
- ½ cup sugar
- Zest of 1 large orange, taken off in strips
- 1 tablespoon whole cloves
- 1 small pineapple
- 3 star fruit

Directions:
1.   Preparing the Ingredients
2.   Put the sugar, orange zest, cloves, and ½ cup water in a small saucepan over medium heat; stir until the sugar dissolves. Bring to a boil, reduce the heat, and gently bubble for 5 to 10 Minutes. Remove from the heat and let sit for at least 30 Minutes and up to several hours to let the flavor develop. When you are happy with the flavor of the syrup, strain it and use or refrigerate in an airtight container; it will keep for at least a week.
3.   If you're using bamboo or wooden skewers, soak them in water for 30 Minutes.
4.   Trim, peel, and core the pineapple, then cut it into 2-inch chunks. Cut the star fruit into ½-inch-thick slices. Skewer the fruit; using 2 skewers makes them easier to turn. Skewer the star fruit through the points of the star on two sides. Brush lightly with the orange-clove syrup.
5.   Bring the griddle grill to medium-high heat. Oil the griddle and allow it to heat until the oil is shimmering but not smoking. Put the skewers on the grill, and cook, until the pineapple chunks brown in spots, 6 to 8 Minutes per side; brush the fruit several times with the syrup while it grills. When the fruit is done, brush it once more with syrup. Transfer to a platter and serve hot or warm.

363.Tasty Herb Mushrooms

Servings: 4
Cooking Time: 10 Minutes
Ingredients:
- 1 lb mushroom caps
- 1 tbsp basil, minced
- 1 garlic clove, minced
- 1/2 tbsp vinegar
- 1/2 tsp ground coriander
- 1 tsp rosemary, chopped
- Pepper
- Salt

Directions:
1.   Preheat the griddle to high heat.
2.   Spray griddle top with cooking spray.
3.   Add all ingredients into the bowl and toss well.
4.   Add mushroom mixture onto the hot griddle top and cook until mushroom is tender.
5.   Serve and enjoy.
Nutrition Info: (Per Serving): Calories 25 ;Fat 0.4 g ;Carbohydrates 4 g ;Sugar 2 g ;Protein 3.6 g ;Cholesterol 0 mg

364.Grilled Cinnamon Toast

Servings: 2
Ingredients:
- ½ cup sugar
- 1 tbsp. cinnamon
- 4 slices bread ¼ cup margarine
- 15 baby marshmallows
- 1 (4.4-oz.) chocolate bar

Directions:
1.   Preparing the Ingredients.
2.   Combine sugar and cinnamon in a bowl. Spread margarine over one side of each slice of bread. Sprinkle with cinnamon and sugar mixture. Arrange two slices of bread onto the Grill Pan, margarine side down. Cover each slice with marshmallows and half of the chocolate bar. Top with remaining two slices of bread.
3.   Grilling
4.   Use Grill Press to cook on both sides, 3 Minutes per side. Serve alone or with a tall glass of milk! As if this couldn't get any better, try a little peanut butter inside!

365.Grill-baked Apple

Servings: 1
Cooking Time: 10 Minutes
Ingredients:
- 1 apple
- 1 tablespoon butter, softened

- 1 tablespoon brown sugar
- ⅛ teaspoon ground cinnamon, or more to taste

Directions:
1. Preparing the Ingredients
2. Remove the core of the apple carefully, without puncturing the bottom or side. Mash the butter, brown sugar, and cinnamon with the back of a fork until thoroughly mixed. Stuff the mixture into the cavity of the apple.
3. Bring the griddle grill to medium-low heat. Oil the griddle and allow it to heat until the oil is shimmering but not smoking. Put the apple on the griddle, and cook until it feels soft when gently squeezed and the filling is melted, 8 to 10 Minutes, depending on its size. Transfer to plate and let cool a few Minutes before serving.

366.Grilled Banana Sundae

Servings: 2
Ingredients:
- Strawberry Sauce
- 8 oz. strawberries
- 2 tsp. sugar
- Pineapple Sauce 8 oz. pineapple rounds ¼ cup light brown sugar
- Sundae Basics

Directions:
1. Preparing the Ingredients.
2. Strawberry sauce: in a small saucepan, combine the grilled strawberries with sugar.
3. Grilling
4. Grill strawberries, pineapple, and banana halves to desired doneness. Set aside. Cook until sugar is dissolved and strawberries are blended. Pineapple sauce: in a separate saucepan, combine the grilled pineapples with light brown sugar. Cook until sugar is dissolved and pineapples are blended. Assemble the sundae: line a dish with grilled bananas. Top with 3 scoops vanilla and / or chocolate ice cream and fruit sauces. Sprinkle with peanuts. Top with chocolate sauce and whipped cream before serving. bananas, halved lengthwise vanilla ice cream chocolate ice cream chocolate sauce ½ cup peanuts, chopped whipped cream. I love using this grilled fruit sauce to flavor my margaritas!

367.Honey Glazed Pineapple

Servings: 5
Cooking Time: 3 Minutes
Ingredients:
- 1 small ripe pineapple
- ¼ cup honey
- ¼ cup fresh lime juice

- 1 tablespoon light brown sugar
- 2 tablespoons chopped fresh mint leaves

Directions:
1. Preparing the Ingredients
2. To peel the pineapple, use a large serrated knife to cut off the bottom and top. Stand the pineapple on one end on a cutting board and begin cutting the skin away from the top toward the bottom. Rotate the pineapple on the board until all of the skin has been removed.
3. Cut the pineapple into slices about I inch thick. Use a paring knife to remove the core and then transfer the slices to a shallow baking dish.
4. Combine the honey and lime juice in a small bowl. Spoon the honey mixture over the pineapple, using the back of the spoon to spread the honey over all of the slices. Turn the slices over to coat both sides. Let the slices marinate for at least 1 hour or up to 8.
5. Sprinkle the brown sugar over the slices.
6. Bring the griddle grill to medium-low heat. Oil the griddle and allow it to heat until the oil is shimmering but not smoking. Grill for about 3 Minutes, until golden brown. Serve hot or at room temperature, sprinkled with the mint.

Nutrition Info: (Per Serving): CALORIES: 135; FAT:5G; PROTEIN:5G

368.Grilled Peaches With Honey

Servings: 4
Cooking Time: 5 Minutes
Ingredients:
- fresh peaches
- fresh honey
- cinnamon to taste
- coconut oil
- plain yogurt or ice cream for topping

Directions:
1. Preparing the Ingredients
2. Slice the peaches lengthwise top to bottom and remove the pits.
3. Drizzle honey on the cut side of the peach and sprinkle with cinnamon.
4. Bring the griddle grill to medium-low heat. Oil the griddle and allow it to heat until the oil is shimmering but not smoking. Set the peaches sliced-side up and grill peaches for a couple Minutes cut side down then flip and brush with coconut oil honey and cinnamon
5. Grill for several Minutes until the skin is starting to brown and pull back.
6. Serve with vanilla ice cream while still warm.

369.Broccoli Fritters

Servings: 4
Cooking Time: 12 Minutes
Ingredients:
- 2 eggs, lightly beaten
- 3 cups broccoli florets, steam & chopped
- 2 garlic cloves, minced
- 2 cups mozzarella cheese, shredded
- 1/4 cup breadcrumbs
- Pepper
- Salt

Directions:
1. Preheat the griddle to high heat.
2. Spray griddle top with cooking spray.
3. Add all ingredients into the large bowl and mix until well combined.
4. Make patties from broccoli mixture and place on hot griddle top and cook until golden brown from both sides.
5. Serve and enjoy.

Nutrition Info: (Per Serving): Calories 124 ;Fat 5.3 g ;Carbohydrates 10.6 g ;Sugar 1.8 g ;Protein 9.7 g ;Cholesterol 89 mg

370.Piña Colada Tacos

Servings: 4
Cooking Time: 10 Minutes
Ingredients:
- ½ ripe pineapple, peeled, cored, and cut into 1-inch cubes
- ¼ cup dark rum
- ¼ cup coconut milk
- 4 tablespoons (½ stick) butter, softened
- 4 7-inch flour tortillas
- 1 tablespoon sugar, or as needed
- Lime wedges for serving (optional)
- ½ cup shredded coconut, toasted

Directions:
1. Preparing the Ingredients
2. 1 Put the pineapple, rum, and coconut milk in a bowl and toss to combine. Let the fruit macerate for at least 20 Minutes, or up to several hours in the refrigerator.
3. If you're using bamboo or wooden skewers, soak them in water for 30 Minutes.
4. Spread the butter on both sides of the tortillas, then sprinkle with the sugar. Thread the pineapple cubes onto 4 skewers, letting excess marinade drip back in the bowl.
5. 2 Bring the griddle grill to medium-high heat. Oil the griddle and allow it to heat until the oil is shimmering but not smoking. Put the skewers on the grill and cook until the pineapple is caramelized, 5 to 8 Minutes per side. Transfer the skewers to a platter.

Put the tortillas on the grill, and cook, turning once, until they lightly brown, 1 to 2 Minutes per side.
6. To serve, put a skewer on top of each tortilla, squeeze with some lime if you like, and sprinkle with toasted coconut. To eat, pull out the skewer.

371.Sweet Potato Pancakes

Servings: 2
Ingredients:
- Wet ¾ cup sweet potato, cooked & pureed
- 2 eggs
- 1 cup buttermilk
- 3 tbsp. butter, melted, for batter

Directions:
1. Preparing the Ingredients.
2. Mix the wet ingredients together and set aside. In a bowl, mix all dry ingredients together. Combine wet ingredients and dry ingredients. Preheat Griddle Pan on medium heat and melt 2 tbsp. butter.
3. Grilling
4. Cook pancakes to desired doneness. Serve with walnut or pecan syrup and bananas. Dry
5. 1 cup flour, 2 tsp. baking powder ½ tsp. salt ½ tsp. cinnamon ¼ tsp. nutmeg, 1 tbsp. brown sugar, 2 tbsp. butter, for Grilling. To Serve walnut or pecan syrup bananas. Griddle Recipe

372.Grilled Apple Bowls

Servings: 4
Ingredients:
- Simple Syrup
- 1 cup sugar
- 1 cup water
- 1 cinnamon stick
- 2 apples, large

Directions:
1. Preparing the Ingredients.
2. Simple syrup: in a saucepan, bring the sugar, water, and cinnamon stick to a boil. Set aside.
3. Cut the apples in half and core with a melon baller. Add to the hot simple syrup. Arrange apples on the Grill Pan, cut side down.
4. Grilling
5. Cook for 3 Minutes. Turn over and continue grilling until tender. Baste with simple syrup. Top the apples with ice cream, caramel sauce, and chopped pecans immediately before serving. 2 cups vanilla ice cream ½ cup caramel sauce ½ cup pecans, chopped. These apples can also be made in advance. After grilling, cool in the refrigerator. When you are ready to serve, warm up in the microwave.

373.Tasty Cauliflower Skewers

Servings: 6
Cooking Time: 14 Minutes
Ingredients:
- 1 large cauliflower head, cut into florets
- 1 onion, cut into wedges
- 1 yellow bell pepper, cut into squares
- 1 fresh lemon juice
- 3 tsp curry powder
- 1/4 cup olive oil
- 1/2 tsp garlic powder
- 1/2 tsp ground ginger
- 1/2 tsp salt

Directions:
1. In a large bowl, whisk together oil, lemon juice, garlic, ginger, curry powder, and salt.
2. Add cauliflower florets and toss until well coated.
3. Preheat the griddle to high heat.
4. Spray griddle top with cooking spray.
5. Thread cauliflower florets, onion, and bell pepper onto the skewers.
6. Place skewers onto the hot griddle top and cook for 6-7 minutes on each side.
7. Serve and enjoy.

Nutrition Info: (Per Serving): Calories 125 ;Fat 8 g ;Carbohydrates 11 g ;Sugar 5 g ;Protein 3.4 g ;Cholesterol 0 mg

374.Caramelized Five-spice Oranges

Servings: 4
Cooking Time: 8 Minutes
Ingredients:
- ¼ cup sugar
- ½ teaspoon five-spice powder
- 2 large oranges
- ¼ cup chopped fresh mint

Directions:
1. Preparing the Ingredients
2. Stir the sugar and five-spice powder together on a small plate. Cut a sliver off the top and bottom of each orange so that it will sit flat on the grates without rolling, then turn them on their sides and cut in half through the equator. Remove any seeds. Press the cut side of each half into the sugar. Let sit until the sugar is absorbed and/or you are ready to grill.
3. Bring the griddle grill to medium-low heat. Oil the griddle and allow it to heat until the oil is shimmering but not smoking. Put the orange halves on the grill, sugared side up, and cook until they are warm all the way through, 6 to 8 Minutes, Turn them over and cook just until the cut sides brown, 2 to 3 Minutes. Transfer to individual serving plates, sprinkle with the mint, and serve with a knife and fork or with grapefruit spoons, if you have them.

375.Whoopie Pies

Servings: 8
Ingredients:
- 1 /3 cup cocoa powder
- 1 ½ cup flour
- 1 tsp. baking soda ½ tsp. salt ¾ cup buttermilk ¾ cup butter ¾ cup brown sugar
- 1 egg ½ tsp. vanilla extract
- Marshmallow Cream Filling

Directions:
1. Preparing the Ingredients.
2. Griddle Recipe
3. Grilling
4. Preheat the oven to 350° F. In a bowl, sift the cocoa powder, flour, baking soda, and salt.
5. In an electric mixer, cream the buttermilk, butter, and brown sugar together. Add the egg and vanilla. Mix until incorporated. Slowly add the flour mixture to the creamed ingredients. Blend. Make first batch of cake halves: arrange eight ¼ cup scoops of cake mix onto the Griddle Pan. Bake 12-15 Minutes or until done. Repeat step 6 to make second batch of cake halves. In the mixer, cream the butter and confectioners' sugar together until creamy. Add the marshmallow and vanilla. Place the marshmallow cream in a piping bag and fill the whoopie pies. ¾ stick butter,1 cup confectioners' sugar, 1 2/3 cup marshmallow cream, 1 tsp. vanilla extract.

376.Watermelon With Honey And Lime

Servings: 4
Cooking Time: 8 Minutes
Ingredients:
- 2 1- to 1½-inch-thick watermelon slices, halved
- Salt
- ¼ cup honey
- Lime wedges for serving

Directions:
1. Preparing the Ingredients
2. Lightly salt the watermelon on both sides, then brush both sides with the honey.
3. Bring the griddle grill to medium-low heat. Oil the griddle and allow it to heat until the oil is shimmering but not smoking. Put the slices on the griddle and cook, turning once, until the watermelon browns in spots, 4 Minutes per side. Transfer to a cutting board. Cut the slices into quarters or smaller wedges. Serve with the lime wedges.

377.Strawberries Romanoff

Servings: 4
Cooking Time: 5 Minutes
Ingredients:
- 1 pound strawberries, hulled
- ¼ cup sugar
- 2 tablespoons Grand Marnier
- 1 pint vanilla ice cream

Directions:
1. Preparing the Ingredients
2. Gently toss the strawberries with the sugar to coat.
3. Bring the griddle grill to medium-low heat. Oil the griddle and allow it to heat until the oil is shimmering but not smoking. Put them on the griddle and cook, rolling them around once, until heated through, about 5 Minutes total.
4. Transfer the strawberries to a bowl. Cut them in halves or quarters, depending on their size, and toss with the Grand Marnier. Let them macerate while you spoon out the ice cream, then divide between the bowls and serve, pouring any liquid from the bowl over the top.

378.Pound Cake & Fruit

Servings: 6
Ingredients:
- 6 slices pound cake
- 3 peaches, sliced & pitted
- 3 bananas, peeled & sliced
- 24 strawberries, large ½ cup simple syrup

Directions:
1. Preparing the Ingredients.
2. Arrange the pound cake, peaches, bananas, and strawberries on the Grill Pan.
3. Grilling
4. Cook on both sides to desired doneness. Toss the fruit with simple syrup. Set aside. Plate the pound cake with grilled fruit. Top with raspberry sauce and whipped cream. Garnish with mint leaves immediately before serving. ¼ cup raspberry sauce, 1 cup whipped cream 6 mint leaves, for garnish. Another delicious variation on this recipe is to slice a corn muffin in half and grill. The fruit and cream complement the corn's sweetness.

379.Grilled Nectarines With Blackberries And Mascarpone

Servings: 2
Cooking Time: 3 Minutes
Ingredients:
- 2 tablespoons honey
- 2 large ripe nectarines, quartered
- ½ teaspoon ground cinnamon
- 1pint blackberries, blueberries, raspberries, or strawberries (if using strawberries, thinly slice them)
- ¼ cup mascarpone

Directions:
1. Preparing the Ingredients
2. Spoon the honey into a small shallow baking dish. Dip the nectarine sections into the honey and then sprinkle the flesh side with the cinnamon.
3. Bring the griddle grill to medium-low heat. Oil the griddle and allow it to heat until the oil is shimmering but not smoking. Grill the nectarines, flesh side down, for about 3 Minutes, until the flesh is crisp, hot, and browned. Serve the nectarines in shallow bowls, topped with the berries and a spoonful of mascarpone.

Nutrition Info: (Per Serving): CALORIES: 162; FAT:7G; PROTEIN:1G

380.Ranch Potatoes

Servings: 2
Cooking Time: 12 Minutes
Ingredients:
- 1/2 lb baby potatoes, wash and cut in half
- 1/4 tsp garlic powder
- 1/2 tbsp olive oil
- 1/4 tsp dill
- 1/4 tsp chives
- 1/4 tsp parsley
- 1/4 tsp paprika
- 1/4 tsp onion powder
- Salt

Directions:
1. Preheat the griddle to high heat.
2. Spray griddle top with cooking spray.
3. Add all ingredients into the mixing bowl and toss well.
4. Spread potatoes on hot griddle top and cook until tender.
5. Serve and enjoy.

Nutrition Info: (Per Serving): Calories 100 ;Fat 3.7 g ;Carbohydrates 14.8 g ;Sugar 0.2 g ;Protein 3.1 g ;Cholesterol 0 mg

381.Jelly Pancake

Servings: 4
Ingredients:
- Pancakes
- 2 eggs
- 1 ½ cups whole milk ½ cup smooth peanut butter

- 1 ¼ cups pancake mix
- Peanut Butter Cream ½ cup smooth peanut butter
- 1 (8-oz.) container whipped topping
- Grape Syrup ¼ cup grape jelly

Directions:
1. Preparing the Ingredients.
2. Griddle Recipe
3. Grilling
4. Preheat the Griddle Pan over medium heat. Make pancake batter: Beat together the egg and milk. Add the peanut butter and Beat until smooth. Mix in the pancake mix. Peanut butter cream: Beat together the peanut butter and whipped topping. Grape syrup: combine the jelly and syrup. Microwave until melted, about 20 seconds. Mix to combine. Ladle a half cup of the pancake batter onto the Pan. Cook until golden brown, about 2 Minutes per side. Continue until all batter is used up. Stack the pancakes, spreading a smear of the peanut butter cream between each pancake. Spry with the grape syrup before serving. ½ cup maple syrup.

382.Sugared Peaches With Candied Ginger Ice Cream

Servings: 4
Cooking Time: 20 Minutes
Ingredients:
- 1 pint vanilla ice cream, softened just a bit
- ¼ cup chopped candied ginger
- 2 or 4 ripe peaches, depending on their size
- 4 tablespoons (½ stick) butter, melted
- ¼ cup Demerara sugar, or more as needed
- Fresh mint sprigs for garnish

Directions:
1. Preparing the Ingredients
2. Put the ice cream and ginger in a bowl and mash together with a wooden spoon until the ginger is mixed throughout the ice cream. This can be done several days ahead; put it back in the ice cream container and freeze at least a couple hours.
3. When you're ready for dessert, cut the peaches in half through the stem end and remove the pits. Brush with the melted butter. Put the sugar on a plate and dredge the cut side of each peach in it.
4. Bring the griddle grill to medium-low heat. Oil the griddle and allow it to heat until the oil is shimmering but not smoking. Put the peaches on the grill, cut side up, and cook until they soften, 10 to 15 Minutes. Turn them cut side down and cook until the sugar caramelizes to a golden brown, 2 to 5 Minutes. Transfer to a platter. To serve, put the warm peaches on plates or in dessert bowls, cut side up. Divide the

ice cream between them, or pass the ice cream at the table. Garnish with the mint.

383.Parmesan Zucchini Patties

Servings: 6
Cooking Time: 30 Minutes
Ingredients:
- 1 cup zucchini, shredded and squeeze out all liquid
- 1/2 tbsp Dijon mustard
- 1 egg, lightly beaten
- 1/4 tsp red pepper flakes
- 1/4 cup parmesan cheese, grated
- 1/2 tbsp mayonnaise
- 1/2 cup breadcrumbs
- 2 tbsp onion, minced
- Pepper
- Salt

Directions:
1. Add all ingredients into the bowl and mix until well combined.
2. Preheat the griddle to high heat.
3. Spray griddle top with cooking spray.
4. Make small patties from the zucchini mixture and place on hot griddle top and cook until golden brown from both sides.
5. Serve and enjoy.

Nutrition Info: (Per Serving): Calories 156 ;Fat 7.7 g ;Carbohydrates 7.9 g ;Sugar 1.2 g ;Protein 10.5 g ;Cholesterol 48 mg

384.Marshmallow Stuffed Banana

Servings: 1
Cooking Time: 5 Minutes
Ingredients:
- 1 banana
- 1/4 cup chocolate chips
- 1/4 cup mini marshmallows

Directions:
1. Take the peeled banana and spread over a 12×12-inch foil sheet.
2. Slice a slit in the banana lengthwise and stuff the slit with chocolate chips and marshmallows.
3. Wrap some foil around the banana to seal it.
4. Prepare and preheat your Griddle Grill set to the medium temperature setting.
5. Once the grill is preheated and place the banana in the grill.
6. Grill each side for 5 minutes.
7. Unwrap your yummy treat, serve and enjoy it!

Nutrition Info: (Per serving): Calories: 372 Fat: 11.8g Carbs: 45.8g Protein: 4g

385.Grilled Pineapple Rings With Ice Cream

Servings: 4
Cooking Time: 4 Minutes
Ingredients:
- 1 whole pineapple, sliced into 6 equal slices
- 6 scoops vanilla bean ice cream
- 6 spoonfuls of whipped cream
- ¼ cup almond slivers, toasted
- ¼ cup sweetened shredded coconut, toasted
- ½ cup caramel sauce
- mint (to garnish)

Directions:
1. Preparing the Ingredients
2. Bring the griddle grill to medium-low heat. Oil the griddle and allow it to heat until the oil is shimmering but not smoking. Grill pineapple until a nice char forms, about 2 Minutes per side.
3. Remove pineapple from grill, top each slice with a scoop of ice cream, a dollop of whipped cream, almonds, and coconut.
4. Drizzle each with caramel sauce, garnish with mint, and serve.

386.Grilled Pears With Gorgonzola, Honey, And Walnuts

Servings: 3
Cooking Time: 8 Minutes
Ingredients:
- 3 pears, ripe but firm
- 2 cups baby arugula
- ½ cup crumbled gorgonzola cheese
- ¼ cup honey
- ¼ cup craisins
- ¼ cup candied walnuts
- 1 Tbsp. olive oil
- 1½ tsp. ground cinnamon

Directions:
1. Preparing the Ingredients
2. Cut each pear in half, remove the core, and dig small "bowl" in each pear half with a standard kitchen spoon or melon baller.
3. Coat each pear half with a light drizzle of olive oil.
4. Place pears cut side down over the heat and grill for 2–3 Minutes or until a light char and grill marks start to form.
5. Fill each pear bowl with a heaping portion of gorgonzola cheese.
6. Bring the griddle grill to medium-low heat. Oil the griddle and allow it to heat until the oil is

shimmering but not smoking. Allow pears to cook until cheese starts to melt, about 5 Minutes.
7. Remove from grill and plate each pear half on a bed of baby arugula.
8. Drizzle with honey, dust with cinnamon, and garnish with craisins and candied walnuts.

387.Grilled Fruit Skewers

Servings: 6
Ingredients:
- 8 strawberries, large
- 2 peaches, sliced thick
- 1 pear, sliced thick
- 1 cup pineapple, cubed
- 1 banana, sliced thick

Directions:
1. Preparing the Ingredients.
2. Skewer the cut fruit.
3. Grilling
4. Grill to desired doneness. Dipping sauce: in a saucepot, bring the heavy cream to a boil. Add the chocolate chips and remove from heat. Mix until creamy, then add vanilla. Serve grilled fruit with chocolate dipping sauce. Chocolate Dipping Sauce 1 cup heavy cream, 1 cup semi-sweet chocolate chips ½ tsp. vanilla extract. Feel free to choose any chocolate you like. Dark and white work well with this recipe.

388.Cauliflower Zucchini Fritters

Servings: 4
Cooking Time: 8 Minutes
Ingredients:
- 2 medium zucchini, grated and squeezed
- 1 tbsp olive oil
- 1/4 cup coconut flour
- 3 cups cauliflower rice
- 1/2 tsp sea salt

Directions:
1. Add all ingredients except oil into the bowl and mix until well combined.
2. Preheat the griddle to high heat.
3. Add oil to the hot griddle top.
4. Make small patties from the mixture and place onto the griddle top and cook for 3-4 minutes on each side.
5. Serve and enjoy.
Nutrition Info: (Per Serving): Calories 90 ;Fat 5 g ;Carbohydrates 8.8 g ;Sugar 5 g ;Protein 4.3 g ;Cholesterol 0 mg

389. Banana Coconut Fritters

Servings: 16
Ingredients:
- 2 bananas, mashed
- 1/3 cup flour ½ tsp. cinnamon
- 2 eggs ½ cup shredded coconut

Directions:
1. Preparing the Ingredients.
2. Combine all ingredients except oil in a bowl. Preheat Griddle Pan for 4 Minutes on medium heat. Coat the Pan with canola oil. Drop heaping tablespoons of fritter batter onto the Pan.
3. Grilling
4. Cook until golden on each side before serving. ½ tsp. baking powder 1 tbsp. brown sugar, 1 tbsp. milk, 3 tbsp. canola oil.

390. Flavors Cauliflower Bites

Servings: 4
Cooking Time: 10 Minutes
Ingredients:
- 1 lb cauliflower florets
- 1 tsp ground coriander
- 1/2 tsp dried rosemary
- 1 1/2 tsp garlic powder
- 1 tbsp olive oil
- 1 tsp sesame seeds
- Pepper
- Salt

Directions:
1. Preheat the griddle to high heat.
2. Spray griddle top with cooking spray.
3. Add cauliflower florets and remaining ingredients into the bowl and toss well and spread on the hot griddle top.
4. Cook cauliflower florets until tender.
5. Serve and enjoy.
Nutrition Info: (Per Serving): Calories 65 ;Fat 4 g ;Carbohydrates 7.1 g ;Sugar 3 g ;Protein 2.6 g ;Cholesterol 0 mg

391. Strawberry Shortcake

Servings: 6
Ingredients:
- 1 angel food cake, sliced into wedges
- ½ stick butter 1 lb. strawberries, cut in half zest of 1 lemon juice of ½ lemon
- Strawberry Shortcake

Directions:
1. Preparing the Ingredients.
2. Brush the cake wedges with butter.
3. Grilling

4. Grill to desired doneness. Grill the strawberries. Let cool before tossing with lemon zest, lemon juice, and 1 tbsp. sugar. Whip the cream with ¼ cup confectioners' sugar and vanilla. Top cake wedges with strawberries and whipped cream immediately before serving. 1 tbsp. sugar 1 ½ cup heavy cream, ¼ cup confectioners' sugar, to whip cream 1 tsp. vanilla extract. I've diced the grilled angel food cake and turned this into an amazing layered trifle when making dessert for a large group!

392. Banana "tostones" With Cinnamon Rum Whipped Cream

Servings: 4
Cooking Time: 3 Minutes
Ingredients:
- FOR THE WHIPPED CREAM:
- 1 cup heavy (whipping) cream
- 3 tablespoons confectioners' sugar
- 1 tablespoon dark rum
- 1 teaspoon ground cinnamon
- FOR THE BANANAS:
- ⅔ cup granulated sugar
- 1 tablespoon ground cinnamon
- 2 teaspoons very finely grated lemon or lime zest
- 4 bananas, chilled in the refrigerator for 1 hour
- 4 tablespoons (½ stick) unsalted butter, melted
- Cooking oil spray
- Fresh mint sprigs (optional), for garnish

Directions:
1. Preparing the Ingredients
2. Make the whipped cream: Place the cream in a chilled mixer bowl or in a large metal bowl. Beat with a mixer until soft peaks form, starting on the slow speed and gradually increasing the speed to high. The total beating time will 6 to 8 Minutes. When soft peaks have formed, add the confectioners' sugar, rum, and cinnamon. Continue beating the cream until stiff peaks form, about 2 Minutes longer. Don't overbeat the cream or it will start to turn to butter. The cinnamon rum whipped cream can be made several hours ahead. Refrigerate it, covered, until ready to serve.
3. Prepare the bananas: Place the granulated sugar, cinnamon, and lemon zest in a shallow bowl and stir to mix.
4. When ready to cook, bring the griddle grill to medium-low heat Lightly coat the grill surface with cooking oil spray. Arrange the pieces of banana upright on the grill, pressing down to flatten the bananas. Grill the bananas until they are crusty and golden brown, 3 to 5 Minutes. After 2 Minutes, brush the tops of the bananas with any remaining butter,

and sprinkle any remaining cinnamon sugar over them.

5. Meanwhile, peel the bananas and cut each crosswise into 1-inch pieces. Dip the ends of each piece of banana in the melted butter, then in the cinnamon sugar, shaking off the excess.

6. Place the banana "tostones" on plates. Garnish each serving with a large dollop of cinnamon rum whipped cream and a mint sprig, if using, and serve at once.

393.Rum-soaked Pineapple

Servings: 6
Cooking Time: 15 Minutes
Ingredients:
- 1/2 cup packed brown sugar
- 1/2 cup rum
- 1 teaspoon ground cinnamon
- 1 pineapple, cored and sliced
- cooking spray
- vanilla ice cream

Directions:
1. Mix the rum with brown sugar and cinnamon in a mixing bowl.
2. Pour this mixture over your pineapple rings and mix well.
3. Let the pineapple rings soak for about 15 minutes and flip the rings after 7 minutes.
4. Prepare and preheat your Griddle Grill setting it at a High-temperature setting.
5. Once your grill is preheated, place your pineapple rings on the grill.
6. Grill it for 4 minutes per side.
7. Serve your pineapple rings with a scoop of ice cream on top.

Nutrition Info: (Per serving): Calories: 143.2 Fat: 0.4g Carbs: 21g Protein: 0.3g

394.Grilled Pear Crisp

Servings: 4
Ingredients:
- 2 pears, cored
- Crisp Topping ¼ cup brown
- sugar ¼ cup flour
- 3 tbsp. butter

Directions:
1. Preparing the Ingredients.
2. Grill pears until tender. About 5 Minutes per side. Make crisp topping: combine brown sugar, flour, butter, walnuts, and cinnamon in a bowl.
3. Grilling
4. Bake in the oven for 15 Minutes at 400° F. Place half a pear into each serving bowl. Immediately

before serving, top with ½ cup vanilla ice cream, 2 tbsp. crisp topping, and 1 tbsp. caramel sauce. 2 tbsp. walnuts ½ tsp. cinnamon, 2 cups vanilla ice cream 4 tbsp. caramel sauce. Feel free to substitute any fruit that is ripe and in season such as local apples or peaches.

395.Straw Berries Pizza

Servings: 8
Ingredients:
- 1 (8-oz.) thin crust pizza dough ¼ cup caramel sauce
- 2 bananas, sliced & grilled
- 8 strawberries, halved & grilled
- 2 tbsp. chocolate sauce

Directions:
1. Preparing the Ingredients.
2. Arrange pizza dough to fit onto the Grill Pan. Cook on both sides to desired doneness.
3. Grilling
4. Spread caramel sauce over the pizza. Layer with bananas and strawberries. Spry with chocolate and raspberry sauces. Top with peanuts. Cut pizza into 8 slices. Serve alone or with your favorite ice cream. 2 tbsp. raspberry sauce ¼ cup peanuts, chopped. Sprinkling toasted coconut or crumbled graham crackers will add extra flavor and crunch!

396.Grilled Peaches Cinnamon

Servings: 4
Cooking Time: 5 Minutes
Ingredients:
- 4 ripe peaches, halved and pitted
- 1/4 cup salted butter
- 1 teaspoon granulated sugar
- 1/4 teaspoon cinnamon

Directions:
1. Mix your sugar, butter and cinnamon in a bowl until smooth.
2. Preheat your griddle grill on the medium temperature setting.
3. Once your grill is preheated, place the peaches on the grill.
4. Grill it for 1 minute per side.
5. Serve the peaches with cinnamon butter on top and enjoy!

Nutrition Info: (Per serving): Calories: 46.4 Fat: 0.1g Carbs: 54.7g Protein: 0.7g

397.Maple-glazed Bananas

Servings: 4

Cooking Time: 5 Minutes
Ingredients:
- 4 bananas
- 3 tablespoons maple syrup
- 6 to 8 tablespoons dark brown sugar or confectioners' sugar
- Ground cinnamon
- 6 tablespoons Hot Fudge Sauce
- 6 tablespoons Cinnamon Caramel Sauce
- Vanilla ice cream (optional), for serving

Directions:
1. Preparing the Ingredients
2. Place the bananas on a work surface and cut each in half lengthwise (leave the skins on). Brush the cut sides with the maple syrup and generously sprinkle brown sugar over them. Lightly dust the cut sides of the bananas with cinnamon.
3. Bring the griddle grill to medium-low heat. Oil the griddle and allow it to heat until the oil is shimmering but not smoking. Arrange the bananas, cut side up, on the hot grill. The bananas will be done after cooking 3 to 5 Minutes until the cut side is caramelized to a dark golden brown and the fruit starts to pull away from the peel. The amount of caramelization you'll get will depend upon your particular contact grill.
4. Transfer the grilled banana halves still in their skins to a platter or plates and place a scoop of vanilla ice cream alongside, if desired. Drizzle Hot Fudge Sauce and/or Cinnamon Caramel Sauce over all, if desired.

398.Grilled Apple Pie

Servings: 4
Ingredients:
- 8 slices white bread
- 4 tbsp. butter, softened
- 2 granny smith apples, cored, halved & sliced thin
- ¼ cup brown sugar 1 tsp. cinnamon ½ cup cream cheese, softened

Directions:
1. Preparing the Ingredients.
2. Brush the bread on one side with butter. In a bowl, combine the apples, brown sugar, and cinnamon. Mix. Spread cream cheese thinly on the unbuttered side of the bread. Assemble the paninis with the apple mixture and second slice of bread.
3. Grilling
4. Grill on each side at medium heat until golden. Cut paninis in half before serving with vanilla ice

cream. 2 cups vanilla ice cream. I love trying different cheeses with this recipe. Yellow cheddar and Brie are my two favorites!

399.Brioche French Toast

Servings: 6
Ingredients:
- 10 eggs ¾ cup half and half
- 2 tsp. cinnamon
- 1 tsp. almond extract ¼ cup maple syrup, to serve
- 1 loaf brioche bread, sliced

Directions:
1. Preparing the Ingredients.
2. In a bowl Whisk the eggs. Mix in half and half, cinnamon, and almond extract. Soak bread in the egg batter for 5 Minutes. Preheat the Griddle Pan on medium heat, 3-4 Minutes. Melt 2 tbsp. butter onto the Pan.
3. Grilling
4. Cook the French toast to desired doneness. Repeat until all are cooked. Serve with maple syrup and butter.1 stick butter. Griddle Recipe.

400.Peanut Butter Sundae

Servings: 4
Ingredients:
- 4 bananas, peeled & sliced into medallions
- 4 large scoops vanilla ice cream ½ cup creamy peanut butter
- Salted Caramel Peanut Butter Sundae

Directions:
1. Preparing the Ingredients.
2. Sprinkle the bananas with cinnamon and cayenne pepper before grilling for a little kick!
3. Grilling
4. Grill bananas on high heat. Scoop ice cream into a serving bowl. Top with bananas, then peanut butter, caramel sauce, and chopped peanuts. Sprinkle lightly with pink sea salt before serving. ½ cup caramel sauce ¼ cup peanuts, chopped pink sea salt, to sprinkle.

401.Yummy Turkey Burger

Servings: 6

Cooking Time: 14 Minutes
Ingredients:
- 1 lb ground turkey
- 1 egg, lightly beaten
- 1 cup Monterey jack cheese, grated
- 1 cup carrot, grated
- 1 cup cauliflower, grated
- 2 garlic cloves, minced
- 1/2 cup onion, minced
- 3/4 cup breadcrumbs
- Pepper
- Salt

Directions:
1. Preheat the griddle to high heat.
2. Spray griddle top with cooking spray.
3. Add all ingredients into the mixing bowl and mix until well combined.
4. Make small patties from mixture and place on hot griddle top and cook until golden brown from both sides.
5. Serve and enjoy.

Nutrition Info: (Per Serving): Calories 299 ;Fat 15.5 g ;Carbohydrates 13.8 g ;Sugar 2.7 g ;Protein 2.7 g ;Cholesterol 121 mg

402.Grilled Doughnut With Ice Cream

Servings: 4
Ingredients:
- 4 apple cider doughnuts, sliced in half
- 2 pears, halved, cored & sliced
- 4 cups vanilla ice cream ½ cup chocolate sauce whipped cream, for serving

Directions:
1. Preparing the Ingredients.
2. Arrange doughnut and pears halves on the Grill Pan.
3. Grilling
4. Cook to desired doneness. Place the ice cream in a small baking pan and cover with plastic wrap. Press flat, about 2 inches thick, then place the pan into the freezer. Cut frozen ice cream into 8 discs the same size as the doughnuts. Place one doughnut half on each dish. Layer with sliced pears and ice cream. Top with a second doughnut half. Repeat to make it a triple decker. Spry with chocolate sauce and whipped cream before serving. The key to this recipe is to use

the best seasonal fruit. Local orchards and farm stands will keep the variety of this recipe endless!

403.Stir Fry Potatoes & Carrots

Servings: 2
Cooking Time: 15 Minutes
Ingredients:
- 1/2 lb potatoes, cut into 1-inch cubes
- 1/2 onion, diced
- 1/2 tsp Italian seasoning
- 1/4 tsp garlic powder
- 1/2 lb carrots, peeled & cut into chunks
- 1 tbsp olive oil
- Pepper
- Salt

Directions:
1. In a large bowl, toss carrots, potatoes, garlic powder, Italian seasoning, oil, onion, pepper, and salt.
2. Preheat the griddle to high heat.
3. Spray griddle top with cooking spray.
4. Transfer carrot potato mixture on hot griddle top and cook until tender.
5. Serve and enjoy.

Nutrition Info: (Per Serving): Calories 201 ;Fat 7.5 g ;Carbohydrates 32 g ;Sugar 8.2 g ;Protein 3.2 g ;Cholesterol 1 mg

404.Banana With Chocolate And Crushed Peanut Brittle

Servings: 4
Cooking Time: 5 Minutes
Ingredients:
- 1 tablespoon butter, softened
- 2 tablespoons crushed or chopped peanut brittle
- 2 tablespoons chopped dark chocolate
- 1 ripe banana
- Ice cream of your choice (optional)

Directions:
1. Preparing the Ingredients
2. Put the butter, peanut brittle, and chocolate in a small bowl and mash together. Slit the banana from top to bottom along one side, through the top peel but not the bottom peel. Pull the banana open enough so you can push the filling into the slit.
3. Bring the griddle grill to medium-low heat. Oil the griddle and allow it to heat until the oil is

shimmering but not smoking. Put the banana on the grill grate slit side up, and cook until the peel turns black, about 5 Minutes. Transfer to a plate.

4.   To serve, eat right from the peel or spoon over ice cream, angel food cake, or vanilla pudding.

405.Naan

Servings: 8 To 12
Cooking Time: 12 Minutes
Ingredients:
- ¼ cup yogurt
- 2 tablespoons good-quality vegetable oil, plus more for the bowl
- 1 tablespoon sugar
- 2¼ teaspoons (1 package) instant yeast
- 3½ cups all-purpose flour, plus more as needed
- ½ cup whole wheat flour
- 2 teaspoons salt
- 1½ cups warm water, plus more as needed
- 5 tablespoons (¾ stick) butter, melted and still warm

Directions:
1.   Preparing the Ingredients
2.   1 Whisk the yogurt, oil, sugar, and yeast together. Stir the flours and salt together in a large bowl. Add the yogurt mixture and combine. Add the water ½ cup at a time, stirring until the mixture comes together in a cohesive but sticky dough; you may need to add another tablespoon or 2 water.
3.   Turn the dough out onto a floured work surface and knead by hand for a minute or so to form a smooth dough. Shape into a round ball, put in a lightly oiled bowl, and cover with plastic wrap. Let rise until doubled in size, 1 to 2 hours. Or you can let the dough rise in the refrigerator for up to 8 hours.
4.   2 Punch the dough down. Using as much flour as necessary to keep the dough from sticking to the work surface or your hands, roll it into a snake about 2 inches in diameter, then tear into 12 equal-sized balls. Space the balls out on the work surface. Cover with plastic wrap or a clean, damp dish towel and let rest for 10 Minutes. Roll each dough ball into an oval roughly 6 to 8 inches long and 3 to 4 inches wide.
5.   3 Bring the griddle grill to medium-high heat. Oil the griddle and allow it to heat until the oil is shimmering but not smoking., put the naan on the grill grate and cook for 6 Minutes, quickly turn with

tongs. The other side will take about the same time or a little less to cook. When you grab it with tongs, the bread should feel firm and springy, and both sides should be browned in spots, with a little charring. Transfer to a platter and immediately brush with the butter. Repeat with the remaining naan and butter and serve as soon as possible.

406.Pain Perdu With Balsamic Strawberries

Servings: 4
Cooking Time: 10 Minutes
Ingredients:
- 3 cups sliced hulled strawberries (about 1½ pounds)
- 2–3 tablespoons sugar
- 1 tablespoon balsamic vinegar
- 2 eggs
- ½ cup milk
- 1 teaspoon vanilla extract
- Pinch salt
- 4 slices bread
- Black pepper (optional)

Directions:
1.   Preparing the Ingredients
2.   1 Put the strawberries in a bowl, sprinkle with 1 to 2 tablespoons of the sugar (depending on their sweetness), and toss gently to coat. Add the vinegar and toss again. Let macerate at room temperature until you're ready for dessert, up to several hours.
3.   2 Beat the eggs lightly in a large shallow bowl, then beat in the milk, the remaining 1 tablespoon sugar, vanilla, and salt. Refrigerate until you're ready to use it (or up to several hours).
4.   3 Bring the griddle grill to medium-low heat. Oil the griddle and allow it to heat until the oil is shimmering but not smoking. Give each slice of bread a quick dip in the egg wash on both sides, put on a large plate, and immediately take out them to the grill. Put the bread on the grill and cook until the bread develops grill marks, 2 to 3 Minutes per side. Transfer to a clean platter. To serve, top each grilled toast with a spoonful of the balsamic strawberries. Let diners add freshly ground black pepper to their strawberries, if they like.

407.Figs With Walnuts And Honey

Servings: 4
Cooking Time: 10 Minutes
Ingredients:
- 8 ripe figs, stemmed
- 2 tablespoons walnut oil or good-quality olive oil
- 8 walnut halves, toasted
- ¼ cup honey

Directions:
1. Preparing the Ingredients
2. Brush the figs with the walnut oil, then cut an X in the stem ends. Push 1 walnut half into each fig.
3. Bring the griddle grill to medium-low heat. Oil the griddle and allow it to heat until the oil is shimmering but not smoking. Put the figs on the grill grate, stem side up, and cook until the fruit softens, 5 to 10 Minutes. Transfer to a platter, drizzle with the honey, and serve.

408.Apricots With Brioche

Servings: 4
Cooking Time: 4 Minutes
Ingredients:
- 2 cups vanilla ice cream
- 2 tablespoons honey
- 4 slices brioches, diced
- 2 tablespoons sugar
- 2 tablespoons butter
- 8 ripe apricots

Directions:
1. Mix the halved apricots with sugar and butter.
2. Prepare and preheat your Griddle Grill on the medium temperature setting.
3. When your grill is preheated, put the brioche slices onto the grill.
4. Grill it for 1 minute per side.
5. Next, grill your apricots in the grill for 1 minute per side.
6. Top your brioche slices with honey, apricot slices, and a scoop of vanilla ice cream.
7. Serve your tasty dessert and enjoy it!

Nutrition Info: (Per serving): Calories: 212 Fat: 9g Carbs: 28g Protein: 4g

VEGETABLE & SIDE DISHES

409.Portobello Caprese Stacks

Servings: 4
Cooking Time: 12 Minutes
Ingredients:
- 4 portobello mushrooms, stems removed and caps wiped clean
- 6 tablespoons good-quality olive oil
- Salt and pepper
- 24 large fresh basil leaves
- 4 tomato slices (each about ¾ inch thick; 2 large tomatoes)
- 4 slices fresh mozzarella cheese (about 4 ounces)
- Balsamic Syrup for serving

Directions:
1. Preparing the Ingredients
2. Brush the mushrooms with the oil and sprinkle with salt and pepper on both sides.
3. Bring the griddle grill to medium-high heat. Oil the griddle and allow it to heat until the oil is shimmering but not smoking. Put the mushrooms and cook until well browned and tender, 6 to 8 Minutes.
4. Transfer the mushrooms to a platter, gill side up. Cover the top with the basil, then add the tomato slices, and finally the mozzarella. Return the stacks directly over the grill, close the lid, and cook until the cheese melts, 2 to 4 Minutes. Serve hot or at room temperature, drizzled with balsamic syrup.

410.Easy Fried Rice

Servings: 2
Cooking Time: 10 Minutes
Ingredients:
- 4 cups rice, cooked
- 2 large eggs
- 2 tbsp green onion, sliced
- 2 tbsp olive oil
- 1 tsp salt

Directions:
1. In a bowl, whisk eggs and set aside.
2. Preheat the griddle to high heat.
3. Spray griddle top with cooking spray.
4. Add cooked rice on hot griddle top and fry until rice separate from each other.
5. Push rice to one side of the griddle top. Add oil to the griddle and pour beaten egg.
6. Add salt and mix egg quickly with rice and cook until rice grains are covered by egg.
7. Add green onion and stir fry for 2 minutes.
8. Serve and enjoy.

Nutrition Info: (Per Serving): Calories 557 ;Fat 19.8 g ;Carbohydrates 79.6 g ;Sugar 0.7 g ;Protein 14 g ;Cholesterol 186 mg

411.Zucchini Antipasto

Servings: 4
Cooking Time: 6 Minutes
Ingredients:
- ¼ cup olive oil
- 3 garlic cloves, minced
- 1 tablespoon fresh thyme leaves or ½ teaspoon dried thyme
- ¼ teaspoon salt
- ¼ teaspoon freshly ground black pepper
- 4 medium zucchini, cut lengthwise into ¼-inch-thick slices
- 1 tablespoon balsamic vinegar

Directions:
1. Preparing the Ingredients
2. Whisk together the olive oil, garlic, thyme, salt, and pepper in a large bowl.
3. Add the zucchini and toss to coat.
4. Bring the griddle grill to medium-high heat. Oil the griddle and allow it to heat until the oil is shimmering but not smoking.
5. Grill for about 6 Minutes, until the zucchini slices have taken on grill marks and are very tender.
6. Serve either hot off the grill or at room temperature, sprinkled with the vinegar.

Nutrition Info: (Per Serving): CALORIES: 156; FAT:14G; PROTEIN:2G

412.Grilled Summer Squash

Servings: 12
Cooking Time: 10 Minutes
Ingredients:
- 1 Summer Squash
- 2 tbsps. Olive Oil
- Sea Salt To Taste

Directions:
1. Slice the squash in half lengthwise. Brush the squash with the olive oil and season with salt.
2. Heat the griddle grill to medium heat, and set the squash cut-side down. Cook for 5 minutes per side until it is tender.
3. Remove from heat and serve.

Nutrition Info: (Per serving):Calories 74, Fat 5.4g, protein 10g, carbs 6.1g

413.Tofu Steaks

Servings: 4
Cooking Time: 10 Minutes
Ingredients:
- 1 block firm or extra-firm tofu (14–16 ounces)
- Good-quality olive oil for brushing
- Salt
- Pepper (optional)

Directions:
1. Preparing the Ingredients
2. Cut the tofu across into 1-inch-thick steaks. Pat dry with paper towels, then brush with oil and sprinkle with salt on both sides.
3. Bring the griddle grill to high heat. Oil the griddle. Put the tofu on the grill and cook, turning once, until the slices develop a crust and release easily from the grate, about 5 Minutes per side. Sprinkle with more salt and some pepper if you like and serve.

414.Stir Fry Bok Choy

Servings: 4
Cooking Time: 5 Minutes
Ingredients:
- 2 heads bok choy, trimmed and cut crosswise
- 1 tsp sesame oil
- 2 tsp soy sauce
- 2 tbsp water
- 1 tbsp butter
- 1 tbsp peanut oil
- 1 tbsp oyster sauce
- 1/2 tsp salt

Directions:
1. In a small bowl, mix together soy sauce, oyster sauce, sesame oil, and water and set aside.
2. Preheat the griddle to high heat.
3. Add oil to the hot griddle top.
4. Add bok choy and salt and stir fry for 2 minutes.
5. Add butter and soy sauce mixture and stir fry for 1-2 minutes.
6. Serve and enjoy.

Nutrition Info: (Per Serving): Calories 122 ;Fat 8.2 g ;Carbohydrates 9.5 g ;Sugar 5 g ;Cholesterol 8 mg

415.Crisp Baby Artichokes With Lemon Aïoli

Servings: 4
Cooking Time: 10 Minutes
Ingredients:
- 2 tablespoons good-quality olive oil
- Grated zest and juice of 1 lemon
- 8 baby artichokes
- ½ cup mayonnaise
- 1 teaspoon minced garlic, or more to taste
- Salt and pepper

Directions:
1. Preparing the Ingredients
2. 1 Whisk the oil and lemon juice in a large bowl. Peel away and discard the outer layers of each artichoke until the leaves are half yellow and half green. With a sharp knife, cut across the top of the artichoke to remove the green tops. Leave 1 inch of stem and use a paring knife or vegetable peeler to trim the bottom so no green remains. Cut the artichoke in half lengthwise from top to bottom. As each artichoke is trimmed, add it to the olive oil mixture and toss to coat evenly; this helps delay discoloring. (You can cover the bowl and refrigerate for up to several hours.)
3. 2 Make the aïoli: Put the mayonnaise, garlic, and lemon zest in a small bowl, sprinkle with salt and pepper, and whisk to combine. Taste and adjust the seasoning.
4. 3 Bring the griddle grill to medium-high heat. Oil the griddle and allow it to heat until the oil is shimmering but not smoking. Put the artichokes cut side down on the grill and cook until tender and charred, 8 to 10 Minutes. Transfer to a plate and serve with the aïoli for dipping.

416.Prosciutto-wrapped Melon

Servings: 8
Cooking Time: 6 Minutes
Ingredients:
- 1 ripe cantaloupe
- Salt and pepper
- 16 thin slices prosciutto

Directions:
1. Preparing the Ingredients
2. 1 Cut the cantaloupe in half lengthwise and scoop out all the seeds. Cut each half into 8 wedges, then cut away the rind from each wedge. Sprinkle with salt and pepper and wrap each wedge with a slice of prosciutto, covering as much of the cantaloupe as possible.
3. 2 Bring the griddle grill to medium-high heat. Oil the griddle and allow it to heat until the oil is shimmering but not smoking. Put the wedges and cook until the prosciutto shrivels, browns, and crisps in places, 4 to 6 Minutes. Serve hot or at room temperature.

417.Grilled Polenta

Servings: 4
Cooking Time: 10 Minutes

Ingredients:
- 2 tablespoons butter, plus more for the pan
- ½ cup milk
- Salt
- 1 cup coarse cornmeal
- Black pepper
- Good-quality olive oil for brushing
- ¾ cup freshly grated Parmesan cheese

Directions:
1. Preparing the Ingredients
2. Generously grease an 8-inch square baking dish or standard loaf pan with butter. Combine the milk with 2 cups of water and a large pinch salt in a medium saucepan over medium heat. Bring just about to a boil, then add the cornmeal in a steady stream, whisking constantly to prevent lumps from forming. Turn the heat down to low and simmer, whisking frequently, until it has the consistency of thick oatmeal, 10 to 15 Minutes. Stir in the butter, taste, and adjust the seasoning with salt and pepper. Pour the polenta into the prepared pan and spread into an even layer. Let stand at room temperature until fully cooled, about 1 hour, or cover and refrigerate overnight.
3. Turn the polenta out onto a cutting board. With a serrated knife, cut it into 1½- to 2-inch squares. Brush the squares with oil on both sides.
4. Bring the griddle grill to medium-high heat. Oil the griddle and allow it to heat until the oil is shimmering but not smoking. Put the polenta squares on the griddle and cook until they brown and are heated through 10 Minutes. Transfer to a platter, immediately sprinkle with the Parmesan, and serve.

418.Stuffed Cabbage With Summer Vegetables

Servings: 4
Cooking Time: 12 Minutes
Ingredients:
- 2 tablespoons good-quality olive oil, plus more for brushing and drizzling
- 1 onion, chopped
- Salt and pepper
- 2 tablespoons minced garlic
- 1 cup thinly sliced snow peas
- 1 cup chopped summer squash
- 1 cup fresh or frozen corn kernels
- 1 large head green or Savoy cabbage (about 4 pounds)
- ¼ cup chopped fresh basil
- Grated zest of 1 lime

Directions:
1. Preparing the Ingredients

2. 1 Put the oil in a large skillet over medium-high heat. When it's hot, add the onion, sprinkle with salt and pepper, and cook, stirring occasionally, until it's soft, about 5 Minutes. Add the garlic and stir until fragrant, about another minute. Add the snow peas, squash, and corn and cook, stirring occasionally, until the squash is just tender, about 5 Minutes. Season to taste with salt and pepper. Remove from the heat.
3. 2 Use a thin-bladed sharp knife to cut a cone-shaped wedge out of the bottom of the cabbage, removing its core. Pull off 12 large, untorn, unblemished leaves and put in a steamer above a couple inches of salted water (you may need to work in batches). Cover and cook until the leaves are just flexible enough to bend, about 5 Minutes. Drain and rinse under cold water to stop the cooking. (Reserve the remaining cabbage leaves for another use.)
4. 3 Stir the basil and lime zest into the filling; taste and adjust the seasoning. To stuff the cabbage leaves, put the leaves, concave side up, on a work surface or cutting board. Make a V-cut in each leaf to remove the tough central stem. Put a heaping ¼ cup or so of filling in the center of a leaf, just above where you cut out the stem. Fold over the sides, then roll up from the stem end, making a little package (like a burrito). Don't roll too tightly; you'll quickly get the hang of it. Skewer the rolls with a toothpick or 2 to hold them together or just put them on a platter seam side down. (You can make the stuffed cabbage to this point up to a day or 2 in advance; cover and refrigerate.)
5. 4 Bring the griddle grill to medium-high heat. Oil the griddle and allow it to heat until the oil is shimmering but not smoking. Brush the rolls with oil on all sides and sprinkle with salt. Put the rolls and cook 6 Minutes, to heat the filling. Transfer to a platter, drizzle with a little more oil, and serve.

419.Asian-spiced Grilled Squash

Servings: 4
Cooking Time: 6 Minutes
Ingredients:
- 1½ pounds butternut or other winter squash
- 2 tablespoons (¼ stick) unsalted butter
- 2 cloves garlic, minced
- 1 scallion, both white and green parts, minced
- 1 tablespoon black or white sesame seeds
- 2 tablespoons maple syrup
- 1 tablespoon soy sauce

Directions:
1. Preparing the Ingredients
2. Peel the squash and remove and discard the seeds. Cut the squash crosswise into ½-inch-thick slices. Place the butter in a small saucepan and melt it over medium heat. Add the garlic, scallion, and

sesame seeds and cook until the garlic has lost its rawness, about 1 minute; do not let the garlic brown. Stir in the maple syrup and soy sauce, bring to a boil, and let boil for 30 seconds.

3.   When ready to cook, brush the squash slices on both sides with some of the butter mixture.

4.   Bring the griddle grill to medium-high heat. Oil the griddle and allow it to heat until the oil is shimmering but not smoking. Place the squash on the hot grill. The squash will be done after cooking 4 to 6 Minutes. You will need to turn the squash so that you can baste both side until browned and tender; it should be easy to pierce with a knife. Baste the squash once or twice with the garlic mixture as it cooks.

5.   Transfer the squash to a platter or plates and serve at once, spooning any remaining butter mixture and, if cooked in a contact grill, any juices that collected in the drip pan over it.

420.Watermelon Steaks With Rosemary

Servings: 4
Cooking Time: 10 Minutes
Ingredients:
- 1 small watermelon
- ¼ cup good-quality olive oil
- 1 tablespoon minced fresh rosemary
- Salt and pepper
- Lemon wedges for serving

Directions:
1.   Preparing the Ingredients
2.   Cut the watermelon into 2-inch-thick slices, with the rind intact, and then into halves or quarters, if you like. If there are seeds, use a fork to remove as many as you can without tearing up the flesh too much.
3.   Put the oil and rosemary in a small bowl, sprinkle with salt and pepper, and stir. Brush or rub the mixture all over the watermelon slices. (You can prepare the watermelon for the grill up to 2 hours ahead; wrap tightly in plastic wrap to keep it from drying out and refrigerate.)
4.   Bring the griddle grill to medium-high heat. Oil the griddle and allow it to heat until the oil is shimmering but not smoking. Put the watermelon on the griddle and cook, turning once, until the flesh develops grill marks and has dried out a bit, 4 to 5 Minutes per side. Transfer to a platter and serve with lemon wedges.

421.Roasted Asparagus

Servings: 4
Cooking Time: 7 Minutes

Ingredients:
- 1 pound medium to thin asparagus, woody stems snapped off and discarded
- 2 tablespoons olive oil
- ¼ teaspoon salt
- ½ teaspoon freshly ground black pepper
- ¼ cup grated Parmesan cheese, preferably freshly grated

Directions:
1.   Preparing the Ingredients
2.   Toss the asparagus with the olive oil, salt, and pepper in a medium bowl.
3.   Bring the griddle grill to medium-high heat. Oil the griddle and allow it to heat until the oil is shimmering but not smoking. Grill the asparagus spears for about 7 Minutes, until they have taken on grill marks and are tender.
4.   Serve hot or at room temperature, sprinkled with the Parmesan.

Nutrition Info: (Per Serving): CALORIES: 102; FAT:9G; PROTEIN:4G; SUGAR:4G

422.Cauliflower With Garlic And Anchovies

Servings: 4
Cooking Time: 10 Minutes
Ingredients:
- 1 head cauliflower (1½–2 pounds)
- 6 tablespoons good-quality olive oil
- 6 oil-packed anchovy fillets, chopped, or more to taste
- 1 tablespoon minced garlic
- ½ teaspoon red chile flakes, or to taste
- (optional)
- Salt and pepper (optional)
- Chopped fresh parsley for garnish

Directions:
1.   Preparing the Ingredients
2.   1 Break or cut the cauliflower into florets about 1½ inches across; put in a bowl.
3.   Put the oil, anchovies, garlic, and red pepper if using it in a small skillet over medium-low heat. Cook, stirring occasionally, until the anchovies begin to break up and the garlic just begins to color, about 5 Minutes. Taste and add more anchovies or some salt and pepper. Pour half of the oil mixture over the cauliflower; toss to coat evenly with it. Bring the griddle grill to medium-high heat. Oil the griddle and allow it to heat until the oil is shimmering but not smoking. Put the florets in a single and cook until the cauliflower is as tender and browned as you like it, 5 Minutes for crisp-tender to 10 Minutes for fully tender. Transfer to a serving bowl, drizzle over the

remaining sauce and the parsley, toss gently, and serve warm or at room temperature.

423.Easy Seared Green Beans

Servings: 6
Cooking Time: 10 Minutes
Ingredients:
- 1 1/2 lbs green beans, trimmed
- 1 1/2 tbsp rice vinegar
- 3 tbsp soy sauce
- 1 1/2 tbsp sesame oil
- 2 tbsp sesame seeds, toasted
- 1 1/2 tbsp brown sugar
- 1/4 tsp black pepper

Directions:
1. Cook green beans in boiling water for 3 minutes and drain well.
2. Transfer green beans to chilled ice water and drain again. Pat dry green beans.
3. Preheat the griddle to high heat.
4. Add oil to the hot griddle top.
5. Add green beans and stir fry for 2 minutes.
6. Add soy sauce, brown sugar, vinegar, and pepper and stir fry for 2 minutes more.
7. Add sesame seeds and toss well to coat.
8. Serve and enjoy.

Nutrition Info: (Per Serving): Calories 100 ;Fat 5 g ;Carbohydrates 11.7 g ;Sugar 3.9 g ;Protein 3.1 g ;Cholesterol 0 mg

424.Fennel-orange Slaw With Rosemary And Pickled Red Onion

Servings: 4
Cooking Time: 10 Minutes
Ingredients:
- ½ cup rice vinegar
- ¼ cup sugar
- 1 small red onion, halved, thinly sliced, and pulled apart
- 2 pounds fennel
- 2 tablespoons good-quality olive oil, plus more for brushing
- 3 navel oranges
- 1 teaspoon minced fresh rosemary
- Salt and pepper

Directions:
1. Preparing the Ingredients
2. Put the vinegar and sugar in a small nonreactive saucepan and bring to a boil. Remove from the heat, add the onion, and stir to combine. Let sit while you prepare the fire. Or you can do this earlier in the day, cover, and let sit at room temperature.
3. Trim the fennel bulbs, reserving the feathery fronds. Cut the fennel in half from stalk end to base; brush with some oil. Cut the peel from the oranges with a small knife, deep enough to remove the white pith. Slice the oranges across into ¼-inch rounds, then cut the rounds into wedges. Put in a large bowl.
4. Bring the griddle grill to medium-high heat. Oil the griddle and allow it to heat until the oil is shimmering but not smoking. Put the fennel on the griddle and cook until the fennel is crisp-tender and browned or charred in spots, 8 to 10 Minutes. Transfer to a cutting board and thinly slice across into crescents. Add to the oranges. Use a slotted spoon to transfer the onion to the bowl; reserve the brine. Mince enough fennel fronds to make 2 tablespoons.
5. Add the oil, 1 tablespoon of the brine, the rosemary, the minced fronds, and some salt and pepper. Toss to coat, taste and adjust the seasoning, and serve. Or prepare the slaw up to a day ahead, cover, and refrigerate.

425.Bacon-wrapped Maple-cinnamon Carrots

Servings: 4
Cooking Time: 30 Minutes
Ingredients:
- ½ cup maple syrup
- 1 Tbsp. fresh ground cinnamon
- 2 lb. carrots (uniform in size, washed and peeled)
- 1 lb. thin-cut bacon
- pinch of salt
- 1 Tbsp. finely chopped parsley, for garnish

Directions:
1. Preparing the Ingredients
2. Whisk together the syrup and cinnamon.
3. Lightly coat carrots with cinnamon-syrup mixture; a basting brush works well for this task.
4. Spiral wrap each carrot with one slice of bacon. Depending on the size of the carrot, two slices may be needed.
5. Apply another coat of the cinnamon-syrup to the outside of the bacon and sprinkle with a pinch of salt.
6. Bring the griddle grill to high heat. Oil the griddle. Place carrots. Ensure you lay the carrots with the tips of the bacon tucked under the carrots to prevent them from unraveling.
7. Reapply another coat of the cinnamon-syrup, and cook additional 15 Minutes or until bacon is crisp and carrots are firm but cooked.
8. Remove from grill, drizzle with any remaining cinnamon-syrup, garnish with parsley, and serve.

426.Pineapple Fried Rice

Servings: 4
Cooking Time: 10 Minutes
Ingredients:
- 3 cups cooked brown rice
- 1/2 cup frozen corn
- 2 carrots, peeled and grated
- 1 onion, diced
- 2 garlic cloves, minced
- 2 tbsp olive oil
- 1/2 tsp ginger powder
- 1 tbsp sesame oil
- 3 tbsp soy sauce
- 1/4 cup green onion, sliced
- 1/2 cup ham, diced
- 2 cups pineapple, diced
- 1/2 cup frozen peas

Directions:
1. In a small bowl, whisk soy sauce, ginger powder, and sesame oil and set aside.
2. Preheat the griddle to high heat.
3. Add oil to the hot griddle top.
4. Add onion and garlic and sauté for 3-4 minutes.
5. Add corn, carrots, and peas and stir constantly for 3-4 minutes.
6. Stir in cooked rice, green onions, ham, pineapple, and soy sauce mixture and stir continuously for 2-3 minutes.
7. Serve and enjoy.

Nutrition Info: (Per Serving): Calories 375 ;Fat 13.3 g ;Carbohydrates 57.6 g ;Sugar 12.7 g ;Protein 9.4 g ;Cholesterol 10 mg

427.Tomatoes Stuffed With Chickpeas And Rice

Servings: 4
Cooking Time: 25 Minutes
Ingredients:
- 4 large, firm fresh tomatoes (12 ounces or more each)
- Salt and pepper
- 2 tablespoons good-quality olive oil, plus more for drizzling
- 2 tablespoons minced ginger
- 1½ cups cooked white rice
- 1 cup cooked chickpeas
- ½ cup chopped fresh mint
- Lime wedges for serving

Directions:
1. Preparing the Ingredients
2. 1 If any of the tomatoes don't sit squarely on the counter, cut a thin slice from the bottom to stabilize it. To core the tomatoes, slice across the top to make a 2-to 3-inch-wide opening. (You can save the tops to put back on after stuffing the tomatoes.) Use a spoon, serrated grapefruit spoon, or melon baller to scoop out the insides, leaving a wall about ¼ inch thick. Discard the woody core and seeds and chop the pulp and bottom slices, saving the juice. Sprinkle the insides of the tomatoes with salt and pepper.
3. 2 Heat the oil in a medium-sized skillet over medium-high heat. Add the ginger and stir until fragrant, 1 to 2 Minutes. Add the tomato pulp and juice, sprinkle with salt and pepper, and cook, stirring occasionally, until most of the liquid has evaporated, 10 to 20 Minutes. Add the rice and chickpeas and stir with a fork until combined. Remove from the heat and stir in the mint; taste and adjust the seasoning. Carefully stuff the mixture into the tomatoes and drizzle the tops with oil. Set the tops back on if you like. (You can make the stuffed tomatoes to this point up to several hours in advance; cover and refrigerate.)
4. 3 Bring the griddle grill to medium-high heat. Oil the griddle and allow it to heat until the oil is shimmering but not smoking. Put the tomatoes on the grill and cook until the tomatoes begin to wrinkle a bit and the filling is hot, 25 Minutes, carefully moving and rotating the tomatoes once for even cooking. Serve hot, warm, or at room temperature with lime wedges.

428.Coleslaw

Servings: 4
Cooking Time: 30 Minutes
Ingredients:
- For the coleslaw
- 1 head shredded green cabbage
- 1 cup shredded carrots
- 2 thinly sliced scallions
- 1 head shredded purple cabbage
- For the dressing
- 1/8 cup white wine vinegar
- 1 tbsp. celery seed
- 1-1/2 cups mayonnaise
- 1 tsp. sugar
- Salt and pepper, to taste

Directions:
1. Set the griddle grill on preheat with the temperature reaching 180 degrees F
2. Now place both carrots and cabbage on a sheet tray and then place it on the grill grates directly
3. Grill it for approx 25 minutes.
4. Remove it from the grill and immediately keep it in the refrigerator so as to cool
5. For the dressing
6. Take a small bowl and mix and the ingredients in it

7. Now, take a large bowl and place cabbage and carrot in it.
8. Pour the dressing over it and stir to coat thoroughly
9. Transfer to a serving dish and sprinkle scallions
10. Serve and enjoy
Nutrition Info: (Per serving):Calories 83, Fat 3.1 g, protein 29g, carbs 14.9 g

429.Grilled Yellow Potatoes

Servings: 4
Cooking Time: 50 Minutes
Ingredients:
- Yellow Potatoes
- Olive Oil
- Sea Salt And Black Pepper To Taste
- Paprika
Directions:
1. Slice the potatoes in half lengthwise, and place them into a large bag or bowl.
2. Drizzle them with olive oil, and stir or shake to coat the potatoes.
3. Add the salt, pepper, and paprika to taste, and stir or shake until completely combined.
4. Preheat the griddle grill to medium, and spray it with oil.
5. Place the potatoes sliced-side down, and grill for several minutes or until you can see grill marks and they feel tender on the cut side.
6. Turn the potatoes over and grill until they are tender through.
7. Remove from heat and serve.
Nutrition Info: (Per serving):Calories 280, Fat 11g, carbs 8g, Protein 4g

430.Stuffed Eggplant With Ginger, Sesame, And Soy

Servings: 4
Cooking Time: 30 Minutes
Ingredients:
- 2 small eggplants (about 8 ounces each)
- ¼ cup minced fresh cilantro
- 2 tablespoons soy sauce
- 1 tablespoon minced fresh ginger
- 1 teaspoon sesame oil
- Lime wedges for serving
Directions:
1. Preparing the Ingredients
2. 1 Cut the eggplants in half lengthwise for long eggplant, or through the equator for globe eggplant. Mix the cilantro, soy sauce, ginger, and oil together well in a small bowl. Work the flavor paste over the cut surfaces of the eggplants, pushing it into the slits.

3. 2 Bring the griddle grill to medium-high heat. Oil the griddle and allow it to heat until the oil is shimmering but not smoking. Put the eggplant halves on the griddle and cook until the skin has crisped, the tops are browned, and the flesh is fork-tender, 25 to 30 Minutes; rotate and turn about halfway through for even cooking. Transfer to a platter and serve hot, warm, or at room temperature with lime wedges.

431.Tomato Melts With Spinach Salad

Servings: 4
Cooking Time: 6 Minutes
Ingredients:
- 1 or 2 large fresh tomatoes (enough for 4 thick slices across)
- 2 tablespoons good-quality olive oil, plus more for brushing
- Salt and pepper
- 2 teaspoons white wine vinegar
- 1 teaspoon Dijon mustard
- 3 cups baby spinach
- 6 slices cheddar cheese (about 4 ounces)
Directions:
1. Preparing the Ingredients
2. Core the tomatoes and cut 4 thick slices (about 1 inch); save the trimmings. Brush them with oil and sprinkle with salt and pepper on both sides. Whisk the 2 tablespoons oil, vinegar, and mustard together in a bowl. Chop the trimmings from the tomatoes; add them to the dressing along with the spinach and toss until evenly coated.
3. Bring the griddle grill to medium-high heat. Oil the griddle and allow it to heat until the oil is shimmering but not smoking. Put the tomato slices and cook for 3 Minutes. Turn the tomatoes and top each slice with a slice of cheddar, and cook until the cheese is melted, 2 to 3 Minutes. Transfer to plates and serve with the salad on top.

432.Baba Ghanoush

Servings: 6
Cooking Time: 30 Minutes
Ingredients:
- 2 medium-large eggplants (about 2 pounds total), with stems on
- ⅓ cup tahini
- ¼ cup fresh lemon juice
- 2 large cloves garlic, or to taste, minced
- Salt and pepper
- 4 pita breads for serving
- Good-quality olive oil for drizzling
- ¼ cup chopped fresh parsley for garnish

Directions:
1. Preparing the Ingredients
2. Pierce the eggplants in several places with a thin knife or skewer.
3. Bring the griddle grill to high heat. Oil the griddle. Put them on the grill. Cook until the eggplants are blackened on all sides and collapsed, 25 to 30 Minutes. Transfer to a bowl.
4. Whisk the tahini and lemon juice in a small bowl until smooth. Stir in the garlic and sprinkle with salt and pepper.
5. When the eggplants are cool enough to handle, peel off and discard the burnt skin. Mash the flesh with a fork. Beat in the tahini mixture until the dip is smooth. Taste and adjust the seasoning. (You can make the dip up to 3 days in advance; cover and refrigerate.)
6. Toast the pita directly over the grill, turning once, until they're warm and have grill marks, 1 to 2 Minutes per side. Cut into wedges. Transfer the baba ghanoush to a shallow serving bowl, drizzle the top with olive oil, sprinkle with the parsley, and serve with the warm pita wedges.

433.Fire-roasted Tomatillo Salsa With Grilled Tortilla Wedges

Servings: 2 Cups
Cooking Time: 10 Minutes
Ingredients:
- 1 pound tomatillos
- 3 scallions, trimmed
- 1 jalapeño chile, seeded and minced
- 2 cloves garlic, minced, or to taste
- ¼ cup chopped fresh cilantro
- 3 tablespoons fresh lime juice, or to taste
- Salt and pepper
- 8 small corn or flour tortillas
- Good-quality olive oil for brushing

Directions:
1. Preparing the Ingredients
2. Remove the husks from the tomatillos, then rinse off the tacky residue and pat dry.
3. Bring the griddle grill to high heat. Oil the griddle. Put the tomatillos and scallions on the grill, and cook until they soften and blacken in spots, turning them to cook evenly, 5 to 10 Minutes total. Transfer to a food processor or blender and add the jalapeño, garlic, cilantro, lime juice, and some salt and pepper; pulse a few times until the mixture comes together but isn't completely smooth. Taste and adjust the seasoning, adding more garlic or lime if you like.
4. Brush the tortillas on both sides with oil. Put them on the grill directly over the fire, close the lid,

and toast, turning once, until they are warm and grill marks develop, 1 to 2 Minutes per side. Cut into wedges and serve with the salsa.

434.Wilted Spinach

Servings: 4
Cooking Time: 1 Minute
Ingredients:
- 8 ounces fresh baby spinach
- 1 tablespoon olive oil
- ¼ teaspoon garlic powder
- ¼ teaspoon salt
- 1 lemon, halved

Directions:
1. Preparing the Ingredients
2. In a medium bowl, toss the spinach with the olive oil, garlic powder, and salt.
3. Bring the griddle grill to medium-high heat. Oil the griddle and allow it to heat until the oil is shimmering but not smoking. Spread the spinach in an even layer over the grill and grill for 30 seconds. The leaves should wilt but retain just a bit of crunch. Transfer to a serving bowl and squeeze a bit of lemon juice on top. Serve immediately.
Nutrition Info: (Per Serving): CALORIES: 44; FAT:4G; PROTEIN:2G

435.Chiles Rellenos With Charred Green Enchilada Sauce

Servings: 4
Cooking Time: 35 Minutes
Ingredients:
- 1¼ pounds tomatillos, husked and rinsed
- 5 large poblano or other mild fresh green chiles
- 3 tablespoons good-quality olive oil
- 2 large onions, chopped
- 5 cloves garlic, minced
- 1 teaspoon dried oregano
- 1 cup vegetable broth or water
- Salt and pepper
- 3 cups grated or shredded Chihuahua or Monterey Jack cheese
- ½ cup chopped fresh cilantro
- ¼ cup fresh lime juice
- Crumbled queso fresco for garnish

Directions:
1. Preparing the Ingredients
2. 1 Bring the griddle grill to medium-high heat. Oil the griddle and allow it to heat until the oil is shimmering but not smoking. Put the tomatillos and 1 of the poblanos on the griddle, and cook the tomatillos until the skins are lightly browned and

blistered, 10 to 15 Minutes. Cook the poblano until it's blackened, 15 to 20 Minutes. When the vegetables are done, transfer them a bowl) When the poblano is cool enough to handle, remove the skin, stem, and seeds. Chop by hand along with the tomatillos, saving the juices.

3.   2 Put the oil in a large, deep skillet over medium heat, add the onions and garlic, and cook, stirring occasionally, until quite soft and golden, 10 to 15 Minutes. Add the tomatillos and poblano, oregano, broth, and a large pinch of salt and pepper; stir and bring to a gentle bubble. Cook, stirring occasionally, until the mixture is slightly thickened, 10 to 15 Minutes. Remove from the heat. Use an immersion blender to purée the sauce in the pan, or very carefully transfer it to a blender, purée, and return it to the pan.

4.   Cut a slit into one side of each of the remaining poblanos, from the stem down to the tip. Carefully remove the seeds without ripping the chiles, then stuff them with the Chihuahua or Jack cheese.

5.   3 Heat the grill for medium. Put the chiles on the griddle, slit side facing up so the cheese doesn't melt out, and cook until the skins have blistered and the flesh is tender, 10 to 15 Minutes. Transfer to a platter. Stir the cilantro and lime juice into the sauce; taste and adjust the seasonings. Spoon the sauce over the chiles, sprinkle with queso fresco, and serve.

436.Stir Fry Mushrooms

Servings: 2
Cooking Time: 10 Minutes
Ingredients:
- 10 oz mushrooms, sliced
- 1/4 cup olive oil
- 1 tbsp garlic, minced
- 1/4 tsp dried thyme
- Pepper
- Salt

Directions:
1.   Preheat the griddle to high heat.
2.   Add 2 tablespoons of oil to the hot griddle top.
3.   Add mushrooms, garlic, thyme, pepper, and salt and sauté mushrooms until tender.
4.   Drizzle remaining oil and serve.
Nutrition Info: (Per Serving): Calories 253 ;Fat 25.6 g ;Carbohydrates 6.2 g ;Sugar 2.5 g ;Protein 4.7 g ;Cholesterol 0 mg

437.Sautéed Vegetables

Servings: 4
Cooking Time: 5 Minutes
Ingredients:
- 2 medium zucchini, cut into matchsticks
- 2 tbsp coconut oil
- 2 tsp garlic, minced
- 1 tbsp honey
- 3 tbsp soy sauce
- 1 tsp sesame seeds
- 2 cups carrots, cut into matchsticks
- 2 cups snow peas

Directions:
1.   In a small bowl, mix together soy sauce, garlic, and honey and set aside.
2.   Preheat the griddle to high heat.
3.   Add oil to the hot griddle top.
4.   Add carrots, snow peas, and zucchini, and sauté for 1-2 minutes.
5.   Add soy sauce mixture and stir fry for 1 minute.
6.   Garnish with sesame seeds and serve.
Nutrition Info: (Per Serving): Calories 160 ;Fat 7.5 g ;Carbohydrates 20.2 g ;Sugar 12.1 g ;Protein 5.3 g ;Cholesterol 0 mg

438.Quinoa Salad With Apples, Brussels Sprouts, And Walnuts

Servings: 4
Cooking Time: 35 Minutes
Ingredients:
- 1 cup quinoa
- Salt and pepper
- 1 pound Brussels sprouts, trimmed and any discolored leaves removed
- 8 tablespoons good-quality olive oil
- 2 apples
- ¾ cup chopped fresh parsley
- 2 tablespoons white wine vinegar
- 2 teaspoons Dijon mustard
- Grated zest of 1 lemon
- 1 cup walnut halves, toasted

Directions:
1.   Preparing the Ingredients
2.   Put the quinoa and ½ teaspoon salt in a saucepan with 1½ cups water, bring to a boil, reduce the heat so the water bubbles gently but steadily, cover, and cook undisturbed until the surface is dotted with holes and the water is almost all absorbed, about 15 Minutes. Turn off the heat and let stand until the kernels are tender and fluffy, 5 to 10 Minutes.
3.   Toss the sprouts and 1 tablespoon of the oil together in a bowl. Sprinkle with salt and pepper to taste and toss again.
4.   Bring the griddle grill to medium-high heat. Oil the griddle and allow it to heat until the oil is shimmering but not smoking. Put the sprouts on the grill grate, and cook until they're fork-tender, 20 to

35 Minutes. Transfer to a bowl. When cool enough to handle, quarter each through the stem.

5. Transfer the quinoa to a large serving bowl. Add the Brussels sprouts. Core the apples and cut them into cubes; add to the bowl along with the parsley. Whisk the remaining 6 tablespoons oil, the vinegar, mustard, and lemon zest together in a small bowl. Taste and season with salt and pepper. Pour over the salad and toss everything to combine. Right before serving, add the nuts. Serve at room temperature.

439.Grilled Tempeh

Servings: 4
Cooking Time: 6 Minutes
Ingredients:
- 1 8-ounce piece tempeh
- Good-quality olive oil for brushing
- Salt
- Pepper (optional)

Directions:
1. Preparing the Ingredients
2. Brush the tempeh with oil and sprinkle with salt on both sides.
3. Bring the griddle grill to high heat. Oil the griddle Put the tempeh and cook until it develops a crust and releases easily from the grates, about 6. Sprinkle with more salt and some pepper if you like, and serve.

440.Radishes With Butter And Sea Salt

Servings: 6
Cooking Time: 6 Minutes
Ingredients:
- 1 pound whole radishes, with greens attached
- 2 tablespoons good-quality olive oil
- 8 tablespoons (1 stick) butter, softened
- 1 to 2 tablespoons sea salt

Directions:
1. Preparing the Ingredients
2. Trim the root ends and remove any discolored leaves from the radishes. Rinse, pat them dry with paper towels, and toss with the oil until completely coated, including the greens.
3. Bring the griddle grill to medium-high heat. Oil the griddle and allow it to heat until the oil is shimmering but not smoking. Put the radishes on the grill, and cook until they warm through and char in places, 4 to 6 Minutes. Transfer to a platter and serve with the butter and salt in small bowls for dipping.

441.Eggplant Salad With Yogurt And Tomatoes

Servings: 4
Cooking Time: 10 Minutes
Ingredients:
- 1 large eggplant (1½ pounds)
- ¼ cup good-quality olive oil, plus more for brushing
- Salt and pepper
- 1½ cups yogurt
- 1 or 2 cloves garlic, minced, to taste
- ¼ cup chopped scallions
- ¼ cup chopped fresh mint
- 1 tablespoon fresh lemon juice, or to taste
- 1 large or 2 medium fresh tomatoes, cut into bite-sized chunks
- Ground sumac for garnish (optional)

Directions:
1. Preparing the Ingredients
2. Peel the eggplant if you like; cut it into ¾-inch slices. Brush with the oil and sprinkle with salt and pepper to taste on both sides.
3. Bring the griddle grill to medium-high heat. Oil the griddle and allow it to heat until the oil is shimmering but not smoking. Put the eggplant on the grill and cook until the slices develop deep grill marks and are tender, 10Minutes; brush the eggplant with more oil if it starts to look dry. Transfer to a cutting board and chop into bite-sized pieces.
4. Put the yogurt, garlic, scallions, mint, and lemon juice in a large bowl and stir to combine. (You can prepare the recipe to this point up to a day before; cover and refrigerate the eggplant and yogurt mixture separately.)
5. Add the tomatoes and eggplant to the yogurt and stir to coat. Serve chilled or bring to room temperature and garnish with sumac if you like.

442.Simplest Grilled Asparagus

Servings: 4
Cooking Time: 10 Minutes
Ingredients:
- 1½–2 pounds asparagus
- 1–2 tablespoons good-quality olive oil or melted butter
- Salt

Directions:
1. Preparing the Ingredients
2. Cut the tough bottoms from the asparagus. If they're thick, trim the ends with a vegetable peeler. Toss with the oil and sprinkle with salt.
3. Bring the griddle grill to medium-high heat. Oil the griddle and allow it to heat until the oil is shimmering but not smoking. Put the asparagus on

the griddle and cook until the thick part of the stalks can barely be pierced with a skewer or thin knife, 8 to 10 Minutes total. Transfer to a platter and serve.

443.Stir Fry Cabbage

Servings: 4
Cooking Time: 5 Minutes
Ingredients:
- 1 cabbage head, tear cabbage leaves, washed and drained
- 2 green onion, sliced
- 1 tbsp ginger, minced
- 2 garlic cloves, minced
- 1 tbsp soy sauce
- 1/2 tbsp vinegar
- 4 dried chilies
- 2 tbsp olive oil
- 1/2 tsp salt

Directions:
1. Preheat the griddle to high heat.
2. Add oil to the hot griddle top.
3. Add ginger, garlic, and green onion and sauté for 2-3 minutes.
4. Add dried chilies and sauté for 30 seconds.
5. Add cabbage, vinegar, soy sauce, and salt and stir fry for 1-2 minutes over high heat until cabbage wilted.
6. Serve and enjoy.

Nutrition Info: (Per Serving): Calories 115 ;Fat 7.3 g ;Carbohydrates 12.7 g ;Sugar 6 g ;Protein 2.9 g ;Cholesterol 0 mg

444.Beets And Greens With Lemon-dill Vinaigrette

Servings: 4
Cooking Time: 45 Minutes
Ingredients:
- 1½ pounds small beets, with fresh-looking greens still attached if possible
- ½ cup plus 2 tablespoons good-quality olive oil
- Salt and pepper
- 3 tablespoons fresh lemon juice
- 4 tablespoons minced fresh dill

Directions:
1. Preparing the Ingredients
2. 1 Cut the greens off the beets. Throw away any wilted or discolored leaves; rinse the remainder well to remove any grit and drain. Trim the root ends of the beets and scrub well under running water. Pat the leaves and beets dry. Toss the beets with 2 tablespoons of the oil and a sprinkle of salt until evenly coated.

3. 2 Bring the griddle grill to medium-high heat. Oil the griddle and allow it to heat until the oil is shimmering but not smoking. Put the beets on the griddle, and cook until a knife inserted in the center goes through with no resistance, 35 to 40 Minutes total. Transfer to a plate and let sit until cool enough to handle.
4. Toss the beet greens in the reserved bowl to coat in oil. Put the greens on the grill and cook until they're bright green and browned in spots, 2 to 5 Minutes total. Keep a close eye on them; if they're on too long, they'll crisp up to the point where they'll shatter. Transfer to a plate.
5. 3 Put the remaining ½ cup oil and the lemon juice in a serving bowl and whisk until thickened. Stir in the dill and some salt and pepper. Peel the skin from the beets and cut into halves or quarters. Cut the stems from the leaves in 1-inch lengths; cut the leaves across into ribbons. Put the beets, leaves, and stems in the bowl and toss with the vinaigrette until coated. Serve warm or at room temperature. Or make up to several hours ahead, cover, and refrigerate to serve chilled.

445.Healthy Zucchini Noodles

Servings: 4
Cooking Time: 10 Minutes
Ingredients:
- 4 small zucchini, spiralized
- 1 tbsp soy sauce
- 2 onions, spiralized
- 2 tbsp olive oil
- 1 tbsp sesame seeds
- 2 tbsp teriyaki sauce

Directions:
1. Preheat the griddle to high heat.
2. Add oil to the hot griddle top.
3. Add onion and sauté for 4-5 minutes.
4. Add zucchini noodles and cook for 2 minutes.
5. Add sesame seeds, teriyaki sauce, and soy sauce and cook for 4-5 minutes.
6. Serve and enjoy.

Nutrition Info: (Per Serving): Calories 124 ;Fat 8.4 g ;Carbohydrates 11.3 g ;Sugar 5.7 g ;Protein 3.2 g ;Cholesterol 0 mg

446.Stir Fry Vegetables

Servings: 4
Cooking Time: 20 Minutes
Ingredients:
- 2 medium potatoes, cut into small pieces
- 3 medium carrots, peeled and cut into small pieces

- 1/4 cup olive oil
- 1 small rutabaga, peeled and cut into small pieces
- 2 medium parsnips, peeled and cut into small pieces
- Pepper
- Salt

Directions:
1. Preheat the griddle to high heat.
2. In a large bowl, toss vegetables with olive oil.
3. Transfer vegetables onto the hot griddle top and stir fry until vegetables are tender.
4. Serve and enjoy.

Nutrition Info: (Per Serving): Calories 218 ;Fat 12.8 g ;Carbohydrates 25.2 g ;Sugar 6.2 g ;Protein 2.8 g ;Cholesterol 0 mg

447.Eggplant Parmesan With Grill-roasted Tomato Sauce

Servings: 4
Cooking Time: 24 Minutes
Ingredients:
- I bet.
- 2 eggplants (¾ to 1 pound each)
- 5 tablespoons good-quality olive oil
- 2 tablespoons balsamic vinegar
- Salt and pepper
- 6 cups cherry or grape tomatoes
- 1 cup freshly grated Parmesan cheese
- About 1 cup packed fresh basil leaves
- 7 ounces mozzarella cheese, thinly sliced

Directions:
1. Preparing the Ingredients
2. Peel the eggplant if you like, and cut each lengthwise into 4 slices not more than ¾ inch thick each. Whisk 4 tablespoons of the oil and the vinegar together with some salt and pepper in a small bowl. Brush the eggplant slices with the oil mixture on both sides. Put them on a baking sheet until you're ready to grill them.
3. Toss the tomatoes with the remaining 1 tablespoon oil and either skewer them or put them in a perforated grill pan and spread them into a single layer.
4. Bring the griddle grill to medium-high heat. Oil the griddle and allow it to heat until the oil is shimmering but not smoking. Put the tomatoes on the grill and cook, turning the skewers or shaking the pan several times, until they start to look wrinkled and get a bit charred in places, 7 to 8 Minutes total. Don't let them cook too long; they should be saucy when you cut them up. Transfer the tomatoes to a bowl.

5. Put the eggplant on the grill and cook until the slices are browned and tender, 10 Minutes.
6. While the eggplant is cooking, chop the tomatoes by hand on a cutting board or in the bowl with an immersion blender, leaving the sauce somewhat chunky. If you chopped by hand, transfer the tomatoes and any juices back to the bowl. Sprinkle the sauce with salt and pepper; taste and adjust the seasoning.
7. As the eggplant is ready, transfer the slices to a platter. Top each slice with 2 tablespoons Parmesan, a layer of basil leaves, and a layer of mozzarella. Return the slices to grill, close the lid, and cook until the mozzarella melts, 4 to 5 Minutes. Return the eggplant to the platter. Reheat the tomato sauce if you like, top the eggplant with the sauce, and serve.

448.Stuffed Winter Squash With Quinoa, Green Beans, And Tomatoes

Servings: 4
Cooking Time: 45 Minutes
Ingredients:
- ¾ cup quinoa
- 2 or 4 winter squash
- 2 tablespoons good-quality olive oil, plus more for brushing and drizzling
- Salt and pepper
- 1 cup chopped cherry or grape tomatoes
- ½ cup thinly sliced green beans (cut across into rounds)
- 2 tablespoons chopped fresh parsley
- 5 cloves garlic, minced

Directions:
1. Preparing the Ingredients
2. Put the quinoa in a saucepan with 1½ cups water, bring to a boil, reduce the heat so the water bubbles gently but steadily, cover, and cook undisturbed until the surface is dotted with holes and the water is almost all absorbed, about 15 Minutes. Turn off the heat and let stand until the kernels are tender and fluffy, 5 to 10 Minutes.
3. Cut the squash in half. If necessary, take a thin slice off the uncut side so the squash half sits on the work surface without rocking. Remove the seeds with a spoon, serrated grapefruit spoon, or melon baller. Brush the interior and cut surface with oil; for varieties with edible skin, also brush the skin. Sprinkle all over with salt and pepper.
4. Bring the griddle grill to medium-high heat. Oil the griddle and allow it to heat until the oil is shimmering but not smoking. Put the squash on the griddle skin side down, and cook until the flesh is just fork tender, 25 Minutes. Turn them cut side down to brown, about 5 Minutes. Transfer to a plate, cut side up.

5. While the squash are on the grill, finish the filling. Put the quinoa, tomatoes, green beans, parsley, garlic, and 2 tablespoons oil in a bowl; sprinkle with salt and pepper and toss with a fork until combined. Cover to keep warm. (You can prepare the filling and partially cook the squash earlier in the day; cover and refrigerate until you're ready to grill; cooking time may be a bit longer.)
6. If necessary, heat the grill for medium direct cooking. Divide the filling between the squash halves. Return to the grill and cook until the filling is hot, 10 to 15 Minutes. Transfer to a platter, drizzle the tops with a little oil if you like, and serve.

449.Elote (spanish Corn On The Cob)

Servings: 4-6
Cooking Time: 10 Minutes
Ingredients:
- Corn On The Cob
- Olive Oil
- Sea Salt To Taste
- Mayonnaise
- Tepín Chili Lime Salt*
- Grated Parmesan Cheese

Directions:
1. Remove the corn from the husk.
2. Brush with olive oil and sprinkle with sea salt.
3. Heat the griddle grill to high, and grill for several minutes, turning the corn over as needed. The corn is done when it begins to wrinkle.
4. Brush with mayo and sprinkle with chili lime salt and parmesan cheese to serve.
5. * Tepín is sold at most Latin markets. You can also substitute with creole seasoning.
Nutrition Info: (Per serving):Calories 164.8, Fat 8.1 g, carbs 6g, protein 13g

450.Grilled Zucchini Squash Spears

Servings: 6
Cooking Time: 15 Minutes
Ingredients:
- 4 midsized zucchini
- 2 springs thyme with the leaves pulled out
- 1 tbsp. sherry vinegar
- 2 tbsps. olive oil
- Salt and pepper as per your taste

Directions:
1. Take the zucchini and cut off the ends
2. Now cut each of them in a half and then cut every half into thirds
3. Take all the leftover ingredients in a midsized zip lock bag and then add spears to it
4. Toss it and mix well so that it coats the zucchini

5. Start the griddle grill to preheat to medium high
6. Remove the spears from the bag and place them directly on the grill grate. Make sure that the side faces downwards
7. Cook for 3 to 4 minutes per side until you can see the grill starts popping up and the zucchini should become tender too
8. Remove from the grill and add more thyme leaves if needed
9. Serve and enjoy
Nutrition Info: (Per serving):Calories 235, Carbs 21g, Fat 16g, Protein 8g

451.Roasted Tomatoes With Hot Pepper Sauce

Servings: 4-6
Cooking Time: 120 Minutes
Ingredients:
- 2 lbs. tomatoes; Roma fresh
- 1 lb. spaghetti
- 2 tbsps. chopped garlic
- 1/2 cup olive oil
- 3 tbsps. chopped parsley
- Salt, hot pepper and black pepper, to taste

Directions:
1. Set the griddle grill to preheat and push the temperature to 400 degrees F.
2. Now take the tomatoes, wash them thoroughly and cut them into halves; lengthwise.
3. Place it on a baking dish while making sure that the cut side faces upwards
4. Sprinkle it with chopped parsley, salt, black pepper, and garlic.
5. Also, put 1/4 cup of olive oil over them
6. Now place it on the grill for 1-1/2 hour
7. The tomatoes will shrink, and the skin is likely to get slightly blackened
8. Now remove the tomatoes from the baking dish and place it on the food processor and puree it well
9. Drop the pasta into the boiling salt water and cook it until it turns tender
10. Drain and toss it immediately with the pureed tomatoes mix
11. Now add the leftover 1/4 cup of raw olive oil along with crumbled hot pepper as per taste
12. Toss well and serve
Nutrition Info: (Per serving):Calories 45, Fat 1g, Carbs 8g, Protein 2g

452.Grilled Eggplant Napoleon

Servings: 4
Cooking Time: 5 Minutes
Ingredients:

- 1 Eggplant sliced lengthwise into half inch slices
- Olive Oil brushed
- Salt to taste
- Heirloom Tomatoes sliced thin
- Lemon squeezed
- Balsamic Vinegar drizzled
- Fresh Basil garnished
- Haloumi cheese sliced to 1/4 inch thick and grilled

Directions:
1. Slice the eggplant thin lengthwise and brush with the olive oil and season with the sea salt.
2. Slice the Halloumi to 1/4 inch and grill on high for one minute per side
3. Turn the griddle grill on high and grill the eggplant for several minutes per side until the grill marks are prevalent.
4. Layer with the eggplant with grilled halloumi, and sliced tomatoes. Squeeze the lemon juice over the top, drizzle the balsamic vinegar, and garnish with slightly torn fresh basil.

Nutrition Info: (Per serving):Calories 232.4, Fat 6.7 g, carbs 9g, Protein 11.2 g

453.Grilled Eggplant With Feta And Lemon

Servings: 4
Cooking Time: 15 Minutes
Ingredients:
- 1 large eggplant, cut into ½-inch slices
- 1 tablespoon salt
- 3 tablespoons olive oil
- 4 ounces feta cheese, crumbled
- ½ teaspoon sweet paprika
- Freshly ground black pepper
- 1 lemon, cut in half

Directions:
1. Preparing the Ingredients
2. Spread the eggplant slices on a rimmed baking sheet and sprinkle with half of the salt. Flip the slices and sprinkle with the remaining salt. Let sit for 15 Minutes to take away some of the bitterness of the eggplant. Transfer the slices to sheets of paper towels and pat dry.
3. Bring the griddle grill to medium-high heat. Oil the griddle and allow it to heat until the oil is shimmering but not smoking. Brush both sides of the eggplant slices with the olive oil. Grill for about 6 Minutes, until the slices have taken on grill marks and are golden brown.
4. Transfer the eggplant to a serving platter and top with the feta, paprika, some pepper, and a squirt of lemon juice. Serve hot or at room temperature.

Nutrition Info: (Per Serving): CALORIES: 204; FAT:17G; PROTEIN:6G

454.Grilled Corn With Soy Butter And Sesame

Servings: 4
Cooking Time: 18 Minutes
Ingredients:
- 3 tablespoons unsalted butter
- 1 scallion, both white and green parts, finely chopped
- 2 tablespoons soy sauce
- 4 ears sweet corn, shucked and cut or broken in half crosswise
- 1 tablespoon toasted sesame seeds

Directions:
1. Preparing the Ingredients
2. Melt the butter in a saucepan over medium heat. Add the scallion and cook until it loses its rawness, about 1 minute (you don't want the scallion to brown). Stir in the soy sauce and remove the saucepan from the heat.
3. Bring the griddle grill to medium-high heat. Oil the griddle and allow it to heat until the oil is shimmering but not smoking.
4. Arrange the ears of corn on the hot Grill. The corn will be done after cooking 2 to 3 Minutes per side (8 to 12 Minutes in all) until nicely browned on all sides, basting it with a little of the soy butter. Use a light touch as you baste; you don't want to drip a lot of butter into the grill.
5. Transfer the corn to a platter. Brush it with any remaining soy butter, sprinkle the sesame seeds over it, and serve at once.
6. To toast sesame seeds, place them in a dry cast-iron or other heavy skillet (don't use a nonstick skillet for this). Cook the sesame seeds over medium heat until lightly browned, about 3 Minutes, shaking the skillet to ensure that they toast evenly. Transfer the toasted sesame seeds to a heatproof bowl to cool.

455.Grilled Sweet Potatoes

Servings: 4
Cooking Time: 10 Minutes
Ingredients:
- Sweet Potatoes
- Olive Oil
- Sea Salt To Taste

Directions:
1. Slice the sweet potatoes in half lengthwise.
2. Brush the entire sweet potato with olive oil and season liberally with sea salt.
3. Heat the griddle grill to high, and grill the sweet potatoes cut-side down for 5–7 minutes. Turn them

over and grill on medium heat until the sweet potatoes are tender through.

4. Let the potatoes relax for several minutes before serving.

Nutrition Info: (Per serving):Calories 160.3, Fat 10.7 g, carbs 6g, Protein 1.1 g

456.Grilled Artichokes With Honey Dijon

Servings: 4-6
Cooking Time: 30 Minutes
Ingredients:
- 6 whole artichokes
- 1/2 gallon water
- 3 Tbsp. sea salt
- olive oil
- sea salt to taste
- 1/4 cup raw honey
- 1/4 cup boiling water
- 3 Tbsp. Dijon mustard

Directions:
1. Cut the artichokes in half lengthwise top to bottom.
2. Mix the 3 tablespoons of sea salt and water together. Place the artichokes in the brine for 30 minutes to several hours before cooking.
3. Heat the griddle grill to medium.
4. Remove the artichokes from the brine, drizzle with olive oil on the cut side, and season with sea salt.
5. Grill for 15 minutes on each side, cut side down first.
6. Turn the grill down to low, and turn the artichokes cut-side down while you mix the honey, boiling water, and Dijon.
7. Turn the artichokes back over, and brush the Dijon mix well over the cut side until it is all absorbed.
8. Serve alongside a protein like salmon, beef, pork, or chicken, or with rice or potatoes for a vegetarian option.

Nutrition Info: (Per serving):Calories 601kcal, Fat 57g, Protein 8g, Carbs 21g

457.Grilled Brussels Sprouts With Balsamic Glaze

Servings: 4
Cooking Time: 10 Minutes
Ingredients:
- brussels sprouts
- olive oil
- sea salt to taste
- balsamic vinegar

Directions:

1. Preparing the Ingredients
2. Cut the sprouts in half lengthwise from top to bottom.
3. Brush with olive oil and season with sea salt.
4. Bring the griddle grill to medium-high heat. Oil the griddle and allow it to heat until the oil is shimmering but not smoking. Grill the sprouts cut-side down for 5 Minutes on each side. Brush the sprouts lightly with balsamic, and grill for a minute or so more to set the vinegar before serving.

458.Vegetarian Paella With Artichokes, Red Peppers, And White Beans

Servings: 8
Cooking Time: 40 Minutes
Ingredients:
- 6 tablespoons good-quality olive oil
- 1 large onion, chopped (2–2½ cups)
- Salt and pepper
- 6 tablespoons minced garlic (9–10 cloves)
- 1 teaspoon smoked paprika (pimentón)
- 2 fresh tomatoes, grated (1½–2 cups)
- 2 tablespoons fresh lemon juice
- 6 baby artichokes
- 2 red bell peppers
- 2 bay leaves
- 2 cups short-grain rice
- 4 cups vegetable broth or water, plus more if needed
- Generous pinch saffron threads, crushed (optional)
- 3 cups cooked cannellini beans

Directions:
1. Preparing the Ingredients
2. 1 Put 4 tablespoons of the oil in a 12-inch or larger deep flameproof skillet or paella pan over medium heat. When it's hot, add the onion and some salt and pepper and cook, stirring occasionally, until very soft, 4 to 5 Minutes. Add 4 tablespoons of the garlic and stir until fragrant, 2 to 3 Minutes. Add the paprika and stir for 1 to 2 Minutes. Add the tomatoes and cook, stirring occasionally, until they soften and most of their liquid evaporates, 15 to 20 Minutes; adjust the heat so the mixture bubbles gently as the sofrito thickens. Remove the pan from the heat if it is ready before you complete the next step. (You can make the sofrito earlier in the day, and refrigerate it; reheat before proceeding).
3. 2 Meanwhile, whisk the remaining 2 tablespoons oil and the lemon juice together in a bowl with some salt. Peel away and discard the outer leaves of each artichoke until the leaves are half yellow and half green. With a sharp knife, cut across the top of the artichoke to remove the green tops.

Leave 1 inch of stem and use a paring knife or vegetable peeler to trim the bottom so no green color remains. Cut the artichoke in half lengthwise from top to bottom. As each artichoke is trimmed, add it to the oil mixture and toss to coat evenly; this helps delay discoloring. (You can cover the bowl with a damp towel and refrigerate for up to several hours.)

4.   3 Bring the griddle grill to medium-high heat. Oil the griddle and allow it to heat until the oil is shimmering but not smoking. Put the red peppers on the grill grate, and cook until their skins are black and blistered all over, 15 to 25 Minutes total. Transfer them to a bowl.

5.   Put the artichokes over the grill, cut side down, and cook until crisp, 5 to 6 Minutes. Transfer to a platter. Cut the artichoke pieces in half. Remove the skins, seeds, and stems from the red peppers and cut them into 1-inch strips.

6.   Return the sofrito to medium heat. When it's hot, add the rice and stir until the grains are fully coated. Add the broth and the saffron if you're using it; stir to combine. Increase the heat to high and cook, stirring occasionally, until steaming but not yet bubbling. Add the beans, then the artichokes and red pepper strips, tucking them into the rice. Taste some of the liquid and adjust the seasoning; if it's a little bland, add some more salt.

7.   After 20 Minutes, check the paella's progress. At this point, the broth should have been absorbed by the rice to the point that the top of the paella is dry; stick a fork down into the rice by the edge of the pan; you should see bubbles. Close the lid.

8.   Check again after another 10 Minutes. Try a forkful of rice. If it's tender and the broth hasn't been fully absorbed, give it a little more time, but keep checking. It should not be soupy at all. In a perfect paella, a tasty crust will develop at the bottom without the rice sticking to the pan. If the rice isn't tender, check on its progress every 10 to 15 Minutes; if it is dry and burning, drizzle with a little more stock.

9.   When the rice is done, bring the paella pan to the table and let it sit for 5 to Minutes before serving family style.

459.Smoky Guacamole

Servings: 4
Cooking Time: 30 Minutes
Ingredients:
- 3 medium or 2 large ripe Hass avocados
- Good-quality olive oil for brushing
- 1 lemon, halved
- ¼ cup minced onion
- ½ teaspoon minced garlic, or to taste

- 1 serrano or jalapeño chile, seeded and minced, or cayenne to taste (optional)
- 1 teaspoon chili powder or any mild pure chile powder like ancho, or to taste
- Salt and pepper
- ¼ cup chopped fresh cilantro for garnish

Directions:
1.   Preparing the Ingredients
2.   Cut the avocados in half. Carefully strike a chef's knife into the avocado pit, then wiggle it a bit to lift and remove it. Repeat with the other avocado(s). Insert a spoon underneath the flesh against the skin and run it all the way around to separate the entire half of the avocado. Repeat with the remaining halves, brush them with oil, and squeeze one of the lemon halves over all so they don't discolor.
3.   Bring the griddle grill to high heat. Oil the griddle. Put the avocados on the grill and cook until grill marks develop, 2 to 3 Minutes per side. Transfer to a bowl and mash with a fork or potato masher. Add the onion, garlic, chile if you're using it, chili powder, salt, pepper, and the juice from the remaining lemon half. Taste and adjust the flavors as necessary.
4.   Garnish with the cilantro and serve right away. Or cover with plastic wrap, pressing it down on the surface to minimize discoloration, and refrigerate for up to 4 hours before garnishing.

460.Italian Zucchini Slices

Servings: 4
Cooking Time: 5 Minutes
Ingredients:
- 2 zucchini, cut into 1/2-inch thick slices
- 1 tsp Italian seasoning
- 2 garlic cloves, minced
- 1/4 cup butter, melted
- 1 1/2 tbsp fresh parsley, chopped
- 1 tbsp fresh lemon juice
- Pepper
- Salt

Directions:
1.   In a small bowl, mix melted butter, lemon juice, Italian seasoning, garlic, pepper, and salt.
2.   Brush zucchini slices with melted butter mixture.
3.   Preheat the griddle to high heat.
4.   Place zucchini slices on the griddle top and cook for 2 minutes per side.
5.   Transfer zucchini slices on serving plate and garnish with parsley.
6.   Serve and enjoy.
Nutrition Info: (Per Serving): Calories 125 ;Fat 12 g ;Carbohydrates 4.1 g ;Sugar 1.9 g ;Protein 1.5 g ;Cholesterol 31 mg

461.Grilled Bbq Tofu

Servings: 2-3
Cooking Time: 20 Minutes
Ingredients:
- Firm Tofu
- Olive Oil
- Sea Salt To Taste
- Bbq Sauce

Directions:
1. Cut the tofu into 1-inch strips, and freeze them.
2. Place the frozen tofu strips on a cookie sheet that is covered with paper towels. Layer more paper towels on top of the tofu, and place another cookie sheet on top. Add weight to press the liquid out of the tofu as it thaws.
3. Once the tofu is completely thawed, brush the strips with olive oil and sea salt.
4. Heat the griddle grill to high, and grill the strips for 10 minutes per side.
5. Brush with BBQ sauce, and return them to the grill for a couple of minutes to set the sauce before serving.

Nutrition Info: (Per serving):Calories 435.7, Fat 32.2 g, carbs 18g, protein 21g

OTHER FAVORITE RECIPES

462.Ancho Griddler Sauce

Servings: 7
Ingredients:
- 6 ancho chilies
- 1 ½ cups cranberry juice
- 3 shallots, minced
- 3 garlic cloves, minced
- 2 tablespoon butter
- 4 cups ketchup
- 1 tablespoon paprika
- 1 tablespoon chili powder
- 1 tablespoon dry mustard
- 1 tablespoon Worcestershire sauce
- ¼ cup red wine vinegar
- ¼ cup brown sugar
- ¼ cup honey

Directions:
1. Preparing the Ingredients.
2. Before handling chilis it's a good idea to Place on rubber gloves, unless you want your skin to burn, that is! Remove the stems from the chilis and discard them. Split the chilis with a sharp knife and Place in a medium bowl. Pour in the hot cranberry juice and let it sit for one hour. Puree in a blender.
3. Grilling
4. In a small saucepan, over medium heat, sauté the shallots and garlic until tender, approximately 5 Minutes, then pour in the cranberry-chili puree and turn the heat up to high. Bring mixture to a boil, then reduce heat to low and simmer for an hour.
5. This sauce is super on beef, pork, venison or wild boar. It's also great on wild turkey, but perhaps a bit spicy for the domestic variety of old Tom. Some Yankees up in New England Place this sauce on their grilled lobster.

463.Skirt Steak & Tomato Tapenade Sandwich

Servings: 6
Cooking Time: 20 Minutes
Ingredients:
- 1 lb. skirt steak
- 1 shallot, peeled & minced
- 3 tbsp. balsamic vinegar 1/4 cup olive oil 1/2 tsp. sea salt

Directions:
1. In a shallow pan, marinate steak with shallots, balsamic vinegar, olive oil, sea salt, and pepper for 1 hour.
2. Combine tapenade ingredients in a bowl. Set aside.

3. Griddle grill the steak to desired temperature. Let rest 10 minutes before slicing.
4. Assemble sliced steak and tapenade open-face on focaccia. Serve with your favorite side dish.
Nutrition Info: (Per serving): Calories: 700 Cal, Fat: 51g Carbs: 20 g Protein: 44 g.

464.Mongo's Mango

Servings: 2
Ingredients:
- 2 tablespoon lime juice
- 2 limes
- zest from one lime, finely chopped
- 1 cup mango chutney
- 1 teaspoon brown sugar
- ¼ cup light corn syrup
- pinch of marjoram
- ⅛ teaspoon red pepper

Directions:
1. Preparing the Ingredients.
2. Peel the limes, saving the zest from one of them. Cut the limes in half, de-seed them and Place them in a food processor. Add lime juice, zest, chutney, and brown sugar. Pulse until the lime is fairly well chopped up, although it will still be chunky.
3. Pour this mixture into a bowl and add the corn syrup, marjoram, and red pepper, and mix well.
4. Pour mixture into sealable glass or plastic containers and refrigerate until ready to use as a marinade, baste or serving sauce. Absolutely superb on halibut, shark and salmon.

465.Griddle Recipe

Servings: 2
Ingredients:
- Grilled Chicken & Pineapple Salad
- Grilled Chipotle Chicken Salad
- Grilled Shrimp Caesar Salad
- Warm Tomato Caprese Grilled Scallops with Green
- Goddess Dressing
- Grilled Watermelon Salad
- Grilled Corn Salad
- Arugula Salad & Grilled Tomato Vinaigrette Grilled Bread Salad
- Marinade
- 3 tbsp. olive oil
- 1 tsp. sea salt ½ tsp. ground black pepper ½ tsp. onion powder ½ tsp. garlic powder ½ tsp. paprika
- 2 tbsp. red wine vinegar

Directions:

1. Preparing the Ingredients.In a bowl, combine marinade ingredients. Marinate chicken in the refrigerator for 1 hour.
2. Grilling
3. Grill the pineapple on both sides until tender. Grill the chicken 6-7 Minutes on each side until cooked. Dressing: in a bowl, combine lemon juice, extra virgin olive oil, sea salt, pepper, and honey. Toss kale and quinoa with dressing. Top with grilled pineapple. Allow chicken to rest before slicing and serving with salad. ¼ pineapple, trimmed & cut into wedges 2 chicken breasts
4. Dressing juice of ½ lemon ¼ cup extra virgin olive oil ½ tsp. sea salt ½ tsp. ground black pepper 1 tsp. honey 3 cups kale. 1 cup quinoa, cooked Eric's Tip: I love to add feta cheese then roll it up in a tortilla for a killer burrito!

466.Tzatziki Lamb Burgers

Servings: 5
Cooking Time: 12 Minutes
Ingredients:
- 1½ pounds boneless lamb shoulder or leg or good-quality ground lamb
- 1 tablespoon chopped fresh oregano
- 1 teaspoon salt
- 1 teaspoon black pepper
- 1 tablespoon minced garlic
- ½ cup Greek yogurt
- 1 tablespoon olive oil, plus more for brushing
- 1 tablespoon red wine vinegar
- 2 tablespoons crumbled feta cheese
- 4 or 5 ciabatta rolls, split, or 8–10 slider buns (like potato or dinner rolls)
- Thinly sliced cucumbers for serving

Directions:
1. Preparing the Ingredients.
2. 1 Put the lamb, oregano, salt, pepper, and garlic in a food processor and pulse until coarsely ground—finer than chopped, but not much. (If you're using preground meat, put it in a bowl with the seasonings and work them together gently with your hands.) Take a bit of the mixture and fry it up to taste for seasoning; adjust if necessary. Handling the meat as little as possible to avoid compressing it, shape the mixture lightly into 4 or 5 burgers or 8 to 10 sliders. Refrigerate the burgers until you're ready to grill; if you make them several hours in advance, cover with plastic wrap.
3. Whisk the yogurt, oil, and vinegar together in a small bowl until smooth. Stir in the feta. Taste and adjust the seasoning with salt and pepper.
4. 2 Bring the griddle grill to high heat. When the griddle is hot, place the burgers and cook for 11 Minutes.

5. Transfer the burgers to a plate. Brush the cut sides of the rolls lightly with oil and toast directly over the griddle, 1 to 2 Minutes. Top with a burger, then several slices of cucumber, a dollop of the sauce, and the other half of the roll. Serve with the remaining sauce on the side.

467.Tempeh Grilling Sauce

Servings: 1
Ingredients:
- 1½ cups thick tomato sauce
- 3 tablespoons honey
- 1 tablespoon molasses
- 1 tablespoon olive oil
- 2 tablespoons soy sauce
- 1 tablespoon paprika
- 1 tablespoon chili powder
- 1 tablespoon mustard
- 1 teaspoon garlic powder
- 1 teaspoon oregano

Directions:
1. Preparing the Ingredients.
2. Combine all the ingredients in a large bowl and mix well. Cover and let mixture stand for at least 1 hour before using. Refrigerate in a tightly sealed bottle if not using right away. Use as a marinade for grilled tofu, seitan or tempeh.

468.Korean Bulgogi Marinade

Servings: 2
Ingredients:
- 1 cup soy sauce
- 1 cup brown sugar
- 3-4 cloves garlic, minced
- 1 inch ginger root, minced
- 2 tablespoons sesame oil
- 1 bunch green onions, finely chopped

Directions:
1. Preparing the Ingredients.
2. In a small saucepan, over low heat.
3. Grilling
4. combine the soy sauce, sugar, garlic, and ginger, and mix until sugar is dissolved. Remove from heat and add the remaining ingredients.
5. This is a super marinade or basting sauce for Tri-tip, beef for sandwiches, and beef ribs. You can use this as a marinade, baste or serving sauce. But since there is sugar in this sauce you can only use it to baste during the last five Minutes the meat is on the Griddle or the sugar will burn.

469.Perfect Honey Bbq Sauce

Servings: 24
Cooking Time: 15 Minutes
Ingredients:
- Ketchup – 1 cup.
- Onion powder – 1 tsp.
- Garlic powder – 1 tsp.
- Smoked paprika – 1 tsp.
- Honey – 2 tbsps.
- Apple cider vinegar –1/4 cup.
- Brown sugar –1/2 cup.
- Black pepper –1/2 tsp.
- Salt – 1 tsp.

Directions:
1. Add all ingredients into the saucepan and heat over a medium heat. Bring to boil. Turn heat to low and simmer for 15 minutes. Remove saucepan from heat and let it cool completely. Pour sauce into an air-tight container and store in the refrigerator for up to 2 weeks.

Nutrition Info: (Per serving):Calories 35, Carbs 9g, Fat 1g, Protein 1g

470.Mini Portobello Burgers

Servings: 4
Cooking Time: 15 Minutes
Ingredients:
- 4 portobello mushroom caps
- 4 slices mozzarella cheese
- 4 buns, like brioche
- For the marinade:
- 1/4 cup balsamic vinegar
- 2 tablespoons olive oil
- 1 teaspoon dried basil
- 1 teaspoon dried oregano
- 1 teaspoon garlic powder
- ¼ teaspoon sea salt
- ¼ teaspoon black pepper

Directions:
1. Whisk together marinade ingredients in a large mixing bowl. Add mushroom caps and toss to coat.
2. Let stand at room temperature for 15 minutes, turning twice.
3. Preheat griddle for medium-high heat.
4. Place mushrooms on the griddle; reserve marinade for basting.
5. Cook for 5 to 8 minutes on each side, or until tender.
6. Brush with marinade frequently.
7. Top with mozzarella cheese during the last 2 minutes of cooking.
8. Remove from griddle and serve on brioche buns.

Nutrition Info: Calories: 248, Sodium: 429 mg, Dietary Fiber: 2.1g Fat: 13.5g, Carbs: 20.3g Protein: 13g

471.Fishies Rub

Servings: 8
Ingredients:
- 1 tablespoon onion powder
- 1 tablespoon white sugar
- 1 tablespoon summer savory
- 1 teaspoon McCormick Imitation Butter Flavor Salt
- 1 teaspoon green tea leaves
- 1 teaspoon finely ground black pepper
- 1 tablespoon lemon granules
- 1 tablespoon ginger powder

Directions:
1. Preparing the Ingredients.
2. In a small bowl mix all the ingredients well with a spoon. Pour into a glass jar which has a shaker top and use to sprinkle on Griddled, broiled or pan-fried fish. Keep in a cool, dry place so spices don't form a useless cake.

472.Easy Fig Jam

Servings: 1
Cooking Time: 40 Minutes
Ingredients:
- 1 pound ripe figs, stems removed
- 1 tablespoon good-quality olive oil
- Sugar (optional)

Directions:
1. Preparing the Ingredients.
2. Heat a Griddle for medium. Make sure the grates are clean.
3. Toss the figs with the oil in a bowl.
4. Place the figs on the grill directly.
5. Grilling
6. Turning once, until soft, 5 to 10 Minutes total. Transfer to a bowl. Use a potato masher or an immersion blender to reduce the figs to a purée, smooth or a little chunky. Taste and adjust the sweetness level with sugar if you like. Eat right away. Or let cool, then store in an airtight container in the refrigerator for up to 5 days.

473.Grilled Chipotle Chicken Salad

Servings: 2
Ingredients:
- Marinade
- 2 chipotle peppers

- 1 clove garlic, peeled & minced ½ tsp. sea salt
- ½ tsp. ground coriander
- 2 tbsp. olive oil
- ½ lime, juiced

Directions:
1. Preparing the Ingredients.
2. Combine all marinade ingredients in a bowl. Marinate chicken in the refrigerator for 1 hour.
3. Combine all dressing ingredients in a bowl. Set aside.
4. Grilling
5. Grill chicken on medium heat 5-7 Minutes per side or until chicken is fully cooked.
6. In a large bowl, toss salad ingredients with dressing. Let chicken rest before slicing and serving over the salad. 2chicken breasts Dressing ¼ cup buttermilk. 1 tbsp. Worcestershire sauce ½ tsp. garlic powder ½ tsp. onion powder, ½ tsp. sea salt, ½ tsp. ground black, pepper ½ tsp. Dijon mustard, 1 tsp. sugar. Salad. 4 cups romaine, chopped ½ cup grape tomatoes, halved ½ red onion, peeled & sliced ½ cucumber, sliced.

474.Kansas City Classic Sauce

Servings: 1
Ingredients:
- ¼ teaspoon allspice
- ¼ teaspoon cinnamon
- ¼ teaspoon mace
- ¼ teaspoon black pepper
- ½ teaspoon curry powder, Oriental preferred
- ½ teaspoon chili powder
- ½ teaspoon paprika
- ¼ cup white vinegar
- ½ teaspoon hot pepper sauce
- 1 cup ketchup
- ⅓ cup dark molasses

Directions:
1. Preparing the Ingredients.
2. Place all of the dry ingredients into a bowl. Add the vinegar and stir. the hot pepper sauce, ketchup, and molasses and mix until the mixture is thoroughly blended. This sauce may be served room temperature or heated.
3. Adds a wonderful zip and burst of flavor to beef brisket, pork tenderloin and lamb chops.

475.Basil Pesto

Servings: 1
Cooking Time: 10 Minutes
Ingredients:
- 2 cups packed fresh basil leaves
- ½ clove garlic, or more to taste, peeled
- 2 tablespoons pine nuts or chopped walnuts
- ½ cup good-quality olive oil, or more as desired
- Salt
- ½ cup freshly grated Parmesan or pecorino Romano (optional)

Directions:
1. Preparing the Ingredients.
2. Place the basil, garlic, nuts, and about ¼ cup oil in a blender or food processor with a pinch of salt. Pulse until finely chopped, stopping to scrape down the side of the container if necessary. Add the rest of the oil gradually while still pulsing. Add more oil if you prefer a thinner mixture. Mix in the cheese by hand just before serving.

476.Korean Bbq Sauce

Servings: 1½
Cooking Time: X
Ingredients:
- ½ cup (120 ml) gochujang
- ¼ cup (60 ml) soy sauce
- ¼ cup (60 ml) mirin/rice wine
- 2 tbsp (30 ml) sesame oil
- 1 tbsp (8 g) gochugaru
- ¼ cup (60 ml) honey
- ¼ cup (60 ml) water

Directions:
1. Preparing the Ingredients..
2. In a large bowl, Beat together the gochujang, soy sauce, mirin, sesame oil, gochugaru, honey and water until thoroughly combined. Store, refrigerated, for up to 2 weeks.

477.Superior Rosemary Polenta

Servings: 4
Ingredients:
- 24-oz. log prepared polenta
- 2 teaspoon extra-virgin olive oil
- garlic salt to taste
- lemon pepper to taste
- 2 tablespoons chopped rosemary

Directions:
1. Preparing the Ingredients.
2. Preheat Griddle on high.
3. Cut the polenta into 12½-inch thick slices. Place the slices on a baking sheet. Brush both sides of the polenta rounds with oil and season lightly with garlic salt, lemon pepper, and sprinkle with chopped rosemary leaves. Lightly oil the grill rack and.
4. Grilling

5. Polenta slices over high heat (500° to 600°) until nicely browned, 3 to 5 Minutes per side.
6. Remove from heat and serve on a heated platter.

478.Jamaican Sauce

Ingredients:
- ½ cup allspice berries
- ½ cup packed brown sugar
- 6-8 garlic cloves
- 4-6 Scotch bonnet peppers *
- 1 tablespoon ground thyme
- 1-2 bunches green onions
- 1 teaspoon cinnamon
- ½ teaspoon nutmeg
- salt and pepper to taste
- 4 tablespoon soy sauce

Directions:
1. Preparing the Ingredients.
2. Place all ingredients in a food processor or blender and liquefy. Pour sauce into a glass jar or plastic container, cover, and keep refrigerated. The sauce will keep forever if refrigerated ! Do not store in metal container as the peppers can eat into the metal and cause contamination.
3. Grilling
4. Use it on chicken, lamb, pork, beef, venison, rabbit or you guessed it: anything that you cook that in any way resembles meat or poultry. This sauce would be overwhelming for most fish dishes, though.
5. Please, please be very careful when handling Scotch bonnet peppers (the hottest peppers on the planet). Use rubber or plastic gloves, whenever you handle peppers, and if these are not available, wash your hands THOROUGHLY after handling. One mistaken rubbing of an eye and you will never forget the experience!

479.Cheese-stuffed Peppers

Servings: 4
Ingredients:
- 8 oz. cream cheese, softened ½ cup pepperoni, chopped
- 2/3 cup Asiago cheese
- 2/3 cup mozzarella cheese
- 2 tbsp. basil, chopped
- 12 mini peppers, cut in half & seeded

Directions:
1. Preparing the Ingredients.
2. In a bowl, combine cream cheese, pepperoni, Asiago, mozzarella and basil. Mix. Stuff the peppers with the cream cheese filling.
3. Grilling

4. Preheat the oven to 400° F. Grill the peppers on medium heat until tender. Place the Grill Pan in the oven for 5-10 Minutes until peppers are cooked through. Sprinkle with scallions before serving. Scallions, for garnish. Wrap the peppers in bacon for awesome poppers!

480.Spiced Lamb Burger

Servings: 4
Cooking Time: 5 Minutes
Ingredients:
- 1¼ pounds lean ground lamb
- 1 tablespoon ground cumin
- ¼ teaspoon ground cinnamon
- ½ teaspoon salt
- ½ teaspoon freshly ground black pepper
- 4 whole wheat pitas
- ½ medium cucumber, peeled and sliced
- ½ cup Simple Garlic Yogurt Sauce

Directions:
1. Preparing the Ingredients.
2. Put the lamb in a medium bowl with the cumin, cinnamon, salt, and pepper. Using a fork, mix the seasonings into the meat and then, with your hands, form the mixture into 4 patties, each about 1 inch thick.
3. Turn control knob to the high position, when the griddle is hot place the burgers and cook for 5 Minutes without flipping. Remove the burgers and cover to keep warm. Put a burger into each pita, stuff a few cucumber slices in there too, and spoon some of the yogurt sauce over the top. Serve immediately.

481.Korean Beef Skewers

Servings: 10
Ingredients:
- 1 lb. beef flank steak, cut into strips
- Marinade ½ cup soy sauce

Directions:
1. Preparing the Ingredients.
2. Combine steak with marinade ingredients in the refrigerator for 2 hours. Skewer steak strips. Preheat the Grill Pan on medium heat for 5 Minutes.
3. Grilling
4. Grill beef skewers on each side to desired doneness. Sprinkle with sesame seeds and crushed red pepper before serving. 1 tbsp. rice vinegar ¼ cup brown sugar 2 tbsp. sesame oil 2 cloves garlic, peeled & minced 4 scallions, sliced. To Serve 1 tsp. sesame seeds,1 tsp. crushed red pepper. Serve with some jasmine rice and bibb lettuce for delicious wraps.

482.Dixie Watermelon Salsa

Servings: 4
Ingredients:
- 6 cups diced watermelon, seeds removed
- 1 ½ cup diced onion
- 4-6 tablespoons jalapeno chilies, seeded and finely chopped
- 3 tablespoons extra virgin olive oil
- 3 tablespoons red wine vinegar
- 2 tablespoons fresh lime juice
- ½ cup finely chopped cilantro salt, to taste

Directions:
1. Preparing the Ingredients
2. In a large stainless steel or glass mixing bowl, combine all ingredients. Mix well. Chill overnight. Use half watermelon which you've hollowed out as a serving dish, and fill with prepared salsa.

483.Tybet's Sauce

Servings: 1
Ingredients:
- 1 can cola (12 oz.) DO NOT USE DIET SODAS
- 1½ cups ketchup
- 1 cup finely chopped onion
- ¼ cup cider vinegar
- ⅛ cup A1 steak sauce
- 1 teaspoon Mexene chili powder
- 2 teaspoon lemon granules
- 1 teaspoon white sugar
- 1 teaspoon salt
- white pepper to taste

Directions:
1. Preparing the Ingredients.
2. In a medium saucepan, over high heat, combine all the ingredients and bring to a boil, stirring often.
3. Grilling
4. Immediately reduce the heat to low and simmer, covered, stirring occasionally, for 30-45 Minutes or until sauce is thickened. Remove pan from heat, let mixture cool, and then store in a tightly covered glass jar or plastic container.

484.Chardonnay Marinade

Servings: 2
Ingredients:
- ½ cup soy sauce
- ½ cup Chardonnay
- ½ cup water
- 1 bunch green onions coarsely chopped
- 5 cloves fresh garlic, coarsely chopped and crushed
- 1 small ginger root, peeled and diced
- 3 tablespoons cane syrup
- fresh ground pepper
- pinch salt
- ½ teaspoon sesame oil

Directions:
1. Preparing the Ingredients.
2. Mix all ingredients in a medium glass or stainless steel bowl. Place in sealable container and set aside until you wish to use this. A great marinade for beef, pork or lamb. Can also be used to baste meat while Grilling.

485.Coffee Rub

Servings: 1
Ingredients:
- ½ cup (125 g) kosher salt
- 3 tbsp (9 g) dark roast ground coffee
- 2 tbsp (14 g) coarsely ground pepper
- 1 tbsp (14 g) turbinado sugar
- ½ tsp chili powder ½ tsp cocoa powder

Directions:
1. Preparing the Ingredients.
2. A savory blend, this rub tastes great on steaks, hamburgers and beef ribs.
3. Add the salt, coffee, pepper, sugar, chili powder and cocoa powder to a small bowl; mix well. Store in an airtight container for up to 6 months.

486.Big Burger

Servings: 4
Cooking Time: 9 Minutes
Ingredients:
- 1¼ pounds lean ground beef
- ½ teaspoon salt
- ½ teaspoon freshly ground black pepper
- Seasoning of your choice (such as a dash of Worcestershire or hot sauce, or 1 teaspoon Spicy Spanish Rub
- 4 slices cheese such as American, cheddar, or Swiss (about 4 ounces), or ¼ cup
- crumbled blue or goat cheese
- 4 toasted buns
- 4 beefsteak tomato slices
- 4 leaves romaine lettuce

Directions:
1. Preparing the Ingredients.
2. Bring the griddle grill to medium-high heat.
3. Put the beef in a medium bowl and add the salt, pepper, and your preferred seasonings. Using a fork, mix the seasonings into the meat and then, with your hands, form the mixture into 4 patties, each about 1 inch thick.

4. When the grill is hot, place the burgers on the Grill and cook for 4 Minutes without flipping. Cooking is complete when the internal temperature of the beef reaches at least 145°F on a food thermometer. If needed, cook for up to 5 more Minutes.

5. Lay the cheese over the burgers and lower the grill. Grill for 30 seconds, just until the cheese melts.

6. Set the burgers onto the bottom halves of the buns, add a slice of tomato and a leaf of lettuce to each burger, and cover with the tops of the buns. Serve immediately.

Nutrition Info: (Per Serving): CALORIES: 510; FAT: 30G; PROTEIN: 36G

487.Alabama Bbq Sauce

Servings: 3½
Cooking Time: X
Ingredients:
- 2 cups (460 g) mayonnaise
- 1 cup (240 ml) white vinegar
- ¼ cup (60 ml) apple juice
- 1 tbsp (15 g) horseradish
- 1 tbsp (15 ml) lemon juice
- 1 tsp cayenne pepper
- 2 tsp (5 g) black pepper

Directions:
1. Preparing the Ingredients.
2. In a large bowl, Beat together the mayonnaise, vinegar, apple juice, horseradish, lemon juice, cayenne pepper and black pepper until thoroughly combined. Store, refrigerated, for up to 2 weeks.

488.Bbq White Sauce

Servings: 16
Cooking Time: 10 Minutes
Ingredients:
- Mayonnaise – 1-1/2 cups.
- Horseradish – 2 tsps.
- Worcestershire sauce – 1 tsp.
- Brown sugar – 1 tbsp.
- Spicy brown mustard – 1 tbsp.
- Onion powder –1/2 tsp.
- Garlic powder –1/2 tsp.
- Apple cider vinegar – 1/4 cup.
- Salt – 1 tsp.

Directions:
1. Add all ingredients into a mixing bowl and whisk until smooth. Pour sauce into an air-tight container and store in the refrigerator for up to 1 week.

Nutrition Info: (Per serving):Calories 156, Carbs 1g, Fat 17g, Protein 1g

489.Rosemary Mustard Marinade

Servings: 1
Ingredients:
- 6 sprigs fresh rosemary
- 1 cup tarragon vinegar
- 6 tablespoon Dijon mustard
- 2 tablespoon minced garlic
- pepper to taste
- salt to taste
- 2 tablespoons olive oil

Directions:
1. Preparing the Ingredients.
2. Beat all ingredients together in a medium bowl. Use this as a marinade for beef, chicken, lamb, pork (shoulder is wonderful in this marinade), or firm fish steaks Marinate at least 6 hours or, preferably, overnight.

490.Black Bean–tomato Salsa

Servings: 2½
Cooking Time: 15 Minutes
Ingredients:
- 1 cup cooked black beans, drained and rinsed if using canned
- ½ cup chopped fresh tomato
- ½ cup fresh corn kernels
- ½ cup chopped red onion
- 1 teaspoon ground cumin
- 1 teaspoon minced garlic, or to taste
- Minced hot fresh chile (like jalapeño, Thai, or habanero), or red chile flakes or cayenne, to taste
- ¼ cup chopped fresh mint
- 2 tablespoons fresh lime juice
- Salt and pepper

Directions:
1. Preparing the Ingredients.
2. Place everything in a bowl with a sprinkle of salt and pepper. Toss to combine, then taste and adjust the seasoning. If possible, let the flavors develop for 15 Minutes or so before serving, but serve within a couple of hours.

491.Grilled Watermelon Salad

Servings: 2
Ingredients:
- 1 (2-in. thick)
- slice watermelon, with rind
- 1 cup micro greens
- 1 tbsp. extra virgin olive oil

- 1 tsp. lemon juice

Directions:
1. Preparing the Ingredients.
2. Grill watermelon on both sides.
3. Grilling
4. In a bowl, toss micro greens with olive oil, lemon juice, sea salt, and pepper. Sprinkle watermelon with feta, red onion, strawberries, and pine nuts. Top with micro greens. Cut into slices before serving. Sea salt & pepper 1 cup feta cheese, 1 small red onion, sliced thin 1 cup strawberries, sliced. 1/3 cup pine nuts. Toasted.

492.Grilled Caesar Salad

Servings: 2

Ingredients:
- Caesar Dressing 1 lemon
- juiced ½ cup olive oil
- 2 egg yolks 6 anchovies
- 1 clove garlic,
- peeled 1 tbsp. mustard
- ½ tsp. Worcestershire sauce salt & pepper to taste
- Croutons 1 cup cubed baguette ½ tbsp. garlic powder ½ tsp. sea salt 2 tbsp. olive oil
- Shrimp Marinade
- 2 tbsp. olive oil
- 1 tsp. sea salt

Directions:
1. Preparing the Ingredients.
2. Caesar dressing: combine egg yolks, anchovies, garlic, and 1 tbsp. lemon juice in a food processor. Very slowly, spry in half of the olive oil (¼ cup). Add remaining olive oil and lemon juice, mustard, and Worcestershire sauce. Season with salt and pepper, to taste. Croutons: in a bowl, toss the cubed bread with garlic powder, sea salt, and olive oil.
3. Grilling
4. Grill croutons on all sides on medium heat. Shrimp marinade: in a bowl, combine olive oil, sea salt, black pepper, and lemon juice. Toss shrimp in marinade. Grill on each side until done. In a bowl, combine romaine, croutons, and ½ cup Caesar dressing. Toss gently. Divide the salad between two plates. Top with six shrimp each. Sprinkle with Parmesan cheese before serving. 1 tsp. black pepper, ground 1 tbsp. lemon juice 12 shrimp, extra large (16-20 size), peeled & deveined To Serve 1 head romaine, chopped ¼ cup Parmesan cheese, grated.

493.Wild Mushroom Asiago Pizza

Servings: 6
Cooking Time: 1 Hour

Ingredients:
- 3 Portobello Mushrooms
- 10 Shiitake Mushrooms
- 10 Oyster Mushrooms
- 1 Pizza Dough, Thin Crust
- 16 Slices Asiago Cheese
- 3 Tbsp. Grana Padano Cheese, Grated

Directions:
1. Use the Griddle grill to tenderize the mushrooms. Chop and set aside.
2. Preheat the oven to 400° F.
3. Arrange dough to fit onto the Grill Pan. Grill both sides, then flip again.
4. Distribute both cheeses, chopped mushrooms, and garlic over the pizza. Sprinkle with truffle salt. Drizzle with olive oil.
5. Finish cooking in the oven for about 10 minutes.
6. Slice pizza before serving with your favorite side dishes.

Nutrition Info: (Per serving):Calories 191, Carbs 18g, Fat 9g, Protein 10g

494.Louisiana Fire Pecans

Servings: 4

Ingredients:
- ½ cup butter
- 2 tablespoons paprika
- 2 tablespoons Worcestershire Sauce
- 2 tablespoons orange juice
- ½ teaspoons granulated garlic
- 1 teaspoons mixed dried Italian seasoning
- 1 ½ teaspoons onion powder
- 1 ½ teaspoons brown sugar
- ¼ teaspoons liquid smoke
- dash of Louisiana hot sauce
- ¼ teaspoons red pepper
- seasoned salt
- 1 pound shelled pecan halves

Directions:
1. Preparing the Ingredients
2. Heat your grill to very high heat. Turn gas burners to high, the grill should be hot enough so your hand can only stay 2-3 inches over it for 1 second.
3. Grilling
4. Mix all ingredients except the nuts in a small saucepan, bringing them to a slow simmer for 5 Minutes, or until mixture is well heated through. Take off burner and add the pecans to the pot, stirring well. Drain the pecans slightly and place on a vegetable grill pan (or you can use a cookie sheet) which has been sprayed with non-stick spray.

5. Place on grill in very hot Griddler for 3-4 Minutes until just browned. Sprinkle with salt, to taste.
6. Serve warm or cold.

495.Grilled Lemon-lime Tempeh

Servings: 4
Ingredients:
- MARINADE:
- ⅛ cup freshly squeezed lime
- ¼ cup freshly squeezed lemon juice
- ¼ cup olive oil
- ¼ teaspoon summer savory
- ¼ teaspoon thyme
- 1 tablespoon raspberry leaves *
- ⅛ teaspoon black pepper
- 16 ounces tempeh
- 1 large sweet onion, sliced
- sliced tomatoes for garnish
- fresh lettuce leaves for garnish
- 4-6 hamburger rolls (whole wheat)
- Heat grill to high, about 400° degrees.

Directions:
1. Preparing the Ingredients.
2. In a small bowl, combine the lime and lemon juice, olive oil, savory, oregano, raspberry leaves, and pepper, mix well and set aside. Cut the tempeh into 1-inch strips and place in a metal or bamboo steamer or over boiling water. Steam for 15-18 Minutes, until heated through. Remove and drain the tempeh, then place it in a 2-4 qt. flat casserole dish or Pyrex baking dish. Pour the marinade over the tempeh add the onions and marinate in the refrigerator for 4-6 hours.
3. Grilling
4. Grill the tempeh and onions over a medium hot (400° to 500°) BBQ grill you've sprayed or coated with oil, basting the tempeh frequently with the marinade. Grill each side until it's heated through and appears a light brown.
5. Serve the tempeh slices and onions on the hamburger rolls. Garnish with onion slices, lettuce, and sliced tomatoes. Have your favorite BBQ sauce ready on the side for those who wish to add it to their grilled sandwiches.

496.Mozzarella Grilled Tomatoes

Servings: 6
Ingredients:
- Olive Oil Marinade ½ cup extra virgin olive oil
- 2 cloves garlic, peeled & minced
- 1 tsp. dried oregano
- ½ tsp. sea salt

- ½ tsp. ground black pepper

Directions:
1. Preparing the Ingredients.
2. Marinade: in a bowl, combine olive oil, garlic, oregano, sea salt, and pepper. Brush the bread on both sides with some of the olive oil marinade. Grill on both sides to desired doneness.
3. Grilling
4. Toss the tomatoes with remaining marinade. Grill to desired doneness. Assemble crostini: arrange mozzarella on top of each slice of bread. Top with tomatoes. Spry balsamic glaze and any leftover olive oil marinade over crostini. Garnish with basil immediately before serving. ½ crusty baguette, sliced into ½ inch rounds 1 cup grape tomatoes, 12 slices fresh mozzarella, 2 tbsp. balsamic glaze, 3 basil leaves, chopped, for garnish

497.Lemon Bbque Glaze

Servings: 1 ½
Cooking Time: X
Ingredients:
- 8 oz can cranberry sauce
- ⅛ teaspoon dried, crushed rosemary
- ¼ cup finely chopped dried cranberries
- ½ cup cranberry juice
- 2 tablespoons lemon juice
- ½ teaspoon finely chopped lemon peel
- ¼ cup honey

Directions:
1. Preparing the Ingredients.
2. In a saucepan, over medium heat, combine all the ingredients and mix constantly while bringing to a boil. Keep over medium heat until the sauce reduces by .
3. Grilling
4. Remove from heat let it cool. Use the sauce to baste turkey, chicken, lamb or pork, several times during the last 5 Minutes on the grill.

498.Jack's Bbq Sauce

Servings: 2
Ingredients:
- ½ pint Jack Daniel's whiskey
- 1 can tomato soup
- 1 tablespoon Worcestershire sauce
- pinch of garlic powder
- 2 tablespoons brown sugar
- 1 teaspoon ground white pepper
- dash of Louisiana Hot Sauce

Directions:
1. Preparing the Ingredients.

2. Mix all ingredients in a medium saucepan, over medium heat,
3. Grilling
4. stirring constantly for 5 Minutes. Remove from heat and pour into a medium bowl to cool. When cooled Place in a sealable glass or plastic bottle.
5. Use this sauce on anything you Griddle, but it's especially good on grilled leg of lamb and grilled lamb riblets.

499.Flank Steak With Balsamic Onion Dressing

Servings: 4
Cooking Time: 20 Minutes
Ingredients:
- 1 Flank Steak
- 1 Tsp. Sea Salt
- 1 Tsp. Ground Black Pepper
- 2 Tbsp. Olive Oil
- Balsamic Onion Dressing

Directions:
1. Rub flank steak with sea salt, pepper, and olive oil.
2. Mix dressing ingredients together.
3. Remove onions from dressing and grill until tender. Cut onions into quarters before returning to the dressing.
4. Griddle grill the steaks to desired temperature.
5. Let steaks rest before slicing. Drizzle with dressing before serving with your favorite side dish.
Nutrition Info: (Per serving):Calories278.8, Protein 96g Carbs 30g Fat 28g

500.Bbq Tofu Cakes

Servings: 4
Ingredients:
- 1 tablespoon arrowroot powder
- ½ cup water
- ¼ cup barley miso
- ½ cup Mirin
- ¼ cup plum sauce
- 1 tablespoon brown sugar
- 2 tablespoons hone
- 12 small Japanese eggplants, or American variety
- 4 Atsu-Age cakes (firm thick deep-fried tofu), available at health food stores
- 8 whole shiitake mushrooms, fresh
- 1 bunch green onions

Directions:
1. Preparing the Ingredients.

2. In a small saucepan, over medium heat on a grill or stovetop burner, Beat together arrowroot and water.
3. Grilling
4. For 2 to 3 Minutes stirring constantly and add miso, Mirin, plum sauce, brown sugar, and honey for 5 Minutes until thickened. Remove from the heat, pour into a medium bowl and let cool. Reserve. Slice each eggplant in half lengthwise (if American variety used slice in ½-inch thick rounds) and trim ends from the green onions. Clean mushrooms. Brush grill with sesame oil to prevent sticking. Cook the Atsu-Age tofu cakes over medium-hot (450° to 550°) 7- 8 Minutes each side until the edges start to crisp and turn brown. While tofu grills, place whole green onions, shiitake mushrooms and eggplant (cut-side down) on the grill and cook for 5 Minutes. Turn and baste with miso sauce. Continue Grilling 5-8 Minutes until eggplant can be pierced easily with a fork. Serve the tofu cakes with the grilled vegetables on top and spry both with the remaining misoplum sauce.

501.Amazing Barbecue Sauce

Servings: 1
Cooking Time: 30 Minutes
Ingredients:
- 1 tablespoon butter
- ¼ cup minced onion
- 1 cup ketchup
- ¼ cup brown sugar
- 2½ tablespoons distilled white vinegar
- 1 tablespoon honey
- 1½ teaspoons yellow mustard (the ballpark stuff)
- 1½ teaspoons Worcestershire sauce
- 1½ teaspoons chili powder (to make your own, see opposite)
- ½ teaspoon cayenne
- Salt and pepper

Directions:
1. Preparing the Ingredients.
2. Melt the butter in a medium saucepan over medium heat. Add the onion and
3. Grilling
4. Stirring occasionally, until softened, 3 to 5 Minutes. Add the remaining ingredients and salt and pepper to taste and Beat to combine.
5. Bring to a boil, then reduce the heat so the mixture bubbles gently. Cook, stirring occasionally, until the flavors develop, 10 to 15 Minutes. Use or let cool and store in an airtight container in the refrigerator for up to a week.

502.Best Vinegar Sauce

Servings: 2½
Cooking Time: X
Ingredients:
- 2 tbsp (30 g) ketchup
- 2 cups (480 ml) apple cider vinegar
- 1 tbsp (15 ml) red hot sauce
- 1 tsp red pepper flakes
- 2 tbsp (28 g) brown sugar
- Salt and pepper to taste

Directions:
1. Preparing the Ingredients.
2. Add the ketchup, vinegar, hot sauce, pepper flakes, brown sugar, salt and pepper to a small pot over low heat; simmer for 10 Minutes, stirring occasionally, until the sugar is dissolved. Strain the sauce and serve. Any unused sauce can be stored in a jar or airtight container in the refrigerator for 2 weeks.

503.Flounder Spaghetti

Servings: 6
Cooking Time: 30 Minutes
Ingredients:
- 1 lb. spaghetti
- 1 lb. flounder fillet
- 4 cloves garlic, sliced 1/4 cup extra virgin olive oil
- 1/2 cup parsley, chopped
- 1/2 tsp. red pepper flakes

Directions:
1. Cook spaghetti according to the box directions.
2. Griddle grill the flounder on medium heat to desired doneness.
3. In a separate pot, sauté the garlic in olive oil until lightly golden.
4. Add cooked pasta, parsley, red pepper flakes, and flounder to the pot. Season with salt and pepper.
5. Serve spaghetti with lemon wedges.
Nutrition Info: (Per serving):Calories 270.2, Fat 10.7 g, carbs 8g, protein 18g

504.Guava Bbq Sauce

Servings: 1
Ingredients:
- 10 oz. guava jelly
- 2 teaspoon dry mustard powder
- ¼ cup lemon juice
- 4 tablespoon white vinegar
- 1 teaspoon cumin
- 2 shallots, minced
- 2 green onions, green part only, minced

- ¼ cup dry sherry
- 3 tablespoon tomato paste
- 2 tablespoon brown sugar
- 1 lemon, sliced thinly

Directions:
1. Preparing the Ingredients.
2. Combine all ingredients in a medium saucepan, stir, and bring to a boil over medium heat. Immediately reduce heat to low and simmer for 30 Minutes.
3. Grilling
4. Remove the sauce from the heat and cool.
5. With a brush, baste pork ribs or fish (salmon and halibut work especially well) several times during the last ten Minutes of Grilling only. Serve extra on the side with freshly sliced lemons floating on the surface.

505.Vital Bar-be-cue Sauce

Servings: 5
Ingredients:
- 1 lg. finely chopped Vidalia onion (or Maui, or Walla Walla)
- 1 cup apple cider vinegar
- ½ cup apple cider
- ¼ cup lemon juice
- ⅓ cup distilled (white) vinegar
- 5 tablespoons prepared yellow mustard
- 3 teaspoons A-1 sauce
- 4 tablespoons honey
- 2 teaspoons brown sugar
- 3 cups ketchup
- 1 teaspoon mesquite seasoning salt *
- 1 teaspoon black pepper
- ¼ pound butter, or margarine

Directions:
1. Preparing the Ingredients.
2. In a medium saucepan mix all ingredients together well, and.
3. Grilling
4. simmer for 10-15 Minutes, stirring often. This sauce works especially well with beef but can be used for just about any Griddle meat, poultry, or fish.

506.Montreal Seasoned Spatchcocked Hens

Servings: 2
Cooking Time: 60 Minutes
Ingredients:
- 1 cornish hen
- 1 tbsp olive oil
- 1 tbsp Montreal chicken seasoning

Directions:
1. Cut the backbone of hens and flatten the breastplate.
2. Brush hen with oil and rub with Montreal chicken seasoning.
3. Wrap hens in plastic wrap and place in the refrigerator for 4 hours.
4. Preheat the griddle to high heat.
5. Spray griddle top with cooking spray.
6. Place marinated hen on hot griddle top and cook for 60 minutes or until internal temperature reaches 180 F.
7. Serve and enjoy.
Nutrition Info: (Per Serving): Calories 228 ;Fat 18 g ;Carbohydrates 0 g ;Sugar 0 g ;Protein 14 g ;Cholesterol 85 mg

507.Red River Rub

Servings: 8
Ingredients:
- Casablanca Rub
- 2 tablespoons paprika
- 1 teaspoon salt
- 1 teaspoon sugar
- ½ teaspoon coarsely ground black pepper
- ½ teaspoon ground ginger
- ½ teaspoon ground cardamom
- ½ teaspoon ground cumin
- ½ teaspoon ground fenugreek
- ½ teaspoon ground cloves
- ¼ teaspoon ground cinnamon
- ¼ teaspoon ground allspice
- ¼ teaspoon cayenne pepper
- RED RIVER RUB
- 1 teaspoon cayenne pepper
- 1 teaspoon curry powder
- 1 teaspoon turmeric
- 1 teaspoon ground ginger
- 1 teaspoon ground cumin
- 1 tablespoon Mexene chili powder
- 1 tablespoon paprika
- dash of nutmeg
- LAST ROUNDUP BEEF RUB
- Caleb Pirtle III, Dallas, Texas
- ½ teaspoon lemon pepper
- ¼ teaspoon ground rosemary
- 4 teaspoons garlic powder
- 4 teaspoons onion powder
- 1 tablespoon Worcestershire powder *
- 1 teaspoon paprika
- 1 teaspoon beef bouillon granules
- 2 teaspoons Montreal Steak Seasoning
- 2 teaspoons salt

- 2 tablespoons black pepper, coarsely ground

Directions:
1. Preparing the Ingredients.
2. Combine all the ingredients in a large bowl, mixing well. Use immediately or store tightly sealed in glass, or plastic, container. Shake before each use to re-mix the spices.

508.Bourbon Salmon

Servings: ¾
Cooking Time: X
Ingredients:
- ½ cup olive oil
- 4 tablespoons good bourbon
- 4 tablespoons rice vinegar
- 1 teaspoon onion powder
- 1 teaspoon dill
- 1 teaspoon brown sugar
- pinch of sea salt
- pinch of white pepper

Directions:
1. Preparing the Ingredients.
2. In a large bowl mix the ingredients and mix until thoroughly blended. After mixing pour into a container and seal, refrigerate until ready to use. If olive oil has thickened when you are ready to use pour liquid into medium saucepan and heat until just warmed through and olive oil is fully liquid again. Can be used as a marinade, baste or sauce. Especially good on salmon, and other fish, but tastes pretty durn good on chicken and pork too!

509.Sweet & Spicy Bbq Sauce

Servings: 40
Cooking Time: 10 Minutes
Ingredients:
- Tomato sauce – 3-1/2 cups.
- White pepper–1/2 tsp.
- Red pepper flakes – 1 tsp.
- Ground mustard – 1 tbsp.
- Onion powder – 1 tbsp.
- Garlic powder – 1 tbsp.
- Paprika – 2 tbsps.
- Soy sauce – 3 tbsps.
- Worcestershire sauce – 3 tbsps.
- Molasses –1/2 cup.
- Brown sugar – 1 cup.

Directions:
1. Add tomato sauce, soy sauce, Worcestershire sauce, molasses, and brown sugar to a saucepan and stir well to combine.

2. Add paprika, white pepper, red pepper flakes, ground mustard, onion powder, and garlic powder and stir to combine.
3. Cook sauce over a medium heat. Bring to boil.
4. Turn heat to medium-low and simmer for 5 minutes. Remove saucepan from heat and let it cool completely.
5. Pour sauce into an air-tight container and store in the refrigerator.
Nutrition Info: (Per serving):Calories 43, Carbs 11g, Fat 1g, Protein 1g

510. Frickles—fried Pickles

Servings: 4
Ingredients:
- 1 cup flour
- 1 cup yellow corn meal
- 1 tablespoons McCormick barbecue seasoning
- ½ cup mustard
- ⅛ cup beer
- 20-30 dill pickle slices

Directions:
1. Preparing the Ingredients
2. These deep fried pickles make a great, if quite surprising appetizer, for any Griddle meal. Serve with icy cold beer in frosted mugs.
3. Combine the flour, cornmeal, and BBQ spice mix and place in a medium bowl. Make a slurry of mustard and beer in a separate medium bowl.
4. Grilling
5. Dip pickle slices in mustard mixture and then in flour/cornmeal. Deep fry at 325° F in peanut or Canola oil until batter is browned. Pickles will float to top when done.
6. Serve as an appetizer with icy cold beer.

511. Sun-dried Tomato And Chicken Flatbreads

Servings: 4
Cooking Time: 7 Minutes
Ingredients:
- 4 flat breads or thin pita bread
- For the topping:
- 1 1/2 cups of sliced grilled chicken, pre-cooked or leftovers
- 1/2 cup sun-dried tomatoes, coarsely chopped
- 6 leaves fresh basil, coarsely chopped
- 3 cups mozzarella cheese, shredded
- 1 teaspoon salt
- 1 teaspoon ground black pepper
- 1 teaspoon red pepper flakes
- Olive or chili oil, for serving

Directions:
1. Preheat the griddle to low heat.
2. Mix all the topping ingredients together in a large mixing bowl with a rubber spatula.
3. Lay flatbreads on griddle, and top with an even amount of topping mixture; spreading to the edges of each.
4. Tent the flatbreads with foil for 5 minutes each, or until cheese is just melted.
5. Place flatbreads on a flat surface or cutting board, and cut each with a pizza cutter or kitchen scissors.
6. Drizzle with olive or chili oil to serve!
Nutrition Info: Calories: 276, Sodium: 1061 mg, Dietary Fiber: 1.9g Fat: 5.7g, Carbs: 35.7g Protein: 19.8g

512. Beet Burgers With Dates And Ginger

Servings: 6
Cooking Time: 10 Minutes
Ingredients:
- 1 pound beets, peeled and grated (about
- 5 cups)
- ½ cup packed pitted dates, broken into
- pieces
- ½ cup almonds
- 1 1-inch piece peeled fresh ginger, cut into coins
- ½ cup bulgur
- Salt and pepper
- ¾ cup boiling red wine or water
- 1 tablespoon Dijon or other mustard
- Cayenne or red chile flakes (optional)

Directions:
1. Preparing the Ingredients
2. 1 Put the beets in a food processor with the dates, almonds, and ginger; pulse until everything is well chopped but not quite a paste. Transfer the mixture to a large bowl and add the bulgur and a sprinkle of salt and pepper. Stir in the boiling wine, mustard, and cayenne to taste if you're using it and cover the bowl with a plate. Let sit for 20 Minutes for the bulgur to soften. Taste and adjust the seasonings. Shape into 12 burgers, put on a platter without touching, and refrigerate for at least 1 hour.
3. 2 Turn control knob to the high position, when the griddle is hot, place the burgers and cook for 10 Minutes without flipping.
4. Serve with your preferred fixings or toppings.

513. Orange Cornish Hen

Servings: 2
Cooking Time: 60 Minutes
Ingredients:

- 1 cornish hen
- 1/4 onion, cut into chunks
- 1/4 orange cut into wedges
- 2 garlic cloves
- 4 fresh sage leaves
- 1 1/2 fresh rosemary sprigs
- For glaze:
- 2-star anise
- 1 tbsp honey
- 1 cup orange juice
- 1/4 fresh orange, sliced
- 1/2 orange zest
- 1.5 oz Grand Marnier
- 1/2 cinnamon stick

Directions:
1. Stuff hen with orange wedges, garlic, onions, and herbs. Season with pepper and salt.
2. Preheat the griddle to high heat.
3. Spray griddle top with cooking spray.
4. Place hen on hot griddle top and cook for 60 minutes or until the internal temperature of hens reaches 165 F.
5. Meanwhile, in a saucepan heat, all glaze ingredients until reduce by half over medium-high heat.
6. Brush hen with glaze.
7. Slice and serve.

Nutrition Info: (Per Serving): Calories 351 ;Fat 12.1 g ;Carbohydrates 29.2 g ;Sugar 40.9 g ;Protein 16 g ;Cholesterol 85 mg

514.Bbq Hen

Servings: 8
Cooking Time: 1 Hour 30 Minutes
Ingredients:
- 1 cornish hen
- 2 tbsp BBQ rub

Directions:
1. Preheat the griddle to high heat.
2. Spray griddle top with cooking spray.
3. Coat hens with BBQ rub and place on hot griddle top and cook for 1 1/2 hours or until the internal temperature of hens reach 165 F.
4. Slice and serve.

Nutrition Info: (Per Serving): Calories 168 ;Fat 11 g ;Carbohydrates 0 g ;Sugar 0 g ;Protein 14 g ;Cholesterol 85 mg

515.Cheddar Jalapeño Stuffed Burger

Servings: 6
Cooking Time: 20 Minutes
Ingredients:

- Burger Mixture
- 2 lb. ground beef
- 1 tsp. sea salt
- 1 tsp. ground black pepper
- 3 tbsp. cilantro, chopped ½ small onion, peeled & minced
- 1 jalapeño, seeded & chopped

Directions:
1. Combine ground beef, sea salt, pepper, cilantro, onion, and jalapeño.
2. Divide ground beef mixture into 4 balls. Stuff each ball with a chunk of cheddar.
3. Rub burgers with olive oil. Griddle grill it for about 5 minutes per side or to desired doneness.
4. Top burgers with sliced cheddar.
5. Spread each roll with margarine. Grill to desired doneness. Serve burgers topped with pickled jalapeños.

Nutrition Info: (Per serving):526.1 calories; 19g fat; 27.2 g protein; 24.4 g carbs

516.Carolina Q Sauce

Servings: 5
Ingredients:
- 4 cups apple cider vinegar
- ¼ cup honey
- ¼ cup yellow mustard
- 4 tablespoons brown sugar
- 4 teaspoons sea salt
- 4 teaspoons crushed red pepper flakes
- 2 teaspoon coarse black pepper

Directions:
1. Preparing the Ingredients.
2. In a large saucepan-
3. Grilling
4. over low heat, add all the ingredients and simmer all for 15-20 Minutes, stirring constantly with a spoon. DON'T BOIL!
5. Remove pan from the heat, and let pan cool to room temperature. Pour mixture into a sealable glass or plastic bottle.
6. Fantastic with smoked ham, pork shoulder, or pork ribs. But should be tried on beef, lamb and chicken too.

517.Caesar Salad Poultry Burgers

Servings: 4
Cooking Time: 15 Minutes
Ingredients:
- ¼ cup mayonnaise
- 2 cloves garlic, 1 minced, 1 peeled and left
- whole

- 2 oil-packed anchovy fillets, drained and mashed
- 2 tablespoons freshly grated Parmesan cheese
- 1 tablespoon fresh lemon juice
- ½ teaspoon Worcestershire sauce
- 1½ pounds ground chicken or turkey
- Good-quality vegetable oil for oiling the grates
- 4 ciabatta rolls, split, or 8–10 slider buns
- Good-quality olive oil for brushing the rolls
- 1 leaves heart of romaine, trimmed

Directions:
1. Preparing the Ingredients.
2. 1 Line a baking sheet with wax paper. Whisk the mayonnaise, minced garlic, anchovies, Parmesan, lemon juice, and Worcestershire together in a small bowl until smooth. Put the chicken in a medium bowl and add 2 tablespoons of the dressing. Cover and refrigerate the remaining dressing. Work the dressing into the chicken with your hands gently but completely. Form the mixture into 4 burgers ¾ to 1 inch thick. Put them on the prepared pan, cover, and refrigerate until firm, at least 1 hour.
3. Turn control knob to the high position, when the griddle is hot, brush the cut sides of the rolls with olive oil. Brush the burgers with oil on both sides, put them on the griddle. Carefully turning once with two spatulas, until browned on the outside and no longer pink in the center, 5 to 7 Minutes per side.
4. 2 For the last couple of Minutes, toast the rolls on the grill, cut side down. To serve, rub the cut side of the top of each roll with the whole garlic clove. Put a burger on the bottom half, add a dollop of the remaining dressing, a leaf of romaine, and the top of the roll.

518.Easy Bbq Sauce

Servings: 10
Cooking Time: 15 Minutes
Ingredients:
- Brown sugar – 1-1/2 cups.
- Onion powder – 2 tsps.
- Paprika – 2 tsps.
- Worcestershire sauce – 1 tbsp.
- Apple cider vinegar –1/2 cup.
- Ketchup – 1-1/2 cups.
- Pepper – 1 tsp.
- Kosher salt – 2 tsps.

Directions:
1. Add all ingredients into a small saucepan and heat over a medium heat. Bring to boil. Turn heat to low and simmer for 15 minutes. Store and serve.
Nutrition Info: (Per serving):Calories 167, Carbs 43g, Fat 3.4g, Protein 1g

519.Traditional Bbq Sauce

Servings: 3
Ingredients:
- 2 cups (480 ml) tomato ketchup
- ¼ cup (60 ml) apple cider vinegar
- ¼ cup (55 g) brown sugar
- 2 tbsp (30 g) yellow mustard
- ¼ cup (60 ml) honey

Directions:
1. Preparing the Ingredients.
2. This is a great sauce recipe to use on beef, ribs and poultry. It is also a starting point for dreaming up your own sauce and flavor profiles. Get creative and feel free to try various combinations. If you like to bring the heat, introduce cayenne or chili powder to the recipe.
3. Combine the ketchup, vinegar, sugar, mustard and honey in a small bowl; mix well. Refrigerate the sauce until ready to use. Any unused sauce can be stored in a jar or airtight container in the refrigerator for 2 weeks.

520.Maryland Crab Cakes

Servings: 4
Ingredients:
- 1 lb. crabmeat, lump
- 1 egg
- 3/4 cup soda crackers, crushed
- 1 tbsp. Dijon mustard
- 1 tsp. seafood seasoning

Directions:
1. Preparing the Ingredients.
2. Mix all the ingredients together except the oil. Form into four 3 oz. cakes.
3. Grilling
4. Pour the oil onto the Griddle Pan. On medium heat, cook crab cakes on both sides until golden. Serve with tartar sauce and lemon wedges. 1 shallot, peeled & minced ¼ cup mayonnaise ½ tsp. ground black pepper 1 red pepper, small dice 2 tbsp. canola oil. To Serve tartar sauce lemon wedges. Griddle Recipe.

521.Cheese-stuffed

Servings: 6
Ingredients:
- ¼ cup bleu cheese
- 10 slices bacon

Directions:
1. Preparing the Ingredients.
2. ¼ cup bleu cheese 1. Preheat the oven to 400° F. ¼ cup cream cheese Mix the cheeses together. Set

aside.20 dates 3. Make a slit, lengthwise, into each date. Stuff with cheese mixture. 10 slices bacon, raw, cut in half 4. Roll each date with bacon. Grill 2-3 Minutes on each side.
3. Grilling
4. Cook in the oven for 8-10 Minutes or until bacon is crispy. I'll add a shelled pistachio or walnut into each date for an extra crunch.

522.Black & Bleu Bites

Servings: 1
Ingredients:
- 1 tablespoon butter
- 1 tablespoon flour
- ¾ cup cream
- ½ cup crumbled bleu cheese
- ½ teaspoon salt
- ½ teaspoon coarsely ground black pepper

Directions:
1. Preparing the Ingredients.
2. In a medium saucepan, melt the butter over medium heat, then mix in the flour until blended. Gradually mix in cream and
3. Grilling
4. Until thickened, about 5 Minutes. Remove from the heat and mix in the remaining ingredients. If not thickened enough, you can gradually add more flour or cornstarch (1 tablespoon at a time) until desired consistency is reached. Oh 'tis wonderful on grilled steaks, grilled chicken breasts, or even hamburger. This sauce doesn't keep well so make it up just before you use it.

523.Classic American Burger

Servings: 6
Cooking Time: 35 Minutes
Ingredients:
- 2 lbs. ground beef, at least 20% fat
- kosher salt
- black pepper
- 1 tomato, sliced
- 1 yellow or red onion, sliced
- 1 head iceberg lettuce, cut into flats
- 6 thick pieces of American or medium cheddar cheese
- 6 seeded buns or potato buns, toasted

Directions:
1. Divide the ground beef into 6 equal loosely formed balls. Press the balls on a flat surface to make patties. Do not over work them.
2. Generously season the patties with salt and black pepper.

3. Heat your griddle to medium-high heat.
4. Place the patties on the griddle and press down to ensure that the surface makes contact. Cook for three to four minutes.
5. Flip the patties and top with cheese. Cook an additional three to four minutes. The cheese should melt by then.
6. Remove the burgers from the griddle and place them on the buns. Top with lettuce, tomato, and onion, as well as your favorite condiments.
Nutrition Info: Calories: 410, Sodium: 305 mg, Dietary Fiber: 0.9g, Fat: 18.8g, Carbs: 4.1g Protein: 53.4g

524.Tempeh Satay

Servings: 4
Ingredients:
- MARINADE:
- ½ cup grated coconut
- ¼ cup orange juice
- 1 tablespoon honey
- ¼ cup tarmari (whole wheat soy sauce)
- ⅛ teaspoon cayenne pepper
- 4 tempeh cutlets
- PEANUT SAUCE:
- ¼ cup smooth peanut butter
- ¼ cup finely chopped roasted peanuts
- 3 tbs. tarmari
- 1 tablespoon Mirin or sherry
- ½ teaspoon rice vinegar
- ⅛ teaspoon garlic powder
- 1 tbs. honey
- 1 cup nonfat yogurt, plain
- ⅛ teaspoon cayenne pepper
- 1 16 oz. can pineapple chunks

Directions:
1. Preparing the Ingredients.
2. To make the marinade, puree ¼ cup of the coconut with the orange juice, honey, tamari and cayenne in a blender until smooth, 2-3 Minutes. Pour the marinade into a shallow baking dish. Cut the tempeh into 1-inch cubes and add it to marinade. Set aside for 30 Minutes.
3. In a small saucepan, Mixtogether the peanut sauce ingredients with a wire whisk, and warm sauce on low heat, for 7-8 Minutes. Do not let boil.
4. Thread the tempeh cubes and pineapple chunks onto bamboo skewers that have been soaked in hot water for 20 Minutes.
5. Grilling
6. Grill the tempeh/pineapple skewers on a grill over medium-heat 3 to 5 Minutes on each side, or until cubes start to get brown edges. Brush the kebabs with marinade 2 to 3 times during Grilling.

When kebabs are browned on all sides they are done. Remove from heat and set on a platter. Sprinkle with the remaining coconut. Serve immediately with warm peanut sauce.

525.Argentinian Beefsteak Sauce

Servings: 1
Ingredients:
- 1 cup chopped Italian parsley
- ½ cup olive oil
- ¼ cup red wine vinegar
- 1 tablespoon garlic, chopped
- 1 teaspoon oregano
- 1 teaspoon red pepper flakes
- ½ teaspoon coarse salt
- Optional:
- 1 tablespoon chopped fresh rosemary
- 1 teaspoon chopped fresh thyme

Directions:
1. Preparing the Ingredients.
2. In a medium bowl mix the ingredients well and let them marinate in the refrigerator for at least a day. You may add thyme and rosemary if you like, but in very small amounts.
3. Remove the mixture form the refrigerator.
4. Grilling
5. In a medium saucepan over high heat boil the liquid for 10 Minutes. Serve the steak sauce in a sauce boat alongside medium rare steaks.

526.Tandoori Tofu Brochettes

Servings: 4
Ingredients:
- 1 pound extra firm tofu, drained
- MARINADE:
- 3 stalks green onion
- 1 tablespoon minced fresh ginger
- 3 garlic cloves
- 1 tablespoon brown sugar
- 1 tablespoon soy sauce
- 1 generous pinch saffron
- ½ cups soy yogurt
- 2 tablespoons chili powder
- 2 tablespoons paprika
- salt to taste
- pepper to taste
- Brochettes:
- 4 small red onions, halved
- ½ pound crimini mushrooms
- 1 pint cherry tomatoes
- 1 green pepper, sliced

- Gently press the tofu to remove excess moisture. Slice the tofu into bite-sized chunks. Set aside.

Directions:
1. Preparing the Ingredients.
2. Place the green onions and ginger in a food processor and process briefly. With the machine running, drop in garlic cloves, one at a time. Process for 30 seconds. Add remaining ingredients. Process for 1 minute and set aside. The marinade will be somewhat chunky. Spoon the onion, mushroom, green pepper and tofu into a Ziploc bag and pour in marinade. Refrigerate overnight.
3. Grilling
4. Heat the grill to medium high (400° to 500°), oil the grill or spray it with non-stick spray. Remove the tofu and vegetables from the refrigerator and thread onto bamboo or metal skewers.. Skewer vegetables and tofu alternately. Place the brochettes on the hot grill, and brush with the remaining marinade. Turn the kabobs once and cook for another 3-5 Minutes. You may need to keep repeating this cycle.

527.Fresh Mango Salsa

Servings: 2½
Cooking Time: 15 Minute
Ingredients:
- 2 or 3 ripe mangoes, peeled, pitted, and cut into ½- to ¾-inch dice (about 2 cups)
- ½ cup chopped fresh basil
- Juice of 1 lime
- Salt and pepper

Directions:
1. Preparing the Ingredients.
2. Place the mango, basil, and lime juice in a small bowl with some salt and pepper. Toss to combine; taste and adjust the seasoning. Leave at room temperature for up to an hour until you're ready to serve.

528.Green Sauce Gremolata

Servings: ½
Cooking Time: 10 Minutes
Ingredients:
- ½ cup chopped fresh parsley
- Grated zest of 1 lemon
- 1 teaspoon minced garlic, or more to taste

Directions:
1. Preparing the Ingredients.
2. Toss the parsley, lemon zest, and garlic together in a small bowl to combine. Use this as soon as you can for the best flavor.

529.Pesto Chicken Paillard

Servings: 6
Cooking Time: 1 Hour
Ingredients:
- 2 chicken breasts, sliced
- lengthwise & pounded 1/4 in. thick 4 tbsp. pesto
- Marinade 1/4 cup olive oil

Directions:
1. Combine chicken with marinade ingredients for 1-2 hours.
2. Using the Griddle Grill, grill the chicken until done. Chicken will cook quickly as it is very thin.
3. Remove chicken from the Grill Pan. Brush with pesto.
4. Combine salad ingredients in a large bowl. Toss.
5. Serve chicken over greens.
Nutrition Info: (Per serving): Calories: 268 Cal Fat: 12 g Carbs: 1 g Protein: 24.1 g

530.Veggie Pesto Flatbread

Servings: 4
Cooking Time: 10 Minutes
Ingredients:
- 2 prepared flatbreads
- 1 jar pesto
- 1 cup shredded mozzarella cheese
- For the topping:
- 1/2 cup cherry tomatoes, halved
- 1 small red onion, sliced thin
- 1 red bell pepper, sliced
- 1 yellow bell pepper, sliced
- 1/2 cup mixed black and green olives, halved
- 1 small yellow squash or zucchini, sliced
- 2 teaspoon olive oil
- ¼ teaspoon sea salt
- ¼ teaspoon black pepper

Directions:
1. Preheat the griddle to low heat.
2. Spread an even amount of pesto onto each flatbread.
3. Top with ½ cup mozzarella cheese each.
4. Mix all the topping ingredients together in a large mixing bowl with a rubber spatula.
5. Lay flatbreads on griddle, and top with an even amount of topping mixture; spreading to the edges of each.
6. Tent the flatbreads with foil for 5 minutes each, or until cheese is just melted.
7. Place flatbreads on a flat surface or cutting board, and cut each with a pizza cutter or kitchen scissors.
8. Serve warm!

Nutrition Info: Calories: 177 Sodium: 482 mg, Dietary Fiber: 1.7g Fat: 11.9g, Carbs: 12.6g Protein: 5.5g

531.All-around Bbq Rub

Servings: ½
Ingredients:
- A great all-around BBQ rub, this mix is good on just about anything from meat to vegetables.
- 2 tbsp (14 g) paprika
- 2 tbsp (20 g) granulated garlic
- 1 tbsp (18 g) kosher salt
- 1 tbsp (5 g) cayenne pepper
- 1 tbsp (7 g) black pepper
- 1 tbsp (14 g) turbinado sugar
- 1 tbsp (7 g) onion powder
- 1 tbsp (3 g) dried oregano
- ½ tbsp (1 g) dried thyme

Directions:
1. Preparing the Ingredients.
2. Add the paprika, garlic, salt, cayenne and black pepper, sugar, onion powder, oregano and thyme to a small bowl; mix well. Store in an airtight container for up to 6 months.

532.New Mexican Salsa Verde

Servings: 1 Cup
Cooking Time: 15 Minutes
Ingredients:
- 4 cloves garlic (leave the skins on),
- skewered on a wooden toothpick or small bamboo skewer
- 1 cup roasted New Mexican green chiles or Anaheim chiles cut into ¼-inch strips (8 to 10 chiles
- 2 tablespoons chopped fresh cilantro
- 2 teaspoons fresh lime juice, or more to
- taste
- ½ teaspoon ground cumin
- ½ teaspoon dried oregano
- Coarse salt (kosher or sea) and freshly
- ground black pepper

Directions:
1. Preparing the Ingredients.
2. Preheat the griddle to high. When ready to cook, lightly oil the grill surface. Place the burgers on the hot griddle. The burgers will be done after cooking 4 to 6 Minutes. Put the garlic cloves until they are lightly browned and tender, 2 to 3 Minutes per side (4 to 6 Minutes in all). Scrape any really burnt skin off the garlic. Place the garlic, chile strips, cilantro, lime juice, cumin, oregano, and 4 tablespoons of

water in a blender and purée until smooth, scraping down the sides of the blender with a spatula.

3. Transfer the salsa to a saucepan and bring to a gentle simmer over medium heat. Let simmer until thick and flavorful, 5 to 8 Minutes, stirring with a wooden spoon. The salsa should be thick (roughly the consistency of heavy cream) but pourable; add more water as needed. Taste for seasoning, adding more lime juice as necessary and salt and pepper to taste; the salsa should be highly seasoned.

533.Seafood Rub

Servings: 2
Ingredients:
- ⅓ cup (88 g) coarse flake salt
- ⅓ cup (36 g) paprika
- ¼ cup (39 g) garlic powder
- ¼ cup (28 g) freshly ground pepper
- 2 tbsp (5 g) dried thyme
- 2 tbsp (7 g) dried rosemary
- 2 tbsp (16 g) ground chipotle pepper
- 2 tbsp (14 g) onion powder

Directions:
1. Preparing the Ingredients.
2. Fresh seafood is the best, and with this rub we try to showcase the depth of flavor in our dish and not overpower it. We want every bite to have the same flavor and depth to which you are accustomed. This rub is fabulous on shrimp and salmon. We also use it when we make a low-country boil. Add the salt, paprika, garlic, pepper, thyme, rosemary, chipotle pepper and onion to a small bowl; mix well. Store in an airtight container for up to 6 months.

534.Layered Beef & Corn Burger

Servings: 6
Cooking Time: 30 Minutes
Ingredients:
- 1 large egg, lightly beaten
- 1 cup whole kernel corn, cooked
- 1/2 cup bread crumbs
- 2 tablespoons shallots, minced
- 1 teaspoon Worcestershire sauce
- 2 pounds ground beef
- 1 teaspoon salt
- 1/2 teaspoon pepper
- 1/2 teaspoon ground sage

Directions:
1. Combine the egg, corn, bread crumbs, shallots, and Worcestershire sauce in a mixing bowl and set aside.

2. Combine ground beef and seasonings in a separate bowl.
3. Line a flat surface with waxed paper.
4. Roll beef mixture into 12 thin burger patties.
5. Spoon corn mixture into the center of 6 patties and spread evenly across within an inch of the edge.
6. Top each with a second circle of meat and press edges to seal corn mixture in the middle of each burger.
7. Grill over medium heat, for 12-15 minutes on each side or until thermometer reads 160°F and juices run clear.
Nutrition Info: Calories: 354, Sodium: 578 mg, Dietary Fiber: 1.2g Fat: 11.1g, Carbs: 12.3g Protein: 49.1g

535."yaller" Sauce

Servings: 2
Ingredients:
- ¾ cup yellow mustard
- ¾ cup red wine vinegar
- ½ teaspoon Worcestershire sauce
- 2 tablespoons butter
- 1½ teaspoons salt
- ¼ cup brown sugar
- 1 teaspoon ground black pepper
- ½ teaspoon Louisiana hot sauce

Directions:
1. Preparing the Ingredients.
2. In a medium saucepan, combine ingredients, stirring to blend.
3. Grilling
4. Over low heat, simmer 30 Minutes, stirring until thoroughly blended Let stand at room temperature for 1 hour before using.

536.Cilantro-mint Chutney

Servings: 1½
Cooking Time: 15 Minutes
Ingredients:
- 1½ cups packed fresh cilantro leaves
- ½ cup packed fresh mint leaves
- 1 or 2 Thai or other hot green chiles, seeded if you like, to taste, or red chile flakes to taste
- 1 1-inch piece fresh ginger, peeled and sliced
- ½ red onion, quartered
- 2 cloves garlic, peeled
- ¼ cup fresh lime juice
- ½ teaspoon salt, or more to taste

Directions:
1. Preparing the Ingredients.

2. Place the cilantro, mint, chiles, ginger, onion, and garlic in a food processor; pulse until finely ground. Add the lime juice and salt and process until nearly smooth; you may need to add up to ¼ cup water to help form a sauce. Taste and adjust the seasoning and serve. Or refrigerate for up to a day, but serve at room temperature.

537. Beer Butte Ranch Sauce

Servings: 5
Cooking Time: 45 Minutes
Ingredients:
- ½ cup white vinegar
- ½ pound bacon grease
- ½ pound butter
- 1 tablespoon freshly ground black pepper
- 1 tablespoon cayenne
- 3 onions, chopped
- ¼ cup Worcestershire sauce
- 3 cups ketchup
- 1 tablespoon salt
- 1 tablespoon celery salt
- 1 tablespoon garlic salt

Directions:
1. Preparing the Ingredients.
2. In a large saucepan, over low heat on stovetop burner, combine all ingredients
3. Grilling
4. And simmer for at least 45 Minutes. Makes sauce for a 20 pound brisket or a whole mess o' beef or pork ribs.

538. Pork Tenderloin Sandwiches

Servings: 6
Cooking Time: 25 Minutes
Ingredients:
- 2 (3/4-lb.) pork tenderloins
- 1 teaspoon garlic powder
- 1 teaspoon sea salt
- 1 teaspoon dry mustard
- 1/2 teaspoon coarsely ground pepper
- Olive oil, for brushing
- 6 whole wheat hamburger buns
- 6 tablespoons barbecue sauce

Directions:
1. Stir the garlic, salt, pepper, and mustard together in a small mixing bowl.
2. Rub pork tenderloins evenly with olive oil, then seasoning mix.
3. Preheat griddle to medium-high heat, and cook 10 to 12 minutes on each side or until a meat

thermometer inserted into thickest portion registers 155°F.
4. Remove from grill and let stand 10 minutes.
5. Slice thinly, and evenly distribute onto hamburger buns.
6. Drizzle each sandwich with barbecue sauce and serve.
Nutrition Info: Calories: 372, Sodium: 694 mg, Dietary Fiber: 2.9g, Fat: 13.4g, Carbs: 24.7g Protein: 37.2g

539. Peach Bbq Sauce

Servings: 24
Cooking Time: 20 Minutes
Ingredients:
- Ketchup –1/4 cup.
- Liquid smoke –1/4 tsp.
- Dry mustard –1/2 tsp.
- Chili powder – 1 tsp.
- Dijon mustard – 1 tbsp.
- Worcestershire sauce – 1 tbsp.
- Balsamic vinegar – 2 tbsps.
- Apple cider vinegar –1/4 cup.
- Soy sauce –1/4 cup.
- Tomato paste – 2 tbsps.
- Honey – 2 tbsps.
- Molasses – 2 tbsps.
- Brown sugar – 3/4 cup.
- Water – 1-1/2 cups.
- Frozen peaches – 1 lb.
- Bourbon – 4 tbsps.
- Jalapeno pepper – 2 tbsps., diced.
- Onion – 1 cup, diced.
- Olive oil – 2 tbsps.
- Black pepper –1/2 tsp.
- Kosher salt –1/2 tsp.

Directions:
1. Heat olive oil in a saucepan over medium heat.
2. Add jalapeno and onion and sauté for 3-4 minutes.
3. Add bourbon and cook for 1 minute.
4. Add 1 cup water and peaches and cook for 10 minutes. Remove saucepan from heat.
5. Pour pan contents into the food processor and process until smooth. Return blended mixture to the saucepan along with remaining ingredients and cook over medium heat for 5 minutes.
6. Remove saucepan from heat and let it cool completely. Pour sauce into an air-tight container and store in the refrigerator.
Nutrition Info: (Per serving):Calories 55, Carbs 9.6g, Fat 1.2g, Protein 0.5g

540.Tofu Steaks Mango Salsa

Servings: 4
Ingredients:
- 1 bunch fresh cilantro
- ⅔ cup white vegetable stock (below)
- ¼ cup lemon juice
- 1 tablespoon crushed red pepper
- ¼ cup minced fresh ginger
- 1 tablespoon brown sugar
- 1 teaspoon blackstrap molasses
- 5 garlic cloves
- black pepper, to taste
- 1 small fresh pineapple
- 2 mangos
- 1 ¼ pound firm tofu, drained, cut lengthwise into four 1-inch thick "steaks"

Directions:
1. Preparing the Ingredients.
2. Chop the cilantro to make ½ cup and set aside 1 tablespoon of it for salsa. In a medium-sized baking dish, combine the chopped cilantro and the stock, lemon juice, red pepper, ginger, sugar, molasses, garlic, and black pepper. Mix and add the tofu. Marinate it for 2 hours at room temperature. Peel the pineapple and mangos, then finely chop, discard pineapple skin and core and mango skin and pit. In a medium serving bowl combine the fruit and 1 tablespoon of the reserved chopped cilantro. Set it aside at room temperature to let the flavors combine.
3. Grilling
4. Prepare the outdoor grill for medium heat Drain tofu, reserving marinade. Lightly oil grill and place tofu on grill over Grill the tofu until lightly browned, 4-5 Minutes, brushing frequently with the marinade and turning once. Serve the tofu steaks with the pineapple and mango mixture.

541.Margherita Pizza

Servings: 6
Cooking Time: 25 Minutes
Ingredients:
- 1 Pizza Dough, Thin Crust
- 2 Tbsp. Basil Pesto
- 2 Tomatoes, Vine Ripe, Sliced
- 14 Slices Fresh Mozzarella
- 1 Clove Garlic, Peeled & Sliced Thin
- 1 Tbsp. Olive Oil

Directions:
1. Preheat the Griddle Pan on high heat.
2. Roll the pizza dough to fit onto the Pan. Cook on one side until golden.
3. Flip the dough. Spread the pesto on top followed by tomato slices, mozzarella slices, and garlic. Drizzle with olive oil.

4. Preheat the broiler.
5. Place the Pan under broiler to melt the cheese and toast the garlic.
Nutrition Info: (Per serving): Calories: 260 Cal Fat: 13g Carbs: 23g Protein: 14g

542.Romesco Sauce

Servings: 2
Cooking Time: 45 Minutes
Ingredients:
- 3 red bell peppers, grill-roasted seeded, and peeled
- ½ cup almonds
- 1 or 2 cloves garlic, peeled
- 1 tablespoon sherry vinegar
- 1 teaspoon smoked paprika (pimentón)
- ¼ cup good-quality olive oil
- Salt and pepper

Directions:
1. Preparing the Ingredients.
2. Place the peppers, almonds, garlic, vinegar, and paprika in a food processor. With the machine running, slowly pour the oil through the feed tube and process until smooth and thick. Season to taste with salt and pepper. Refrigerate in an airtight container for up to 5 days.

543.Grilled Vegetable Pizza

Servings: 6
Cooking Time: 10 Minutes
Ingredients:
- 8 small fresh mushrooms, halved
- 1 small zucchini, cut into 1/4-inch slices
- 1 small yellow pepper, sliced
- 1 small red pepper, sliced
- 1 small red onion, sliced
- 1 tablespoon white wine vinegar
- 1 tablespoon water
- 4 teaspoons olive oil, divided
- 1/2 teaspoon dried basil
- 1/4 teaspoon sea salt
- 1/4 teaspoon pepper
- 1 prebaked, 12-inch thin whole wheat pizza crust
- 1 can (8 ounces) pizza sauce
- 2 small tomatoes, chopped
- 2 cups shredded part-skim mozzarella cheese

Directions:
1. Preheat your griddle to medium-high heat.
2. Combine mushrooms, zucchini, peppers, onion, vinegar, water, 3 teaspoons oil and seasonings in a large mixing bowl.

3. Transfer to griddle and cook over medium heat for 10 minutes or until tender, stirring often.
4. Brush crust with remaining oil and spread with pizza sauce.
5. Top evenly with grilled vegetables, tomatoes and cheese.
6. Tent with aluminum foil and griddle over medium heat for 5 to 7 minutes or until edges are lightly browned and cheese is melted.
7. Serve warm!
Nutrition Info: Calories: 111, Sodium: 257 mg, Dietary Fiber: 1.7g Fat: 5.4g, Carbs: 12.2g Protein: 5g

544.Turkey Pesto Panini

Servings: 2
Cooking Time: 6 Minutes
Ingredients:
- 1 tablespoon olive oil
- 4 slices French bread
- 1/2 cup pesto sauce
- 4 slices mozzarella cheese
- 2 cups chopped leftover turkey
- 1 Roma tomato, thinly sliced
- 1 avocado, halved, seeded, peeled and sliced

Directions:
1. Preheat griddle to medium-high heat.
2. Brush each slice of bread with olive oil on one side.
3. Place 2 slices olive oil side down on the griddle.
4. Spread 2 tablespoons pesto over 1 side of French bread.
5. Top with one slice mozzarella, turkey, tomatoes, avocado, a second slice of mozzarella, and top with second half of bread to make a sandwich; repeat with remaining slices of bread.
6. Cook until the bread is golden and the cheese is melted, about 2-3 minutes per side.
7. Serve warm with your favorite salad or soup.
Nutrition Info: Calories: 1129, Sodium: 1243 mg, Dietary Fiber: 10g, Fat:70.9g, Carbs: 53.2g Protein: 73g

545.Beach Peanut Salad

Servings: 4
Ingredients:
- 1 small head of cabbage, finely chopped
- 2 cups finely chopped unsalted peanuts (or pecans or walnuts)
- 1 teaspoons butter
- 1 teaspoons mustard
- 1 teaspoons brown sugar
- 1 teaspoons whole wheat flour

- ¾ teaspoons pepper
- 4 tablespoons apple cider vinegar
- 2 egg yolks, Whisken salt

Directions:
1. Preparing the Ingredients
2. In a medium bowl mix the chopped cabbage and peanuts together and set aside.
3. Grilling
4. Cream the butter, mustard, sugar and flour together until a thick paste, then add the pepper and mix in the vinegar. In a double boiler heat this mixture while stirring, until very thick. Add Whisken egg yolks, salt to taste, and mix thoroughly. When mixed and while still warm, pour over nuts and cabbage, toss gently and serve.

546.Marvelous Margarita Glaze

Servings: 1
Ingredients:
- ½ cup triple sec
- ½ cup lime juice
- ½ cup tequila
- ½ cup honey
- pinch of salt

Directions:
1. Preparing the Ingredients.
2. Mix all ingredients in a medium saucepan over low heat.
3. Grilling
4. Stirring constantly, for 4 to 5 Minutes. When the glaze is thoroughly mixed, remove from the heat and cool. When cooled you can bottle or use the glaze straight from the pan to brush over chicken, fish, or shellfish.
5. Try basting shrimp with this, or use this as a dip for cooked chicken wings or shrimp. One more way to use is to spryd the glaze on grilled oysters or clams, after the shells have opened.

547.Chicken Satay

Servings: 10
Ingredients:
- Peanut Sauce
- 1 cup peanut butter
- 2 tbsp. shallots, minced
- 2 tbsp. brown sugar ½ tsp. curry
- 1 tbsp. soy sauce

Directions:
1. Preparing the Ingredients.
2. Peanut sauce: combine peanut butter, shallots, brown sugar, curry, soy sauce, mirin, lime juice, and garlic. Mix. Marinate chicken in peanut sauce for 4 hours in the refrigerator.

3. Grilling
4. Preheat the Grill Pan on medium heat for 5 Minutes. Skewer the chicken. Grill on both sides until done. Top skewers with chopped peanuts and scallions before serving. 1 tbsp. mirin rice wine, 1 lime, juiced,1 clove garlic, peeled & minced, 2 chicken breasts, sliced thin. Garnish ½ cup peanuts, chopped scallions, chopped. I love to substitute the chicken for shrimp then toss them with chilled sesame noodles.

548.Chipotle Burgers With Avocado

Servings: 4
Cooking Time: 5 Minutes
Ingredients:
- 1¼ pounds lean ground beef
- 2 tablespoons chipotle puree
- ½ teaspoon salt
- ¼ teaspoon freshly ground black pepper
- 4 slices cheddar cheese (about 4 ounces)
- 1 avocado, halved, pitted, and sliced
- ¼ head iceberg lettuce, shredded
- 4 hamburger buns, toasted

Directions:
1. Preparing the Ingredients.
2. Put the beef in a medium bowl and add the chipotle puree, salt, and pepper. Using a fork, mix the seasonings into the meat and then, with your hands, form the mixture into 4 patties, each about 1 inch thick.
3. Turn control knob to the high position, when the griddle is hot, place the burgers and cook for 4 Minutes without flippin. Topping each burger with a slice of cheese and cook for 1 minute more, until the cheese melts. Remove the burgers and cover to keep warm.
4. Top each burger with a few slices of avocado and some shredded lettuce before sandwiching between a bun.
5. Chipotle Puree: Put canned chipotles and their liquid in a blender or food processor and process until smooth. The puree can be covered with plastic wrap and refrigerated for up to 2 weeks. This stuff is hot-hot-hot, so a little goes a long way. I use it in meat marinades and dips. The puree is sold in some grocery stores, in ethnic mark.
Nutrition Info: (Per Serving): CALORIES: 590; FAT: 38G; PROTEIN: 37G

549.Steak Seasoning

Servings: 1
Ingredients:
- ½ cup (125 g) kosher salt
- ½ cup (80 g) granulated garlic
- ¼ cup (55 g) turbinado sugar
- ¼ cup (28 g) ground black pepper, café grind (see here)

Directions:
1. Preparing the Ingredients.
2. Add the salt, garlic, sugar and black pepper to a small bowl; mix well. Store in an airtight container for up to 6 months.
3. This is a great steak rub or seasoning. It's best to apply this to meat 30 Minutes prior to Grilling.

550.Grilled Bread Salad

Servings: 4
Ingredients:
- Vinaigrette ½ cup extra virgin olive oil
- ¼ cup red wine vinegar
- 1 clove garlic, peeled & minced

Directions:
1. Preparing the Ingredients.
2. In a bowl, combine the olive oil, vinegar, and garlic. Mix. Season with salt and pepper.
3. Grilling
4. Grill the bread on both sides. Cut into quarters. Toss grilled bread with vinaigrette and remaining ingredients immediately before serving. Salt and pepper 1 French baguette, sliced 1-inch thick 1 lb. large cherry tomatoes, quartered, 2 cucumbers, quartered & cut into 1-inch medallions. 1 medium red onion, halved & sliced ¼ cup fresh basil, chopped.

CPSIA information can be obtained
at www.ICGtesting.com
Printed in the USA
LVHW010533030621
689213LV00003B/35